LEARN JAPANESE WITH MANGA

A SELF-STUDY LANGUAGE BOOK FOR BEGINNERS

Volume One

Marc Bernabé

TUTTLE Publishing

Tokyo | Rutland, Vermont | Singapore

Marc Bernabé, the author of the two-volume course *Learn Japanese with Manga*, is a manga and anime translator who teaches Japanese language and etiquette courses for non-Japanese. He is the co-founder of the manga- and anime-specialized translation agency Daruma Serveis Lingüístics SL and the Japan culture center Espai Daruma. He has also published several Japan-related books.

Gabriel Luque is the illustrator of the manga story *Rakujō*. Professor of Visual Arts, his work has appeared in various publications including the *World of Warcraft* and *Starcraft* manga series from Tokyopop. In 2011 his artwork was selected for Udon Entertainment's Megaman Tribute Artbook. In 2017 he was nominated for Best Comic Artist in the Carlos Trillo Awards in his native Argentina. He currently works as a storyboard creator for movies and advertisements, as a freelance comic artist, and as a concept artist for animation, video games, toys and collectibles. **www.artstation.com**

Ken Niimura is the illustrator of the manga story *Kage*, co-written with Marc Bernabé. A Spanish-Japanese cartoonist and illustrator, he has a unique style informed by his international background. He has worked with clients such as Amazon, Google, McDonald's, Marvel Comics, Apple, L'Oreal, DC Entertainment, Shogakukan, Slate, The Apatow Company, Tezuka Pro, Image Comics, Kodansha and NHK Broadcasting Station among others. His book *I Kill Giants*, written by Joe Kelly, won the International Manga Award and was adapted into a film in 2019 starring Zoe Saldana. His series *Umami* earned him an Eisner Award to the Best Digital Comic. Ken Niimura's work has been translated into twelve languages. He lives and works between Japan and Europe. **www.niimuraweb.com**

Other illustrations in volumes 1 and 2:
Guillermo March
Studio Kōsen
Xian Nu Studio

Translation: **Olinda Cordukes**

Table of Contents

へへへへへへ
へへへへへへ。

気をつけろな

ぼくが壊した

Introduction

It is possible that some readers, not acquainted with the manga and anime world, will wonder why Japanese manga comic strips have been chosen to illustrate the lessons in these two volumes of books *Learn Japanese with Manga*.

The first reason is that the lessons that make up this course were originally published in a well-known Japanese comic book and anime magazine in Spain. When the magazine's editor-in-chief at the time asked me to produce a monthly Japanese course, I thought this should somehow be in line with the general subject matter of the magazine. Drawing inspiration from the lessons in the now defunct American magazine *Mangajin*, where every month a linguistic subject was explained using manga as examples, I managed to find a formula, which involved developing a course in Japanese with a fixed structure. This structure consisted of a page of theory with vocabulary and grammar tables and a page of examples taken directly from Japanese manga, to illustrate and expand what had just been explained. To my surprise, the idea worked perfectly well, allowing the course to be published without a break for thirty issues of the magazine (almost three years). All this allowed for the publication of these books, a largely improved compilation of the contents in the magazine.

The second reason we use manga to teach Japanese in these two volumes is because manga is a big phenomenon, not only in Japan, but throughout the world. Manga, with its enormous subject variety, is an ideal window through which to observe Japanese society and its mentality.

The word *manga* literally means "spontaneous and meaningless drawings." By extension, the West has adopted this word with the meaning of "Japanese comic-book." However, the popularity of manga in Japan is incomparable to similar genres in Western countries. If a comparison must be made, the manga phenomenon could possibly meet its match in the movie industry. A successful manga author is able to charge a real fortune and, in fact, the best-known authors are among the wealthiest people in Japan.

Here are some facts you may not know about the Japanese manga industry:

a) The sales value of comics, or manga, in Japan was estimated at almost 676 billion Japanese yen in 2021, up by more than 10 percent compared to the previous year. The market size increased for the fourth year in a row (*Annual Report on the Publication Market 2022*).

b) Weekly manga magazines and manga serials have amazing sales figures in Japan. The manga series *Jujutsu Kaisen* (lit. "Sorcery Fight") sold approximately 30.9 million volumes in Japan from November 2020 to November 2021, making it the best-selling manga series in the country during that time period (statista.com).

c) In Japan there are manga of all genres, for all ages and social strata, including children, teenagers, older women, laborers, office workers, etc. There are even erotic and pornographic manga.

In Japan manga tend to be published initially in thick and cheap weekly magazines, in the form of serials of about twenty pages per episode. When a weekly series is successful, it's usually then compiled in a volume of about two-hundred pages called a 単行本 ***tankōbon***. This ecosystem is maintained in digital form. Actually, in 2021, the digital manga market size was already almost double than the traditional printed book market.

All in all, manga is a very important phenomenon in Japan. Through these comic books—with a degree of caution and an analytical spirit—we can study not just the Japanese language but Japanese culture and idiosyncrasies too!

Be sure to read through the next section carefully to get an idea of how this method works and how this two-volume course is structured. I hope *Learn Japanese with Manga* will help you to learn about Japanese language culture. It is a great honor for me to be your ***sensei***.

How to use *Learn Japanese with Manga*

This two-volume series is designed for the self-study of the spoken, colloquial Japanese used in manga, so that you will be able to understand a Japanese comic book or anime series in the original, with the help of a dictionary.

With the focus on the informal oral language of manga, you will study many aspects of Japanese not usually taught in conventional courses or textbooks at such an early stage, for instance, the different personal pronouns (Lesson 7), emphatic particles at the end of sentences (Lesson 17), or verbs in their simple form (Lesson 20). Difficulty increases as the lessons progress, so I recommend studying the lessons in order, and moving on to the next lesson only when you are familiar with the contents of the previous lessons. To make studying easier and speedier, you'll find Roman alphabet (***rōmaji***) transcription of all words and sentences in lessons 1–30 in this first volume, even though we recommend that you learn the hiragana and katakana alphabets as soon as possible so as not to get into bad habits which will be difficult to correct later on.

The thirty-five lessons

Volume 1 consists of thirty-five lessons, each divided into three main parts:

a) **theory:** a detailed explanation of the lesson's subject matter often with grammar or vocabulary tables which help summarize and reinforce what has been explained.

b) **manga examples:** from real Japanese manga, to illustrate and expand what has been explained in the theory pages. The system used to analyze each sentence is the following:

Tenchi: この本はとても面白いですね。
kono hon wa totemo omoshiroi desu ne.
this book SP very interesting EP
This book is very interesting, isn't it?

First line: exact transcription of the original Japanese text.
Second line: transcription of the text into the Western alphabet (***rōmaji***).
Third line: literal translation, word for word. (The meaning of the abbreviations SP, EP and others can be found in the glossary on page 9.)
Fourth line: translation of the text into natural-sounding English.

From Lesson 31 onwards, manga example sentences are not given in ***rōmaji***, as we expect that by now, you can read hiragana, katakana and many kanji easily. For more difficult kanji, hiragana transcriptions, known as ***furigana***, are written directly over the kanji.

c) **exercises:** these are always related to the lesson's subject matter, and the answers can always be obtained or deduced from the content of the lesson they belong to. The answers to the exercises can be found online by following the link on page 9.

On translations

There are many example sentences throughout the book, as well as many manga examples, with their corresponding word-for-word translations into English. Sometimes, the sentences we offer may not sound very natural, since we have chosen more literal translations for an easier understanding of their formation. Trying to create a more natural English translation of every sentence would be a good exercise: it would help you consolidate concepts, make and in-depth analysis of the Japanese sentence, and think about it as a whole rather than a mere group of words and grammatical patterns.

Online materials

This book comes with comprehensive online materials which can be accessed using the link on page 9:

1. **Answers to the Exercises:** detailed answers to all the exercises included in the book.
2. **Kanji Compilation:** a compilation of 260 kanji characters, with stroke order and five compound words each. The study of these characters is essential to acquire a sound basis for a subsequent, more in-depth study of the language.
3. **Glossary of Onomatopoeia:** a useful reference tool for readers of manga in their original version.
4. **Vocabulary Index:** an index of almost 1,000 Japanese vocabulary words that appear throughout the book, in alphabetical order.
5. **Audio Files:** Key words and sentences recorded by native Japanese speakers to help you achieve authentic pronunciation. Sections of the text that have online audio recordings are indicated by the headphones logo.

略称集 Glossary of abbreviations

CP: Companion Particle, (who with), for example と ***to***

DOP: Direct Object Particle (what), for example, を ***o*** (Lesson 16)

DP: Direction Particle (where to), for example, へ ***e*** (Lesson 16)

EP: Emphatic Particle. Most end-of-sentence particles state emphasis or add a certain nuance, for example, ね ***ne***, よ ***yo***, ぞ ***zo***, etc. (Lesson 17)

GER: Gerund, or "-ing form," usually rendered as the ***-te*** form of the Japanese verb (Lesson 24)

IOP: Indirect Object Particle, for example, に ***ni*** (Lesson 16)

POP: Possessive Particle (whose), for example, の ***no*** (Lesson 16)

PP: Place Particle (where), for example, で ***de***, に ***ni*** (Lesson 16)

Q?: Question particle. Shows that the sentence is a question, for example, か ***ka*** (Lesson 17)

SBP: Subordinate Sentence Particle. This particle is used as a link between a subordinate sentence and the main sentence, for example と ***to***

SP: Subject Particle (who), for example, が ***ga*** (Lesson 16)

SUF.: Suffix for a person's name, for example, さん ***san***, くん ***kun***, etc. (Lesson 15)

TOP: Topic Particle. Shows that the previous word is the topic, for example, は ***wa*** (Lesson 16)

TP: Time Particle (when), for example, に ***ni*** (Lesson 16)

To Access the Online Materials:

1. Check to be sure you have an internet connection.
2. Type the URL below into your web browser.

www.tuttlepublishing.com/learn-japanese-with-manga-volume-1

For support, you can email us at info@tuttlepublishing.com.

Lesson 1 • 第1課

Learning the Hiragana Alphabet

The first step we will take on our manga journey will be to learn a little about the Japanese writing system: we are obviously talking about those unfamiliar-looking characters which many of you may have encountered. In these few first lessons you will learn the two basic syllabaries, hiragana and katakana.

The Japanese writing system

Memorizing the hiragana and katakana alphabets is the essential first step in learning to read Japanese. Most Japanese textbooks use ***rōmaji***—that is, the "Romanized" alphabet—to teach the beginner. However, *if* you wish to learn Japanese at all levels and, especially, if you wish to be able to read magazines or comic books, your study must include learning how to read and write the two Japanese syllabaries. This will be the first step toward a sound learning of the language. You must get used to Japanese characters as soon as possible, so we will start with the writing basics. Japanese has two "alphabets" or "syllabaries" called hiragana and katakana. A Japanese character usually equals a two-letter syllable in our language (that is why hiragana and katakana are called "syllabaries.") Thus, the character か is read ***ka***. There is only one exception: the sound "n," the only consonant sound that can go on its own.

Both hiragana and katakana have 46 syllabic symbols, each equivalent to its corresponding symbol in the other syllabary in pronunciation—but written differently. For instance, the hiragana character ち and the katakana character チ are both read ***chi***. It may seem strange or unnecessary, but less so when you consider that we have a very similar system in the Western alphabet: upper case and lower case letters. Try thinking about "a" and "A," or between "g" and "G." Do they look the same?

In addition to hiragana and katakana, Japanese also uses kanji: ideograms taken from Chinese during the period from the 3rd to the 6th century AD. Kanji represent concepts rather than sounds. There are many kanji (an estimated number of more than 50,000) but "only" about 3,000 are usually and frequently used, out of which 2,136 are considered "common use" (Lesson 3) and must compulsorily be studied at school. The subject of this first lesson is the hiragana syllabary, the fundamental first step in learning how to read and write Japanese.

On Japanese writing

Before we get started, it's worth knowing a few basic things about Japanese writing. As you probably know, Japanese can be written using the traditional style (vertically and from right to left), but it can also be written using the Western style (horizontally and from left to right).

Although newspapers and manga, for example, tend to use the traditional style, both methods are generally used in Japan nowadays, perhaps with a slight predominance of the Western style over the traditional. Therefore, it is essential to become familiar with both.

You will find that many books, magazines, comic books and printed material in general are read "backwards." In other words, the front cover of a Japanese book is placed where we would usually find the back cover, and that is why they are read left to right, just the opposite of Western books. If you think about it, this is not so odd; Arabic books, for that matter, are opened the same way.

Japanese punctuation marks are also different. A period is written with a small circle (。) and comas point upwards, the opposite from what we are used to (、). In addition, Japanese uses square brackets (「 and 」) as quotation marks. However, there are several other punctuation marks which are exactly the same as the Western alphabet, such as question marks (？) and exclamation marks (！).

Hiragana

After this general introduction to Japanese writing, we will fully go into the subject we are dealing with in this first lesson: the hiragana syllabary. Pay attention to the table on the following page, because you will need to learn it well: it is essential to learn how to read and write hiragana fluently as soon as possible.

Bear in mind you must follow a particular stroke order to write each one of the characters (it may not seem so, but stroke order is very important). At the end of this lesson you will find a writing guide for each of the basic hiragana characters, showing the stroke order for each character.

The hiragana syllabary is used more than katakana because it is used to write strictly Japanese words. Katakana is mainly used for words of foreign origin (as we will see in Lesson 2). Hiragana is used when a word can't be written in kanji (either because the kanji character is not officially recognized as a kanji of "common use," or because the writer doesn't remember the corresponding kanji). Also, particles (Lesson 16) and grammatical endings are written using hiragana characters.

Hiragana is what Japanese children learn first when they study how to write; therefore, many children's reading books are entirely written in this syllabary. Later, as children increase their knowledge, katakana and kanji are introduced.

Complete list of hiragana characters

Basic sounds					Additional sounds					Combined sounds		
あ *a*	い *i*	う *u*	え *e*	お *o*								
か *ka*	き *ki*	く *ku*	け *ke*	こ *ko*	が *ga*	ぎ *gi*	ぐ *gu*	げ *ge*	ご *go*	きゃ *kya* ぎゃ *gya*	きゅ *kyu* ぎゅ *gyu*	きょ *kyo* ぎょ *gyo*
さ *sa*	し *shi*	す *su*	せ *se*	そ *so*	ざ *za*	じ *ji*	ず *zu*	ぜ *ze*	ぞ *zo*	しゃ *sha* じゃ *ja*	しゅ *shu* じゅ *ju*	しょ *sho* じょ *jo*
た *ta*	ち *chi*	つ *tsu*	て *te*	と *to*	だ *da*	ぢ *ji*	づ *zu*	で *de*	ど *do*	ちゃ *cha*	ちゅ *chu*	ちょ *cho*
な *na*	に *ni*	ぬ *nu*	ね *ne*	の *no*						にゃ *nya*	にゅ *nyu*	にょ *nyo*
は *ha*	ひ *hi*	ふ *fu*	へ *he*	ほ *ho*	ば *ba* ぱ *pa*	び *bi* ぴ *pi*	ぶ *bu* ぷ *pu*	べ *be* ぺ *pe*	ぼ *bo* ぽ *po*	ひゃ *hya* びゃ *bya* ぴゃ *pya*	ひゅ *hyu* びゅ *byu* ぴゅ *pyu*	ひょ *hyo* びょ *byo* ぴょ *pyo*
ま *ma*	み *mi*	む *mu*	め *me*	も *mo*						みゃ *mya*	みゅ *myu*	みょ *myo*
や *ya*		ゆ *yu*		よ *yo*								
ら *ra*	り *ri*	る *ru*	れ *re*	ろ *ro*						りゃ *rya*	りゅ *ryu*	りょ *ryo*
わ *wa*				を *(w)o*								
ん *n*												

Syllabary description

There are 46 basic sounds, which you can see in the first column of the above syllabary. First learn these characters, because later on you will find it infinitely easier to learn by heart the so-called "additional" sounds.

Note: You have probably noticed that there are two ***ji*** sounds (じ and ぢ) and two ***zu*** sounds (ず and づ.) These are, indeed, pronounced exactly the same way, but their usage is different. For the time being, let's say that we will almost always use じ and ず, and hardly ever the other two.

In the second column we see the list of additional sounds—the word "additional" is used to refer to sounds that are derived from other sounds. Note that the ***ka*** (か) syllable is almost the same as ***ga*** (が), but ***ga*** has two small lines on the top right-hand corner of the syllable (the voicing mark); the same applies when we go from the ***s*** line to the ***z*** one, from ***t*** to ***d***, and from ***h*** to ***b***.

Notice, too, that to obtain the ***p*** sound we must place a small circle on top of the characters in the ***h*** line, for example, は (***ha***) → ぱ (***pa***).

In the third column, we find "combined" sounds, combinations of the characters in the ***i*** column (き ***ki***, し ***shi***, ち ***chi***, に ***ni***, ひ ***hi***, み ***mi***, り ***ri***) with those in the ***y*** line (や ***ya***, ゆ ***yu***, よ ***yo***), the second character written in a smaller size. These combinations are used to represent more complex sounds, such as ちゃ ***cha***, ひょ ***hyo*** or ぎゅ ***gyu***.

There is no ***l*** sound in Japanese. So, whenever we need to write or pronounce a non-Japanese word with the letter ***l*** in it, we will have to replace it with a soft ***r***. The name ***Lance***, for example, would be pronounced ***Ransu***. No, this is not wrong, nor have you misread anything. Because of this pronunciation difficulty, many Japanese seem to find themselves misunderstood when they travel abroad. Words such as "right" and "light," or "fry" and "fly," tend to sound the same, or even worse, "please sit" may become "please shit"! This can cause some startling or awkward conversations.

Don't worry about it for the moment, because we will <u>never</u> use hiragana to transcribe our names into Japanese. (We will see more about this in Lessons 2 and 8.)

Pronunciation

Japanese is pronounced with very few sounds, all of them very simple and basic. Let's have a look at the pronunciation of key Japanese sounds:

- ***a*** as in "f<u>a</u>ther."
- ***i*** as in "mach<u>i</u>ne."
- ***u*** as in "rec<u>u</u>perate."
- ***e*** as in "s<u>e</u>t."
- ***o*** as in "c<u>o</u>operate."
- ***g*** is always pronounced as in "get" and never as in "gentle."
- ***r*** is always in pronounced in the Spanish fashion (not the rolling trill, don't worry). It's somewhere between the ***l*** and the ***r*** and can be the most difficult sound to get right.
- ***ch*** as in "church."
- ***tsu*** as in the tz-u part of "Ri<u>tz U</u>ruguay"

漫画例 Manga Examples

We are now going to take a look at some examples of hiragana usage. During this course of study we will always see examples inspired by real Japanese manga to illustrate the explanations that have been given in the opening pages of each lesson. A manga example is worth a thousand words, as you might say.

Manga Example 1: Yawning

This first example shows us Katsuko waking up and saying: ***fuwaa...*** The drawing and the character's pose make the meaning of this onomatopoeia obvious, so we don't need to expand on this.

Katsuko: ふわぁっ
fuwaa...
(Onomatopoeia for a yawn.)

This manga example shows just how easy it is to practice reading hiragana with any Japanese manga you can get hold of. Onomatopoeia and sound effects written in the hiragana syllabary abound on the pages of manga; recognizing them and starting to read them, although you may not clearly understand their meaning, is already a very satisfactory first step and good motivation to pursue your Japanese studies with enthusiasm. (You have an online Glossary of Onomatopoeia accessible via the link on page 9.)

Note: You may have noticed the small, curious ***tsu*** (っ) character at the end of the exclamation. This means the sound stops abruptly; that is, it ends sharply. You will often find the small ***tsu*** (っ), indicating a sharp ending, in comic books, where it is profusely used. However, you will hardly find this sound effect in any other type of text.

Manga Example 2: Laughing

Here we see Tatsu and Mifu the instant they meet. Their reaction is most curious: what exactly do those sounds written in hiragana indicate?

Mifu: あはははははははははは。
ahahahahahahahahahahaha
(Onomatopoeia for laughing.)

Tatsu: へへへへへへへへへへへへへ。
hehehehehehehehehehehehe
(Onomatopoeia for laughing.)

They're giggles. Onomatopoeia for sounds produced by manga human characters (laughs, sounds of puzzlement, screams, etc.) are usually written in hiragana, unlike sounds caused by human acts, objects and animals (barks, explosions, blows, etc.), which are usually written in katakana, as we will see in Lesson 2.

However, don't take this as an inflexible rule; depending on the author and his or her taste, the use of hiragana and katakana in manga can vary greatly.

Manga Example 3: Grammatical particles

In this third example we find two of the most characteristic uses of the hiragana syllabary. With this syllabary we write grammatical particles, the units which constitute the true "skeleton" of a sentence. Grammatical particles, essential in Japanese grammar (as we will see in Lesson 16), are always written in hiragana. Here we have an example of one of them, が ***(ga)***, which is used to mark the subject of the sentence, that is, the person who is performing the action, in this case, ぼく ***boku*** ("I"). Verb endings are also written in hiragana to indicate present tense, past tense, etc. In this case, the hiragana した (***shita***), indicating the past tense (Lesson 20), has been added to the kanji 壊. Thus, 壊した (***kowashita***) means "I broke."

Kazuhiro: ぼくが壊した！？
boku ga kowashita!?
I broke it!?

Manga Example 4: Hiragana, katakana and kanji combined

This final example scarcely bears any relation to the rest of this first lesson. It shows us one of the most curious characteristics of the Japanese language. We are talking about the usage of the three Japanese writing forms in the same sentence: hiragana, katakana and kanji.

Note the whole text is written in hiragana, the true "skeleton" of a sentence, apart from ハンサム ***hansamu***—which comes from English and is, therefore, written in katakana (Lesson 2)—and the name 杉本明 ***Sugimoto Akira***, written in kanji with the corresponding reading alongside in small hiragana characters called ***furigana***. ***Furigana*** is often used in texts aimed at children or young people—such as ***shōnen*** comic books (for boys) or ***shōjo*** comic books (for girls)—to give young readers who still haven't mastered kanji some help that will enable them to comfortably read the text. Of course, these kinds of manga can be very useful for reading practice for a student of Japanese!

J.M. Ken Niimura

Tarō: わしよりハンサムなのは杉本明だけだ
washi yori hansamu na no wa sugimoto akira dake da
I more handsome than sugimoto akira only be.
Only Akira Sugimoto is more handsome than me.

Sugimoto: わーいありがとうへへへ…。
waai arigatō he he he...
wow! thanks he he he
Well, thanks! He, he, he.

Note 1: Sugimoto's T-shirt says ***aho***, which means "stupid" (Lesson 23).

Note 2: Japanese names are used in the order surname + given name, not the other way round. Here, 杉本 ***Sugimoto*** is the surname and—明 ***Akira*** the given name, so in the West he would be called "Akira Sugimoto."

Vocabulary: ***Washi*** = "I" (used mainly by older males, Lesson 7) | ***yori*** = "more than" | ***hansamu-na*** = "handsome" (from the English word) | ***dake*** = "only" | ***da*** = verb "to be," simple form (Lesson 7) | ***arigatō*** = "thanks").

Exercises 練習

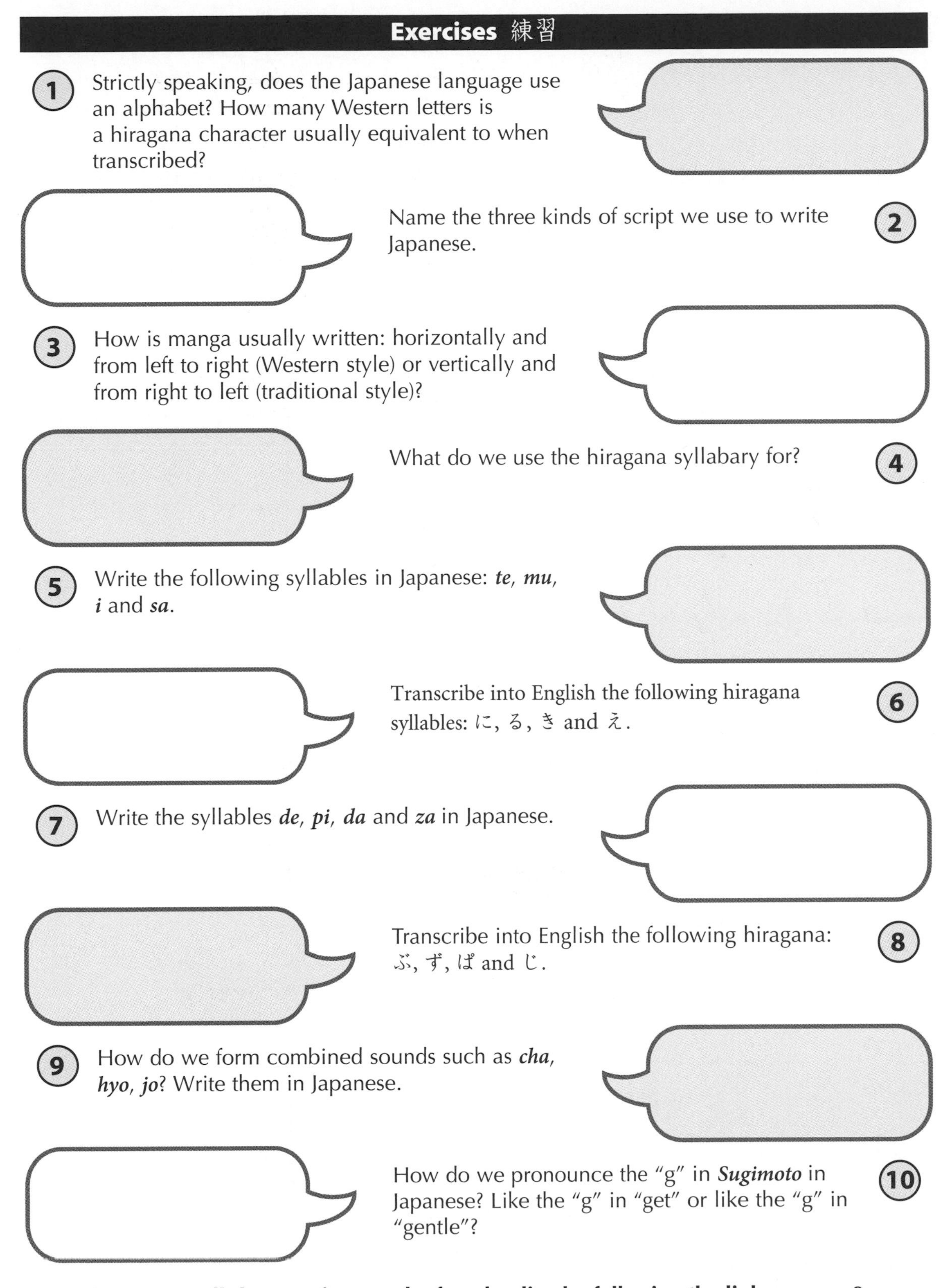

1. Strictly speaking, does the Japanese language use an alphabet? How many Western letters is a hiragana character usually equivalent to when transcribed?

2. Name the three kinds of script we use to write Japanese.

3. How is manga usually written: horizontally and from left to right (Western style) or vertically and from right to left (traditional style)?

4. What do we use the hiragana syllabary for?

5. Write the following syllables in Japanese: ***te***, ***mu***, ***i*** and ***sa***.

6. Transcribe into English the following hiragana syllables: に, る, き and え.

7. Write the syllables ***de***, ***pi***, ***da*** and ***za*** in Japanese.

8. Transcribe into English the following hiragana: ぶ, ず, ぱ and じ.

9. How do we form combined sounds such as ***cha***, ***hyo***, ***jo***? Write them in Japanese.

10. How do we pronounce the "g" in ***Sugimoto*** in Japanese? Like the "g" in "get" or like the "g" in "gentle"?

— Answers to all the exercises can be found online by following the link on page 9. —

a	あ
i	い
u	う
e	え
o	お
ka	か
ki	き
ku	く
ke	け
ko	こ
sa	さ
shi	し
su	す
se	せ
so	そ
ta	た
chi	ち
tsu	つ
te	て
to	と
na	な
ni	に
nu	ぬ
ne	ね

no	の			
ha			は	
hi	ひ			
fu				ふ
he	へ			
ho				ほ
ma			ま	
mi		み		
mu			む	
me		め		
mo			も	
ya			や	

yu		ゆ		
yo		よ		
ra		ら		
ri		り		
ru	る			
re		れ		
ro	ろ			
wa		わ		
wo			を	
n	ん			

Lesson 2 • 第2課

Learning the Katakana Alphabet

In Lesson 1 we saw how hiragana is strictly used to write Japanese native words. So, what do we use katakana for? In this lesson we will study the usage of this second syllabary, and as well some extra features of hiragana.

Foreign words

Katakana has a rather limited use, and in fact Japanese children first learn hiragana, and then, in due time, they learn katakana. Learning katakana, however, is essential to reading Japanese, so don't leave its study until the last minute: start studying the table on the facing page as soon as possible. Believing this is a "minor" syllabary and that it is not worth studying properly is a serious mistake.

Basically, katakana is used to write foreign words which have been adapted to the rather limited Japanese phonetics. Thus, "computer" becomes コンピュータ ***konpyūta***, "part-time work" becomes アルバイト ***arubaito***, and "prêt-à-porter" becomes プレタポルテ ***puretaporute***.

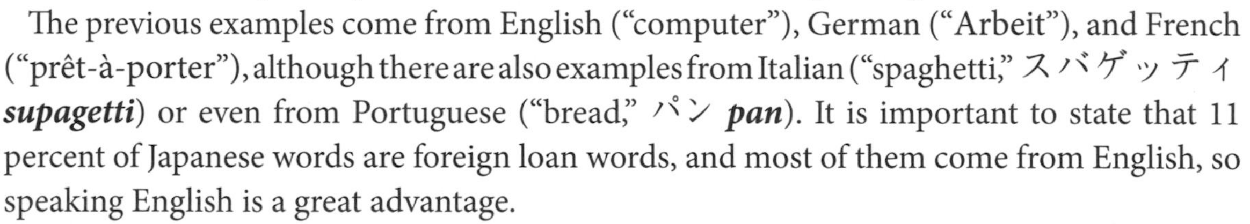

The previous examples come from English ("computer"), German ("Arbeit"), and French ("prêt-à-porter"), although there are also examples from Italian ("spaghetti," スパゲッティ ***supagetti***) or even from Portuguese ("bread," パン ***pan***). It is important to state that 11 percent of Japanese words are foreign loan words, and most of them come from English, so speaking English is a great advantage.

Watch out: pay special attention to the differences between シ ***shi*** and ツ ***tsu***, and between ン ***n*** and ソ ***so***, which are easily confused.

Another use of katakana is as an emphasizing element of a particular word in a sentence (a bit like our italics). Finally, this syllabary is also used for onomatopoeia, so finding words written in katakana on the pages of any comic book is extremely frequent.

People's names

All non-Japanese or non-Chinese names of people and places—including names of cities or geographical areas—must be written in katakana. First of all, the sounds of the word we want to write in Japanese must be transcribed into Japanese phonetics.

The main problem is Japanese has no individual consonant sounds—apart from the ***n***. Therefore, for each consonant pronounced on its own in its original language, we will add a ***u*** (***u*** after a consonant has a very soft pronunciation in Japanese). The only exceptions are ***t*** and ***d***, where we will add an ***o***.

Thus, yours truly's name (Marc) becomes ***Maruku*** マルク, Sandra becomes ***Sandora*** サンドラ, and Alfred becomes ***Arufureddo*** アルフレッド (remember ***l*** doesn't exist and must be replaced with an ***r***.)

Don't worry if transcriptions seem difficult now, because we will expand on the subject of foreign name conversion into katakana later on in Lesson 8.

Complete list of katakana characters

Basic sounds	Additional sounds	Combined sounds
ア *a*, イ *i*, ウ *u*, エ *e*, オ *o*		
カ *ka*, キ *ki*, ク *ku*, ケ *ke*, コ *ko*	ガ *ga*, ギ *gi*, グ *gu*, ゲ *ge*, ゴ *go*	キャ *kya*, キュ *kyu*, キョ *kyo* ギャ *gya*, ギュ *gyu*, ギョ *gyo*
サ *sa*, シ *shi*, ス *su*, セ *se*, ソ *so*	ザ *za*, ジ *ji*, ズ *zu*, ゼ *ze*, ゾ *zo*	シャ *sha*, シュ *shu*, ショ *sho* ジャ *ja*, ジュ *ju*, ジョ *jo*
タ *ta*, チ *chi*, ツ *tsu*, テ *te*, ト *to*	ダ *da*, ヂ *ji*, ヅ *zu*, デ *de*, ド *do*	チャ *cha*, チュ *chu*, チョ *cho*
ナ *na*, ニ *ni*, ヌ *nu*, ネ *ne*, ノ *no*		ニャ *nya*, ニュ *nyu*, ニョ *nyo*
ハ *ha*, ヒ *hi*, フ *fu*, ヘ *he*, ホ *ho*	バ *ba*, ビ *bi*, ブ *bu*, ベ *be*, ボ *bo* パ *pa*, ピ *pi*, プ *pu*, ペ *pe*, ポ *po*	ヒャ *hya*, ヒュ *hyu*, ヒュ *hyo* ビャ *bya*, ビュ *byu*, ビョ *byo* ピャ *pya*, ピュ *pyu*, ピョ *pyo*
マ *ma*, ミ *mi*, ム *mu*, メ *me*, モ *mo*		ミャ *mya*, ミュ *myu*, ミョ *myo*
ヤ *ya*, ユ *yu*, ヨ *yo*		
ラ *ra*, リ *ri*, ル *ru*, レ *re*, ロ *ro*		リャ *rya*, リュ *ryu*, リョ *ryo*
ワ *wa*, ヲ *(w)o*	**Only found in katakana**	ヴァ *va*, ヴィ *vi*, ヴ *vu*, ヴェ *ve*, ヴォ *vo*, ドゥ *du*, ティ *ti* ファ *fa*, フィ *fi*, フェ *fe*, フォ *fo*, シェ *she*, ジェ *je*, チェ *che*
ン *n*		

Short and long vowels

In the previous lesson, we left aside some hiragana characteristics. These characteristics can also be applied to katakana so we will explain them now. We are talking about long vowels and double sounds.

"Long vowels," as their name suggest, are pronounced a little longer than an average (short) vowel. This subtle difference is very important in a language such as Japanese whose phonetic range is limited, since the difference between ***kūso*** ("empty," "vain") and ***kuso*** ("shit") is based on this distinction. You need to be very careful with your pronunciation if you don't want to find yourself in an awkward situation!

To indicate vowel lengthening we write a hiragana ***u*** (う) after hiragana sounds ending in ***o*** or ***u***, for example, くうそ ***kūso***, がっこう ***gakkō*** (which is not pronounced "*gakkow*" but "*gakkoh*.")

However, in katakana we will use a dash: ニューヨーク ***Nyūyōku***, Madrid マドリード ***Madoriido***.

Throughout this course, whenever we need to transcribe a Japanese word into our alphabet, we will use an accent called a macron on top of ***u*** and ***o*** to indicate this vowel lengthening: ***ū*** and ***ō***.

Double sounds

"Double" sounds are consonants that have a longer and/or more abrupt sound than normal ones. This effect is indicated by a small ***tsu*** character before the consonant to be doubled, both in hiragana (っ) and katakana (ッ). We only double those hiragana starting with the following consonants: ***k***, ***s***, ***t***, ***ch***, ***g***, ***z***, ***d***, ***b*** and ***p***. For example: しゅっぱつ ***shuppatsu*** ("starting," "departure") | きっさてん ***kissaten*** ("coffee shop") | まっちゃ ***matcha*** ("green tea") | ラケット ***raketto*** ("racket") | マッサージ ***massaaji*** ("massage.")

And now, to finish the syllabaries, we will say that if you find the learning of hiragana and katakana difficult, there are many textbooks on the market that devote themselves to learning these two syllabaries..

Some basic vocabulary

Yes はい ***hai***
No いいえ ***iie***
Good morning おはようございます ***ohayō gozaimasu***
Good afternoon こんにちは ***konnichi wa***
Good evening こんばんは ***konban wa***
Thank you ありがとう ***arigatō***
Goodbye さようなら ***sayōnara***
You're welcome どういたしまして ***dō itashimashite***
Please おねがいします ***onegai shimasu***
Go ahead / Here you are どうぞ ***dōzo***
That's right そうです ***sō desu***
I understand わかりました ***wakarimashita***
I don't understand わかりません ***wakarimasen***
Excuse me すみません ***sumimasen***

漫画例 Manga Examples

We are now going to see some examples of the widespread usage of the katakana syllabary in Japanese. We will see two kinds of examples: onomatopoeia and foreign words, which mostly come from English and have been introduced into the Japanese language.

Manga Example 1: Explosions and blows

Onomatopoeic sounds which are not voices or screams are almost always written in katakana. For instance, blows, explosions and mechanical noises belong to this category. In a manga, the katakana used for these kinds of sound is often difficult to recognize for someone who is not very used to them, because authors usually deform them to obtain the most spectacular possible effects, as you can see in the two examples below). However, with some practice you will learn to identify and read them quite effortlessly.

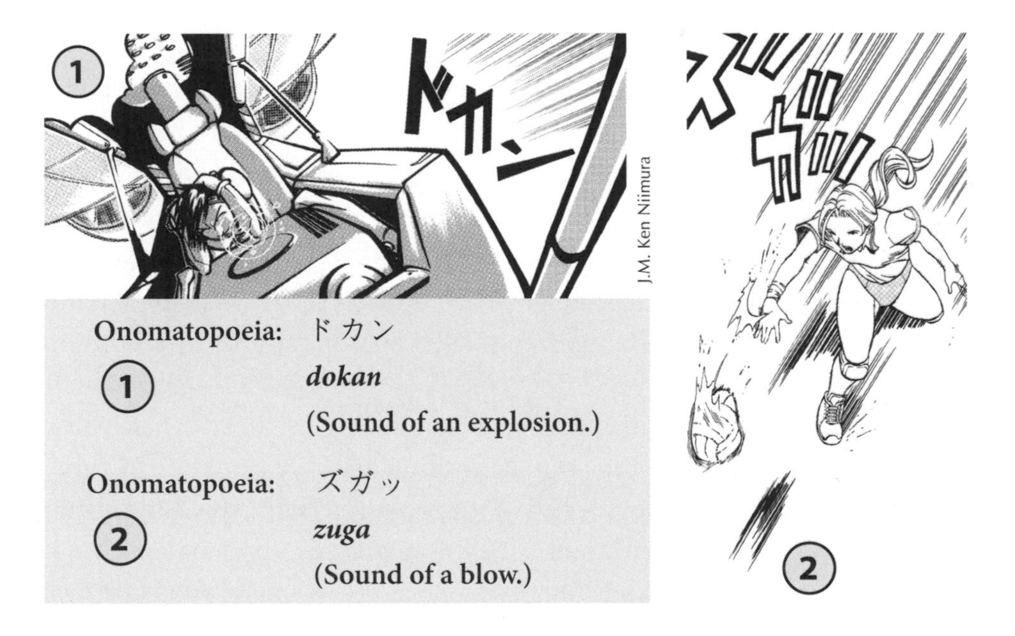

Onomatopoeia: ドカン
① ***dokan***
(Sound of an explosion.)

Onomatopoeia: ズガッ
② ***zuga***
(Sound of a blow.)

The problem with onomatopoeia lies more in understanding it than in reading it, because it is usually radically different from Western onomatopoeia. Take a look at the pictures: where we would say "boom!" the Japanese say ドカン ***dokan***, and where we would say "smack!" or "slam!" they say ズガッ ***zuga***. It's just a matter of practice.

Note: Remember the small ***tsu*** (ッ) at the end of ***zuga*** indicates the sound ends abruptly.

Manga Example 2: Book titles and names of magazines

Here we have three manga and magazine covers where katakana is used. Using English words or expressions in titles is not uncommon, especially when they are aimed at young readers: in Japan, English exerts a powerful attraction and sounds modern and "cool."

Title: ファン ① *fan* Phan

Title: イーブニング ② *iibuningu* Evening

Title: ロストユース ③ *rosuto yūsu* Lost Youth

In picture ① we have ファン (literally *Fan*, but transcribed *Phan*), a non-Japanese name, which is, therefore, written in katakana (Japanese names are almost always written in kanji). In ② and ③ we have words taken directly from English: "evening" and "lost youth."

With these three examples you must already have noticed the way Japanese tend to "twist" English words when they transcribe them into katakana, to a point where they are hardly recognizable.

Don't worry if you don't even recognize the original English word when you read a katakana transcription. Getting used to "katakanization" is only a matter of time. You will eventually find you are able to recognize the foreign words transcribed into katakana, and vice-versa: that is, you will be able to transcribe foreign words into katakana.

There are many onomatopoeia and foreign expressions in manga, so start practicing as soon as possible!

Exercises 練習

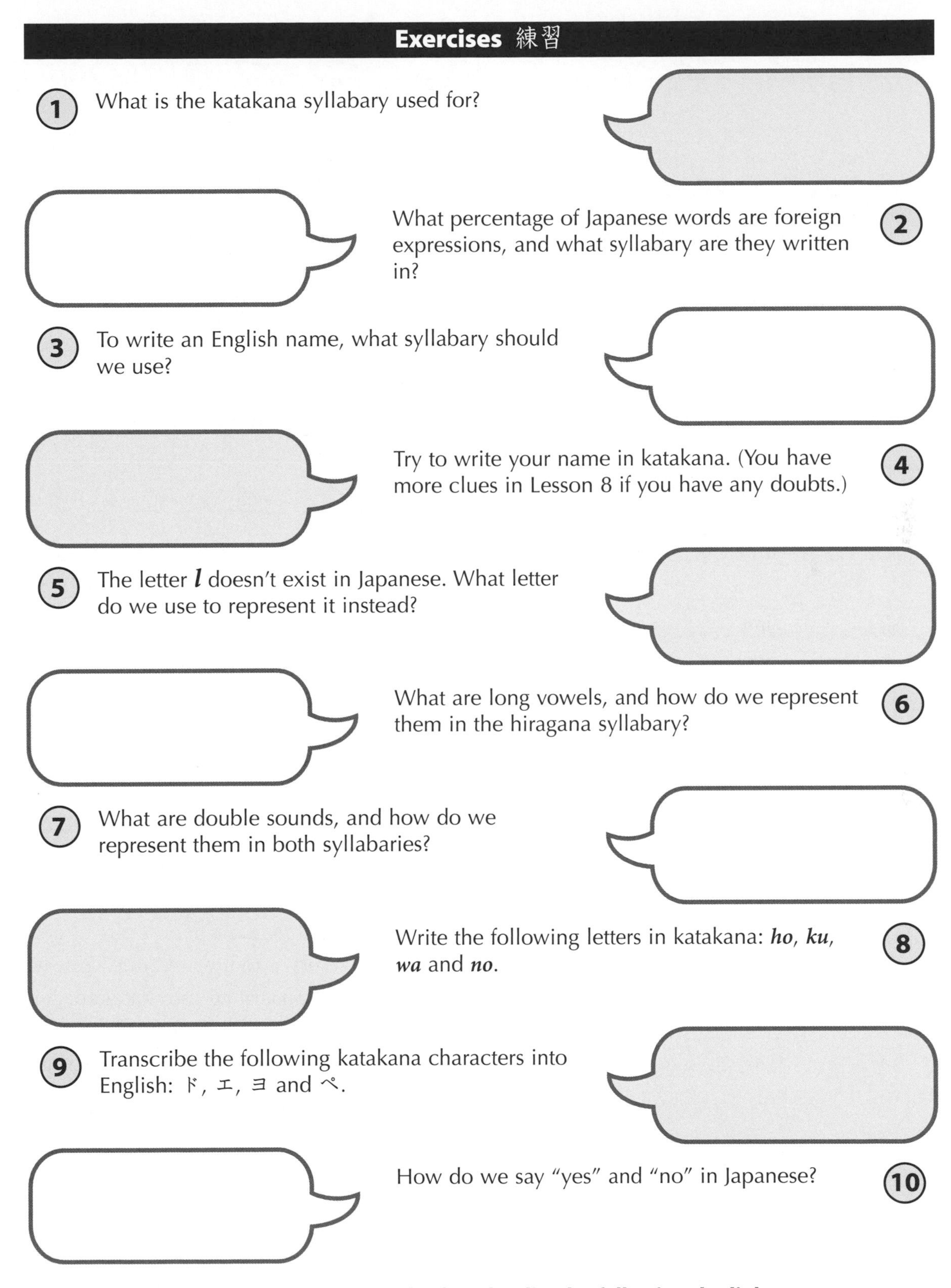

1. What is the katakana syllabary used for?

2. What percentage of Japanese words are foreign expressions, and what syllabary are they written in?

3. To write an English name, what syllabary should we use?

4. Try to write your name in katakana. (You have more clues in Lesson 8 if you have any doubts.)

5. The letter ***l*** doesn't exist in Japanese. What letter do we use to represent it instead?

6. What are long vowels, and how do we represent them in the hiragana syllabary?

7. What are double sounds, and how do we represent them in both syllabaries?

8. Write the following letters in katakana: ***ho***, ***ku***, ***wa*** and ***no***.

9. Transcribe the following katakana characters into English: ド, エ, ヨ and ペ.

10. How do we say "yes" and "no" in Japanese?

— Answers to all the exercises can be found online by following the link on page 9. —

a	ア	***su***	ス
i	イ	***se***	セ
u	ウ	***so***	ソ
e	エ	***ta***	タ
o	オ	***chi***	チ
ka	カ	***tsu***	ツ
ki	キ	***te***	テ
ku	ク	***to***	ト
ke	ケ	***na***	ナ
ko	コ	***ni***	ニ
sa	サ	***nu***	ヌ
shi	シ	***ne***	ネ

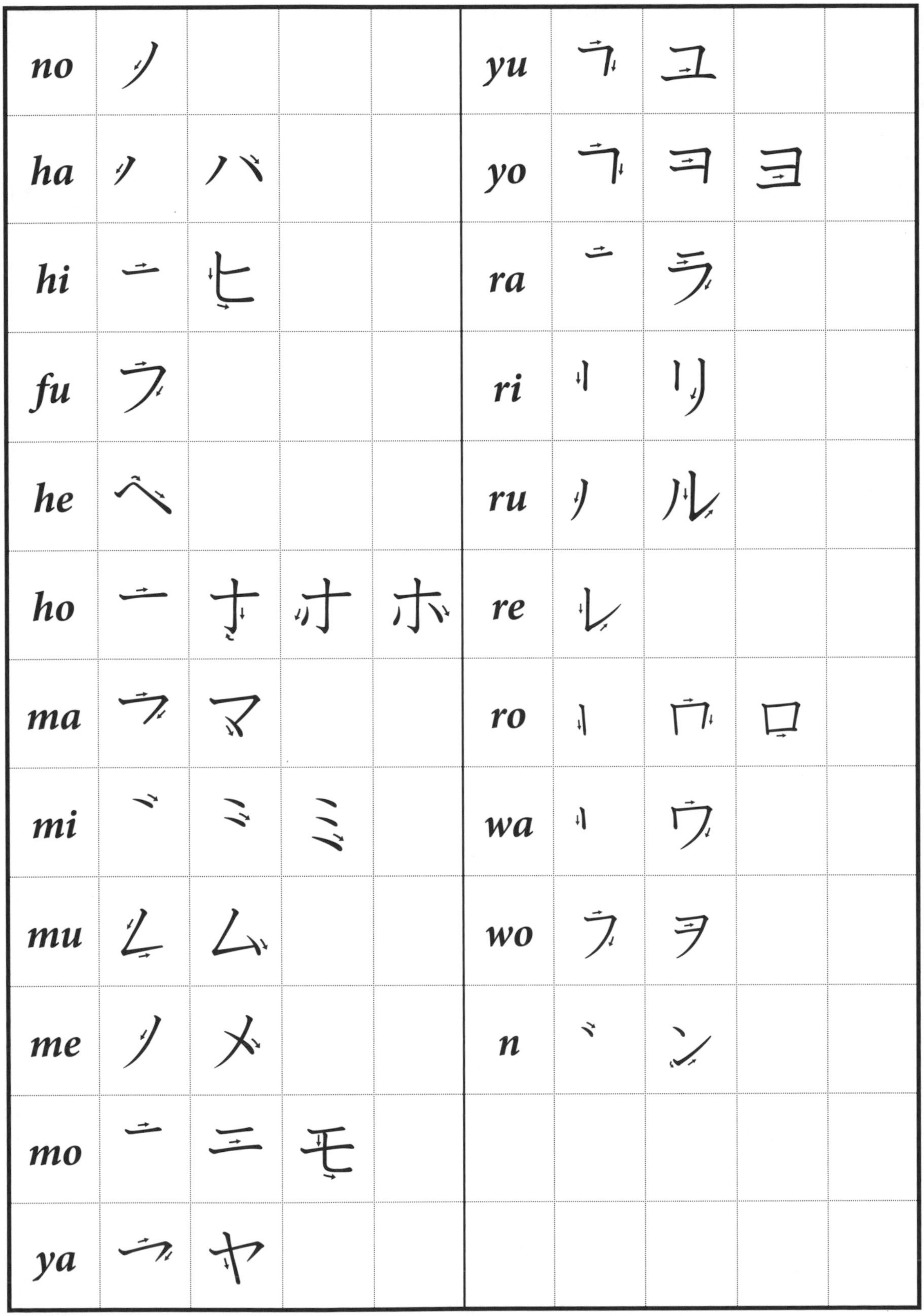

no	ノ	*yu*	ユ
ha	ハ	*yo*	ヨ
hi	ヒ	*ra*	ラ
fu	フ	*ri*	リ
he	ヘ	*ru*	ル
ho	ホ	*re*	レ
ma	マ	*ro*	ロ
mi	ミ	*wa*	ワ
mu	ム	*wo*	ヲ
me	メ	*n*	ン
mo	モ		
ya	ヤ		

Lesson 3 • 第3課

Learning the Kanji Characters

In this lesson we are going to deal with one of the most complex as well as essential subjects in the Japanese language: we are talking about the Chinese characters known as kanji.

A little bit of history

In China, five thousand years ago, a type of writing based on drawings was invented. These drawings represent different material or abstract concepts. This is not unusual in human history, you need only to look at the Egyptian hieroglyphics to understand that Chinese is not an isolated case. The unusual fact about Chinese characters is that their writing didn't become progressively simpler, forming in the end an alphabet which merely represented sounds.

This was the case with Roman writing, which had its origin in Phoenician, filtering through Greek. In China, the function of ideograms was to express both sound and meaning, unlike Western writing, which simply expresses sound.

Obviously, the form of these characters is different now from the original one. They started off as more or less realistic drawings of things, and with use, they were stylized and became simpler, developing into their actual forms today, as we can see in the table on the right.

How some characters were formed

Ideogram	Modern character	Meanings
	木	tree
	林	woods
	森	forest
	日	sun, day
	月	moon
	明	bright
	山	mountain
	鳥	bird
	島	island

Chinese and Japanese

Until the 4th century of our era, the inhabitants of the Japanese archipelago didn't have any writing system. At that time Chinese writing came to Japan via Korea. In the beginning, only a few educated people could read Chinese and all they read was scriptures on Buddhism and philosophy. But Chinese ideograms were gradually used to write Japanese. There was a problem here, however: the Japanese language already existed, (it just had no writing system), and Chinese characters were imported along with their pronunciation (with substantial changes due to the limited Japanese phonetics). So now there were two or more different ways to read the same character.

For example, the character representing *mountain,* 山 can be pronounced the "Japanese way," that is ***yama***, or the "Chinese way," ***san***. And this is where we find one of the most typical reading mistakes in Japanese, as the word 富士山, which means "Mount Fuji," is pronounced ***Fuji-san*** and not ***Fuji-yama*** as we might mistakenly think!

On'yomi and kun'yomi

These different ways of pronouncing a character are called ***on'yomi*** (the reading which comes from Chinese) and ***kun'yomi*** (the original Japanese reading.) How can we tell the word 富士山 is pronounced ***Fuji-san*** and not, for instance, ***Fuji-yama*** or ***Tomishi-san*** or ***Fūshi-yama*** or any other perfectly possible reading of this three-kanji combination?

The answer is: we can't. But we have clues: when a character is on its own in a sentence, it is usually read the ***kun'yomi*** way, if it is accompanied by other kanji, it is usually read the ***on'yomi*** way. People and proper place names are usually always read the ***kun'yomi*** way. This rule works 90 percent of the time. (But careful with the remaining 10 percent!)

Example: the character 新 (new)

Take a look at this example, because it will be very helpful in understanding how kanji and their ***on'yomi*** and ***kun'yomi*** readings work:

その新しい新聞はおもしろいです。
Sono atarashii shinbun wa omoshiroi desu.
That new newspaper is interesting.

sono = "that" | ***atarashii*** = "new" | ***shinbun*** = "newspaper" | ***wa*** = topic particle | ***omoshiroi*** = "interesting" | ***desu*** = "to be."

We see the character 新 appears twice in the sentence but it has a different pronunciation each time. The first time it is pronounced the ***kun'yomi*** way, ***atara(shii)***: the word ***atarashii*** is an adjective which means "new." Notice that this character is on its own in the sentence. So, in keeping with the clues we have just given you, it is logical to pronounce it the ***kun'yomi*** way.

The second time it is read ***shin***, that is, the ***on'yomi*** way, and it comes with another kanji (聞), which means "to hear." 新 shin ("new") and 聞 ***bun*** ("to hear") together form the word 新聞 shinbun ("newspaper,") which is something that "gathers new events (things that have been heard)." In this case, the two characters together form a single word. Therefore, we will pronounce them the ***on'yomi*** way.

Japanese and nihongo

Let's analyze the word ***nihongo***, which is the name given to the Japanese language. In kanji, this word is written 日本語. The first kanji, 日 ***ni***, means "day," "sun." The second one, 本 ***hon***, means "origin," "root," and the third one, 語 ***go***, "language." In Japanese, Japan's name is ***Nihon***—although it can also be read ***Nippon***—and we write it like this: 日本. And what have "sun" and "origin" got to do with Japan? Doesn't the expression "the land of the rising sun" ring a bell? So this is where it comes from. Therefore, ***nihongo*** means "the language of the land of the rising sun," in other words, "Japanese."

Kanji are complex

Mastering kanji writing and reading is an important challenge, since there are many similar characters, and, besides, we must bear in mind ***on'yomi*** and ***kun'yomi*** readings. There are quite easy kanji, like the one for "person" 人 (***hito***, ***nin***, or ***jin***, with two strokes), but there are also complicated ones, like the one for "machine" 機 (***ki***, sixteen strokes.) In the online Kanji Compilation that can be accessed via the link on page 9, you will find 160 kanji with their stroke order, ***on'yomi*** and ***kun'yomi*** readings, as well as several examples of compound kanji words.

How many kanji are there?

There are technically over 45,000 or 50,000 kanji, but don't worry, "only" about 3,000 are normally used. There is a list of 2,136 kanji called the ***Jōyō Kanji*** or "common use kanji," which are those that are used in newspapers. If a kanji not included in the list is used, its reading must be given in hiragana in small characters above each character (these hiragana readings on top of the kanji are called ***furigana***.)

Some easy kanji: numerals and interesting words					
一	***ichi***	1	人	***hito***	person
二	***ni***	2	男	***otoko***	man
三	***san***	3	女	***onna***	woman
四	***yon/shi***	4	月	***tsuki***	moon, month
五	***go***	5	火	***hi***	fire
六	***roku***	6	水	***mizu***	water
七	***nana/shichi***	7	木	***ki***	tree
八	***hachi***	8	金	***kane***	money
九	***kyū/ku***	9	土	***tsuchi***	earth, soil
十	***jū***	10	日	***hi***	day, sun
百	***hyaku***	100	山	***yama***	mountain
千	***sen***	1,000	川	***kawa***	river
万	***man***	10,000	田	***ta***	rice field

漫画例 Manga Examples

We will now see some examples of kanji usage: the first two examples show us the most common difficulties we will find when studying kanji. In them we will meet King Slime, who can't read nor write kanji very well.

Manga Example 1: The error of writing an extra stroke

What is Shigeo laughing about in this example? He's laughing about Slime's mistake: instead of writing the kanji for "king," 王, he has written the kanji for "ball," 玉. Notice how the only difference between "king" and "ball" is a single stroke, which goes almost unnoticed. What Slime really wanted to write on his autograph was "Great King Slime, Space King." The kanji for 王 "king" is read ***ō*** and the kanji for 玉 "ball" is read ***tama***.

Guillermo March

Autograph:	しげおくんえ	うちゅーの玉者スライム大玉
①	***Shigeo-kun e***	***uchū no tamaja suraimu ootama***
	Shigeo (SUF.) for	space POP ball person slime big ball
	For Shigeo	**Great "Ball" Slime, the Space Ball.**

Guillermo March

Note: The hiragana ***ku*** in ***Shigeo-kun*** (picture 1) is written the wrong way round. The correct way to write it is く. Also, ***e***, which means "for" (Lesson 16) should be へ, not え.

Moral of the story: Be very careful with your strokes, you can't write too many and you can't leave any out, as you run the same risks as King Slime!

Shigeo: みんなみんなー！このひと「宇宙のタマジャ」だって！「スライムオオタマ」だって！

② ***minna minna kono hito "uchū no tamaja" datte! "suraimu ootama" datte!***

everyone everyone this person "space POP ball person" be say! "slime great ball" be say!!

Hey, look! This guy's name is "Space Ball"! He's a "Great Slime Ball"!!

Manga Example 2: Errors when reading kanji: *on'yomi* and *kun'yomi*

What mistake has King Slime? He has misread the kanji on the planet. Instead of using the ***on'yomi*** (Chinese reading) for the planet Mars (***kasei***), he has used the ***kun'yomi*** (***hiboshi***). Remember: if a kanji is on its own, it is usually read the ***kun'yomi*** way, and if it is with other kanji, it is read the ***on'yomi*** way. His subject has immediately realized and corrected him.

Guillermo March

Slime: あのヒボシをよくみてよ！
ano hiboshi o yoku mite yo!
that hiboshi DOP well see EP!
Take a good look at that Hiboshi!

Subject: カセイとよむのです 大王様
kasei to yomu no desu daiō-sama
kasei read be great king (SUF.)
It says Kasei, your Highness...

"Fire" (火) is read ***hi*** on its own (***kun'yomi***), and ***ka*** when it is combined with other kanji (***on'yomi***). "Star" (星) is read ***hoshi*** in ***kun'yomi***, and ***sei*** in ***on'yomi***. Therefore, 火星 ***kasei***, the Japanese name for the planet Mars, literally means "fire star." In this case, the readings ヒボシ ***(hiboshi)*** and カセイ ***(kasei)*** are written in katakana to make them stand out in the sentence; here, katakana is used in a similar manner as our quotation marks.

Moral of the story: Be careful with the ***on'yomi*** and ***kun'yomi*** readings of kanji!

Manga Example 3: Kanji in manga

This panel has two easy kanji: one is "father" 父, and the other is "to die" 死. Also, we are given the ***furigana*** reading, something very frequent in ***shōnen*** and ***shōjo*** manga (aimed at teenage readers who may not have mastered the more difficult kanji).

Rinrin: お父さん！お父さん！死んじゃいやぁ！
Otōsan! Otōsan! Shinja iyaa!
Father! Father! Don't die!

Exercises 練習

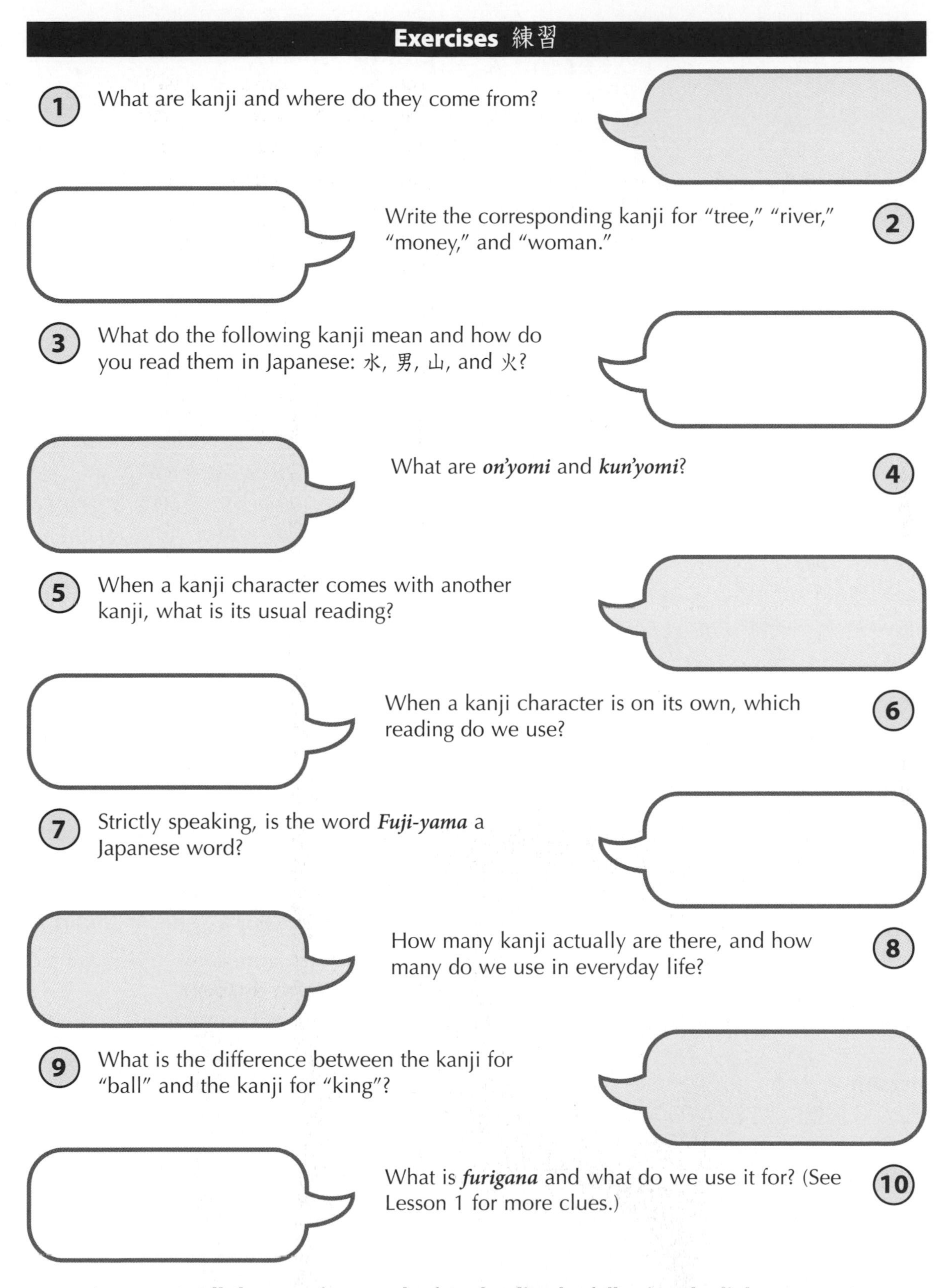

1. What are kanji and where do they come from?
2. Write the corresponding kanji for "tree," "river," "money," and "woman."
3. What do the following kanji mean and how do you read them in Japanese: 水, 男, 山, and 火?
4. What are ***on'yomi*** and ***kun'yomi***?
5. When a kanji character comes with another kanji, what is its usual reading?
6. When a kanji character is on its own, which reading do we use?
7. Strictly speaking, is the word ***Fuji-yama*** a Japanese word?
8. How many kanji actually are there, and how many do we use in everyday life?
9. What is the difference between the kanji for "ball" and the kanji for "king"?
10. What is ***furigana*** and what do we use it for? (See Lesson 1 for more clues.)

— Answers to all the exercises can be found online by following the link on page 9. —

Lesson 4 • 第4課

Basic Expressions

In this lesson we will give a short list of basic expressions so that you will begin to feel you are studying Japanese. We already gave a very basic list in Lesson 2, and some of those expressions are repeated here. But, of course, in this lesson we will learn many more new expressions.

Greetings

Here are some common greetings:

おはようございます ***ohayō gozaimasu***	Good morning (until about 11 am)
こんにちは ***konnichi wa***	Good afternoon (from 11 am to 6pm)
こんばんは ***konban wa***	Good evening (from about 6 pm on)
おやすみなさい ***o-yasumi nasai***	Good night (when going to bed)
お元気ですか？ ***o-genki desu ka?***	How are you?
はい、元気です ***hai, genki desu***	I'm fine.

Introducing oneself

Using this conversation as a model, we will learn how to introduce ourselves:

Person A:
はじめまして。私の名前は ______ です。 よろしくお願いします。
あなたの名前は何ですか？

Hajimemashite. Watashi no namae wa ______ desu. Yoroshiku o-negai shimasu. Anata no namae wa nan desu ka?

How do you do? My name is ______. Pleased to meet you. What's your name?

Person B:
私の名前は ______ です。 こちらこそよろしく。

Watashi no namae wa ______ desu. Kochira koso yoroshiku.

My name is ______. Pleased to meet you (too).

Put your name in the corresponding place, and you can introduce yourself in Japanese!.

Thank you

The most basic way of saying "thank you" is: ありがとう ***arigatō.*** But there are many more combinations, such as this very formal one:

どうもありがとうございます。 ***Dōmo arigatō gozaimasu.***
Thank you very much.

The next one is a little less formal than the previous one:
ありがとうございます。 ***Arigatō gozaimasu.*** Thank you.

Or there is this very informal and simple one, useful in almost any situation:
どうも。 ***Dōmo.*** Thanks.

The answer to any expression of thanks usually is:
どういたしまして。 ***Dō itashimashite.*** You're welcome.

Or a simpler one: いいえ。 ***Iie.*** That's okay.

Asking for prices

Knowing how to ask for prices is important for survival in Japan, so this is what we will study next. Study the following conversation between a shop assistant and customer.

いらっしゃいませ。 ***Irasshaimase.*** Welcome./Can I help you?

これはいくらですか？ ***Kore wa ikura desu ka?*** How much is this?

これは ______ 円です。 ***Kore wa ______ en desu.*** It's ______ yen.

Don't worry, we know you can't count in Japanese yet. This will be solved in the next lesson! If we find the price is all right and we want to buy something, we will say:

これをください。 ***Kore o kudasai.*** This one, please.
Or:
これをお願いします。 ***Kore o o-negai shimasu.*** I would like this, please.

Farewells

The best known way of saying goodbye is: さようなら ***sayōnara***. But it is not the most usual, in fact you seldom hear it in Japan. Expressions like "see you later" are more common than the typical "goodbye." Combinations with ***mata*** are frequent:

それでは（それじゃ）、また明日会いましょう。
Sore de wa (sore ja), mata ashita aimashō. Well, let's meet again tomorrow.

Here are some shorter, everyday colloquial expressions:

じゃ、また明日。 ***Ja, mata ashita.*** Well, see you tomorrow.

じゃ、また！ ***Ja, mata!*** Well, see you later!

またね！ ***Mata ne!*** See you later!

バイバイ！ ***Baibai!*** Bye bye!

Other useful expressions

はい ***hai*** yes

いいえ ***iie*** no

すみません ***sumimasen***
sorry/excuse me

ごめんなさい ***gomen nasai***
sorry

やった！
Yatta!
Yes!/I did it!

おめでとうございます ！
Omedetō gozaimasu
Congratulations!

We will conclude this lesson with a list of kanji bringing the total we've introduced so far to 53. Notice that the last four words in the table are formed by two kanji instead of one.

Short list of useful kanji							
何	なに	***nani***	what?	心	こころ	***kokoro***	heart
子	こ	***ko***	child	春	はる	***haru***	spring
円	えん	***en***	yen	夏	なつ	***natsu***	summer
右	みぎ	***migi***	right	秋	あき	***aki***	fall
左	ひだり	***hidari***	left	冬	ふゆ	***fuyu***	winter
上	うえ	***ue***	up	東	ひがし	***higashi***	east
下	した	***shita***	down	西	にし	***nishi***	west
中	なか	***naka***	center	南	みなみ	***minami***	south
目	め	***me***	eye	北	きた	***kita***	north
口	くち	***kuchi***	mouth	学生	がくせい	***gakusei***	student
手	て	***te***	hand	先生	せんせい	***sensei***	teacher
耳	みみ	***mimi***	ear	学校	がっこう	***gakkō***	school
鼻	はな	***hana***	nose	大学	だいがく	***daigaku***	university

漫画例 Manga Examples

Fluently mastering basic greetings in Japanese at an early stage in your studies is very important. In the manga examples, as usual, we will see samples of real usage of some of the most basic and useful expressions. Study them thoroughly.

Manga Example 1: Morning greeting

J.M. Ken Niimura

Yui:	おはよう	***ohayō***
Tetsuya:	おはよ	***ohayo***
	Good morning.	

This is the morning greeting, generally used until 11 am or noon, when it is replaced by ***konnichi wa*** ("hello.") ***Ohayō*** is a colloquial simplification of the formal expression ***ohayō gozaimasu***, and is widely used in everyday conversation between friends.

Note: Notice that Tetsuya doesn't pronounce the long ***o***. This has the effect of making him sound more informal.

Manga Example 2: Afternoon greeting

J.M. Ken Niimura

This greeting is usually said from noon until late in the afternoon (around 6 or 7 pm.) This is easily one of the most useful Japanese greetings there is, so memorize it as soon as possible.

Note: The syllable は is not pronounced ***ha*** here, which is how it should be read according to the hiragana table in Lesson1. Here it is pronounced ***wa***. In Lesson 16 we will gain more insight on this.

Professor Shinobu: こんにちは
konnichi wa
Hello.

Manga Example 3: Evening greeting

Konban wa is the evening greeting, used from around 6 or 7 pm. As in Manga Example 2, the syllable は is pronounced ***wa*** and not ***ha***.

Guillermo March

Note: The word ***ōji*** means "prince" and ***-sama*** is a honorific suffix for people's names. We will study these suffixes in Lesson15.

Mary: こんばんは　王子様
konban wa ōji-sama
Good evening, my prince.

Manga Example 4: Expression of gratitude

Here we see a very common way of saying thank you: ***dōmo arigatō***. There are other ways of expressing gratitude, but this is a very useful expression and it always sounds good.

J.M. Ken Niimura

Takashi: どうもありがとう
dōmo arigatō
Thank you very much!
博士によろしく
hakase ni yoroshiku
Give the doctor my regards.

Manga Example 5: Farewell

In its literal translation, the expression in this manga example means something like "take care of your spirit." It is actually used to say goodbye to someone, telling them to take care. Therefore, "take care" is a more exact translation. However, the form of the expression used in this manga example is not used in contemporary colloquial language. The most usual expression, the one that you should use, is 気をつけて ***(ki o tsukete)***.

J.M. Ken Niimura

Ken: 気をつけろな
ki o tsukero na
Take care!

Exercises 練習

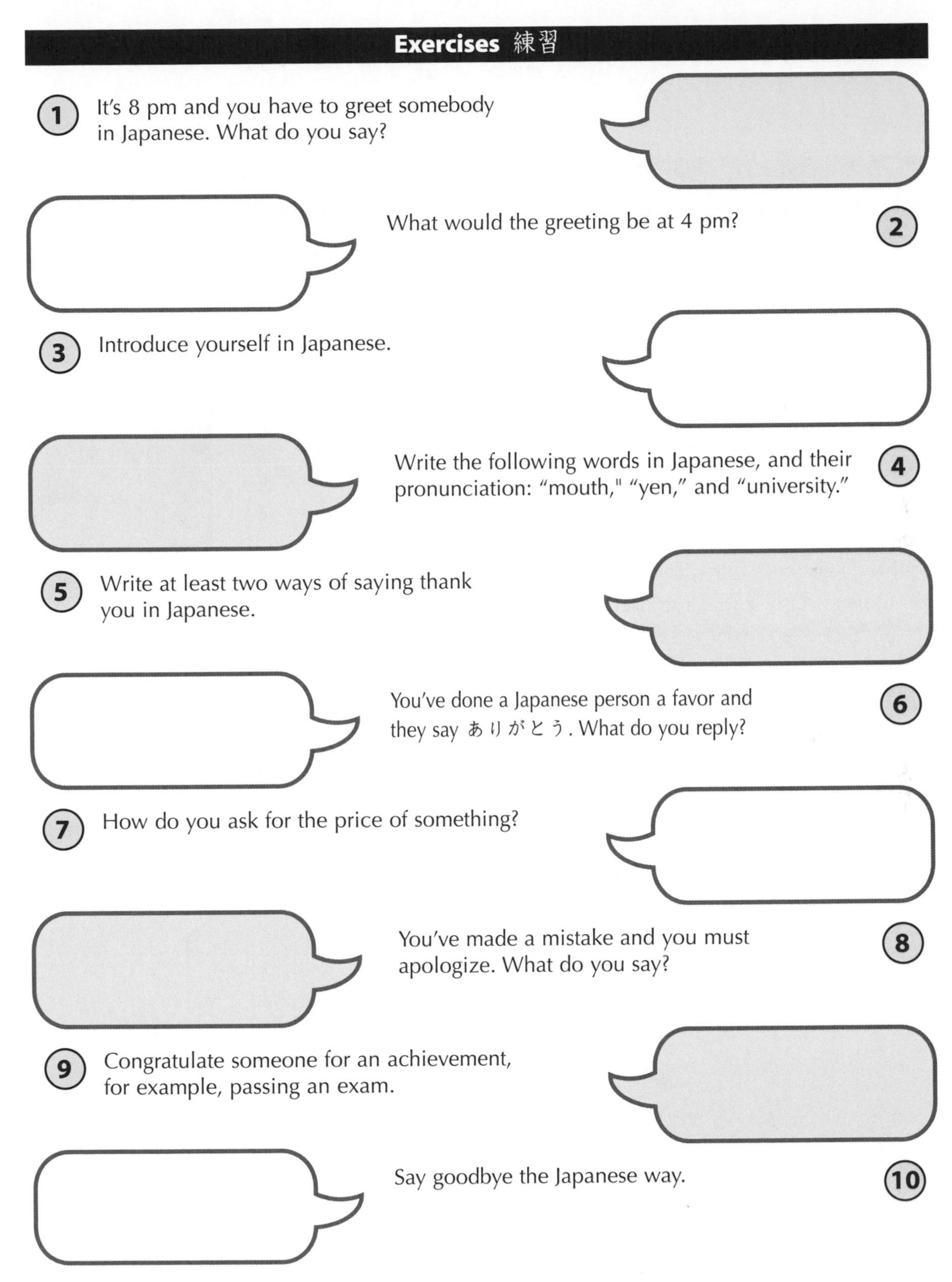

1. It's 8 pm and you have to greet somebody in Japanese. What do you say?

2. What would the greeting be at 4 pm?

3. Introduce yourself in Japanese.

4. Write the following words in Japanese, and their pronunciation: "mouth," "yen," and "university."

5. Write at least two ways of saying thank you in Japanese.

6. You've done a Japanese person a favor and they say ありがとう. What do you reply?

7. How do you ask for the price of something?

8. You've made a mistake and you must apologize. What do you say?

9. Congratulate someone for an achievement, for example, passing an exam.

10. Say goodbye the Japanese way.

— Answers to all the exercises can be found online by following the link on page 9. —

Lesson 5 • 第5課

Numbers

We are now going to study numbers in this lesson, something very useful for countless things, especially when you're shopping! Get ready, because you will need to memorize quite a few new words.

Do the Japanese use "our" numbers?

First of all, we must point out that, even though Japanese has a series of kanji which corresponds to each number and that numbers can be written in kanji, nowadays this way of representing them is not used very often. To our relief, the Japanese basically use Arabic numerals, just like us. (But, watch out, because they are pronounced the Japanese way, of course!) We are going to study the numbers with the help of three different tables. The first two tables show the numbers in Arabic numerals, then in kanji, next in hiragana, and finally in ***rōmaji***, so it is easier for you to memorize them.

Table number 1

In the first table we will see the numbers from 1 to 19, in other words, units and tens. You must memorize numbers 1 to 10 one by one. Just notice that numbers 0, 4, 7 and 9 have two different pronunciations: you can use whichever you like, they are both correct and valid.

Tens, that is, numbers from 10 to 19, are very easy if you already know the units: all you need to do is add ***jū*** (10) before the units. For example, number 15 is called ***jū go*** (ten-five). Unlike English, where "teen" is added after the number: 16 = sixteen (six-ten).

Short list of useful kanji							
0	○	れい/ゼロ	***rei/zero***	10	十	じゅう	***jū***
1	一	いち	***ichi***	11	十一	じゅういち	***jū ichi***
2	二	に	***ni***	12	十二	じゅうに	***jū ni***
3	三	さん	***san***	13	十三	じゅうさん	***jū san***
4	四	し/よん	***shi/yon***	14	十四	じゅうし/じゅうよん	***jū shi/jū yon***
5	五	ご	***go***	15	十五	じゅうご	***jū go***
6	六	ろく	***roku***	16	十六	じゅうろく	***jū roku***
7	七	しち/なな	***shichi/nana***	17	十七	じゅうしち/じゅうなな	***jū shichi/jū nana***
8	八	はち	***hachi***	18	十八	じゅうはち	***jū hachi***
9	九	く/きゅう	***ku/kyū***	19	十九	じゅうく/じゅうきゅう	***jū ku/jū kyū***

Table 2: Tens, hundreds, thousands, etc.											
10	十	じゅう	***jū***	100	百	ひゃく	***hyaku***	1,000	千	せん	***sen***
20	二十	にじゅう	***ni jū***	200	二百	にひゃく	***ni hyaku***	2,000	二千	にせん	***ni sen***
30	三十	さんじゅう	***san jū***	300	三百	さんびゃく	***san byaku***	3,000	三千	さんぜん	***san zen***
40	四十	よんじゅう	***yon jū***	400	四百	よんひゃく	***yon hyaku***	4,000	四千	よんせん	***yon sen***
50	五十	ごじゅう	***go jū***	500	五百	ごひゃく	***go hyaku***	5,000	五千	ごせん	***go sen***
60	六十	ろくじゅう	***roku jū***	600	六百	ろっぴゃく	***roppyaku***	6,000	六千	ろくせん	***roku sen***
70	七十	ななじゅう	***nana jū***	700	七百	ななひゃく	***nana hyaku***	7,000	七千	ななせん	***nana sen***
80	八十	はちじゅう	***hachi jū***	800	八百	はっぴゃく	***happyaku***	8,000	八千	はっせん	***hassen***
90	九十	きゅうじゅう	***kyū jū***	900	九百	きゅうひゃく	***kyū hyaku***	9,000	九千	きゅうせん	***kyū sen***

10,000	一万	いちまん	***ichi man***	1,000,000	百万	ひゃくまん	***hyaku man***
100,000	十万	じゅうまん	***jū man***	10,000,000	千万	せんまん	***sen man***

Table number 2

Now numbers start getting a bit more complicated. In this table we have tens, hundreds, thousands, and in the bottom part, the "ten-thousands." Tens have no secret, they consist of "number + 10." That is, number 60 is ***roku jū***, "six tens" in its literal translation, and 30 is ***san jū***, "three tens."

Hundreds and thousands are just like in English. The number 500 is ***go hyaku***, "five hundred," 900 is ***kyū hyaku***, "nine hundred," and 2,000 is ***ni sen***, "two thousand." Pay attention to the somewhat special readings of 300, 600, 800, 3,000, and 8,000.

Let's move onto the "ten-thousands." What is this? It's an expression we have made up to define the number ***man***. Eastern cultures don't have the same concept we have for large numbers. While we interpret the number 10,000 as "ten thousand," they say this number is ***1 man***. Therefore, in Japanese number 10,000 is called ***ichi man***. Make sure you don't say ***jū sen***, literally "ten thousand," because it is completely wrong in Japanese. It is extremely easy to get confused with this number, especially when you get to larger numbers. A million in Japan is interpreted as ***hyaku man***, "one hundred ***man***," and ten million as ***sen man***, "one thousand ***man***."

For your reference, we will give you even larger numbers that are not in the table, but which you might come across someday: 億 ***oku*** (100,000,000, one hundred million) and 兆 ***chō*** , (1,000,000,000,000, a trillion.) For example: 三十億 ***san jū oku***, "three billion," 三兆 ***san chō***, "three trillion."

Table number 3

In this last table we can see the composition process of much more complex numbers. Look carefully at how each number is "assembled": it isn't particularly difficult, but you can get a little mixed up in the beginning.

Here's an example to get you into the right frame of mind. How do you say 34,267 in Japanese? Let's see first how many ***man*** ("ten-thousands") there are. Since there are three, let's start from ***san man***, 30,000; then we have 4 thousands (***yon sen***, 4,000). At the moment we have ***san man yon sen***, 34,000.

Table 3: How to form complex numbers

								一	1	いち ***ichi***
							十	一	11	じゅういち ***jū ichi***
						八	十	一	81	はちじゅういち ***hachi jū ichi***
					百	八	十	一	181	ひゃくはちじゅういち ***hyaku hachi jū ichi***
				五	百	八	十	一	581	ごひゃくはちじゅういち ***go hyaku hachi jū ichi***
			千	五	百	八	十	一	1,581	せんごひゃくはちじゅういち ***sen go hyaku hachi jū ichi***
		三	千	五	百	八	十	一	3,581	さんぜんごひゃくはちじゅういち ***san zen go hyaku hachi jū ichi***
一	万	三	千	五	百	八	十	一	13,581	いちまんさんぜんごひゃくはちじゅういち ***ichi man san zen go hyaku hachi jū ichi***
七	万	三	千	五	百	八	十	一	73,581	ななまんさんぜんごひゃくはちじゅういち ***nana man san zen go hyaku hachi jū ichi***
					百			一	101	ひゃくいち ***hyaku ichi***
					百		十		110	ひゃくじゅう ***hyaku jū***
		三	千					一	3,001	さんぜんいち ***san zen ichi***
		三	千			八	十		3,080	さんぜんはちじゅう ***san zen hachi jū***
七	万			五	百			一	70,501	ななまんごひゃくいち ***nana man go hyaku ichi***

Then, there are 2 hundreds (***ni hyaku***, 200), 6 tens (***roku jū***, 60), and finally one 7 (***nana***). If we put it all together, we find 34,267 is pronounced ***san man yon sen ni hyaku roku jū nana***. It's simpler than it looks, isn't it?

Now, the other way around. How would we write in numbers something like ***go man san zen roppyaku ni jū hachi***? Let's see, ***go man*** = 50,000, ***san zen*** = 3,000, ***roppyaku*** = 600, ***ni jū*** = 20, and ***hachi*** = 8. Therefore, the answer is 53,628. Written in kanji it would be even easier. Take a look: ***go man*** = 五万, ***san zen*** = 三千, ***roppyaku*** = 六百, ***ni jū*** = 二十 and ***hachi*** = 八. If we put all the kanji together, we will have 五万三千六百二十八, which is the equivalent in Japanese writing to the number 53,628.

Be careful, because Western numbers are often combined with kanji, especially when dealing with round numbers. For example, you may come across 3千 ***san zen*** (3,000), or 500万 ***go hyaku man*** (5,000,000).

When it comes to giving the price of something, we will always find the kanji 円 after a number. This character, pronounced ***en***, means "yen," the Japanese currency. If an object is marked 4千円 (***yon sen en***), then we will know its price is 4,000 yen. Mastering numbers and the kanji 円 is a matter of survival!

漫画例 Manga Examples

In the manga examples in this lesson we have chosen frames that show good examples of numbers, even if the level of the rest of the language is quite high. So don't worry if you can't understand all the text, just look carefully at the numbers, our focus for this lesson.

Manga Example 1: 8 million

This manga example features the character Rage, who is surprised at the power of the enemy fleet. The part of the text we'd like to highlight is the number 八百万 ***happyaku man***, where we have the kanji for 万 ***man***, which, as you probably remember, means 10,000. If 八 ***hachi*** is 8, and 百 ***hyaku*** is 100, then, number 八百万 will be 800 times 10,000, that is, 8 million. Although its literal meaning is "8 million," the Japanese use this number to convey that some quantity is very large, uncountable or infinite. It's like saying in English "a thousand and one" or "a million and one," as in the sentence "I've got a million and one things to do"; rather than giving the actual figure, we simply wish to give an exaggerated number for a more dramatic effect.

About ordinal numbers: Forming ordinal numbers in Japanese is very simple. All you have to do is place the word 第 ***dai*** before the number. We see Rage talks about the sixth division and she says ***dai roku kikōgun***. We can find more examples in the Japanese titles which head all the lessons in this book, for example, the title of this lesson: 第5課. This means, of course, fifth lesson.

Rage: 帝国第六機甲軍が…
Teikoku dai roku kikōgun ga...
empire sixth division armored...
The Empire's sixth armored division…
八百万の艦隊が…
happyaku man no kantai ga...
eight-hundred-man squadrons...
Has eight million squadrons…

Manga Example 2: 20 million

Here we see how an executive tries to get a singer to terminate her contract by bribing her. What we want to look at in this example is the number 二千万 ***ni sen man***, literally translated "two thousand ten-thousands" (attention to 万 = 10,000), that is, 20 million. Be very careful with the number 万 ***man***, as it is very easy to get confused.

Guillermo March

Hashizaki: 二千万ある
ni sen man aru
two thousand ***man*** there are
Here are 20 million.

契約破棄の違約金だ
keiyaku haki no iyakukin da
contract cancellation compensation
It's a compensation for the cancellation of your contract.

受け取りたまえ
uketoritamae
accept (*command form*)
You must take it.

Manga Example 3: A strange watch

This strange watch was the prize in a magazine contest. It is curious how the numbers are written the Japanese way and not the Western way, as they usually are on Japanese watches. In addition, the small circle in the bottom right corner features an inscription with another number. Here, we see the number 100, ***hyaku***, next to 人, the kanji for "person," which we studied in Lesson 3. This means there were one hundred watches for one hundred lucky people. The way of writing the same expression using Japanese numbers would be 百人 ***hyaku nin***.

Watch:	十二	三	六	九	Box:	100人
	jū ni	***san***	***roku***	***kyū***		***hyaku nin***
	twelve	three	six	nine		One hundred people

Exercises 練習

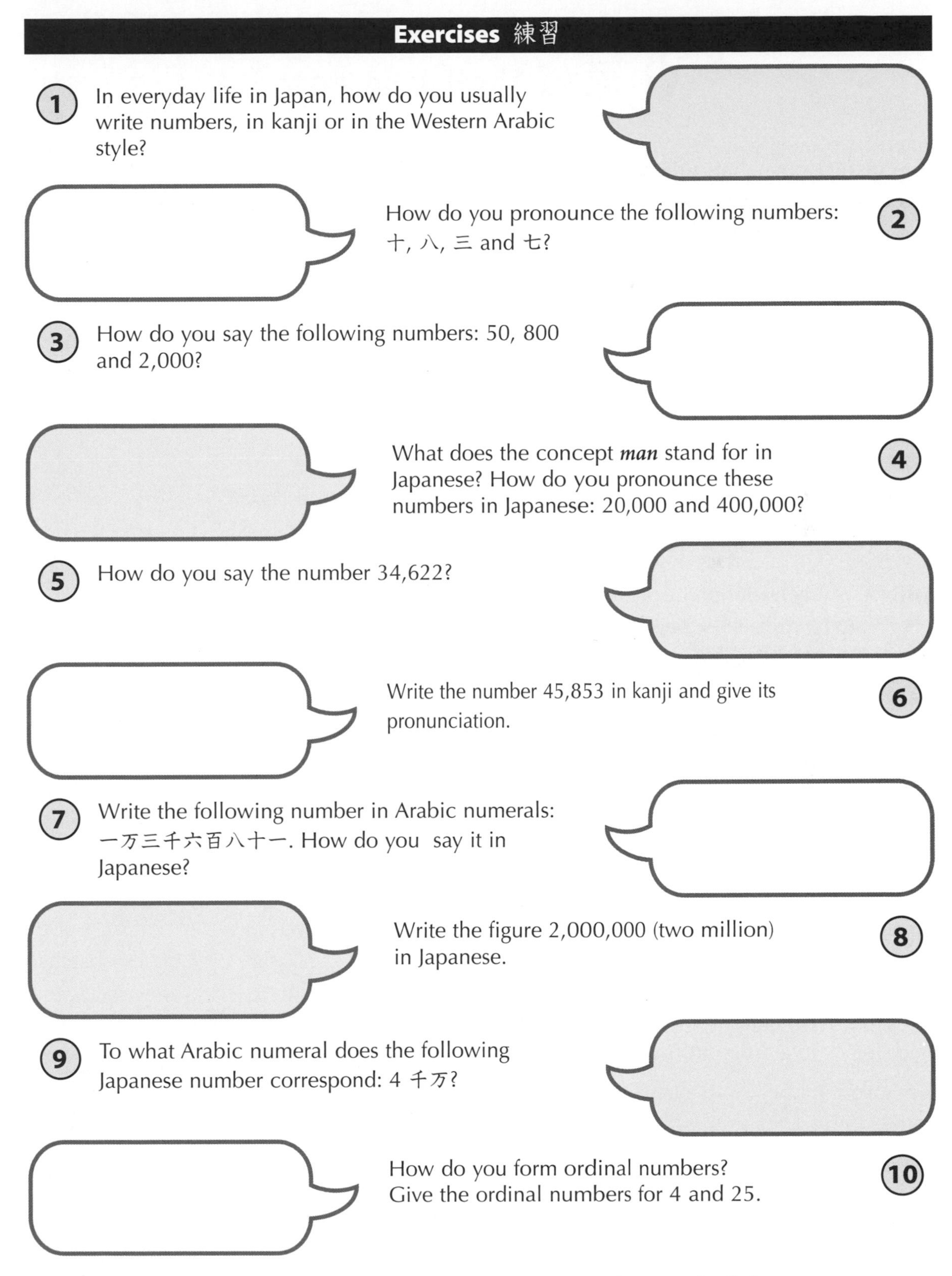

1 In everyday life in Japan, how do you usually write numbers, in kanji or in the Western Arabic style?
2 How do you pronounce the following numbers: 十, 八, 三 and 七?
3 How do you say the following numbers: 50, 800 and 2,000?
4 What does the concept *man* stand for in Japanese? How do you pronounce these numbers in Japanese: 20,000 and 400,000?
5 How do you say the number 34,622?
6 Write the number 45,853 in kanji and give its pronunciation.
7 Write the following number in Arabic numerals: 一万三千六百八十一. How do you say it in Japanese?
8 Write the figure 2,000,000 (two million) in Japanese.
9 To what Arabic numeral does the following Japanese number correspond: 4 千万?
10 How do you form ordinal numbers? Give the ordinal numbers for 4 and 25.

— Answers to all the exercises can be found online by following the link on page 9. —

落城 The Rakujō Story

The manga story that runs through the first 30 lessons takes place on the distant planet of Saka, which was devastated by defeat in a war a few years earlier. Nevertheless, Saka still has an air of splendor, a remnant of its once highly developed civilization and an echo of its once regal reign over the galaxy. On the planet Saka there is a great fortress, apparently impregnable, where Saka's leaders, Yodo and her son, Hide, are taking refuge. The governor of the galaxy, Yasu, is looking for an excuse to attack and take control of Saka. But in order to take control of this proud and rebellious planet, he has to defeat Saka's fierce general Yuki, who has arrived with his troops to defend the last fortress . . .

Characters

Yuki: Brave and faithful general, loyal to his leaders, Yodo and Hide.

Yodo: A woman of strong character, as beautiful as she is obstinate. She is mother to Hide, and is relentless in imposing her own opinions upon him.

Hide: Young leader of the planet Saka. Being a rather timid and fainthearted man, he tends to let himself be persuaded by his mother's overbearing will.

Yasu: Present governor of the galaxy, an extremely cunning and ruthless strategist. He will not let anybody prevent him from gaining absolute control over the galaxy.

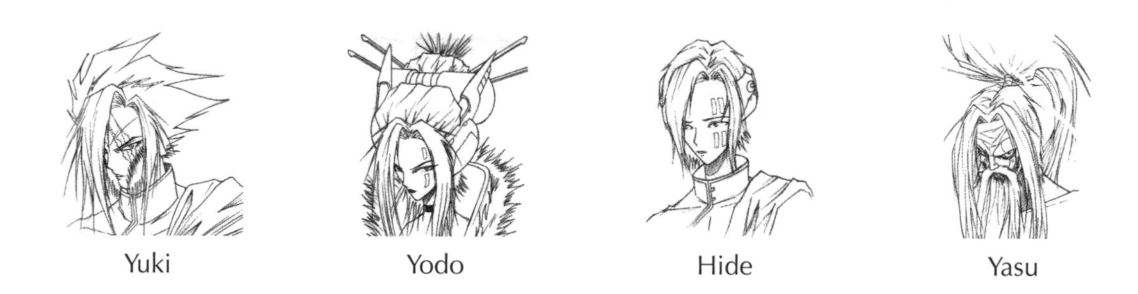

Yuki Yodo Hide Yasu

Watch out: When the sides of the panel are painted **black**, what is narrated in these panels takes place in a different time period to that of the story being told, either in the past or in the future.

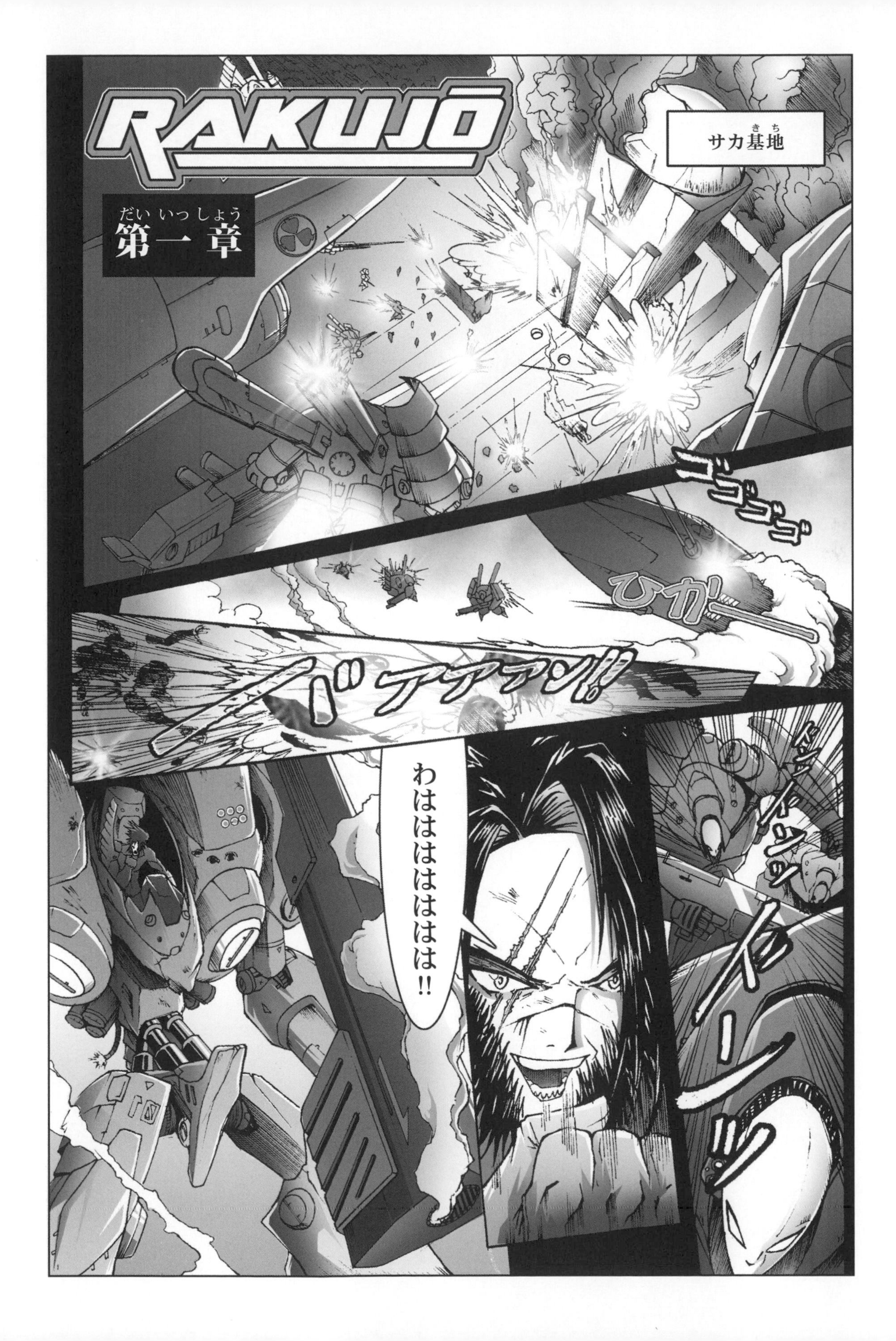
RAKUJŌ
だい いっしょう
第一章
サカ基地
きち
ゴゴゴゴ
ひか〜
バアアアン!!
わはははははは!!

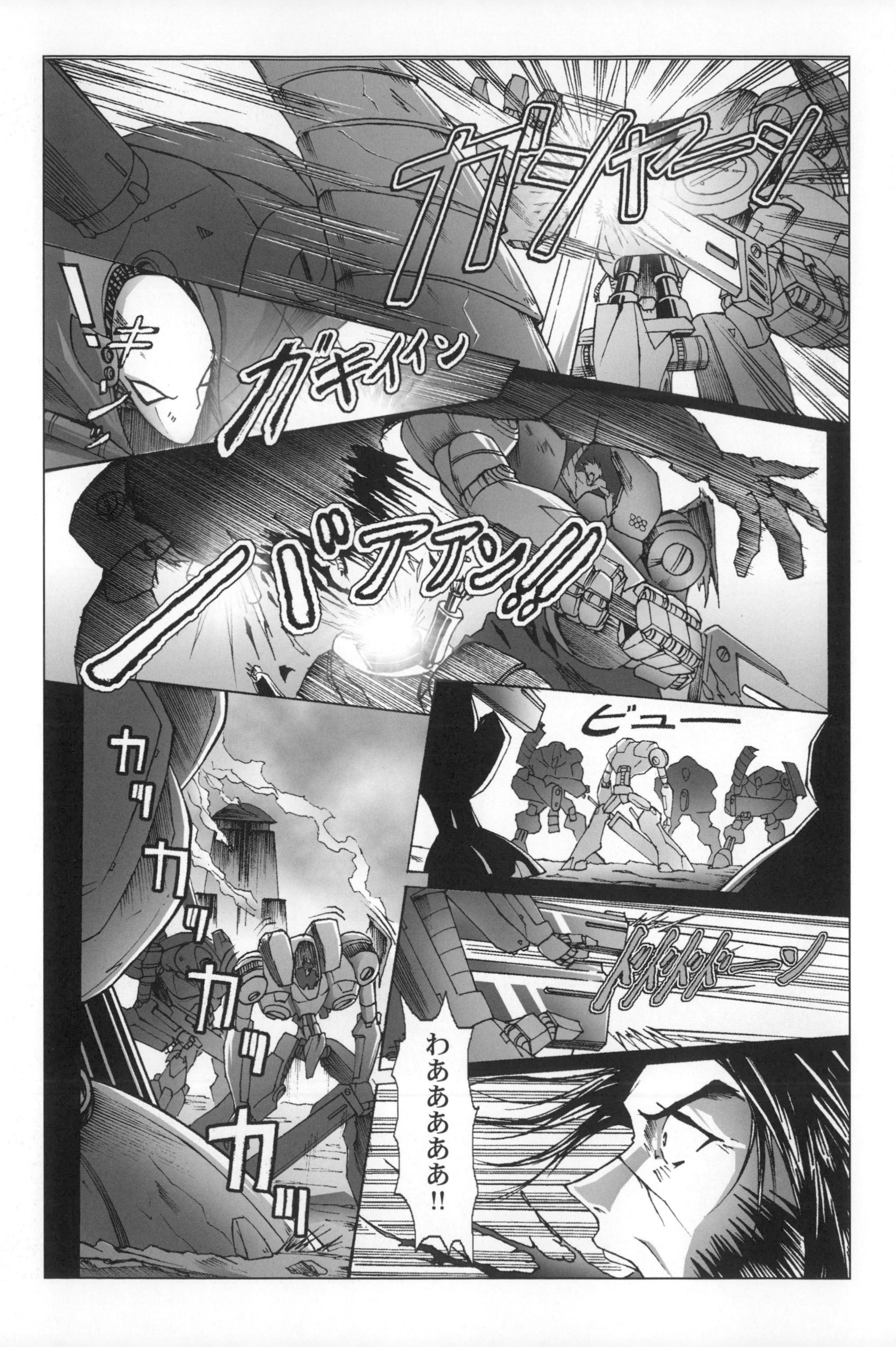
ガギャーン
ガキイイン
バアアン!!
ビュー
カッカッカッカッカッ
ドドドドーン
わあああああ!!

こんにちは、ヒデ。元気？
はい、元気です。
あ、おはようございます。
よろしくおねがいします、リーダー
はじめまして、私の名前はユキです。

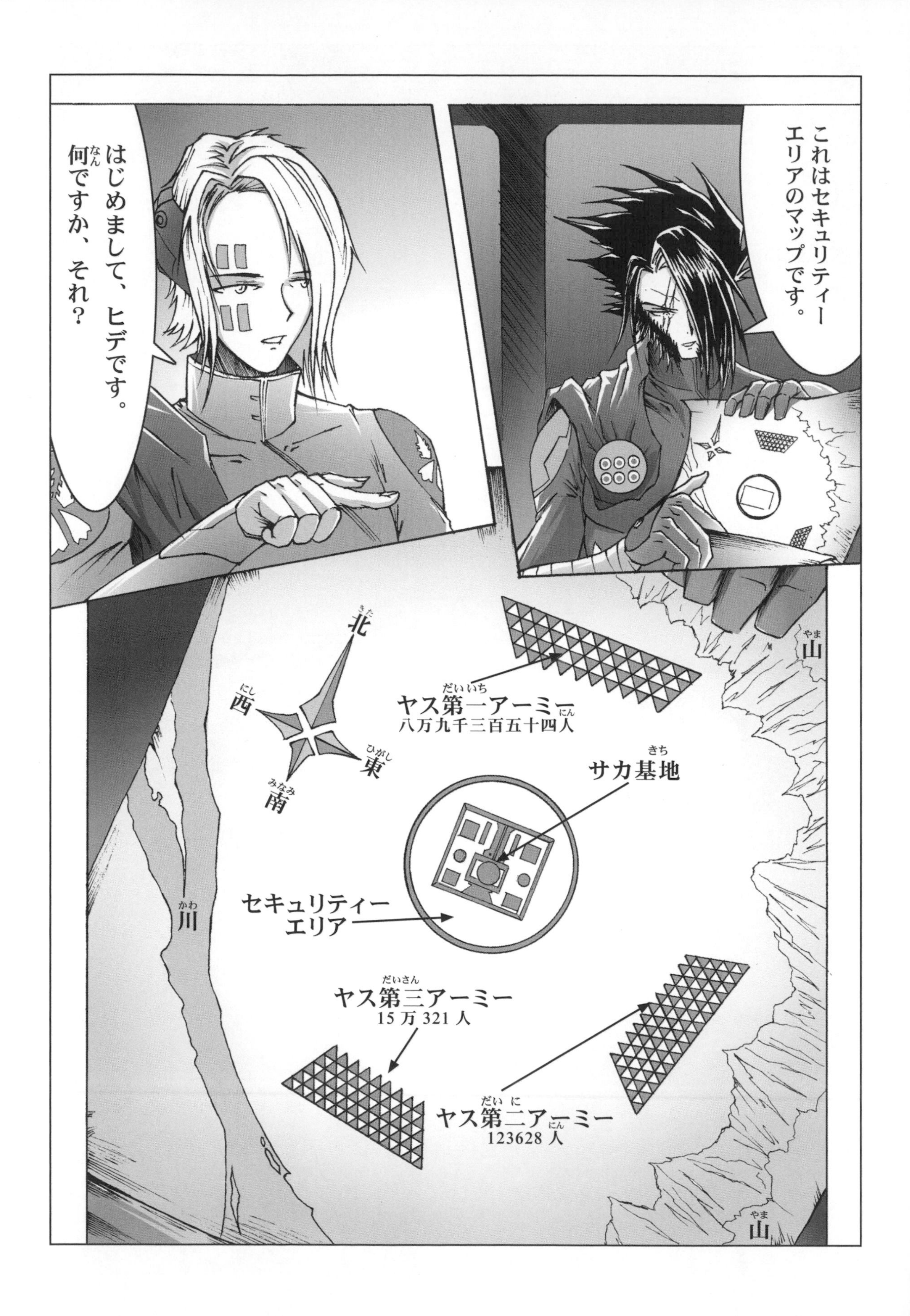
これはセキュリティーエリアのマップです。
はじめまして、ヒデです。何ですか、それ？
北
西
東
南
ヤス第一アーミー
八万九千三百五十四人
サカ基地
セキュリティーエリア
川
山
ヤス第三アーミー
15万321人
ヤス第二アーミー
123628人
山

Review for Lessons 1–5

Answers to all the review exercises can be found online by following the link on page 9.

Important: We are assuming that you have already mastered both of the Japanese syllabaries, hiragana and katakana, to perfection. Therefore, you won't have the help of ***rōmaji*** in these exercises. Good luck!

RAKUJŌ – New vocabulary 新しい単語

章(しょう)	chapter, episode	エリア	area
基地(きち)	(military) base	マップ	map
リーダー	leader	アーミー	army
セキュリティー	security		

1. Based on what you have read in the first episode of ***Rakujō***, what sound or action do you think the following onomatopoeia represent?

カッカッカッカッ	____________	わはははは	____________
ゴゴゴゴゴ	____________	ドドドーン	____________
ガキィィィン	____________	ビュー	____________

2. What is the name of the man who introduces himself to Hide at the end of page 3?

3. How many men make up Yasu's first army? How about the third army?

4. How many men are in each of Yasu's armies?

5. Choose the right answer:

a) What greeting would you use at 2 pm?

1. こんばんは　2. こんにちは　3. こんにちわ　4. こんぱんは

b) What do you say when you go to bed at night?

1. おやすみなさい　2. おはよう　3. こんばんは　4. バイバイ

c) If you had to congratulate someone, what expression would you use?

1. すみません　2. じゃね、また　3. おめでとうございます　4. どうも

d) How would a young man say goodbye to a classmate whom he'll be seeing soon?

1. またね！　2. さようなら！　3. まだね！　4. ごめんなさい！

e) What is the standard answer to the greeting お元気(げんき)ですか？

1. まあ、ね　2. はい、元気(げんき)です　3. 気(き)をつけて
4. よろしくお願(ねが)いします

6. A friend says ありがとう！ to you. What do you answer? And what do you answer if a person you hardly know says ありがとうございます?

7. What is the meaning of 気(き)をつけて and in what kind of situations do we use it?

8. It's 8 am, and you go into a store. Write the conversation you have with the storekeeper, following the prompts.

You:	おはようございます	(Good morning.)
Storekeeper:	______________	(Welcome.)
You:	______________	(How much is this?)
Storekeeper:	______________	(It's 343 yen.)
You:	______________	(383 yen?)
Storekeeper:	______________	(No, 343 yen.)
You:	______________	(I'll take it, please.)
Storekeeper:	______________	(Thank you very much.)
You:	______________	(You are welcome.)
Storekeeper:	______________	(Goodbye.)

9. Practice writing the hiragana below.

た	ニ	ナ	た	た		ふ			
あ	ニ	ナ				き			
む	ニ					え			
ゆ						ち			
す						ね			
は						を			
お						ま			
け						か			

10. Link each hiragana character with its corresponding reading in ***rōmaji***.

の	***mi***	ちゃ	***zu***
き	***sa***	ぺ	***cha***
く	***ku***	じょ	***ne***
さ	***no***	づ	***wa***
じ	***pa***	わ	***ga***
し	***ji***	が	***zu***
み	***ki***	ず	***jo***
ぱ	***shi***	ね	***pe***

11. Transcribe each hiragana character into ***rōmaji*** and vice versa.

い *i* ______	う ______	じゅ ______	***to*** と ______	***be*** ______	***chu*** ______
ぞ ______	な ______	ちゃ ______	***o*** ______	***go*** ______	***rya*** ______
ぽ ______	ぬ ______	りょ ______	***pe*** ______	***wa*** ______	***gyu*** ______
か ______	を ______	きゃ ______	***ru*** ______	***zu*** ______	***ja*** ______
り ______	ん ______	みゅ ______	***mo*** ______	***shi*** ______	***byo*** ______

12. Transcribe the following words in hiragana into ***rōmaji***.

おんがく	***ongaku***	いちご	______	つなみ	______
さかな	______	ちゃのゆ	______	でんしゃ	______
りょかん	______	いしばし	______	くいだおれ	______
いいわけ	______	けいさつかん	______	ふつかよい	______
したぎ	______	いきじごく	______	かみのけ	______
どろぼう	______	とうきょう	______	きっぱり	______
くうしゅう	______	ぎょうざ	______	まっちゃ	______
がんりゅう	______	さっぽろ	______	きょうみ	______
したっぱ	______	ぎゅうにゅう	______	いろっぽい	______

13. Transcribe the following words in ***rōmaji*** into hiragana.

nihongo	にほんご	***meitantei***	______	***jitabata***	______
shamisen	______	***nemawashi***	______	***kannushi***	______
nagoyaka	______	***tsuyu***	______	***tabako***	______
tanpopo	______	***pakuri***	______	***ebisu***	______
momiage	______	***tebukuro***	______	***donzoko***	______
kyūri	______	***jakkan***	______	***assari***	______
jūdō	______	***kenkyū***	______	***buchō***	______
gunyagunya	______	***kyūshū***	______	***yappari***	______
kyakka	______	***rōmaji***	______	***kyūdō***	______

14. If there are any mistakes in the following transcriptions, correct them.

かがや	***ka~~n~~aya*** (g)	おのはら	***anohara***	あっぱれ	***appawa***
こっぱ	***kobba***	さぼてん	***kiboten***	はだか	***hodaka***
ぶらり	***purari***	こわっぱ	***koneppa***	うなりごえ	***unerigoe***
りょうほう	***ryōhō***	のうぎょう	***nūgyō***	まみれ	***momiwa***

15. Practice writing the katakana below.

ホ	一	十	才	ホ	シ				
チ	一	二			ク				
サ	一				ウ				
ロ					メ				
マ					ソ				
ヨ					ン				
ナ					ラ				
ネ					オ				

16. Link each katakana character with its corresponding reading in ***rōmaji***.

デ	***so***	チャ	***pu***
オ	***a***	ジ	***shu***
ソ	***n***	プ	***su***
マ	***ma***	ミョ	***ji***
ン	***de***	ス	***re***
ム	***zo***	ロ	***cha***
ゾ	***o***	シュ	***ro***
ア	***mu***	レ	***myo***

17. Transcribe each katakana character into ***rōmaji*** and vice versa.

カ ***ka***	エ ______	ギュ ______	***ze*** ゼ	***no*** ______	***pyu*** ______
ド ______	ワ ______	リャ ______	***u*** ______	***n*** ______	***ja*** ______
ツ ______	フ ______	チャ ______	***ke*** ______	***wa*** ______	***myo*** ______
メ ______	ク ______	ピョ ______	***ji*** ______	***yu*** ______	***byu*** ______
ル ______	ポ ______	ジョ ______	***bi*** ______	***mi*** ______	***sho*** ______

18. Transcribe the following words in katakana into ***rōmaji***.

パンダ	panda	ミルク	________	ワシントン	________
ロリコン	________	ピアノ	________	ゼネラル	________
ギャル	________	ジャンボ	________	タンゴ	________
マラソン	________	ギリシア	________	ソーダ	________
オランダ	________	シャワー	________	ギブアップ	________
キャラバン	________	クリーナー	________	ハーモニー	________
バグダッド	________	ルノアール	________	フットボール	________
キューピッド	________	マトリックス	________	チャーミング	________
マスコット	________	アットマーク	________	ホットポット	________

19. Transcribe the following words in ***rōmaji*** into katakana.

furansu	フランス	***shatsu***	________	***gurume***	________
pasokon	________	***arabama***	________	***igirisu***	________
maiwaifu	________	***neruson***	________	***myunhen***	________
remon	________	***kyaria***	________	***napori***	________
nūdo	________	***apaato***	________	***gyappu***	________
kōhii	________	***kūdetaa***	________	***raamen***	________
pureeyaa	________	***kukkii***	________	***piramiddo***	________
chachacha	________	***biitoruzu***	________	***kyasshu***	________
supittsu	________	***jaanarisuto***	________	***doraiyaa***	________

20. If there are any mistakes in the following transcriptions, correct them.

シューマイ	***sh~~aa~~mai*** (ū)	ソナタ	***tsunata***	レバー	***rebaa***
ミスター	***misukū***	アンドラ	***asodora***	メキシコ	***mekinko***
ノウハウ	***souhawa***	ケース	***keenu***	キャンセル	***kyanseru***
ビッグマン	***pigguman***	サッカー	***sakkaa***	ナニワ	***naniu***

Kanji

一	二	三	四	五	六	七	八	九
(1)	(2)	(3)	(4)	(5)	(6)	(7)	(8)	(9)
十	百	千	万	円	東	西	南	北
(10)	(11)	(12)	(13)	(14)	(29)	(30)	(31)	(32)

21. Practice writing the kanji below. Find the stroke order in the online Kanji Compilation section via the link on page 9.

南	一	十	十丨							
四	丨									
円										
北										
万										

22. Link each kanji with its meaning.

東 ⟶	east	百	west
六	south	九	ten
万	six	西	nine
円	ten thousand	北	hundred
南	yen	二	north
一	one	十	two

23. Link each kanji with its most common reading.

北	なな	十	みなみ
七	ご	三	さん
千	いち	西	よん
東	きた	万	はち
五	ひがし	南	まん
一	せん	四	じゅう
円	えん	八	にし

24. Write the following numbers in kanji and give their reading in ***furigana***.

8	八 (はち)	3	_____	9	_____
16	_____	12	_____	24	_____
35	_____	47	_____	50	_____
88	_____	111	_____	897	_____
7,200	_____	3,874	_____	1,011	_____

25. Give the reading of the following numbers, and write them in Arabic numerals.

三	さん	(3)	五	_____	( )
十九	_____	( )	八十	_____	( )
五十八	_____	( )	九十五	_____	( )
百二	_____	( )	三百五十七	_____	( )
八千五十一	_____	( )	千二百三十三	_____	( )

26. Write the following numbers in kanji and give their reading in ***furigana***.

3,783	三千七百八十三 (さんぜんななひゃくはちじゅうさん)	10,940	_____
24,851	_____	300,340	_____
834,901	_____	108,234	_____
560,205	_____	1,280,785	_____
75,034,026	_____	834,201,016	_____

27. Give the reading of the following numbers, and write them in Arabic numerals.

二万六千二百三	にまんろくせんにひゃくさん	(26,203)
五万七百二十九	_____	( )
十八万五千五百三十二	_____	( )
三百八十七万五千二百十四	_____	( )
二億三千二百万五千百十二	_____	( )

Lesson 6 • 第6課

Days and Months

In the previous lesson we studied numbers. Now, we are going to study the days of the week, the days of the month and the months. You may find it hard to believe, but lessons 5 and 6 have a lot in common, so you should review the previous lesson thoroughly before you carry on.

Days of the week

The first table shows us how to say the days in Japanese. First is the kanji, then the hiragana and, finally, the ***rōmaji*** transcription.

Note that all days have the 曜日 ***yōbi*** part in common, because ***yōbi*** means "day of the week." The kanji before ***yōbi*** shows the original meaning of each of the days of the week, as you can see on the bottom part of the table. Therefore, Monday would be the "moon day (月)," Tuesday the "fire day (火)," and so on...

Days of the week			
Monday	月曜日	げつようび	***getsuyōbi***
Tuesday	火曜日	かようび	***kayōbi***
Wednesday	水曜日	すいようび	***suiyōbi***
Thursday	木曜日	もくようび	***mokuyōbi***
Friday	金曜日	きんようび	***kin'yōbi***
Saturday	土曜日	どようび	***doyōbi***
Sunday	日曜日	にちようび	***nichiyōbi***
月 moon | 火 fire | 水 water | 木 tree | 金 metal | 土 earth | 日 sun			

A brief remark

Remember in Lesson 3 when we talked about kanji and their different readings according to the kanji position in the sentence? Did you notice anything odd in the table above? That's right, the word "Sunday," in Japanese, is 日曜日 ***nichiyōbi***, and the same kanji, 日, is read both ***nichi*** and ***bi*** in the same word. That's because the same character, depending on the context, can mean "sun" and "day." The first time it appears (pronounced ***nichi***) it refers to "sun," and the second time (pronounced ***bi***) it refers to "day." Therefore, Sunday is "sun day." (Hey, just like English!)

The exact same thing happens with the character 月, which can mean "moon," as in 月曜日 ***getsuyōbi***, "moon day"; or "month," as in 四月 ***shigatsu***, literally "month number 4," that is "April" (as we will soon see).

Days of the month

There are no specific names for the days of the month in English, we simply say "the first" or "the twenty-fifth"; that is, we use numbers alone. In Japanese, names for the days of the month do exist, at least from one to ten. From the eleventh on, we simply use the regular number and all you need to do is add the word ***nichi*** (which in this context means "day.") Therefore, if today were the 26th, we would say ***kyō wa ni jū roku nichi desu*** ("today is the 26th") (***kyō*** = today | wa = subject particle | ***ni jū roku*** = 26 | ***nichi*** = day | ***desu*** = verb to be.) For precisely this reason, you need to know the numbers very well, as we mentioned in the introduction. If you haven't done this already, first study Lesson 5 thoroughly.

The table below shows the special words for days 1 to 10 of the month. Notice how the kanji are simply those which correspond to the numbers plus the kanji for day (日), but the reading for the 4th (四日) is not ***yon nichi*** (***yon*** = 4 | ***nichi*** = day) but ***yokka***... You have just come across one of the big obstacles in Japanese: special readings for kanji. The are some words, like those which correspond to the first ten days of the month, with special readings, and you have no choice but to learn them by heart. (Be careful! "Day 4" 四日 ***yokka*** / "day 8" 八日 ***yōka***.)

Days of the month and months							
1	一日	ついたち	***tsuitachi***	January	一月	いちがつ	***ichi gatsu***
2	二日	ふつか	***futsuka***	February	二月	にがつ	***ni gatsu***
3	三日	みっか	***mikka***	March	三月	さんがつ	***san gatsu***
4	四日	よっか	***yokka***	April	四月	しがつ	***shi gatsu***
5	五日	いつか	***itsuka***	May	五月	ごがつ	***go gatsu***
6	六日	むいか	***muika***	June	六月	ろくがつ	***roku gatsu***
7	七日	なのか	***nanoka***	July	七月	しちがつ	***shichi gatsu***
8	八日	ようか	***yōka***	August	八月	はちがつ	***hachi gatsu***
9	九日	ここのか	***kokonoka***	September	九月	くがつ	***ku gatsu***
10	十日	とおか	***tooka***	October	十月	じゅうがつ	***jū gatsu***
11	十一日	じゅういちにち	***jū ichi nichi***	November	十一月	じゅういちがつ	***jū ichi gatsu***
12	十二日	じゅうににち	***jū ni nichi***	December	十二月	じゅうにがつ	***jū ni gatsu***
14	十四日	じゅうよっか	***jū yokka***				
17	十七日	じゅうしちにち	***jū shichi nichi***				
19	十九日	じゅうくにち	***jū ku nichi***				
20	二十日	はつか	***hatsuka***				
?	何日？	なんにち？	***nan nichi?***	What month?	何月？	なんがつ？	***nan gatsu?***

From the 11th on, as we mentioned before, there is no problem, except with the 14th, which is not jū ***yon nichi***, but ***jū yokka***. And again with the 24th, which is pronounced ***ni jū yokka***, and not ni ***jū yon nichi***. Finally, pay attention to the 17th and the 19th, which are pronounced ***jū shichi nichi*** and ***jū ku nichi*** respectively, and not ***jū nana nichi*** nor ***jū kyū nichi***, which would be the other possible readings. Oh, and the 20th has a special pronunciation too! It is ***hatsuka*** instead of ***ni jū nichi***.

Months

At last something easy in Japanese! The Japanese don't have month names like we do (March, July, etc.), they use numbers 1 to 12 to name them instead, followed by the word 月 ***gatsu***, which means "month." Therefore, "July" is ***shichi gatsu*** in Japanese, that is, "seventh month." It's easy, isn't it? If you can count to 12 in Japanese, then saying the months should be no problem for you.

The table opposite lists all the months. You just need to pay attention to the pronunciation of "April," "July" and "September." They are pronounced ***shi gatsu, shichi gatsu***, and ***ku gatsu***, respectively, and not ***yon gatsu***, ***nana gatsu***, or ***kyū gatsu***, which would seem to be likely options. Remember how in the previous lesson we saw numbers 4, 7, and 9 which have two different pronunciations? Here we can only use one of them.

On years

Although the Japanese recognize the Western calendar (which started in remembrance of the birth of Christ), they still use the Japanese imperial calendar. For instance, while the Western world lived in year 2000 A.D., in Japan they lived in the year 12 of the Heisei era.

This doesn't mean they don't use our calendar in everyday life. Western influence has overcome tradition and, nowadays, "year 2000" is used as often as "year 12 of the Heisei era." However, in official documents, the tendency to almost always use the Japanese nomenclature instead of the Western one is still very strong.

The obvious question is: what is the basis for the Japanese way of counting years? The answer is in the reigns of the emperors. 1989 was the first year of the Heisei era because it was then that the present emperor, Akihito, came to the throne.

To end this lesson, we will see some of the most recent eras and their emperors.

Meiji era	明治	(1868–1912)	Emperor Mutsuhito
Taishō era	大正	(1912–1926)	Emperor Yoshihito
Shōwa era	昭和	(1926–1989)	Emperor Hirohito
Heisei era	平成	(1989–2019)	Emperor Akihito
Reiwa era	令和	(2019–)	Emperor Naruhito

漫画例 Manga Examples

In this section of manga examples we will first study a couple of manga panels, as usual; then, we will break down the characteristics of a page from a Japanese calendar to help you learn how to express the date correctly.

Manga Example 1: December 28th

Studio Kōsen

The part we are interested in is, of course, the date: 12月28日 ***jū ni gatsu ni jū hachi nichi***. 12月, literally "month 12," is "December," and 28日 is "day 28." Thus, we have "December twenty-eighth."

Narrator:	１２月２８日	東京立川競輪場
	jū ni gatsu ni jū hachi nichi	***Tōkyō Tachikawa keirin-jō***
	12 month twenty-eight day	Tōkyō Tachikawa bicycle race place
	December twenty-eighth	**Tachikawa cycle track, Tokyo**
	競輪ＧＰ′９７ Ｓ級シリーズ	
	keirin GP kyū jū nana S-kyū shiriizu	
	bicycle race GP '97 S class series	
	Grand Prix in cycling '97, S series	

Manga Example 2: June 26th

Studio Kōsen

Sign:	6月26日	土曜日
	roku gatsu ni jū roku nichi	***doyōbi***
	six month twenty-six day	Saturday
	June twenty-sixth	**Saturday**

Here we have 6月26日 ***roku gatsu ni jū roku nichi***, that is "June twenty-sixth." Notice how you say the month first and then the day.

A Japanese calendar

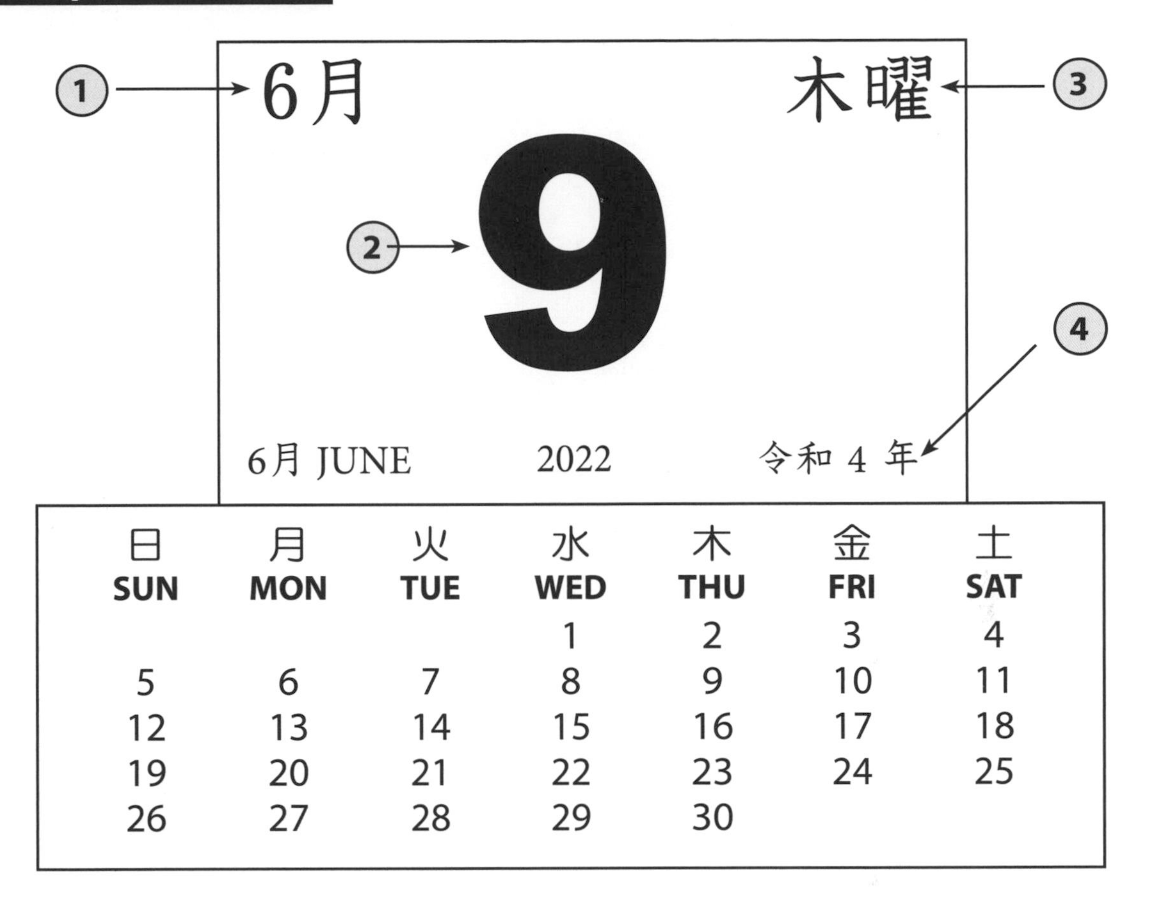

Let's analyze the elements of this calendar page one by one:

① 6 月 ***rokugatsu***. This is June's name (its literal translation would be "sixth month.") Under the number 9 we see the exact same word once more, but this time it comes with the English translation, "June."

② 9 ***kokonoka***. This is how we read number 9 when we are talking about the day of the month (be careful, as it is one of the special readings). It also is an abbreviated form, as it would usually be written 9日, with the kanji for "day" next to it.

③ 木曜 ***mokuyō***. This word means "Thursday." Its literal translation would be "tree day." Here we find an abbreviated form, without the kanji for "day" (日), the complete form being 木曜日 ***mokuyōbi***.

④ 令和 4 年 ***reiwa yo nen***. Literally, "year four of Reiwa." (Note the special pronunciation of the word 4 here.) Reiwa is the name of the present era, which started when Emperor Naruhito came to the throne in 2019. The Western year, 2022 is also included.

⑤ 日月火水木金土 These are the most abbreviated possible forms for the days of the week. You simply write the first kanji and forget about 曜日 ***yōbi***.

Exercises 練習

1. Translate the words 金曜日, 月曜日 and 木曜日 into English.

2. Write the seven days of the week in Japanese and indicate the pronunciation of each.

3. What do the kanji 土, 火 and 木 mean?

4. Why can the kanji have two different readings, even in the same word, 日曜日 (***nichiyōbi*** "Sunday")?

5. Write the following date in Japanese and its pronunciation: May 15th.

6. Translate the following date into English: 三月三日. How do you read this date?

7. Write the twelve months of the year in Japanese and indicate the pronunciation of each.

8. How do you say "the 6th" in Japanese? And how about "the 11th"?

9. In what year did the Reiwa era begin?

10. To what Western calendar year does the year 20 of the Shōwa era correspond? Refer to page 61 to help you in your calculations!

— Answers to all the exercises can be found online by following the link on page 9. —

Lesson 7 • 第7課

Personal Pronouns

In this lesson we will slightly change our approach: instead of studying endless (though very useful) vocabulary lists, we will look at one of the most curious characteristics of Japanese: personal pronouns. How do we say "I," "you," "she," "we" and other personal pronouns in Japanese?

Before we start...

Before we start, a few important things need clarifying so this lesson can be understood. First of all, you should know Japanese is a very hierarchical language: depending on the social position of the person talking and the one listening, the speaker will use certain words which he or she would never use in other situations. Further on, we will give you some examples so you can get a clearer idea.

Second, Japanese spoken by men can be quite different from that spoken by women. There are expressions, words, and constructions which a man would never use, and vice versa.

A basic understanding of these characteristics of Japanese culture is essential to get an idea of how the language works.

Isn't there a single word for "I"?

In Indo-European languages there is only one first person singular pronoun. It's the "I" in English, "yo" in Spanish, "ich" in German, "je" in French, "eu" in Portuguese, and so on. The same doesn't happen in Japanese: there is a huge variety of pronouns, both in first and second person. The third person is an exception (we will see why later).

First person			
	Singular (I)	Plural (we)	
Very formal	わたくし *watakushi*	わたくしども *watakushidomo*	わたくしたち *watakushitachi*
Formal	私 *watashi*	わたしたち *watashitachi*	われわれ *wareware*
Informal	僕 *boku* ♂ あたし *atashi* ♀	僕たち *bokutachi* ♂ 僕ら *bokura* ♂	あたしたち *atashitachi* ♀ あたしら *atashira* ♀
Vulgar	俺 *ore* ♂	俺たち *oretachi* ♂	俺ら *orera* ♂

Depending on whether you are a man or a woman, and depending on who you are talking to, you will use a different personal pronoun (in the table on the previous page you have the most common ones). Here are a few simple examples of which pronoun certain people would use in certain situations:

a) A 50-year-old Osaka-born employee in an important company.
   1. If he is talking to his boss: ***watashi***
   2. If he is talking to his wife: ***washi***
b) A 20-year-old girl.
   1. If she is talking to her boyfriend: ***atashi***
   2. If she is talking to her teacher: ***watashi***
c) A 25-year-old male student.
   1. If he is talking to another student: ***ore***
   2. With the father of a friend: ***boku***

Second person

The second person singular pronoun, "you," is very similar in use to the first person pronoun, with terms that are used in formal situations and others in colloquial situations. For example: to someone I don't know: ***anata*** | A girl to a close female friend: ***anta*** | A boy to his girlfriend: ***kimi*** | A boy to a male friend: ***omae***, etc.

Second person				
	Singular (you)		Plural (you)	
Formal	あなた *anata*		あなたがた *anatagata*	あなたたち *anatatachi*
Informal	君 *kimi* ♂		君たち *kimitachi* ♂	君ら *kimira* ♂
Vulgar	お前 *omae* ♂	あんた *anta*	お前たち *omaetachi* ♂ お前ら *omaera* ♂	あんたたち *antatachi* あんたら *antara*

But, very often, instead of the pronoun, there is a tendency to use the person's name, title or profession of the person one is directly addressing. Let's see some examples:

Talking to a teacher:

先生は頭がいいです。 ***Sensei wa atama ga ii desu.***
You are intelligent. (Literally: "The teacher is intelligent.")
(***sensei*** = teacher | ***atama ga ii*** = intelligent | ***desu*** = verb "to be")

Talking to Mr. Tanaka:

田中さんは頭がいいです。 ***Tanaka-san wa atama ga ii desu.***
You are intelligent. (Literally: "Mr. Tanaka is intelligent.")

Although we are using the words ***sensei*** ("teacher") and ***Tanaka-san*** ("Mr. Tanaka"), and it may seem we are talking about a third person, it is very possible that this is, in fact, a face-to-face conversation with the professor and Mr. Tanaka themselves.

Third person

The third person, "he" or "she," is a special case. Traditionally, the Japanese don't use these pronouns much; instead, they use the name or title of the person. The sentences above, about the teacher and Tanaka-san, could also be sentences referring to a third person. In that case, they would take a literal meaning: "The teacher is intelligent," and "Mr. Tanaka is intelligent." The only way to know is through the context.

Still, there are third person pronouns that can be used in all contexts and registers: 彼 ***kare*** "he," and 彼女 ***kanojo*** "she." Be careful with these pronouns, as they also mean "boyfriend" and "girlfriend," depending on the context. The sentence 彼女は頭がいいです ***kanojo wa atama ga ii desu*** can mean both "She is intelligent" and "My girlfriend is intelligent."

The plural and other pronouns

The first and second person plural pronouns "we" and "you" are similar to the singular as far as use is concerned, as you can see in the tables on pages 65 and 66. As for the third person, the plural personal pronouns are 彼ら ***karera***, "they," when talking about men and 彼女たち ***kanojotachi***, "they," when talking about women.

There are other less used pronouns which we might come across. For example:

わし ***washi*** ("I") Men over 50 (often dialectal).
あっし ***asshi*** ("I") Men in very informal / vulgar situations.
オイラ ***oira*** ("I") Country men (basically used in parodies).
拙者 ***sessha*** ("I") Ancient samurai (in films, comic books, etc.).
きさま ***kisama*** ("you") Used threateningly against a rival by men.
てめえ ***temee*** ("you") Very vulgar and threatening, used by men.

A last piece of advice that a non-native speaker of Japanese might find helpful is to use 私 ***watashi*** ("I") and あなた ***anata*** ("you") in all situations, until you have a better command of the language. For now, it is a safe way to speak which ensures you will never make a mistake. Besides, the person you are talking to will think you are most polite.

漫画例 Manga Examples

In this manga example section, let's study the use of personal pronouns in manga, which, as you'll see, is extremely varied.

Manga Example 1: First person singular

On this first page we will see two ways of saying "I." One is ***boku***, used by young men in neither very formal nor very colloquial situations. The second one is ***ore***, also used by men, but with a more rough and informal nuance than ***boku***. Women never use these two pronouns, except in some manga (not in real life).

Guillermo March

Keita: やだよ オレあんなカオになりたくないもん
ya da yo ore anna kao ni naritakunai mon
Unpleasant! I that kind of face don't want to become
No way! I don't want to look like that.

Suzuki: オレもだよ！
ore mo da yo!
me too be EP!
Me neither!

Studio Kōsen

Dong: こいつは僕が殺す...
koitsu wa boku ga korosu...
this guy I kill
I'll kill him!

Studio Kōsen

Blade: 俺は...ちがう...
ore wa... chigau...
I wrong
I'm wrong...

Manga Example 2: Second person singular

In this second section we will see two ways of saying "you." The first one is ***omae***, exclusively used by men, since it is a rather rough and informal word which a woman would never use. The second is ***kimi***, quite informal but very common. You must be careful when you choose a pronoun to address a second person: the safest way to address the person is to use his or her name plus a suffix of respect (see Lesson 15), his or her title (professor, director, etc.), or to use ***anata*** ("you.")

J.M. Ken Niimura

Hara:	さ…さつき	お前 たばこを吸うのか…
	Sa... Satsuki	***omae tabako o suu no ka...***
	Sa... Satsuki	you tobacco smoke Q?
	Sa... Satsuki	**D... do you smoke?**

Kishiwada:	誰かね 君は？
	dare ka ne kimi wa?
	who Q? EP you TOP?
	And who are you?
Amaterasu:	女神のアマテラスと申します！
	megami no amaterasu to mōshimasu!
	goddess Amaterasu POP I am called!!
	I am Amaterasu, the goddess.

J.M. Ken Niimura

Manga Example 3: First person plural

To conclude, a last example which shows us the usage of "we." The speaker is a girl and the sentence is a serious one. We keep the pronoun ***watashitachi*** (formal) for this type of more formal and serious situation.

Studio Kōsen

Girl:	私たちっ 別れましょう
	watashitachi wakaremashō
	we are going to split
	I want to split up.
Boy:	ええっ 何故だ！？
	ee! naze da!?
	eh? why!?
	What? Why?!

Exercises 練習

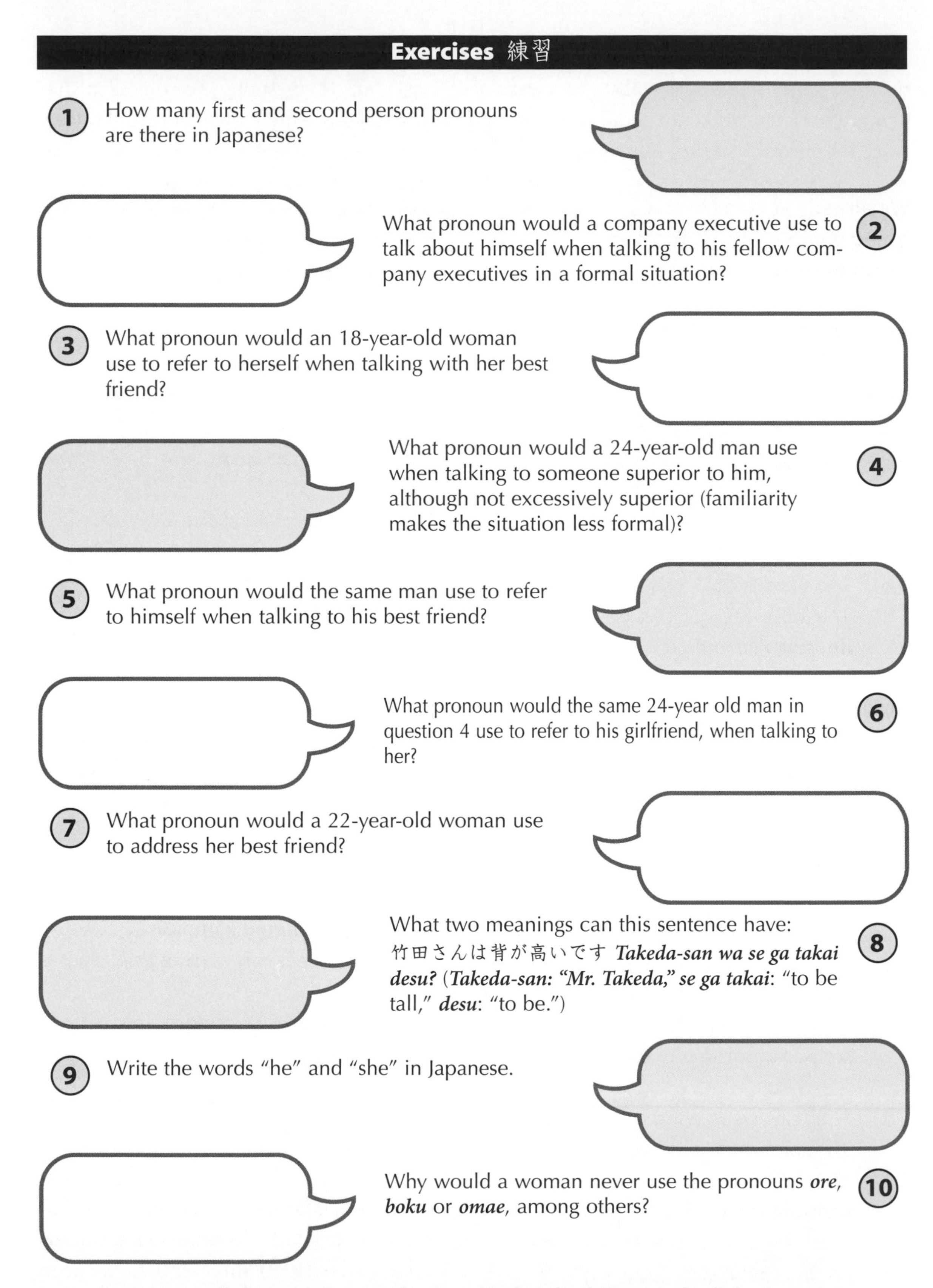

1. How many first and second person pronouns are there in Japanese?

2. What pronoun would a company executive use to talk about himself when talking to his fellow company executives in a formal situation?

3. What pronoun would an 18-year-old woman use to refer to herself when talking with her best friend?

4. What pronoun would a 24-year-old man use when talking to someone superior to him, although not excessively superior (familiarity makes the situation less formal)?

5. What pronoun would the same man use to refer to himself when talking to his best friend?

6. What pronoun would the same 24-year old man in question 4 use to refer to his girlfriend, when talking to her?

7. What pronoun would a 22-year-old woman use to address her best friend?

8. What two meanings can this sentence have: 竹田さんは背が高いです ***Takeda-san wa se ga takai desu?*** (***Takeda-san***: ***"Mr. Takeda,"*** ***se ga takai***: "to be tall," ***desu***: "to be.")

9. Write the words "he" and "she" in Japanese.

10. Why would a woman never use the pronouns ***ore***, ***boku*** or ***omae***, among others?

— Answers to all the exercises can be found online by following the link on page 9. —

Lesson 8 • 第8課

Katakana Special

We already saw in Lesson 2 how the katakana syllabary basically works; now we are going to go into this topic in greater depth, because one lesson is not enough. We recommend that you review Lesson 2 as a reminder before carrying on.

The phonetic limitations of Japanese

First, make sure you are familiar with the characteristics of Japanese pronunciation (Lesson 1) to be able to make good transcriptions into katakana and to interpret words written in that syllabary. Japanese has certain phonetic characteristics which make the exact transcription of foreign words almost impossible. These are the most distinct characteristics:

a) Japanese has no single consonants; a consonant must always be paired wit a vowel as part of a syllable. The exception is ***n***, which can go on its own.
b) The sounds ***l***, ***x*** ("ks,") ***ny***, and ***v*** don't exist.
c) The following syllables don't exist in Japanese: ***fa***, ***fe***, ***fi***, ***fo***, ***she***, ***che***, ***je***, ***ti***, ***zi***, ***di***, ***tu***, ***du***, ***tyu***, ***fyu*** and ***ye***.

Strategies to overcome phonetic limitations

Due to the phonetic limitations of Japanese, a transcription system for foreign words exists, following certain more or less established rules. We will study these rules by means of questions and answers:

1) *What is the basis for transcribing? Pronunciation or the way the original word is written?*
   It is the original pronunciation and never the way it is written. Examples:
   コンピュータ ***konpyūta***. It comes from computer. Since it comes from English, it is transcribed according to the English pronunciation.
   オランダ ***oranda***. It comes from the Portuguese "Holanda" (Holland), so it is transcribed according to its original Portuguese pronunciation.

2) *How can we transcribe a consonant on its own?*
   The solution lies in choosing the column from the katakana table which most resembles the original pronunciation, and then choosing the character which stands for that consonant + ***u***. ***U*** in Japanese has a very weak pronunciation, so it goes almost unnoticed. For example, to transcribe the word "crack," notice how there are two k sounds on their own (they come with no vowels). To transcribe these k on their own, we need

to go to the k column in the katakana syllabary and choose ***k*** + ***u*** (ク ***ku***). Thus, the word "crack" would become クラック ***kurakku***. Another example: to transcribe the ***s*** sound, we need to choose the katakana ス ***su***, as in the final sound in the word "service," which would be サービス ***saabisu***. There is one exception to this rule: since the ***tu*** and ***du*** combinations don't exist (we find the ツ ***tsu*** and ヅ ***zu*** sounds instead) we need to use katakana ト ***to*** and ド ***do*** to transcribe the ***t*** and ***d*** sounds on their own, for example, ヒント ***hinto*** (hint) and ベッド ***beddo*** (bed). There are more exact but less used transcriptions for ***tu*** or ***du***, introduced in section 6, opposite.

3) *How do we represent long sounds?*
   With a dash. A dash means the previous vowel is pronounced for a little longer than a single one, for example: バレーボール ***bareebōru*** (volleyball), カレー ***karee*** (curry), ヒーター ***hiitaa*** (heater).

4) *How are double consonants represented?*
   We have many words in English where a consonant is pronounced more strongly than usual: these kinds of consonants are called "double" consonants. To represent this effect, a small ***tsu*** character is used before the consonant to be doubled, for example: カーペット ***kaapetto*** (carpet), スリッパ ***surippa*** (slipper), ポケット ***poketto*** (pocket).

5) *How do we represent sounds that don't exist in Japanese?*
   Sounds that don't exist in Japanese have to be replaced with the sound that most resembles the original pronunciation.
   a) ***l***: This sound is replaced with ***r***, which, as you will remember, always has a soft pronunciation in Japanese, for example: ボール ***bōru*** (ball), レンズ ***renzu*** (lens).
   b) ***x*** ("ks"): We will always use the two katakana letters クス ***kusu***, for example: ファックス ***fakkusu*** (fax), ボックス ***bokkusu*** (box.)
   c) ***v***: Traditionally the ***v*** sound in English words was transcribed the same way as the ***b*** sound, irrespective of the fact that it is pronounced as a cross between ***b*** and ***f***. Thus, the word "violin" was transcribed バイオリン ***baiorin***. In recent years, though, there is a tendency to use the katakana ***u*** with two little slashes (ヴ ***vu***) to represent this sound more faithfully. Unfortunately, however, both ブ and ヴ are still pronounced exactly the same way: ***bu***. To transcribe ***va***, ***ve***, ***vi***, and ***vo***, we will add a smaller ***a***, ***e***, ***i***, or ***o***, respectively, after ヴ. Thus we have ヴァ ***va***, ヴェ ***ve***, ヴィ ***vi*** and ヴォ ***vo***. ***Vu*** will remain as it is, ヴ. Nowadays, the word "violin" is usually written ヴァイオリン ***vaiorin***. Other examples are エヴァンゲリオン ***evangerion*** (Evangelion) and ヴェロニカ ***veronica*** (Veronica).

6) *If the combinations* ***fa***, ***fe***, ***fi***, ***fo***, ***she***, ***che***, ***je***, ***ti***, ***di***, ***tu***, ***du***, ***ye***, ***tyu***, ***fyu*** *don't exist, how do we transcribe words containing these sounds?*

   There is a series of rules which can be applied in these cases, but the most common strategy is using a katakana character plus a smaller size vowel next to it.

   a) Sounds with ***f***: The only character with the ***f*** pronunciation in the katakana table is フ ***fu***. To transcribe ***f*** syllables + vowel (except for ***fu***, since we already have フ), we will use フ ***fu*** + the corresponding vowel next to it, written in a smaller size, for example: ファ ***fa*** (***fu*** + small ***a***), フィ ***fi*** (***fu*** + small ***i***). Examples in real words include ファン ***fan*** (fan) and フォント ***fonto*** (font).
   b) ***She***, ***che*** and ***je***: To make ***she*** we use katakana ***shi*** + small ***e*** (シェ); to make ***che*** we use katakana ***chi*** + small ***e*** (チェ); and to make ***je*** we use katakana ***ji*** + small ***e*** (ジェ), for example: チェス ***chesu*** (chess), ジェット ***jetto*** (jet).
   c) ***Ti***, ***di***: The transcription is ***te*** or ***de*** + small ***i*** (ティ ***ti***, ディ ***di***), for example, スパゲッティ ***supagetti*** (spaghetti"), ディスク ***disuku*** (disk).
   d) ***Tu***, ***du***: These are rather special sounds because they can be transcribed in several ways. The most common way of transcribing ***tu*** is using katakana ツ ***tsu***, as in ツアー ***tsuaa*** (tour). We may also come across the transcription トゥ (***tu*** = ***to*** + small ***u***), for example: テゥモロー ***tumorō*** (tomorrow), トゥアレグ ***tuaregu*** (Tuareg). The ***du*** sound is seldom used, but should we need to transcribe it and want to be as faithful as possible to the original (where a simple transcription using ド ***do*** would not do), we would probably use the combination ドゥ (***du*** = ***do*** + small ***u***) for example, ドゥーリトル ***dūritoru*** (Doolittle), ドゥオーモ ***duōmo*** (duomo).
   e) ***Tyu*** and ***fyu***: We add a small katakana ュ ***yu*** to チ ***chi*** for ***tyu*** (チュ) and to ヒ ***hi*** for ***fyu*** (ヒュ), for example: チューバ ***chūba*** (tuba), ヒューズ ***hyūzu*** (fuse).
   f) ***Ye***: We write it with the two katakana sounds ***ie***, for example: イエス ***iesu*** (yes), イエロー ***ierō*** (yellow), イエメン ***iemen*** (Yemen.)
   g) ***Ny*** (*gn* in French and Italian, *ñ* in Spanish, *nh* in Portuguese): The last sound in this long list is ***ny***. To transcribe this sound, we will use the character ニ ***ni*** plus a small ャ ***ya***, ュ ***yu***, or ョ ***yo***, for example: ラザーニャ ***razaanya*** (lasagna), ニョッキ ***nyokki*** (gnocchi), ギニョール ***ginyooru*** (guignol).

漫画例 Manga Examples

In this section of manga examples we will look at some uses of katakana and study how foreign words are transformed when they become Japanese, often with extravagant pronunciations that are far from the original!

Manga Example 1: Foreign place names

Studio Kōsen

We said in Lesson 2 that katakana is used to transcribe non-Japanese (and non-Chinese) names of people and places. Here we have an example of a place name: Broadway. The word has been transformed into Japanese as ***burōdouee***; remember the transcription must be as faithful as possible to the original English pronunciation.

Cindy: なにをしにブロードウエーまでいったのだろう**...**
nani o shi ni burōdouee made itta no darō...
what do Broadway to go I wonder...
I wonder why he went to Broadway...

Manga Example 2: Foreign people's names

Guillermo March

In this second example we have the transcription of a foreign person's name into Japanese. As Captain George is not a Japanese name, we use the katakana syllabary to transcribe it. The full name has to be adapted to the Japanese pronunciation following the rules we have studied on the previous pages. Thus, Captain George is transcribed as ***kyaputen jōji***. Now, try writing your own name in Japanese!

Captain George: キャプテンジョージ！
kyaputen jōji!
Captain George!!
I'm Captain George!!

Manga Example 3: Foreign expressions (1)

J.M. Ken Niimura

In this example the word "stadium" is used. Notice how the Japanese word is transcribed according to the English pronunciation (***sutajiamu***), and not to its written equivalent.

Keiko: 一郎 スタジアムの中に入るんだ！
Ichirō sutajiamu no naka ni hairu n da
Ichirō stadium in enter
Ichirō! Let's go into the stadium!

Ichiro: いま手が離せねえんだよ！
ima te ga hanasenee n da yo
now hand release (neg.)
I can't now, I'm busy!

Manga Example 3: Foreign expressions (2)

Here we see the word ***sentaa***, from the English word "center." Although Japanese has its own word for center with the same meaning, 中心 ***chūshin***, to the Japanese it sounds cooler and more modern if you use an English word instead.

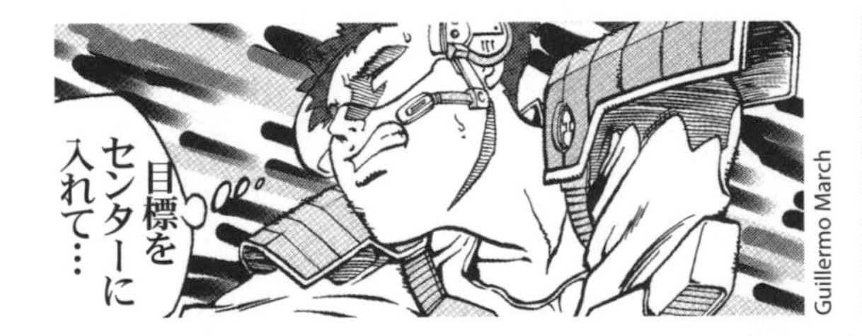

Guillermo March

Kurō: 目標をセンターに入れて...
mokuhyō o sentaa ni irete...
target center put in...
Center the target and...

Manga Example 4: Onomatopoeia and foreign expressions

In this manga example we have two ways of using katakana. The first one is for the word ***arukōru***, which comes from the foreign word "alcohol." The second, for the word ***hikku***, represents the sound for hiccups, and, therefore, is an onomatopoeia (remember katakana is very often used to represent onomatopoeia, Lesson 2).

Guillermo March

Tetsu: アルコールの臭い？
arukōru no nioi?
alcohol smell?
Can I smell alcohol?

Ryōko: ヒック
hikku
(hiccups sound)
Hic!

Exercises 練習

1. What is the katakana syllabary used for?

2. Japanese syllabaries are based on consonant and vowel combinations, but is there an exception to this rule?

3. How do we transcribe isolated consonants into Japanese? For example, if we have to write the consonant ***s*** in Japanese, what do we do?

4. If we are to transcribe the consonants ***t*** and ***d***, what do we do?

5. What are double consonants and how do we represent them in katakana? Give an example.

6. Since ***f*** doesn't exist in Japanese, how do we transcribe the syllable ***fi***?

7. How do we transcribe the syllable ***ti*** into Japanese?

8. Transcribe the English word "American" into Japanese.

9. Transcribe the English word "family" into Japanese.

10. Write your own name in Japanese.

— Answers to all the exercises can be found online by following the link on page 9. —

Lesson 9 • 第9課

Basic Grammar

Having seen in the previous lessons how the writing system works, as well as some of the special features of the Japanese language, we will now start exploring grammar, starting with the most basic verb: "to be."

The verb "to be": present affirmative

In Japanese, the verb "to be" is ***desu*** (formal), and ***da*** (informal/vulgar). Let's start by having a look at a few very simple sentences where this verb has an essential role:

これはりんごです。
Kore wa ringo desu.
This is an apple.
それはテーブルです。
Sore wa teeburu desu.
That is a table.
あれはとりです。
Are wa tori desu.
That over there is a bird.
どれがボールペンですか？
Dore ga bōrupen desu ka.
Which is the ballpoint pen?

Verb "to be" (です)		
	Formal	Simple
Present	です ***desu***	だ ***da***
Past	でした ***deshita***	だった ***datta***
Negative	ではありません ***de wa arimasen*** じゃありません ***ja arimasen***	ではない ***de wa nai*** じゃない ***ja nai***
Past negative	ではありませんでした ***de wa arimasen deshita*** じゃありませんでした ***ja arimasen deshita***	ではなかった ***de wa nakatta*** じゃなかった ***ja nakatta***

As you can tell from the examples, the verb ***desu*** always goes at the end of the sentence. In Japanese the verb must always go at the end, with no exceptions. In addition, Japanese verbs don't have singular and plural forms. In the case of the verb "to be," the verb will always be ***desu*** and its form will not change whether I'm talking about myself (僕はジョンです ***boku wa jon desu***, "I am John") or whether I'm talking about someone else (彼らはバカです ***karera wa baka desu***, "they are idiots").

Note: the ***u*** in ***desu*** is hardly pronounced. Thus, the example sentence "I am John" in the paragraph above is actually pronounced something close to ***boku wa jon des***.

Kosoado

You must have noticed there are several very similar words in the example sentences above: これ ***kore***, それ ***sore***, あれ ***are*** and どれ ***dore***. These words respectively mean "this," "that" (close), "that" (far) and "which." You'll notice they all have the same root (***re***) and before this ***re*** we find the prefixes ***ko-***, ***so-***, ***a-*** and ***do-***. There are several more words like these in Japanese, where the prefixes ***ko-*** (indicating something close to the speaker), ***so-*** (close to the listener), ***a-*** (far from both), and ***do-*** (question) go before the root. For the time being, study these three groups in depth, because they will be extremely useful:

- これ ***kore*** "this"; それ ***sore*** "that"; あれ ***are*** "that over there"; どれ ***dore*** "which."
  For example: それは犬です ***sore wa inu desu*** "That is a dog."
- この ***kono*** "this x"; その ***sono*** "that x"; あの ***ano*** "that x over there"; どの ***dono*** "which x."
  For example: この犬は大きいです ***kono inu wa ookii desu*** "This dog is big."
- ここ ***koko*** "here"; そこ ***soko*** "there"; あそこ ***asoko*** "over there"; どこ ***doko*** "where."
  For example: あそこに犬がいる ***asoko ni inu ga iru*** "There is a dog over there."

The particle wa

Sometimes, after a noun we find the hiragana は ***ha***. It is an important grammatical particle which comes after a noun to indicate the "topic" in a sentence. We will devote Lesson 16 to studying the various particles in Japanese, because it is essential to understand them clearly.

Note: When we find a は working as topic particle (marking the topic we are talking about in the sentence), we will pronounce it ***wa***, although we write it with the hiragana ***ha***.

Past affirmative

"To be" can be conjugated in the present or past, affirmative or negative, formal or informal (see table on page 77). It's simpler than you may think: the only thing that changes is the verb form at the end of the sentence. Let's look at some examples:

これはりんごでした	それはテーブルでした
kore wa ringo deshita	***sore wa teeburu deshita***
This was an apple.	That was a table.

As you can see, the past tense of the verb "to be" is でした deshita, and, like its present affirmative equivalent です ***desu***, it goes at the end of the sentence. **Note:** The "***i***" in ***deshita*** is hardly pronounced. Thus, でした is pronounced "***deshta***."

Present negative

Let's look now at the negative, which is not so complicated either. It is just a question of replacing です ***desu*** with ではありません ***de wa arimasen*** or じゃありません ***ja arimasen***. **Note:** ***Ja arimasen*** is less formal than ***de wa arimasen***.

これはりんごではありません	それはテーブルじゃありません
kore wa ringo de wa arimasen	***sore wa teeburu ja arimasen***
This is not an apple.	That is not a table.

Past negative

The past negative form of the verb "to be" is ではありませんでした ***de wa arimasen deshita*** or じゃありませんでした ***ja arimasen deshita*** (the latter being less formal).

これはりんごではありませんでした
kore wa ringo de wa arimasen deshita
This was not an apple.

それはテーブルじゃありませんでした
sore wa teeburu ja arimasen deshita
That was not a table.

Question form

The question form in Japanese is not difficult: simply place ***ka*** at the end of the sentence and a questioning intonation when you say it.

これはりんごですか？
kore wa ringo desu ka?
Is this an apple?

それはテーブルですか?
sore wa teeburu desu ka?
Is that a table?

The word 何 ***nan*** or ***nani*** means "what":

これは何ですか?
kore wa nan desu ka?
What is this?

それはりんごです
sore wa ringo desu
That is an apple.

Simple form (AKA: informal form / dictionary form / casual form)

The simple, shortened form of the verb "to be" is often used in informal conversation:

これはりんごだった
kore wa ringo datta
This was an apple.

それはテーブルじゃない
sore wa teeburu ja nai
That is not a table.

あれはとりではなかった
are wa tori de wa nakatta
That was not a bird.

Some vocabulary					
Japanese	**Rōmaji**	**Meaning**	**Japanese**	**Rōmaji**	**Meaning**
りんご	***ringo***	apple	ふで	***fude***	writing brush
テーブル	***teeburu***	table	パソコン	***pasokon***	computer
とり	***tori***	bird	レモン	***remon***	lemon
ボールペン	***bōrupen***	ballpoint pen	本（ほん）	***hon***	book
ばか	***baka***	idiot	うた	***uta***	song
テレビ	***terebi***	television	しゃしん	***shashin***	photo
いす	***isu***	chair	アニメ	***anime***	cartoon
ねこ	***neko***	cat	マンガ	***manga***	comic book
いぬ	***inu***	dog	おかね	***o-kane***	money

漫画例 Manga Examples

As usual, in the manga examples section, we will illustrate the grammar points studied in this lesson with manga panels. Let's look at some examples showing different forms of the verb "to be."

Manga Example 1: Present affirmative form (formal)

Studio Kōsen

We see here the simplest form of the verb "to be": です ***desu***, the present affirmative. Remember that we hardly pronounce the ***u***, and we will say something closer to ***des***.

Desu is perceived as formal: we use it when talking to strangers (like here, where Ayako talks to some boys she doesn't know), or people who are hierarchically or socially superior to us. It's like using the "Mr.," "Mrs.," or "Miss" title with someone.

Ayako: そして私があなた達のコーチです。
soshite watashi ga anatatachi no kōchi desu
Then I SP you POP coach be
I am your coach, then.

Manga Example 2: Present affirmative form (informal)

Guillermo March

We can see here two special features we have learned in this lesson. First, we have the verb "to be" in its simple present affirmative form, だ ***da***, with exactly the same meaning as です ***desu***, but much more informal. On the other hand, we have これ ***kore***, which means "this" and which you should learn together with それ ***sore*** "that"; あれ ***are*** "that over there"; and どれ ***dore*** "which."

Kenji: あった！これだ！
atta! kore da!
found! this be!
I found it! This is it!

Manga Example 3: Present negative form (formal)

Here we see the present negative form ではありません ***de wa arimasen***, which means "not be." Its simple negative form can be ではない ***de wa nai*** or じゃない ***ja nai*** (we will see this last form in most manga). In addition, we can also see the farewell expression お気をつけて ***o-ki o tsukete***, which we saw in Lesson 4.

J.M. Ken Niimura

Irumi: 世の中 正しいことばかりではありません。お気をつけて。
yo no naka tadashii koto bakari de wa arimasen. o-ki o tsukete
world inside correct thing only not be. take care.
Not everything in the world is good. Take care.

Manga Example 4: Question form (formal present affirmative)

Guillermo March

Here we have the verb です ***desu*** again, this time in the question form. All we need to do is add the hiragana か ***ka*** after a sentence in any form (present / past affirmative, present / past negative, in their formal and informal versions) to make a question.

Kurō: これも 父の仕事ですか。
kore mo chichi no shigoto desu ka
this also father job be Q?
Is this . . . my father's job as well?

Manga Example 5: Past affirmative form (informal)

Studio Kōsen

To conclude, let's see the past form of the verb "to be" in its simple form: だった ***datta***, its formal form being でした ***deshita***. Use of the simple or formal form depends on the context. In a conversation with friends we will use the former, and in more formal situations, the latter.

Anne: 総理大臣って変な顔の人だった
sōri daijin tte hen-na kao no hito datta
Prime Minister weird face POP person was
The Prime Minister was a person with a weird face.

Exercises 練習

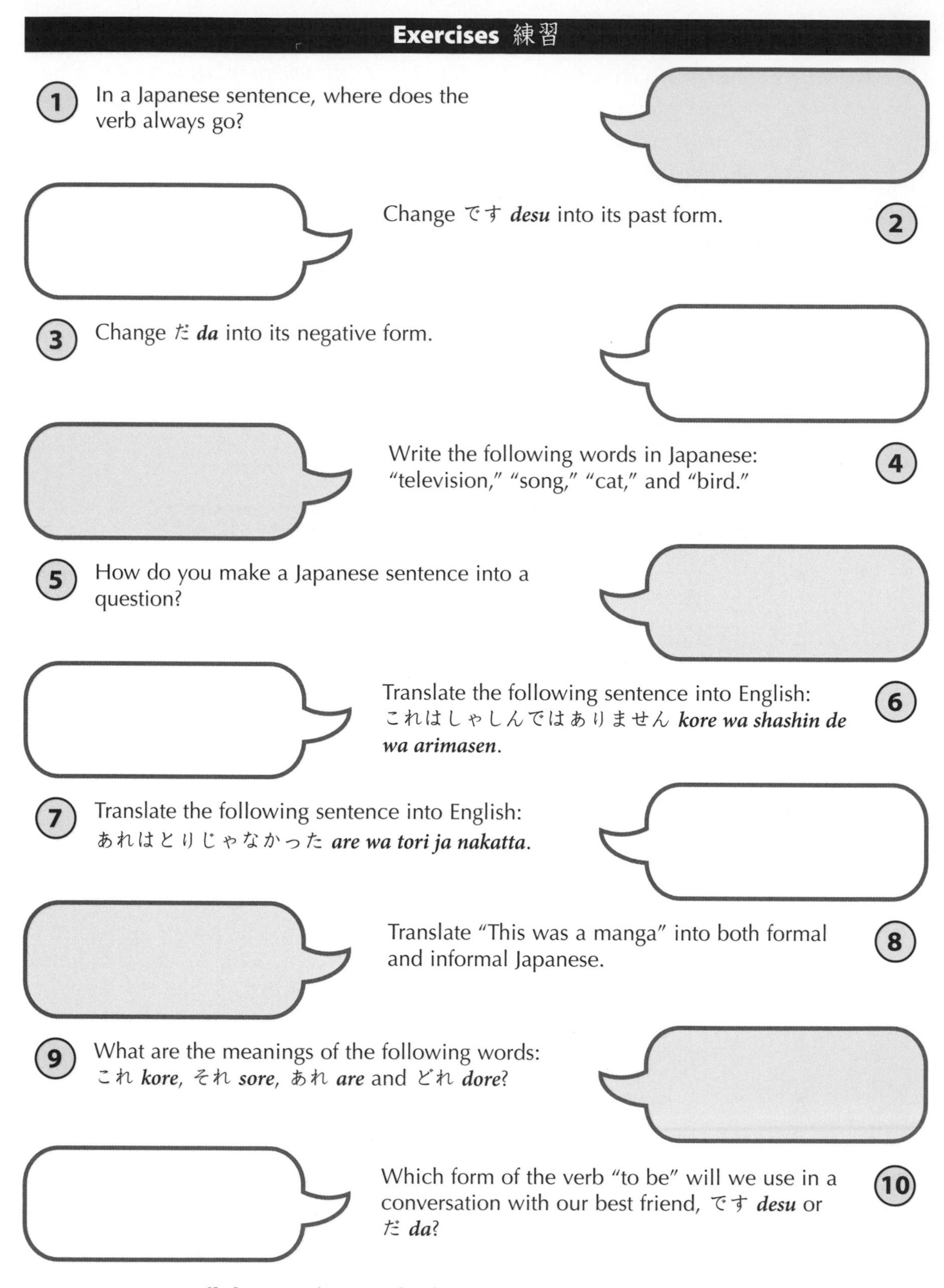

1. In a Japanese sentence, where does the verb always go?

2. Change です ***desu*** into its past form.

3. Change だ ***da*** into its negative form.

4. Write the following words in Japanese: "television," "song," "cat," and "bird."

5. How do you make a Japanese sentence into a question?

6. Translate the following sentence into English: これはしゃしんではありません ***kore wa shashin de wa arimasen***.

7. Translate the following sentence into English: あれはとりじゃなかった ***are wa tori ja nakatta***.

8. Translate "This was a manga" into both formal and informal Japanese.

9. What are the meanings of the following words: これ ***kore***, それ ***sore***, あれ ***are*** and どれ ***dore***?

10. Which form of the verb "to be" will we use in a conversation with our best friend, です ***desu*** or だ ***da***?

— Answers to all the exercises can be found online by following the link on page 9. —

Lesson 10 • 第10課

The Four Seasons

This lesson deals with the four seasons and different meteorological phenomena, giving you the opportunity to add lots of new words to your vocabulary. Don't forget that in the online Vocabulary Index that can be accessed via the link on page 9, you have a full list of all the vocabulary that appears throughout the lessons.

The geography of Japan

Japan, pronounced 日本 ***Nihon*** or ***Nippon*** in Japanese, is situated in the planet's northern hemisphere, and that means the seasons are more or less the same as in the northern states of America or in the UK, that is, in July and August it is summer, in January and February it is winter, etc.

Japan is situated in an area of great meteorological activity; therefore, the four seasons are clearly marked, and there are seasons with heavier rain than others and seasons of high humidity. Besides, you probably know Japan is in one of the areas with the most tectonic activity on earth, and this means there's a great risk of earthquakes (地震 ***jishin***).

With regard to temperatures (温度 ***ondo***), we will point out that Japan, being a group of islands covering a long distance from north (北 ***kita***) to south (南 ***minami***), has a wide range of climates.

For example, 北海道 Hokkaidō, the northernmost island, has an almost Siberian climate, extremely cold in winter and cool in summer, whereas 沖縄 Okinawa, the group of islands in Japan's far south, has an almost tropical climate.

Climate

Besides 北海道 Hokkaidō, the other three large, main islands of Japan (本州 Honshū, 四国 Shikoku, and 九州 Kyūshū), have various climates according to their latitude. However, generally speaking, their climates are all similar to the northern states of the US. Winter (冬 ***fuyu***) is moderately cold, and summer (夏 ***natsu***) is very hot.

For example, in 京都 Kyōto, a city situated more or less in the center of Japan, in the middle of the largest island of Honshū, summers are very hot and humid (蒸し暑い ***mushiatsui***), with temperatures easily reaching 97–98 °F (36 °C). But winters in the Kyoto area are cold and temperatures below freezing point are not unusual. By the way, they use degrees centigrade, or Celsius (°C), in Japan and not Fahrenheit, like in the US.

Meteorological peculiarities

In Japan, the four seasons, spring (春 ***haru***), summer (夏 ***natsu***), fall (秋 ***aki***), and winter (冬 ***fuyu***), are very different, and each has its own characteristics. It is very cold (寒い ***samui***) in winter; cherry blossom (桜 ***sakura***) blooms in spring; it is very hot (暑い ***atsui***) in summer; and, in autumn, the leaves of the trees (especially the maple tree) take on red, orange and yellow tones, the so-called 紅葉 ***kōyō*** (autumn colors).

Rain and snow

It rains quite often in Japan, which means there are hardly ever water restrictions, despite the widespread custom of indulging in お風呂 ***o-furo***, a daily bath in a deep bathtub.

Rain (雨 ***ame***) is especially frequent in summer and early fall. Mid-June to mid-July is the rainy season (梅雨 ***tsuyu***), when it rains almost every day. September is typhoon (台風 ***taifū***) season, with heavy storms and torrential downpours.

With regard to snow (雪 ***yuki***), it doesn't snow much along the east-facing Pacific Ocean coast, where the largest cities are. But in Hokkaidō and along the west-facing Sea of Japan coast it snows very heavily during the winter months.

Some vocabulary

Japanese	Rōmaji	Meaning	Japanese	Rōmaji	Meaning
冬	***fuyu***	winter	日	***hi***	sun
春	***haru***	spring	星	***hoshi***	star
夏	***natsu***	summer	月	***tsuki***	moon
秋	***aki***	fall	梅雨	***tsuyu***	rainy season
寒い	***samui***	cold	嵐	***arashi***	storm
涼しい	***suzushii***	cool	雲	***kumo***	cloud
暑い	***atsui***	hot	晴れ	***hare***	sunny
暖かい	***atatakai***	warm	くもり	***kumori***	cloudy
風	***kaze***	wind	きり	***kiri***	fog
台風	***taifū***	typhoon	ひょう	***hyō***	hail
雨	***ame***	rain	紅葉	***kōyō***	autumn leaves
雪	***yuki***	snow	桜	***sakura***	cherry blossom

These two sentences may come in handy:

今日は雨が降っています ***Kyō wa ame ga futte imasu***. "It's raining today."
今日は雪が降っています ***Kyō wa yuki ga futte imasu***. "It's snowing today."

Some more geography

To end this part of the lesson, we will talk about Japanese geography so we can have an idea of the layout of the country and where its main cities are. Japan (日本 ***Nihon*** or ***Nippon***) is a country formed by almost 7,000 islands, but there are four which are by far the largest and therefore most important ones. They are 本州 Honshū, 北海道 Hokkaidō, 九州 Kyūshū and 四国 Shikoku, from largest to smallest, respectively. In addition, in the far south of the archipelago we will find the 沖縄 Okinawa islands.

Most of the main cities are on the largest island of Honshū. In fact, only two of the eleven cities with a population of over a million are not in Honshū: they are 札幌 Sapporo in Hokkaidō and 福岡 Fukuoka in Kyūshū. The other cities with a population over one million are 東京 Tōkyō, 横浜 Yokohama, 大阪 Ōsaka, 名古屋 Nagoya, 神戸 Kōbe, 京都 Kyōto, 川崎 Kawasaki, 広島 Hiroshima, さいたま Saitama and 仙台 Sendai. However, at the time of writing, 北九州 Kitakyūshū (in Kyūshū) is close to reaching the million number mark.

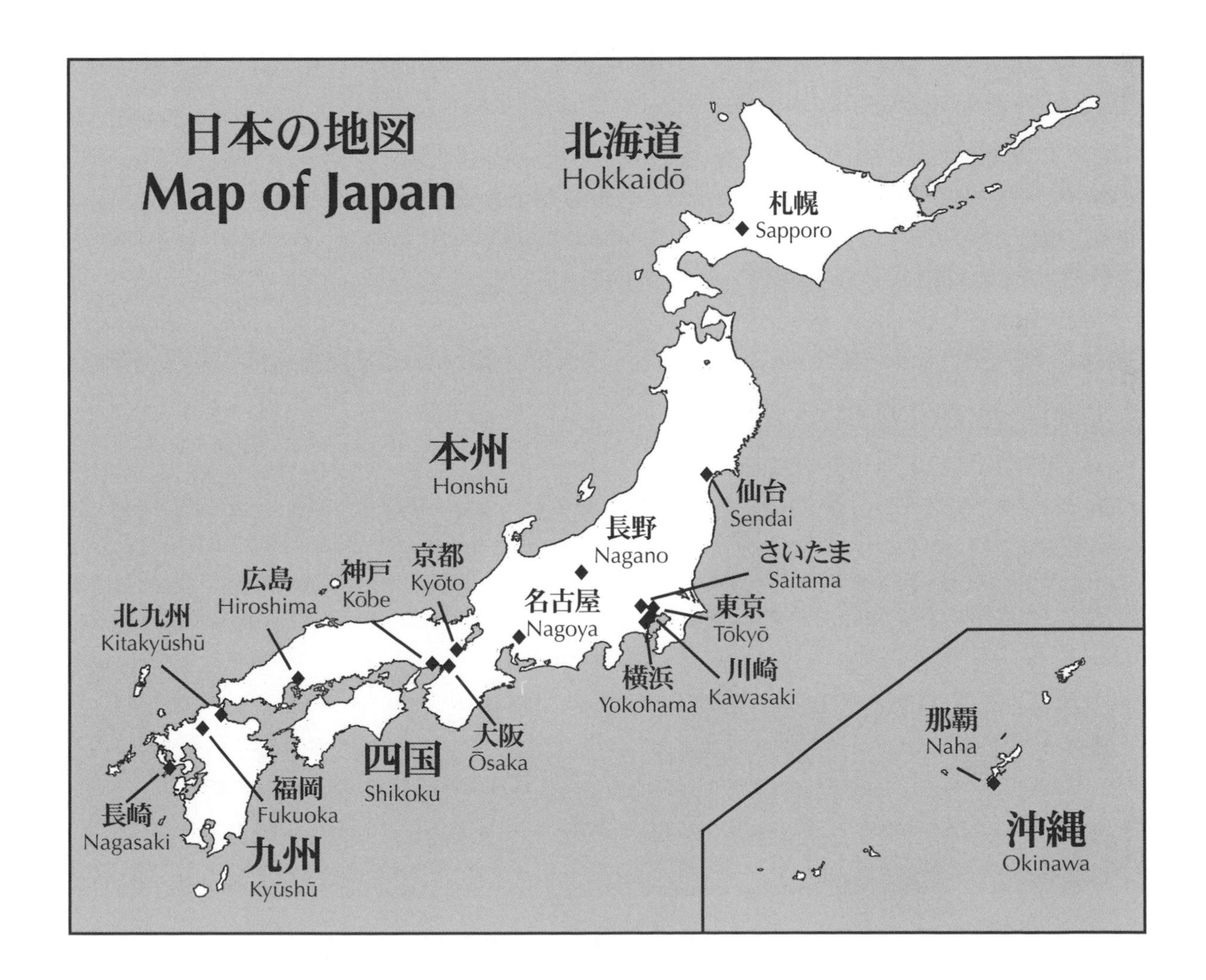

漫画例 Manga Examples

Let's now move onto the manga examples section, where we will see manga panels with vocabulary related to meteorology and geography. It is always satisfying to see what we have just studied being used in real manga!

Manga Example 1: Snow

Guillermo March

In this example we have the word 雪 ***yuki***, which means "snow," along with a construction which would be the equivalent in this context to the English verb "to snow": 雪が降る ***yuki ga furu***, literally "snow falls." We see here a somewhat different form, 雪が降り始めた ***yuki ga furihajimeta***, "it started snowing." The suffix ***hajimeru*** is placed after a verb to add the meaning "to start to."

Jack: その年の最初の雪が降り始めた**...**
sono toshi no saisho no yuki ga furihajimeta...
that year first snow start falling...
The first snowfalls of that year had begun...

Manga Example 2: I'm cold

We have here the word 寒い ***samui***, a very common adjective, which means "cold." Study this useful word well, together with its opposite, 暑い ***atsui***, "hot"; they may help you strike up a conversation. For example: 寒いですね ***samui desu ne*** ("It's cold, isn't it?") is a good way to make a connection with someone.

Studio Kōsen

John: どうしたジェシカ？
dōshita jeshika?
what is the matter Jessica?
What's the matter, Jessica?

Jessica: ううん なんだか寒いだけ
uun nanda ka samui dake
nothing a little bit cold just
Nothing, I'm just a little bit cold.

Manga Example 3: Wind and typhoon

In this example we have two words related to the weather: they are 風 ***kaze***, "wind," and 台風 ***taifū***, "typhoon." Talking about the wind, the word 神風 ***kamikaze*** (literally "divine wind") probably sounds familiar to you: this word came into being toward the end of the thirteenth century to describe the very timely gales and sudden storms which frustrated attempts to invade Japan by Kublai Khan's Mongolian army fleet.

Chieko:	風が静まったわよ。	**Takuya:**	台風はどうしたんだ！？
	kaze ga shizumatta wa yo		***taifū wa dōshita n da!?***
	Wind calm down EP EP		typhoon TOP what happened!?
	The wind has died down.		**What happened to the typhoon?!**

Manga Example 4: Some geography

In this last example we will review Japanese geography. Here Keita is talking about サッポロ Sapporo ramen, a particularly delicious regional version of the much-loved noodle dish. Then, Keita talks about going to 北海道 Hokkaidō. If you take a look at the map on page 85, you'll see Hokkaidō is the large island in the north of Japan, and that its capital is 札幌 Sapporo. This city has a population of almost two million.

Keita: サッポロラーメン 食べたい。できれば 家族そろって北海道へ...

sapporo raamen tabetai. dekireba kazoku sorotte hokkaidō e...

Sapporo ramen eat want. if I could family gather Hokkaidō to...

I'd like to eat Sapporo ramen. If I could, I'd go with my family to Hokkaidō...

Exercises 練習

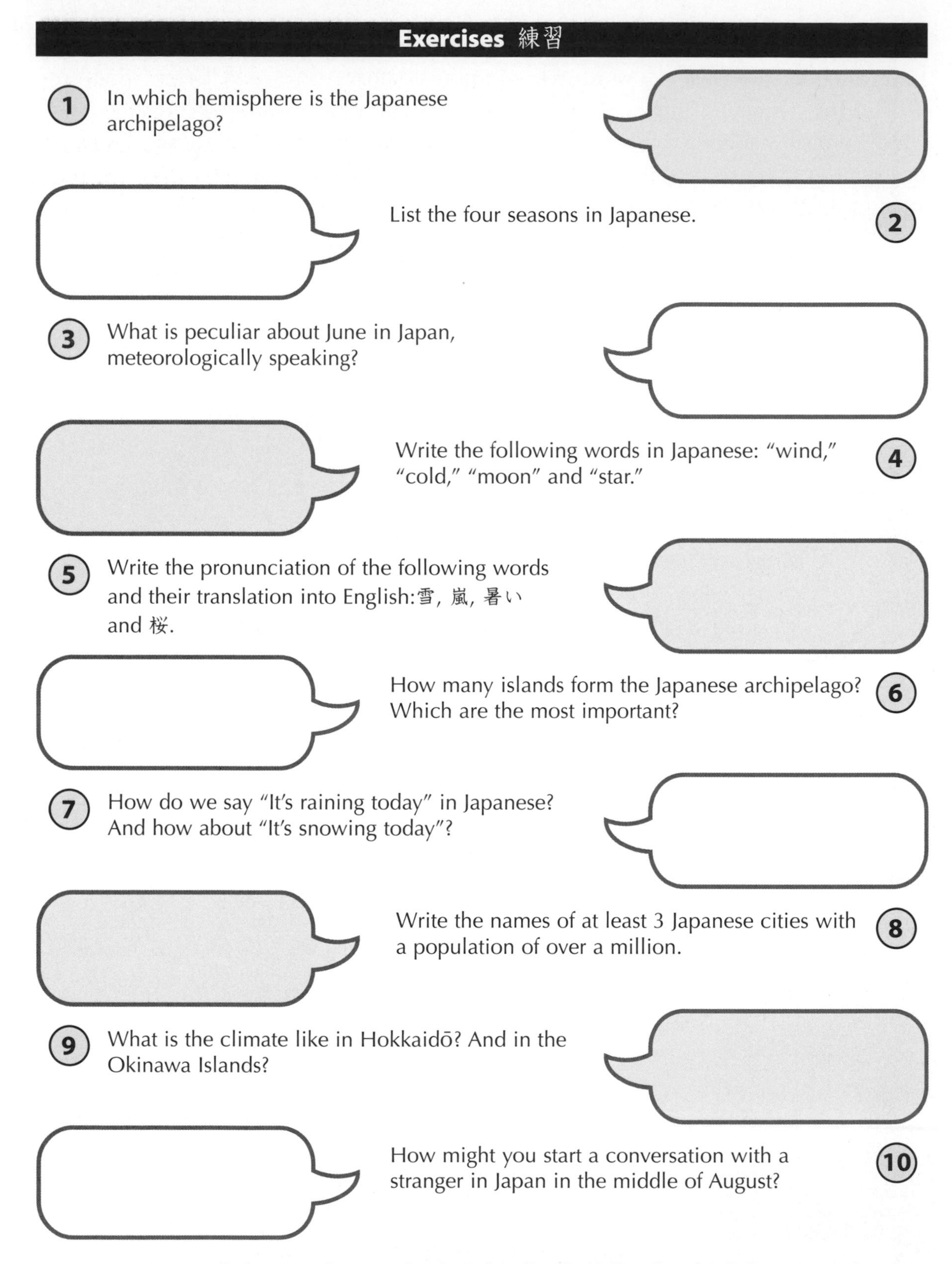

1 In which hemisphere is the Japanese archipelago?
List the four seasons in Japanese. 2
3 What is peculiar about June in Japan, meteorologically speaking?
Write the following words in Japanese: "wind," "cold," "moon" and "star." 4
5 Write the pronunciation of the following words and their translation into English:雪, 嵐, 暑い and 桜.
How many islands form the Japanese archipelago? Which are the most important? 6
7 How do we say "It's raining today" in Japanese? And how about "It's snowing today"?
Write the names of at least 3 Japanese cities with a population of over a million. 8
9 What is the climate like in Hokkaidō? And in the Okinawa Islands?
How might you start a conversation with a stranger in Japan in the middle of August? 10

— Answers to all the exercises can be found online by following the link on page 9. —

RAKUJŌ
第二章
銀河350*年9月6日
サイボーグです。
ここに何がいるの？
これはヤス・アーミーです。
サイボーグ？ロボットじゃないの？
ロボットではありません。メガファイトヴァイオレントサイボーグです。
いいえ、あたたかいです。
おまえ、今、外は暑い？
*銀河1年＝2153年

十日か…
雨が降りはじめました。しかし、十日に台風が来ます。
天気は？
ライフルではありませんでした。キャノンでした。
ザ
それはサカ基地のキャノンです。
キャノン？ライフルじゃなかった？
雨か…
きみ、これは何？

今日はきりか…
今日はここでキャンプだ。
よし！ヤス・アーミー!!アタックだ!!
ありがとうございます!!!
シャッ
おまえは東のアーミーのリーダーだ!!
それでは、さようなら！
はい!!わかりました！
チカッ
ピッ
all systems ON LINE
カチャッ

ザァアアアアアアアアアァ――――
敵だ!!
敵だ!!!
敵だ！
ピッピッ
ピッピッ
YASU
53890072
20 x
サー、
敵です!!!
カッ
ばんざい
ばんざい
ばんざい
ばんざい
ばんざい
ばんざい
ばんざい
サカ基地、
バンザイ!!!

Review for Lessons 6–10

Answers to all the review exercises can be found online by following the link on page 9.

RAKUJŌ – New vocabulary 新しい単語

銀河(ぎんが)	galaxy	キャノン	cannon
サイボーグ	cyborg	ライフル	rifle
ロボット	robot	キャンプ	camp
メガ	mega- (prefix)	よし！	All right!
ファイト	fight	アタック	attack
ヴァイオレント	violent	わかりました	Sure, I get you
外(そと)	outside	敵(てき)	enemy
しかし	however	サー	sir
来(き)ます	to come	バンザイ(万歳)	hurrah!

1. In what year of the Western calendar does the action in this episode take place?

2. What is the weather like at the Saka base now? (Say it in Japanese.)

3. What will happen in four days, weather-wise?

4. Which personal pronoun does Hide use when he talks to Yuki? How about Yodo when she talks to Yuki? Why do you think they use these specific pronouns and not different ones?

5. Does Hide use the plain or polite form of です when he speaks with Yuki? Why?

6. What is the form of the verb in Hide's sentence ライフルじゃなかった? Write all possible forms for the verb in this sentence:

Plain present	________________
Polite present	ライフルです
Plain past	________________
Polite past	________________

Plain negative ____________________

Plain negative (2 forms) ____________________

Polite negative ____________________

Plain past negative ____________________

Plain past negative (2 forms) ____________________

Polite past negative ____________________

Polite past negative (2 forms) ____________________

7. Yuki's answer to Hide's question is ライフルじゃなかった. Change this answer into a question in both forms, plain and polite.

8. Based on Lesson 8 and using as an example some of the English-origin words in katakana that we have seen in this episode of ***Rakujō***, try transcribing the following words into katakana.

cybot	サイボット	shake	______
cybernet	______	fake	______
scandal	______	Venus	______
ham	______	guerrilla	______
check	______	tiramisu	______

9. Write the following dates in Japanese along with their reading in ***furigana***, as in the example.

13th March	３月１３日 (さんがつじゅうさんにち)	4th April	______
12th June	______	10th August	______
6th May	______	26th January	______
17th July	______	1st December	______
20th September	______	24th February	______

10. It's important to know the names of Japanese eras (based on the reign of the emperors) as they are still commonly referred to. According to what you studied in Lesson 6, to what years of the Western calendar do the following Japanese years correspond?

平成(へいせい)17年(ねん)	2005	昭和(しょうわ)30年(ねん)	______
明治(めいじ)5年(ねん)	______	平成(へいせい)2年(ねん)	______
大正(たいしょう)10年(ねん)	______	昭和(しょうわ)51年(ねん)	______

11. Link the following words based on their similarity in concept or association of ideas. Bear in mind the passage of seasons in Japan (check Lesson 10 if you have any doubts).

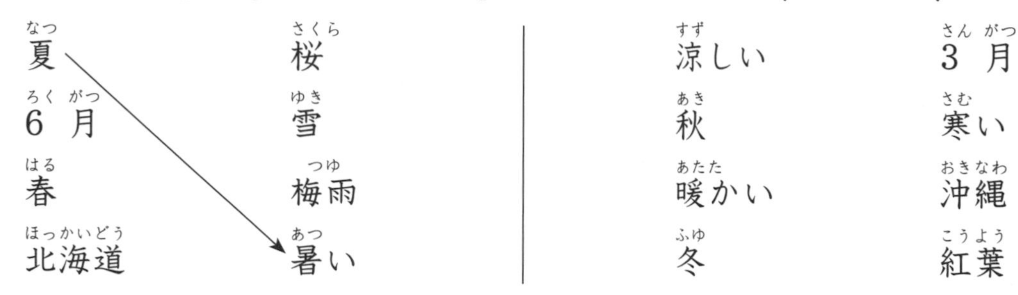

12. Place the pronouns in the table on the right in their corresponding box.

	singular	plural
1st person	私(わたし)	
2nd person		

私(わたし)	あなた
お前(まえ)ら	僕(ぼく)
君(きみ)	俺(おれ)たち
われわれ	わし
お前(まえ)	あんたたち

13. Transcribe these words into katakana according to the rules studied in Lessons 2 and 8.

Randy	ランディ	Sylvia	______
California	______	George	______
Chuck	______	Dionysus	______
Constantinople	______	Stephanie	______
Canyon	______	Jodie	______

14. Choose the right answer.

a) ____はボールペンです。
1. その　2. それ　3. あそこ　4. あの

b) ____に筆(ふで)がある。（ある ="there is/are"）
1. あそこ　2. あれ　3. この　4. これ

c) 彼女(かのじょ)は ____ ですか。
1. この　2. どの　3. あれ　4. どこ

d) ____ は何(なん)ですか。
1. あれ　2. どの　3. この　4. どれ

15. Complete the following sentences with the most suitable ***kosoado*** pronoun.

a) これ は写真(しゃしん)です。(close to the speaker)

b) ____________ は雪(ゆき)ですか。(far from both speakers)

c) ____________ に鳥(とり)がいる。("there is/are," close to the speaker)

d) **A:** ボールペンはどこですか。　| **B:** __________だ！(close to B)

e) **A:** __________ 人(ひと)が先生(せんせい)ですか。　| **B:** あの人(ひと)です。(far from both speakers)

f) ____________ 犬はばかです！(close to the speaker)

16. Give the form of the verb です indicated for each sentence.

a) あれはテーブル　でした。(formal past)

b) その人(ひと)は学生(がくせい)　____________。/ ____________。(formal negative; 2 options)

c) 今日(きょう)は土曜日(どようび)　____________。(formal question)

d) これはお金(かね)　____________。/ ____________。(simple negative; 2 options)

e) その人(ひと)は先生(せんせい)　____________。/ ____________。(formal neg. question; 2 options)

f) それは一万円　____________。(simple past)

g) その猫(ねこ)はばか　____________。/ ____________。(simple past neg.; 2 options)

h) あれはレモン　____________。(formal past question)

17. Mr. Akiyama is going on a business trip to several world cities. On the page from his notebook below you can see a list of his travel plans. Use this information to fill in the blanks in the sentences. Write the missing kanji in the empty brackets.

a) 秋山(あきやま)さんは火曜日(かようび)に<u>ローマ</u>です。

b) むいか (六日) は<u>水曜日(すいようび)</u>です。

c) 秋山(あきやま)さんは ________ にパリです。

d) ________ は土曜日(すいようび)です。

e) 秋山(あきやま)さんは日曜日(にちようび)に ________ です。

f) 秋山(あきやま)さんはいつか (   ) に ________ です。

g) 秋山(あきやま)さんはよっか (   ) にアムステルダム ________。

h) 秋山(あきやま)さんはここのか (   ) に ________ です。

i) ようか (   ) は________じゃありません。

旅行予定

3日(日) 東京(とうきょう)
4日(月) ロンドン
5日(火) ローマ
6日(水) バルセロナ
7日(木) パリ
8日(金) アムステルダム
9日(土) 上海(シャンハイ)

18. Complete each sentence with the appropriate personal pronoun from the box below.

a) 私(わたし)の名前(なまえ)はトモコです。(1st sing. | woman, to a stranger)

b) ________ の名前(なまえ)は山田(やまだ)と秋本(あきもと)です。(1st pl. | politicians, among them)

c) ________ の名前(なまえ)は風之介(かぜのすけ)です。(1st sing. | samurai, to a stranger)

d) ________ の名前(なまえ)は何(なん)ですか。(2nd sing. | 40-year-old man, to a young woman)

e) ________ の名前(なまえ)はエミカです。(3rd sing. | girl, to a stranger)

f) ________はばかじゃない！(1st pl. | young men, to some friends)

g) ________はばかだった(3rd pl. | young men, to each other)

彼(かれ)ら	君(きみ)	~~私(わたし)~~	俺(おれ)ら	彼女(かのじょ)	拙者(せっしゃ)	われわれ

Kanji

日 (16)	月 (17)	火 (18)	水 (19)	木 (20)	金 (21)	土 (22)	春 (86)	夏 (87)	秋 (88)	冬 (89)
年 (54)	人 (15)	男 (33)	女 (34)	子 (35)	私 (82)	山 (42)	川 (43)	田 (44)	本 (74)	雨 (138)

19. Practice writing the kanji below. Find the stroke order in the online Kanji Compilation section via the link on page 9.

水										
男										
年										
春										
雨										

20. Link each kanji with its most common reading (usually, the ***kun'yomi***).

冬 → ふゆ	ほん	人	ひと
本	ふゆ	秋	あき
男	ひ	夏	かわ
田	た	火	こ
木	おとこ	子	ひ
日	き	川	なつ

21. Choose the correct kanji or kanji combination for each reading.

a) はる
1. 春　2. 巻　3. 舂　4. 泰

b) つき
1. 日　2. 目　3. 月　4. 円

c) だんじょ
1. 男子　2. 男女　3. 男山　4. 男人

d) わたし
1. 利　2. 秋　3. 科　4. 私

22. Choose the correct reading for each kanji combination.

a) 木曜日
1. どようび　2. げつようび　3. きんようび　4. もくようび

b) 日本人
1. にっぽんしん　2. にっぽんじん　3. にほんしん　4. にはんじん

c) 雨水
1. あめみず　2. あまみす　3. あまみず　4. あめみづ

23. Give the hiragana readings of the following words, and give their meaning.

人	ひと	person	秋	______	______
山	______	______	平成(へいせい)3年	______	______
女子	______	______	水曜(よう)日	______	______
春休(やす)み	______	______	六日	______	______
冬眠(みん)	______	______	油(ゆ)田	______	______

24. Write the following words in kanji, and give their meaning.

なつ	夏	summer	おんな	______	______
つき	______	______	かわ	______	______
あめ	______	______	か曜(よう)び	______	______
しがつ	______	______	わたし	______	______
はつか	______	______	ごねん	______	______

Lesson 11 • 第11課

Nouns

We are going to deal with some more grammar in this lesson—nouns. This will not be very difficult, since nouns in Japanese are quite simple. We will also take this opportunity to add some more vocabulary to your stock!

Japanese nouns

As you know, a noun is a word used to refer to a person, place, thing or concept. Needless to say, nouns are the basis of the vocabulary of any language and the more you learn, the more ideas you will be able to express in Japanese. But don't forget the grammar! There is no point in knowing lots of words without being able to connect them coherently.

What is so special about Japanese nouns for us to devote a whole lesson to them? First, if we know how to use nouns, we can learn a great deal of vocabulary in Japanese, something which is now absolutely necessary. Second, Japanese nouns have certain characteristics which make them different to English nouns.

Characteristics of nouns

Japanese nouns have neither gender (masculine / feminine) nor number (singular / plural). To give a clear example, we will say that the English words "boy," "boys," "girl," and "girls" are equivalent to the Japanese word 子 ***ko***, without distinction between one or more, male or female. This peculiarity makes Japanese nouns at once easy to master (because they don't change) and difficult to interpret (because they can only be understood in context).

For example, the sentence これは子です ***kore wa ko desu*** can have up to four different meanings: a) this is a boy, b) this is a girl, c) these are boys, and d) these are girls.

Of course, this can lead to confusion. If we want to specify whether something or someone is male or female, or whether there is one or several, we will have to make a more complex sentence as in the following examples:

a) これは男の子が一人です
kore wa otoko no ko ga hitori desu
This is one boy.

b) これは女の子が一人です
kore wa onna no ko ga hitori desu
This is one girl.

c) これは男の子が五人です
kore wa otoko no ko ga go nin desu
These are five boys.

d) これは女の子が五人です
kore wa onna no ko ga go nin desu
These are five girls.

However, these kinds of sentence are not generally used, unless determining gender or number is absolutely necessary. Usually, the context will clarify what we are talking about.

When you finish this lesson, and you have learned how "counters" work (see below), try forming your own sentences using the animal, fruit and vegetable names in the table below. You can use the sentences we have just studied as a base.

Animals, fruits and vegetables					
Japanese	**Rōmaji**	**Meaning**	**Japanese**	**Rōmaji**	**Meaning**
犬	***inu***	dog	バナナ	***banana***	banana
猫	***neko***	cat	りんご	***ringo***	apple
鳥	***tori***	bird	なし	***nashi***	pear
馬	***uma***	horse	すいか	***suika***	watermelon
牛	***ushi***	cow / bull	オレンジ	***orenji***	orange
さる	***saru***	monkey	みかん	***mikan***	mandarin
うさぎ	***usagi***	rabbit	いちご	***ichigo***	strawberry
羊	***hitsuji***	sheep	レモン	***remon***	lemon
へび	***hebi***	snake	もも	***momo***	peach
ぶた	***buta***	pig	トマト	***tomato***	tomato
魚	***sakana***	fish	じゃがいも	***jagaimo***	potato
くま	***kuma***	bear	たまねぎ	***tamanegi***	onion
あり	***ari***	ant	レタス	***retasu***	lettuce
ライオン	***raion***	lion	ピーマン	***piiman***	green pepper
ぞう	***zō***	elephant	きのこ	***kinoko***	mushroom
しか	***shika***	deer	にんにく	***ninniku***	garlic
とら	***tora***	tiger	かぼちゃ	***kabocha***	pumpkin
りゅう	***ryū***	dragon	まめ	***mame***	bean

Counters

This brings us to how to count things in Japanese. Notice how in the sentences at the bottom of the facing page we used the word 人 ***nin***? This is the "counter" for people (with the exception of 一人 ***hitori***, one person, and 二人 ***futari***, two people). The use of counters is as follows: "thing to be counted + particle ***ga*** + number + counter + verb." For example:

これは紙が三枚です
kore wa kami ga san mai desu
These are three sheets of paper.
kami = paper | ***san*** = 3 | ***mai*** = counter

There are many counters and they change depending on the properties of the things we wish to give the number of. In Lesson 25 we will make a more comprehensive study of counters, but for the time being, here are some of the main ones:

人 ***nin***	for people	枚 ***mai***	for flat things
匹 ***hiki***	for small animals	本 ***hon***	for long things
台 ***dai***	for machines	冊 ***satsu***	for books, magazines, etc.

To conclude, we recommend that you thoroughly study the two vocabulary tables in this lesson: learning all these words will give you enough basic vocabulary to be able to form your own sentences in the lessons that follow.

A few nouns					
Japanese	**Rōmaji**	**Meaning**	**Japanese**	**Rōmaji**	**Meaning**
くるま	***kuruma***	car	レストラン	***resutoran***	restaurant
じてんしゃ	***jitensha***	bicycle	おかし	***o-kashi***	candy
カメラ	***kamera***	camera	おちゃ	***o-cha***	tea
しんぶん	***shinbun***	newspaper	コーヒー	***kōhii***	coffee
たばこ	***tabako***	tobacco	ごはん	***gohan***	cooked rice
きって	***kitte***	stamp	こめ	***kome***	uncooked rice
えんぴつ	***enpitsu***	pencil	パン	***pan***	bread
ボールペン	***bōrupen***	ballpoint pen	スープ	***sūpu***	soup
きょうしつ	***kyōshitsu***	classroom	うた	***uta***	song
にわ	***niwa***	garden	えいが	***eiga***	movie
たてもの	***tatemono***	building	てがみ	***tegami***	letter
びょういん	***byōin***	hospital	やすみ	***yasumi***	rest
トイレ	***toire***	toilet	パーティー	***paatii***	party
いえ	***ie***	house	ざっし	***zasshi***	magazine
かみ	***kami***	paper	あさ	***asa***	morning
にく	***niku***	meat	ひる	***hiru***	noon
くだもの	***kudamono***	fruit	ゆうがた	***yūgata***	evening
やさい	***yasai***	vegetables	よる	***yoru***	night

漫画例 Manga Examples

As an introduction to these manga examples, it's worth knowing that nouns are usually written in kanji, and since their form never changes, they are the easiest words to look up in a dictionary.

Manga Example 1: Blood and tears

J.M. Ken Niimura

In this example we find two nouns, 血 ***chi*** ("blood") and 涙 ***namida*** ("tear"). As we can see, it doesn't say whether there is one tear or several, but we are pretty sure from the context there is more than one, hence the translation in the plural form. We also find the possessive particle の ***no***, which we will study in Lesson 16.

> **Yūsuke:** 血の… 涙
> ***chi no... namida***
> blood POP tear
> Tears of... blood.

Manga Example 2: "Heart" and review of Lesson 7

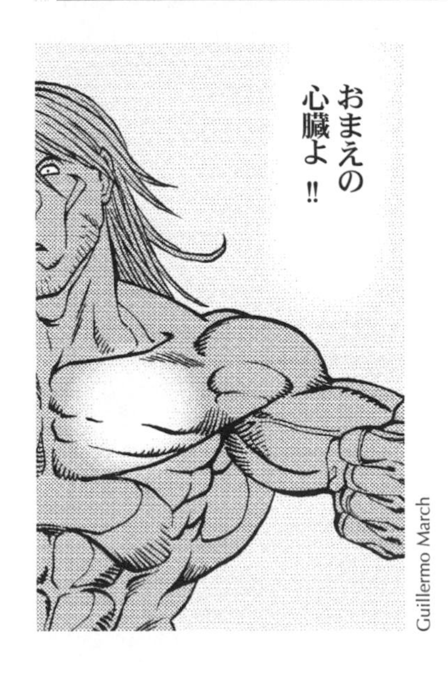

Guillermo March

Remember the word おまえ ***omae*** from Lesson 7? This pronoun means "you," but it has a superiority nuance: the speaker feels superior to the person they are speaking to (so this is something we should refrain from using). In this panel we also have the noun 心臓 ***shinzō***, which means "heart," and the particle の ***no*** appears again. The ending particle よ ***yo*** is used for emphasis (see Lesson 17).

> **Kamada:** おまえの心臓よ!!
> ***omae no shinzō yo!!***
> you POP heart EP!!
> It's your heart!!

Manga Example 3: Several nouns

Studio Kōsen

We see here some more nouns, like ヤツ ***yatsu*** ("person," in a vulgar sense, more or less equivalent to "guy"), 酒 ***sake*** (the word for any alcoholic drink in the broad sense, or "Japanese sake" specifically), 女 ***onna*** (woman), 悦楽 ***etsuraku*** (pleasure), and 日々 ***hibi*** (day after day). Notice how we have translated the word 女 ***onna*** as "women," in the plural due to the context: the speaker is obviously referring to more than one woman, and the two women in the picture also give us a clue.

Kudō: 歯向かうヤツを殺す!!
hamukau yatsu o korosu!!
Defy person DOP kill!!
I'll kill whoever defies me!!

酒と女と悦楽の日々!!
sake to onna to etsuraku no hibi!!
alcohol & woman & pleasure POP day after day!!
A life of drink, women, and pleasure!!

Manga Example 4: People counter

J.M. Ken Niimura

In this example we have a couple of interesting things. First of all, the counter 人 ***nin***, which, together with 七 ***shichi*** (seven), forms the word 七人 ***shichinin***; that is, "seven people." Second, the example talks about a 使者 ***shisha*** (messenger). Therefore, 七人の使者 ***shichinin*** no shisha means "seven messengers." This is a very clear example of the use of counters.

Finally, take a look at the form of the quotation marks in the lower speech bubble, which are totally different from those we use in English.

Mai: おそらく...『七人の使者』
osoraku... "shichinin no shisha"
...maybe... "seven people POP messenger"
They might be... "The Seven Messengers."

Exercises 練習

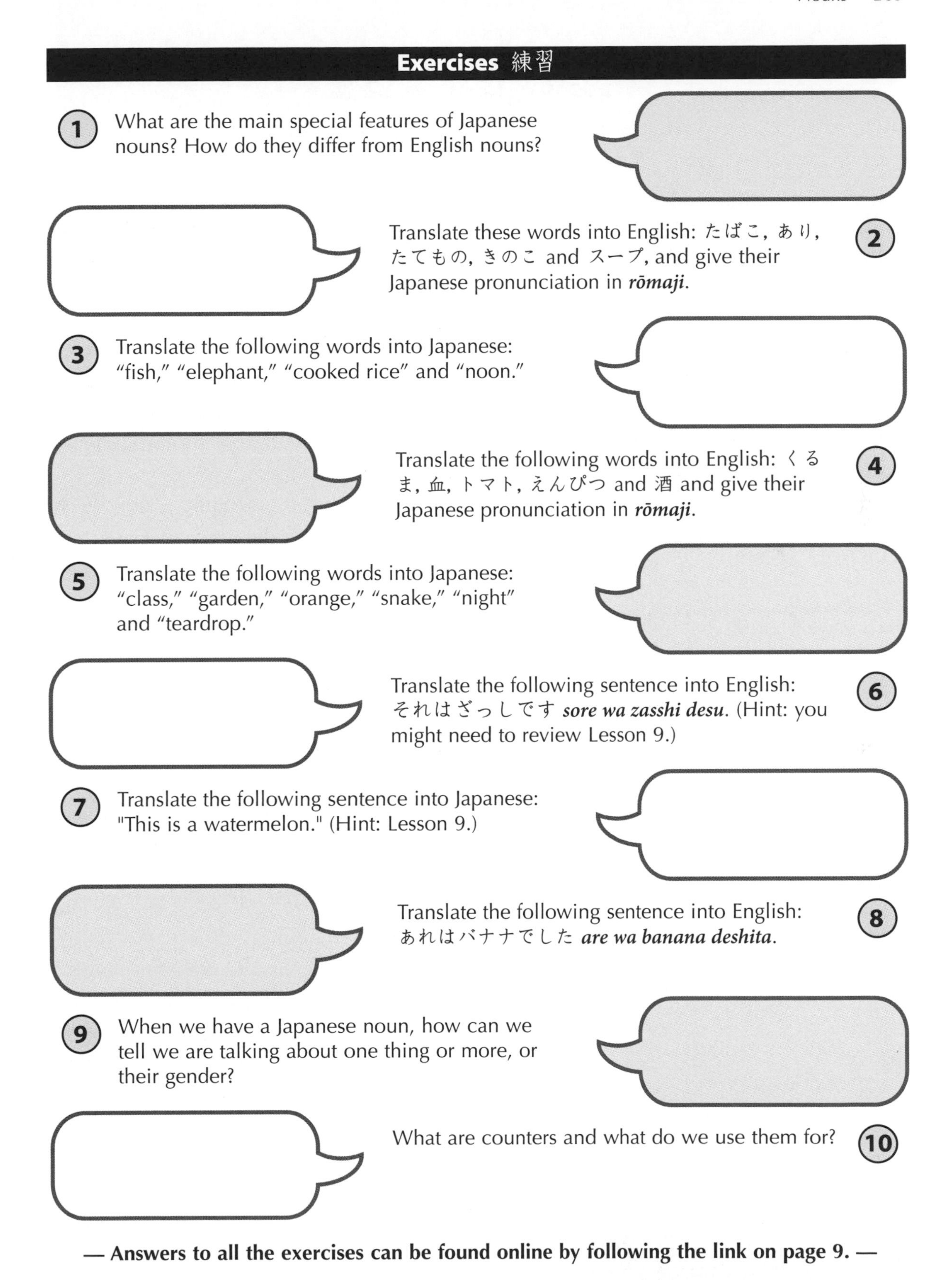

1. What are the main special features of Japanese nouns? How do they differ from English nouns?

2. Translate these words into English: たばこ, あり, たてもの, きのこ and スープ, and give their Japanese pronunciation in ***rōmaji***.

3. Translate the following words into Japanese: "fish," "elephant," "cooked rice" and "noon."

4. Translate the following words into English: くるま, 血, トマト, えんぴつ and 酒 and give their Japanese pronunciation in ***rōmaji***.

5. Translate the following words into Japanese: "class," "garden," "orange," "snake," "night" and "teardrop."

6. Translate the following sentence into English: それはざっしです ***sore wa zasshi desu***. (Hint: you might need to review Lesson 9.)

7. Translate the following sentence into Japanese: "This is a watermelon." (Hint: Lesson 9.)

8. Translate the following sentence into English: あれはバナナでした ***are wa banana deshita***.

9. When we have a Japanese noun, how can we tell we are talking about one thing or more, or their gender?

10. What are counters and what do we use them for?

— Answers to all the exercises can be found online by following the link on page 9. —

Lesson 12 • 第12課

What's the Time?

In this lesson, we will learn how to tell the time and some related expressions. As you might have deduced, this topic has a lot to do with numbers, so we recommend that you thoroughly review Lesson 5 before you start.

Some special readings

First, you must study the table on page 108, and note that many of words to do with telling the time have irregular readings. For example, the kanji 四時 is pronounced ***yo ji*** and not ***yon ji*** or ***shi ji***, which would be other possible options. Likewise, 六分 is pronounced ***rop-pun*** and not ***roku fun***.

Especially in the case of the kanji 分, we must point out its basic reading is ***fun***, but in certain cases, for phonetical reasons, it is pronounced ***pun***. This is the case with 1 分, 3 分, 4 分, 6 分, 8 分 and 10 分, which are respectively pronounced ***ippun***, ***san pun***, ***yon pun***, ***roppun***, ***happun***, and ***juppun / jippun*** (10 分 has two valid readings).

To master telling the time in Japanese you need to carefully study the correct pronunciations of the kanji for hours and minutes, since there are many exceptions.

今、八時です
ima, hachi ji desu
It's now eight o'clock

今、五時十五分すぎです
ima, go ji jū go fun sugi desu
It's now a quarter past five

今、三時半です
ima, san ji han desu
It's now half past three

今、十一時十五分まえです
ima, jū ichi ji jū go fun mae desu
It's now a quarter to eleven

Telling the time

Telling the time in Japanese is really very easy: there are only a few points to bear in mind, and they aren't necessarily essential. We will explain why shortly.

When someone asks for the time, the best way to start your answer is with 今 ***ima***, which means "now." Then you say the time, and finish with the verb です ***desu***, which, as you probably remember, means "to be" (Lesson 9).

Now look at the first clock on the facing page so we can practice telling the o'clock times. Just follow the pattern 今、X時です ***ima, x ji desu***, replacing "x" with a number. For example: 今、九時です ***ima, ku ji desu*** means "it is now nine o'clock."

Other constructions

There are three other basic constructions: half past, a quarter past, and a quarter to. Look at the illustrations of the clocks once more to understand the explanation in a more visual way.

Half past: Add 半 ***han*** after 時 ***ji***. Thus, the basic pattern is: 今、X時半です ***ima, x ji han desu***. Example: 今、三時半です ***ima, san ji han desu***, "It is now half past three."

A quarter past: Add 十五分すぎ ***jū go fun sugi*** after 時 ***ji***, so the basic pattern is 今、X時十五分すぎです ***ima, x ji jū go fun sugi desu***. Example: 今、十二時十五分すぎです ***ima, jū ni ji jū go fun sugi desu***, "It is now a quarter past twelve."

A quarter to: Add 十五分まえ ***jū go fun mae*** after 時 ***ji***, so the basic pattern is 今、X時十五分まえです ***ima, x ji jū go fun mae desu***. Example: 今、七時十五分まえです ***ima, shichi ji jū go fun mae desu***, "It is now a quarter to seven."

Some information to better understand these constructions: 半 ***han*** means "half," すぎ ***sugi*** means "to exceed," and まえ ***mae*** means "before." Not so difficult, right?

Still simpler

Actually, none of what we have just explained is essential, since you can say the time using shorter phrases. For example, for 6:30 you can either say 六時半です ***roku ji han desu*** ("It is half past six") or 六時三十分です ***roku ji san juppun desu*** ("It is six thirty"). Here are some more examples:

今、二時十二分です ***ima, ni ji jū ni fun desu***, "It is now two twelve."
今、十時五十七分です ***ima, jū ji go jū nana fun desu***, "It is now ten fifty-seven."

Sample conversation

Let's now have a look at a basic conversation, which you can use as a model:

A: すみませんが...
sumimasen ga...
Excuse me...

B: はい、何でしょうか?
hai, nan deshō ka?
Yes, can I help you?

A: 今、何時ですか？
ima, nan ji desu ka?
What's the time, please?

B: ええ...今、X時Y分です
ee... ima, x ji y fun desu
Mmm... It's now x y.

A: ありがとうございます
arigatō gozaimasu
Thank you very much.

B: どういたしまして
dō itashimashite
You're welcome.

Hours	時 *(ji)*	Minutes	分 *(fun)*
一時	***ichi ji***	一分	***ippun***
二時	***ni ji***	二分	***ni fun***
三時	***san ji***	三分	***san pun***
四時	***yo ji***	四分	***yon pun***
五時	***go ji***	五分	***go fun***
六時	***roku ji***	六分	***roppun***
七時	***shichi ji***	七分	***nana fun***
八時	***hachi ji***	八分	***happun***
九時	***ku ji***	九分	***kyū fun***
十時	***jū ji***	十分	***jippun/juppun***
十一時	***jū ichi ji***	十一分	***jūippun***
十二時	***jū ni ji***	十二分	***jū ni fun***
何時？	***nan ji?***	何分？	***nan pun?***

This conversation could easily be taking place right now anywhere in Japan. All you need to do is change the x and y for the corresponding hour and minute, and you will be able to calmly tell the time. Give it a try!

Take a look, anyway, at how to ask for the time, because you will find this useful too: 今、何時ですか？ ***ima, nan ji desu ka?*** "What's the time (now)?"

AM and PM

To conclude, you will probably wonder how to tell whether we are referring to morning or afternoon time. There are two strategies for this.

The first is to use the twenty-four clock. For example, if we want to say 6:00 pm, we can say 今、十八時です ***ima, jū hachi ji desu***, "It is now eighteen hours." However, the most common strategy by far, is to use the time adverbs 午前 ***gozen*** or 朝 ***asa*** ("morning," from 5 to 11 am), 昼 ***hiru*** ("noon," 12 pm), 午後 ***gogo*** ("afternoon," from 1 pm till evening), 夕方 ***yūgata*** ("evening"), 夜 ***yoru*** ("night," from evening to midnight), and 深夜 ***shin'ya*** ("dawn," from 1 to 4 am). The particle の ***no*** is not needed with ***gozen*** and ***gogo***:

今、午前９時半です ***ima, gozen ku ji han desu***, "It is now 9:30 a.m."
今、深夜の３時です ***ima, shin'ya no san ji desu***, "It is now three in the morning."

漫画例 Manga Examples

We will use the manga examples in this section to review what we have studied on the previous pages and to expand on what we've learned so far by having a look at a more colloquial way of telling the time.

Manga Example 1: 3:30

In this example we have two times, 3時24分 ***san ji ni jū yon pun*** (3:24) and 3時半 ***san ji han*** (half past 3). In the second case, we could also say 3時30分 ***san ji san juppun*** (3:30). Notice too the word タイムリミット ***taimu rimitto***, which comes from the English word "time limit."

Kei:	3時24分…タイムリミットは3時半…	それまでにやらなきゃ…
	san ji ni jū yon pun... taimu rimitto wa san ji han...	***sore made ni yaranakya...***
	3 h 24 min.... time limit 3 hour half...	then before do...
	It's 3:24... The time limit is half past 3..	**It must be done by that time...**

Manga Example 2: 6:10

Shunsuke is talking about a clock, hence the usage of the verb 指す ***sasu***, which means "to point" or, in this context, "the clock hands point to the time." The time indicated is 6時10分 ***roku ji juppun*** (10 past 6), but, without knowing the context, we can't tell whether it is morning or afternoon.

Shunsuke:	6時10分を指していたよ
	roku ji juppun o sashite ita yo
	six hours indicate EP
	The time was 6:10.

Manga Example 3: "What's the time?"

We will use this example to illustrate two of the points we saw earlier in the lesson.

The first point is how to ask the time: We have already seen the formal way, that is, 今、何時ですか？ ***Ima, nan ji desu ka?*** In this example, Hiroshi uses the informal way (slightly rough, but OK among friends), 今何時だ？ ***Ima nan ji da?*** Notice how he uses だ ***da***, the simple form of the verb です ***desu*** ("to be," Lesson 9), used to imply familiarity with the person he is speaking to.

The second point is Miyuki's answer: 12時10分 ***ju ni ji juppun***, "10 past 12." As you can see, knowing the numbers (Lesson 5) is essential to be able to tell the time.

Hiroshi: そうだ 今何時だ!?
sō da ima nan ji da!?
that be now what time be!?
That's right! What's the time?!

Miyuki: 12時10分よ！
jū ni ji juppun yo!
12 hours 10 minutes EP!
It's 10 past 12!

Manga Example 4: The two "afternoons" in Japanese

Our last example, besides giving a new way of saying the time (in this case, 3時 ***san ji***, "three o'clock"), shows us how to use a time adverb that refers to a particular time of day.

Here, the word 午後 ***gogo*** (afternoon) makes it clear Sayoko is talking about 3 pm and not 3 am (when she would use the word 深夜 ***shin'ya***, dawn.)

午後 ***gogo*** is used to refer to the part of the day which goes from noon till sunset: this is the "afternoon." From then on, it is 夕方 ***yūgata***, which means "evening." It works just like English, which is good news!

Sayoko: よっしゃ！ 午後の３時にしよう！！
yossha! gogo no san ji ni shiyō!!
OK! afternoon POP 3 hours to decide on!
OK! Let's do it at 3 o'clock in the afternoon!

Exercises 練習

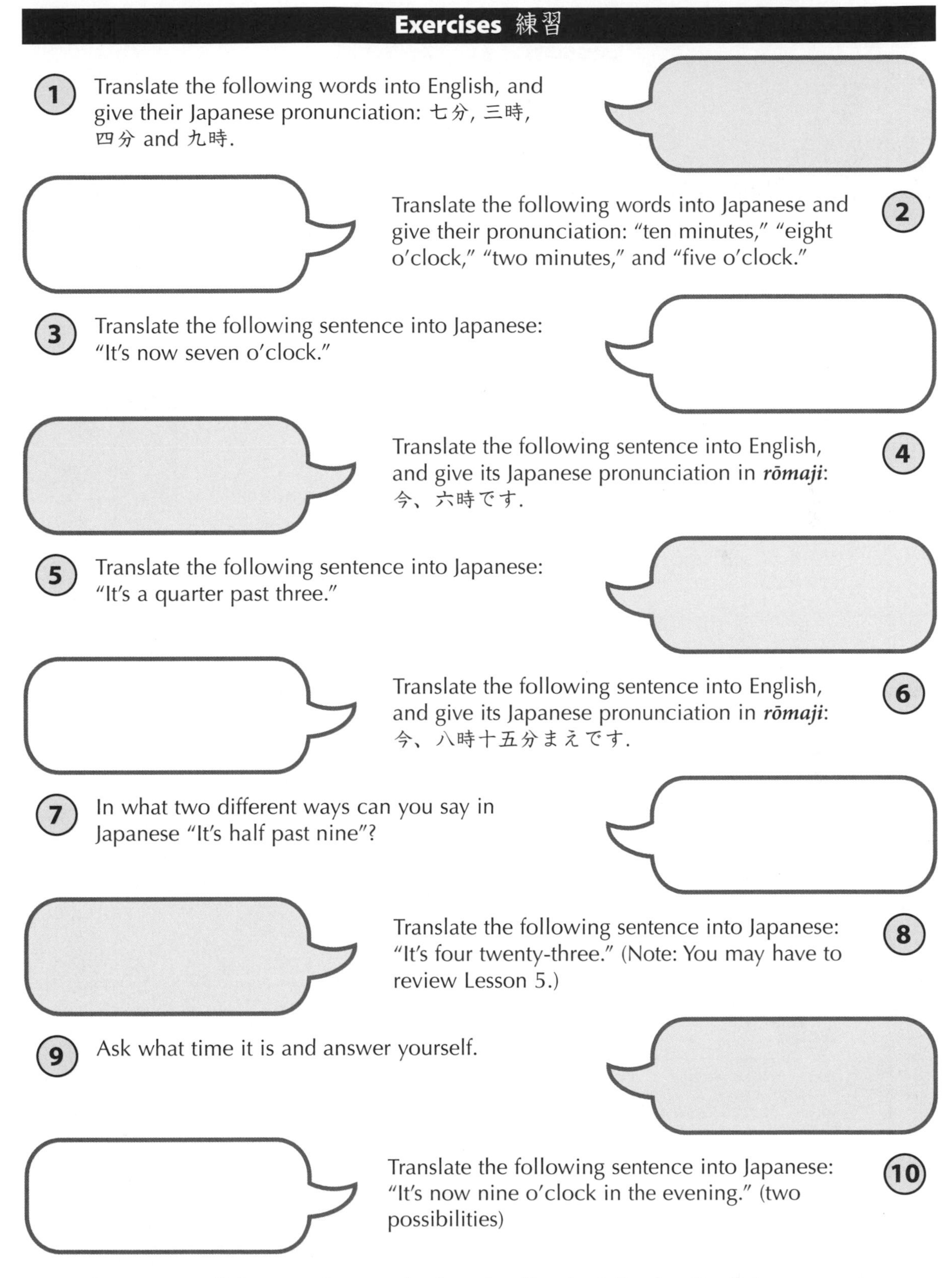

1. Translate the following words into English, and give their Japanese pronunciation: 七分, 三時, 四分 and 九時.
2. Translate the following words into Japanese and give their pronunciation: "ten minutes," "eight o'clock," "two minutes," and "five o'clock."
3. Translate the following sentence into Japanese: "It's now seven o'clock."
4. Translate the following sentence into English, and give its Japanese pronunciation in ***rōmaji***: 今、六時です.
5. Translate the following sentence into Japanese: "It's a quarter past three."
6. Translate the following sentence into English, and give its Japanese pronunciation in ***rōmaji***: 今、八時十五分まえです.
7. In what two different ways can you say in Japanese "It's half past nine"?
8. Translate the following sentence into Japanese: "It's four twenty-three." (Note: You may have to review Lesson 5.)
9. Ask what time it is and answer yourself.
10. Translate the following sentence into Japanese: "It's now nine o'clock in the evening." (two possibilities)

— Answers to all the exercises can be found online by following the link on page 9. —

Lesson 13 • 第13課

-i Adjectives

We have reached Lesson 13, where we will learn one of two kinds of Japanese adjectives: the *-i* adjectives. As you know, an adjective is a word that describes a noun. For example, in the phrase "expensive coat," the word "expensive" is an adjective describing the quality of the coat.

What is an "-i" adjective?

In Japanese there are two kinds of adjectives, referred to as ***-i*** adjectives and ***-na*** adjectives.

Why these names? Well, ***-i*** adjectives all end in the sound い ***i***, with no exceptions. This guarantees that when you see a word which ends with い, you can be almost certain that it is an adjective. Obviously, ***-na*** adjectives end in な ***na***, and we will devote Lesson 14 to the study of ***-na*** adjectives.

The good news is that in Japanese, like in English, adjectives always go before the noun they modify, with no exceptions. This means that it will not be necessary for an English native speaker to think about the position of adjectives when constructing sentences in Japanese, as literal translations from English will work just perfectly.

Take a look at these examples: 高い木 ***takai ki***, "tall tree" (***takai*** = "tall," ***ki*** = "tree"), 青い空 ***aoi sora***, "blue sky" (***aoi*** = "blue," ***sora*** = "sky"). Notice how the structure is exactly the same as in English: adjective first, and then noun.

Some *-i* adjectives					
Japanese	Rōmaji	Meaning	Japanese	Rōmaji	Meaning
小さい	***chiisai***	small	黄色い	***kiiroi***	yellow
大きい	***ookii***	big	高い	***takai***	tall / expensive
やさしい	***yasashii***	easy / kind	安い	***yasui***	cheap
むずかしい	***muzukashii***	difficult	低い	***hikui***	low
白い	***shiroi***	white	新しい	***atarashii***	new
赤い	***akai***	red	古い	***furui***	old
青い	***aoi***	blue	暗い	***kurai***	dark
黒い	***kuroi***	black	明るい	***akarui***	bright

Inflection of -i adjectives					
		Affirmative		Negative	
		desu form	Simple form	*desu* form	Simple form
Present	Rule	いです	い	~~い~~くないです	~~い~~くない
	Example	安いです	安い	安くないです	安くない
	Rōmaji	***yasui desu***	***yasui***	***yasukunai desu***	***yasukunai***
	Translation	It's cheap.		It isn't cheap.	
Past	Rule	~~い~~かったです	~~い~~かった	~~い~~くなかったです	~~い~~くなかった
	Example	安かったです	安かった	安くなかったです	安くなかった
	Rōmaji	***yasukatta desu***	***yasukatta***	***yasukunakatta desu***	***yasukunakatta***
	Translation	It was cheap.		It wasn't cheap.	

-i adjectives are inflected

Not only are there ***-i*** adjectives and ***-na*** adjectives which work in different ways, but ***-i*** adjectives are inflected, meaning that they are conjugated in the same way as verbs.

Fortunately there are only four kinds of inflection: present affirmative, past affirmative, present negative and past negative. In addition, there are also formal versions (the ***desu*** form, which we use with people we don't know, older people, or people who are hierarchically superior), and informal versions (the simple form, which we use with family and friends), making a total of eight forms to study for each adjective. The formation of all eight forms is illustrated in the table above, using the adjective 安い ***yasui***, "cheap."

Don't worry about the distinction between the ***desu*** and simple forms: to make the formal version (***desu*** form) of an ***-i*** adjective simply add the verb です ***desu*** at the end.

The four inflections

Let's look at the four forms, in their informal version, one by one, with examples.

Present affirmative: This is the easiest form; it is the adjective as you have studied in the vocabulary lists, with no changes. Since it is the most basic form, it is also called the "infinitive" of the adjective. For example: "old house" 古い家 ***furui ie*** (***furui*** = "old," ***ie*** = "house"); "white book" 白い本 ***shiroi hon*** (***shiroi*** = "white," ***hon*** = "book").

Past affirmative: In this case, the final い ***i*** in the adjective is replaced with かった ***-katta***, the past ending. For example: "house that was old" 古かった家 ***furukatta ie***; "book that was white" 白かった本 ***shirokatta hon***.

Present negative: Replace the final い ***i*** of the infinitive with the negative ending くない ***-kunai***. For example: "house that isn't old" 古くない家 ***furukunai ie***; "book that isn't white" 白くない本 ***shirokunai hon***.

Past negative: This is a combination of the previous two inflections. The final い ***i*** in the infinitive is replaced with くな ***-kuna-***, the negative ending, + かった ***-katta***, the past ending. For example: "house that wasn't old" 古くなかった家 ***furukunakatta ie***; "book that wasn't white" 白くなかった本 ***shirokunakatta hon***.

Just like a jigsaw puzzle, isn't it? Now try to practice the inflections on the adjectives in the table on page 112. When you are done, try with the adjective あたたかい ***atatakai*** (warm). This one is really a tongue twister!

Sentences with the verb "to be"

Remembering Lesson 9 is essential to understand this lesson perfectly, since we will assume you already know the points that were explained in that lesson.

As mentioned earlier, if we place the verb です ***desu*** after an inflected adjective, we obtain a formal sentence. Before we study the examples below, make sure you have mastered the words この ***kono*** (this), その ***sono*** (that), and あの ***ano*** (that one over there), which we studied in Lesson 9.

このかばんは重いです
kono kaban wa omoi desu
This bag is heavy.
(***kaban*** = "bag," ***omoi*** = "heavy")

あのマンガはおもしろくないです
ano manga wa omoshirokunai desu
That manga is not interesting.
(***omoshiroi*** = "interesting")

その犬は危なかったです
sono inu wa abunakatta desu
That dog was dangerous.
(***inu*** = "dog," ***abunai*** = "dangerous")

あの肉はおいしくなかったです
ano niku wa oishikunakatta desu
That meat wasn't good.
(***niku*** = "meat," ***oishii*** = "good," "delicious")

As you can see, the adjectives are inflected, while the verb "to be" always remains the same, that is, in its infinitive form (it is not conjugated). **Note:** You only need to remove the verb です ***desu*** to obtain the same sentences in their informal version; for instance, その犬は危なかった ***sono inu wa abunakatta***, "That dog was dangerous."

Warning!

A sentence like this is completely wrong:

その犬は危ないでした ***sono inu wa abunai deshita***, "That dog was dangerous."

This is because, instead of changing the form of the adjective, which would give us the correct construction, the form of the verb has been changed. You have to take care with this special characteristic of ***-i*** adjectives, as constructing wrong sentences is extremely easy.

漫画例 Manga Examples

Welcome back to more manga examples! As usual, in this section we have selected a variety of manga panels that will further illustrate the grammar points you have studied on the previous pages of this lesson, in this case, the use of *-i* adjectives.

Manga Example 1: Present affirmative (infinitive)

As we have seen, in informal spoken language the verb ***desu*** is usually left out when using ***-i*** adjectives, as illustrated clearly in this example. When translating into English, leaving the adjective on its own wouldn't sound natural ("handsome," in this case) and so something must be added, as in our suggestion: "He's handsome." The adjective かっこいい ***kakkoii*** is a word used by women when referring to a handsome man. A beautiful woman would be 美しい ***utsukushii*** (also an ***-i*** adjective).

Guillermo March

Sakura: かっこいい . . .
kakkoii
handsome
He's handsome . . .

Manga Example 2: Past affirmative

The main word here is 悪かった ***warukatta***, the past affirmative form of the adjective 悪い ***warui***, "bad." In the translation, we have used the verb "to choose," which doesn't appear in the original script. The literal translation would sound unnatural if we hadn't done so.

Studio Kōsen

Rie: 相手が悪かったわ
aite ga warukatta wa
rival SP bad EP
You chose a bad rival...

Manga Example 3: Present negative

Here we have よくない ***yokunai***, the present negative inflection of the ***-i*** adjective いい ***ii*** (good). As you can see, this adjective is slightly irregular: instead of いくない ***ikunai***, it is よくない ***yokunai*** (this is the only irregular adjective there is). Its inflections are: present: いい ***ii***, past; よかった ***yokatta*** (sometimes translated as "thank goodness"); present negative: よくない ***yokunai***; and past negative: よくなかった ***yokunakatta***. As this is and extremely common adjective, you should learn its inflections by heart.

J.M. Ken Niimura

Wolf:	あ！その肉あまってんのか…？	よくないな、それ！
	a! sono niku amatten no ka...?	***yokunai na, sore!***
	oh! that meat left EP Q?	good EP that!!
	Oh! Was there still that meat left?	**That's not good!!**

Manga Example 4: Past negative

Studio Kōsen

Mio: 忠臣くん　あたしがこわくなかった？
tadaomi-kun atashi ga kowakunakatta?
Tadaomi (SUF.) me SP not afraid Q?
Tadaomi, weren't you afraid of me?

To end this lesson, we will see an ***-i*** adjective in its past negative form. The adjective is こわくなかった ***kowakunakatta***, and its simple form is こわい ***kowai***, which means "scary." Its other possible inflections are: present negative こわくない ***kowakunai***, and past affirmative こわかった ***kowakatta***.

This panel also illustrates a point mentioned in Lesson 7. The girl, Mio, doesn't use the second person pronoun (you) to address the boy; she uses his name, "Tadaomi." A literal translation would be "Tadaomi was not afraid of me?" as though she were talking about a third person. This way of addressing people is quite normal in Japanese, so try to remember it.

Exercises 練習

1. What are ***-i*** adjectives? Why are they referred to by this name?

2. In what position do the Japanese adjectives always go, before the noun or after?

3. Translate the following words into English and give their Japanese pronunciation in ***rōmaji***: 赤い, 古い, 大きい and 高い

4. Translate the following words into Japanese and give their pronunciation in ***rōmaji***: "small," "blue," "dark," "cheap."

5. Give two examples of ***-i*** adjectives in the past form.

6. And how about the negative form? Give two examples.

7. What's the past form of the adjective 白い ***shiroi***, "white"?

8. Give the present, past, negative and past negative forms of the adjective 黒い ***kuroi***, "black."

9. Translate the following sentence into Japanese: "This mountain is low." (mountain: 山 ***yama***.)

10. What is wrong with this sentence? この猫はおとなしいではありません ***kono neko wa otonashii de wa arimasen?*** (***neko***: "cat"; ***otonashii***: "docile" [***-i*** adj.].)

— Answers to all the exercises can be found online by following the link on page 9. —

Lesson 14 • 第14課

-na Adjectives

In the previous lesson we talked about one of two kinds of adjectives in the Japanese language: the *-i* adjectives. Now we are going to talk about the second kind, the *-na* adjectives. Before you start, we recommend that you thoroughly review Lessons 9 and 13.

What are "-na" adjectives?

As we explained in the previous lesson, there are two kinds of adjectives in Japanese: ***-i*** and ***-na*** adjectives. The former are called ***-i*** adjectives because they always end with the sound い ***i***. Well, ***-na*** adjectives, as you might have guessed, get their name from the fact that they all end with the syllable な ***na***, with no exceptions (although in dictionaries you will usually find them listed without な ***na***). Have a look at the vocabulary table below.

Just like ***-i*** adjectives, ***-na*** adjectives always go before the noun they modify, without exceptions. Take a look at the examples: "clumsy carpenter" 下手な大工 ***heta-na daiku*** (***heta-na*** = "clumsy," ***daiku*** = "carpenter"); "the woman I like" 好きな女 ***suki-na onna*** (***suki-na*** = "that one likes (to like)," ***onna*** = "woman").

-na adjectives are NOT inflected

What are the differences then between one kind of adjective and the other, if up to this point we have seen that they both occupy the same place in the sentence? Here we come to the most important point concerning the differences between the two kinds of Japanese adjectives.

Some *-na* adjectives					
Japanese	**Rōmaji**	**Meaning**	**Japanese**	**Rōmaji**	**Meaning**
大変な	***taihen-na***	serious, difficult	安全な	***anzen-na***	safe
しずかな	***shizuka-na***	calm	上手な	***jōzu-na***	skillful
きれいな	***kirei-na***	pretty	下手な	***heta-na***	clumsy
ひまな	***hima-na***	with spare time	大切な	***taisetsu-na***	important
丈夫な	***jōbu-na***	healthy, strong	有名な	***yūmei-na***	famous
元気な	***genki-na***	cheerful, strong	大丈夫な	***daijōbu-na***	sure, safe
親切な	***shinsetsu-na***	kind	好きな	***suki-na***	to like
危険な	***kiken-na***	dangerous	きらいな	***kirai-na***	to dislike

Forms of *-na* adjectives					
		Affirmative		Negative	
		desu form	Simple form	*desu* form	Simple form
Present	Rule	~~な~~です	~~な~~だ	~~な~~ではありません	~~な~~ではない
	Example	有名です	有名だ	有名ではありません	有名ではない
	Rōmaji	***yūmei desu***	***yūmei da***	***yūmei de wa arimasen***	***yūmei de wa nai***
	Translation	Is famous.		Is not famous.	
Past	Rule	~~な~~でした	~~な~~だった	~~な~~ではありませんでした	~~な~~ではなかった
	Example	有名でした	有名だった	有名ではありませんでした	有名ではなかった
	Rōmaji	***yūmei deshita***	***yūmei datta***	***yūmei de wa arimasen deshita***	***yūmei de wa nakatta***
	Translation	Was famous.		Was not famous.	

In Lesson 13 we saw the four ***-i*** adjective forms: present affirmative, past affirmative, present negative, and past negative. We add the verb です ***desu*** ("to be") after these forms to make a formal sentence. Without です ***desu***, the sentence becomes informal. Well, ***-na*** adjectives are not inflected: the verb is inflected instead, as seen in the table above: so reviewing Lesson 9 and knowing by heart the different forms of the verb です ***desu*** is important.

How do -na adjectives work?

This lack of inflection means handling ***-na*** adjectives is much simpler than handling ***-i*** adjectives. All you need to do to construct sentences such as "this book is important" is conjugate the verb です ***desu***, and (read carefully now) remove the な ***na*** ending of the adjective.

Notice in the table above we have the "formal" (***desu*** form) and "simple" forms: as with ***-i*** adjectives, the first is used in formal situations, and the second in casual ones. The simple form is used more often by far in manga—and you can learn more about this in Lessons 19 and 20.

Sentences with the verb "to be"

Consider these examples:

1. この本は大切です
kono hon wa taisetsu desu
This book is important.
(***hon*** = "book," ***taisetsu-na*** = "important")

2. 私は魚が大嫌いでした
watashi wa sakana ga daikirai deshita
I didn't like fish at all.
(***watashi*** = "I," ***sakana*** = "fish," ***kirai-na*** = "not like")

3. あの道は危険ではない
ano michi wa kiken de wa nai
That road isn't dangerous.
(***michi*** = "road," ***kiken-na*** = "dangerous")

4. その花はきれいじゃなかった
sono hana wa kirei ja nakatta
That flower wasn't pretty.
(***hana*** = "flower," ***kirei-na*** = "pretty")

Sentence 1 is formal present affirmative, 2 is formal past affirmative, 3 is informal present negative, and 4 is informal past negative. Remember, the では ***de wa*** part of ではありません ***de wa arimasen*** and ではない ***de wa nai*** can be contracted into じゃ ***ja*** (Lesson 9), as in sentence 4. (You may have noticed that ***-na*** adjectives work like nouns, so if you've studied Lessons 9 and 11 well, you should be able to make those kinds of sentence.)

When do we leave -na as it is and when do we remove it?

As you have seen, な ***na*** sometimes disappears, and sometimes stays. We keep な ***na*** when the ***-na*** adjective comes before a noun, as we have already seen in the example "clumsy carpenter," 下手な大工 ***heta-na daiku***. However, we remove な ***na*** when the ***-na*** adjective comes before the verb です ***desu***, for example, "this carpenter is clumsy" この大工は下手です ***kono daiku wa heta desu***.

As you can see, the ***-na*** adjective we have used is the same, 下手な ***heta-na*** (clumsy). We keep な ***na*** in the first example, whereas in the second one we remove it.

Warning!

In Lesson 13 we said ***-i*** adjectives could go without the verb です ***desu*** in informal situations, for example:

試験はむずかしかった（です）
shiken wa muzukashikatta (desu)
The exam was difficult.
(***shiken*** = "exam," ***muzukashikatta*** = "was difficult")

With ***-na*** adjectives, the verb です ***desu*** must always be there, whether in the simple form or in the formal form, as in these examples:

Simple form: 試験は大変だった
shiken wa taihen datta
The exam was difficult.

Formal form: 試験は大変でした
shiken wa taihen deshita
The exam was difficult.

Here, the words むずかしい ***muzukashii*** (***-i*** adjective) and 大変な ***taihen-na*** (***-na*** adjective) are synonymous, but the lower examples, which use the ***-na*** adjective, needs the verb です ***desu***.

On the other hand, the ***-i*** adjective can go without です ***desu***, making the sentence less formal. Remember that if we keep です ***desu***, the sentence is formal.

漫画例 Manga Examples

As usual, in the manga examples in this section we will see both the practical usage and the theoretical usage of *-na* adjectives, taking the opportunity to review what we have studied earlier in the lesson.

Manga Example 1: Present affirmative

J.M. Ken Niimura

Here we have the simple present affirmative of a です ***desu*** sentence with a ***-na*** adjective. The simple form is frequently used in manga. The ***-na*** adjective here is 大丈夫な ***daijōbu-na***, which is very commonly used in Japanese. It cannot directly be translated into English, but its meaning would be "it's all right," "I'm okay," or "don't worry."

Tomoko: 大丈夫だよ
daijōbu da yo
well / correct be EP
It's okay. / Don't worry.

Manga Example 2: Present negative

We see here the simple present negative form of the adjective 元気な ***genki-na*** ("strong," "healthy," "well"). The ***de wa*** part of ***genki de wa nai*** can be contracted, becoming ***ja***: in this case, ***genki ja nai***.

In addition, Ken is talking in the Kantō dialect of the Tokyo area, and so we have yet another contraction, dialectal this time: ***nai*** becomes ***nee***. Thus, ***genki de wa nai*** here becomes ***genki ja nee***.

Guillermo March

Ken: なんだ、元気じゃねーか？
nanda, genki ja nee ka?
what be, healthy be Q?
What's wrong? Aren't you OK?

Manga Example 3: Past negative

あたし
ちっともイヤ
じゃなかった
Guillermo March

Nanako: あたし ちっともイヤじゃなかった
atashi chittomo iya ja nakatta
I nothing unpleasant not be
I didn't find it unpleasant at all.

Here is another instance of a sentence with a ***-na*** adjective, this time in the past negative form. The ***-na*** adjective is ***iya-na***, written in katakana in this example, but usually written in kanji: 嫌な ***iya-na***.

According to the dictionary, this very common adjective in manga means "unpleasant," "offensive," "lousy," "nasty," "disgusting," or "repulsive." Wow!

Note: Notice also in this panel the colloquial contraction we saw in Example 2: the ***de wa*** part of ***de wa nakatta*** becomes ***ja*** (***ja nakatta***).

Manga Example 4: When do we keep *-na*?

To end this lesson's manga examples, we will study an instance of when we do not remove the な ***na*** part of ***-na*** adjectives. As we said earlier in this lesson, we only keep な ***na*** when there's a noun after the adjective, as in this case, where we have the noun ***yokan*** "foreboding." Therefore, as Tamiko correctly says, the sentence is not ***iya yokan ga suru***, but ***iya-na yokan ga suru***. The sentence would be wrong without な ***na***.

The adjective here is ***iya-na*** once more, as in the previous example, but this time it is written in kanji instead of katakana.

嫌な予感が
するわ…
Studio Kōsen

Tamiko: 嫌な予感がするわ...
iya-na yokan ga suru wa...
unpleasant foreboding SP do EP
I have a horrible foreboding...

Exercises 練習

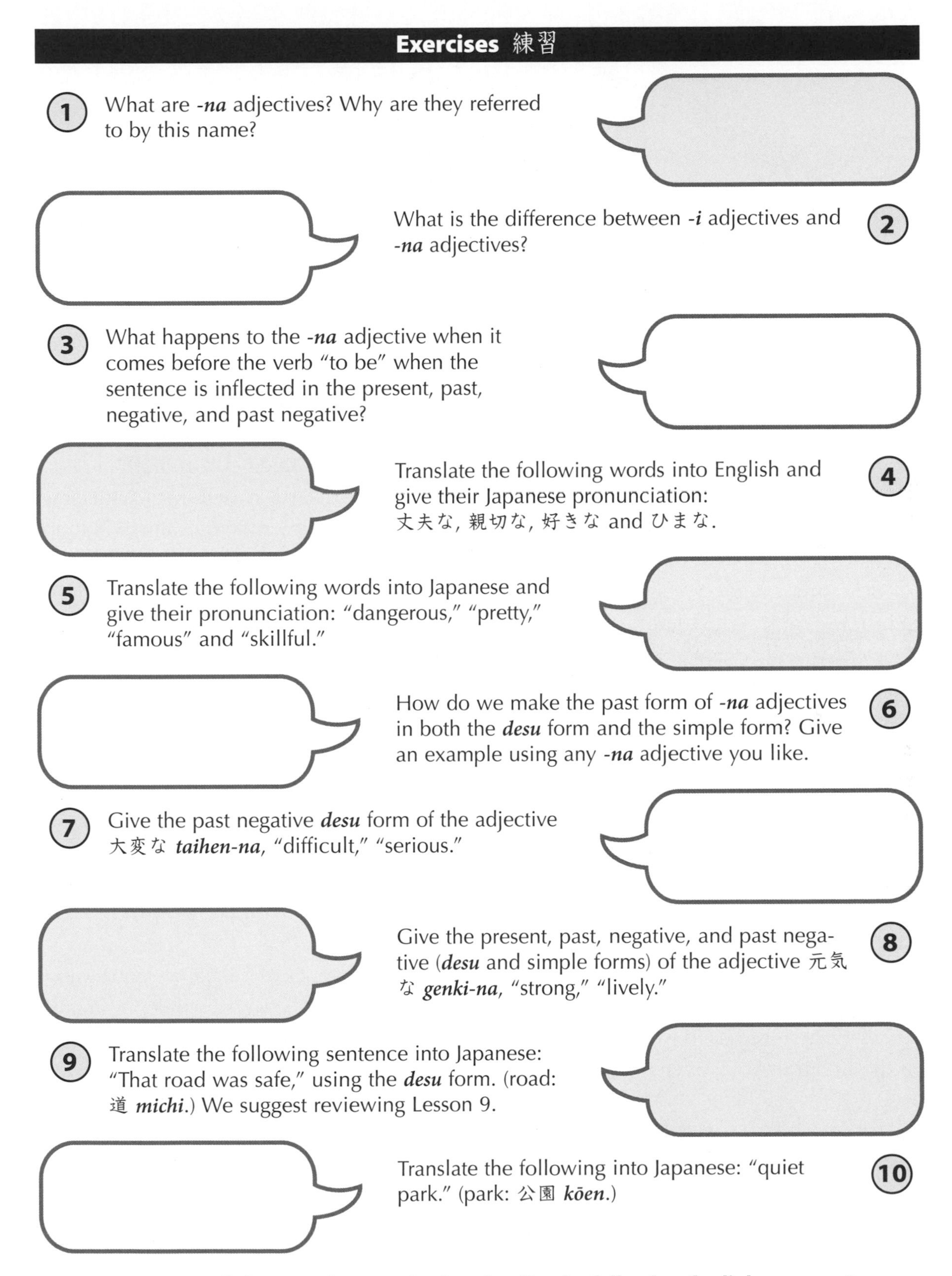

1. What are ***-na*** adjectives? Why are they referred to by this name?

2. What is the difference between ***-i*** adjectives and ***-na*** adjectives?

3. What happens to the ***-na*** adjective when it comes before the verb "to be" when the sentence is inflected in the present, past, negative, and past negative?

4. Translate the following words into English and give their Japanese pronunciation: 丈夫な, 親切な, 好きな and ひまな.

5. Translate the following words into Japanese and give their pronunciation: "dangerous," "pretty," "famous" and "skillful."

6. How do we make the past form of ***-na*** adjectives in both the ***desu*** form and the simple form? Give an example using any ***-na*** adjective you like.

7. Give the past negative ***desu*** form of the adjective 大変な ***taihen-na***, "difficult," "serious."

8. Give the present, past, negative, and past negative (***desu*** and simple forms) of the adjective 元気な ***genki-na***, "strong," "lively."

9. Translate the following sentence into Japanese: "That road was safe," using the ***desu*** form. (road: 道 ***michi***.) We suggest reviewing Lesson 9.

10. Translate the following into Japanese: "quiet park." (park: 公園 ***kōen***.)

— Answers to all the exercises can be found online by following the link on page 9. —

Lesson 15 • 第15課

Name Suffixes

In this lesson we will study the suffixes that are used after people's names, another curious feature of the Japanese language that stems from the fact that Japan is a hierarchical society with deeply rooted traditions.

Social hierarchy

In theory Japan is an egalitarian society, but in practice social statuses are quite marked, mainly between people of different ages. For example, the relationship between a 先輩 ***senpai*** "senior" and 後輩 ***kōhai*** "junior" or between a 先生 ***sensei*** "teacher" and a 学生 ***gakusei*** "student" is clearly defined, and reflected in the language used between both parties.

For example, a 25-year-old man will talk in an informal-vulgar way with his friends, but with his teacher his way of talking will change. With friends, the man in question will most probably use 俺 ***ore*** to refer to himself, whereas with his teacher he will probably use 私 ***watashi***, or 僕 ***boku***. We already touched on these hierarchies in Lesson 7, but in this lesson we will look at them more closely.

Suffixes for people's names

Japanese has several characteristics which are totally different from Western languages. One of them is the use of suffixes after people's names. That is, in Japanese, when we refer to someone by their given name or surname, we must almost always add a suffix after that name.

The most common and well known suffix is さん ***-san***. For example, if we refer to Mr. Tanaka, we will not just say ***Tanaka***, but always ***Tanaka-san***. For example, the sentence "Tanaka is handsome" would be 田中さんはかっこいいです ***Tanaka-san wa kakkoii desu*** (***kakkoii*** = "handsome"; ***desu*** = "to be,").

It is very important to add the suffix さん ***-san*** after the names of people we don't know well or are not too familiar with, as well as after the names of people who are older or hierarchically superior to us. If we don't abide by this rule, we may be seen as rude, or, depending on the situation, even offensive.

Different kinds of suffixes depending on the formality

From what we have just explained, you can tell that the suffix さん ***-san*** implies a certain formality: it would more or less be equivalent to adding Mr., Mrs., or Ms. to somebody's name in English. There are also other options, which we will now explain in order from the most formal to the least:

～殿 ***-dono***: This is an extremely formal and archaic suffix that has the nuance of "Lord" or "Lady." Nowadays, it is only used in samurai films or on very few, extremely formal occasions. Try not to use it, unless you want to sound like a samurai.

～様 ***-sama***: Very formal suffix, used mainly in written language or in the client-clerk relationship: a shop clerk usually addresses a customer as お客様 ***o-kyaku-sama***, literally "honored customer." Letters are always addressed to 田中様 ***Tanaka-sama*** (make sure you don't use ***-san*** in letters or written documents in general). The suffix ***-sama*** is also used when a subject is talking to a king. In the past, children would address their parents using ***-sama***.

～氏 ***-shi***: The suffix 氏 ***-shi*** is used on very few occasions, mostly in newspapers on the television news. It is used to refer to someone with respect and who holds a social position above your own. It is also a quite impersonal form of address.

～さん ***-san***: The most common name suffix. See facing page.

～君 ***-kun***: This suffix is quite often used when a senior speaks to a junior, or when the former is referring to the latter. However, it is also used among young people when they are not too familiar with each other yet. It it is not as strong as ***-san***. It is usually attached to male names, and if the speaker is a woman, it shows some familiarity or even affection toward the male she is addressing.

～ちゃん ***-chan***: Affectionate suffix used with children's names. It is also used among adolescent girls, when the speakers know each other very well. Take care not to use it with a man, because it would sound as if you were talking to a child.

The name alone: Finally, among fairly close friends, young people, family members, etc., people are usually called by their name alone. Take care when using someone's name without any suffix: it has to be a very close friend and, preferably someone young. If not it is better to use ***-san***, ***-kun*** or even ***-chan*** if you are talking to young girls or children.

A couple of warnings

The easiest option for a foreigner who hasn't mastered Japanese yet is to always use さん ***-san***, in order to avoid misunderstandings. Be careful: none of these suffixes are ever used to refer to oneself. If you are introducing yourself, for example, a sentence like 私はジェームズです ***watashi wa Jeemuzu desu***, "I am James," is correct. It would be a terrible mistake to say 私はジェームズさんです ***watashi wa Jeemuzu-san desu***.

Addressing someone using his or her title

In spite of having such a variety of suffixes, the most correct way of addressing someone is to use a suffix which shows his or her relationship to the speaker; a sort of "title" similar to "Sir," but much more commonly used.

Some of the most common of these titles are: 先生 ***sensei***, "teacher," "medical doctor" or, very often a person one respects, with prestige, experience or knowledge in a particular field, for example, 田中先生 ***Tanaka-sensei***, "Professor Tanaka" or "Doctor Tanaka"); 夫人 ***fujin*** "Mrs.," for example, 田中夫人 ***Tanaka-fujin***, "Mrs. Tanaka"; 社長 ***shachō***, "company director," for example, 田中社長 ***Tanaka-shachō***, "Director Tanaka"); 課長 ***kachō***, "section head"; 部長 ***buchō***, "head of department"; 選手 ***senshu***, "(sports) player," "athlete."

Shop names

As you can see, this lesson's vocabulary table deals with different shop names, and even some restaurant names. What relationship does this have with the suffixes used for people's names? First take a look at the table, and you will see that all shop names specified here end with the kanji 屋 ***ya***, which means "shop."

However, when talking about a specific store, the suffix さん ***-san*** is very often added: This is a very curious honorific use. For example, saying 本屋さんへ行く ***hon'ya-san e iku***, "I'm going to the bookshop" is very common.

Shops and restaurants					
Japanese	**Rōmaji**	**Meaning**	**Japanese**	**Rōmaji**	**Meaning**
本屋	***hon'ya***	bookshop	おかし屋	***o-kashiya***	confectionary shop
文房具屋	***bunbōguya***	stationery store	電気屋	***denkiya***	appliance store
肉屋	***nikuya***	butcher's shop	くつ屋	***kutsuya***	shoe shop
魚屋	***sakanaya***	fish shop	居酒屋	***izakaya***	pub
八百屋	***yaoya***	grocery store	お弁当屋	***o-bentōya***	bento shop
果物屋	***kudamonoya***	fruit store	すし屋	***sushiya***	sushi restaurant
パン屋	***pan'ya***	bakery	ラーメン屋	***raamen'ya***	ramen restaurant
ケーキ屋	***keekiya***	cake shop	うどん屋	***udon'ya***	udon restaurant

Notes: ***bentō***: ready-made food placed in a lunch box for take-out
rāmen and ***udon***: two kinds of very popular noodles

漫画例 Manga Examples

Let's make use of the manga examples in this lesson to study some of the suffixes that are used with people's names. They have no direct translation into English but give very important nuances to Japanese sentences.

Manga Example 1: *-san*

We start with the most common suffix: さん ***-san***. When Ayumi meets her old boss, she calls him by his name and adds the suffix ***-san***. Since Okunishi is older than her, and her boss as well, the use of ***-san*** to show respect is compulsory here: it's like calling him "Mr."

Ayumi: 奥西さん！
Okunishi-san!
Okunishi (SUF.)
Mr. Okunishi!

Manga Example 2: *-kun*

Miho: 気をつけてね 茂くん!!
ki o tsukete ne Shigeru-kun!!
take care EP Shigeru (SUF.)!!
Take care, Shigeru!!

In this example we see the suffix くん ***-kun***, which sometimes we will see written in kanji as 君. Miho, the girl, affectionately adds ***-kun*** to Shigeru's name. The suffix ***-kun*** actually has two quite different uses: on the one hand, we have its affectionate use, usually when addressing young men (as in this example), and, on the other hand, it can be used by a senior person when he addresses a junior or a subordinate. We will only see ***-kun*** after a girl's name if its use corresponds to the latter case.

Manga Example 3: *-senpai*

As we saw at the start of this lesson, a frequent way of showing respect is by using the person's title instead of the usual suffixes ***-san***, ***-sama***, etc.

Here we see the suffix 先輩 ***-senpai***, a very Japanese concept which cannot be translated into English, and which more or less means "person who studies or works with me, but who started earlier, and is more experienced." It is always much more correct (and it sounds better) if you use someone's "title" when addressing them, rather than ***-san***.

Tetsuharu:	麻美先輩!!
	Asami-senpai
	Asami (SUF.)
	Asami!!

Manga Example 4: *-dono*

In this last example, we have some ancient Japanese: the samurai way of speaking, to be precise. Notice how Nagatomo addresses the person he is speaking to as 綾香殿 ***Ayaka-dono***. The suffix ***-dono*** is archaic, not used nowadays (except in extremely formal written documents). To convey the nuance of deep respect and "ancientness" given by ***-dono*** when we translate, we have chosen to use "thee" instead of "you," and we have substituted "Lady" for "Ms." **Note:** The verb でござる ***de gozaru*** is the archaic equivalent of です ***desu*** ("to be," Lesson 9).

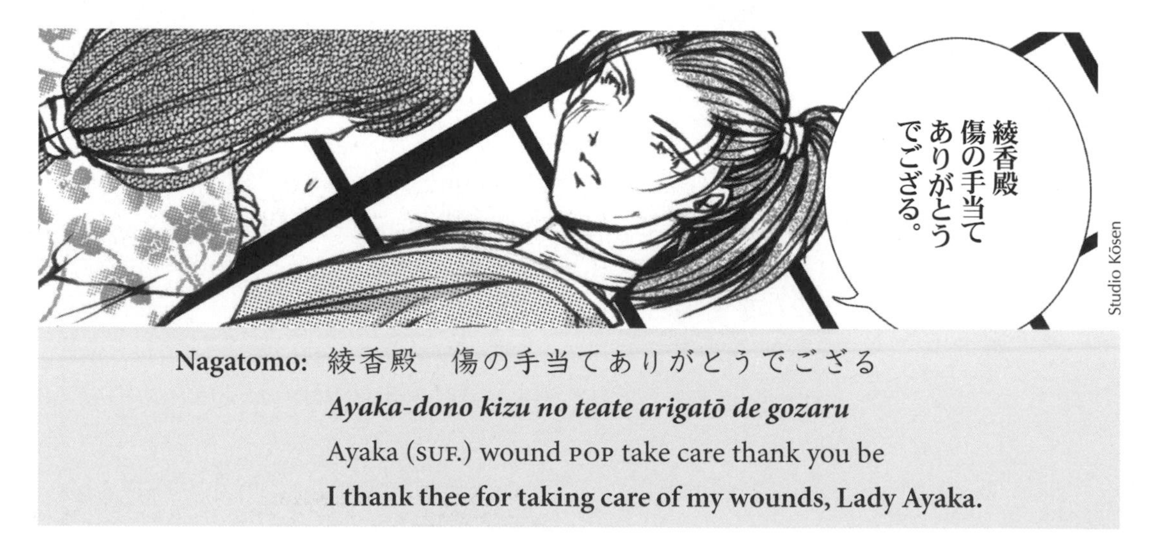

Nagatomo:	綾香殿　傷の手当てありがとうでござる
	Ayaka-dono kizu no teate arigatō de gozaru
	Ayaka (SUF.) wound POP take care thank you be
	I thank thee for taking care of my wounds, Lady Ayaka.

Exercises 練習

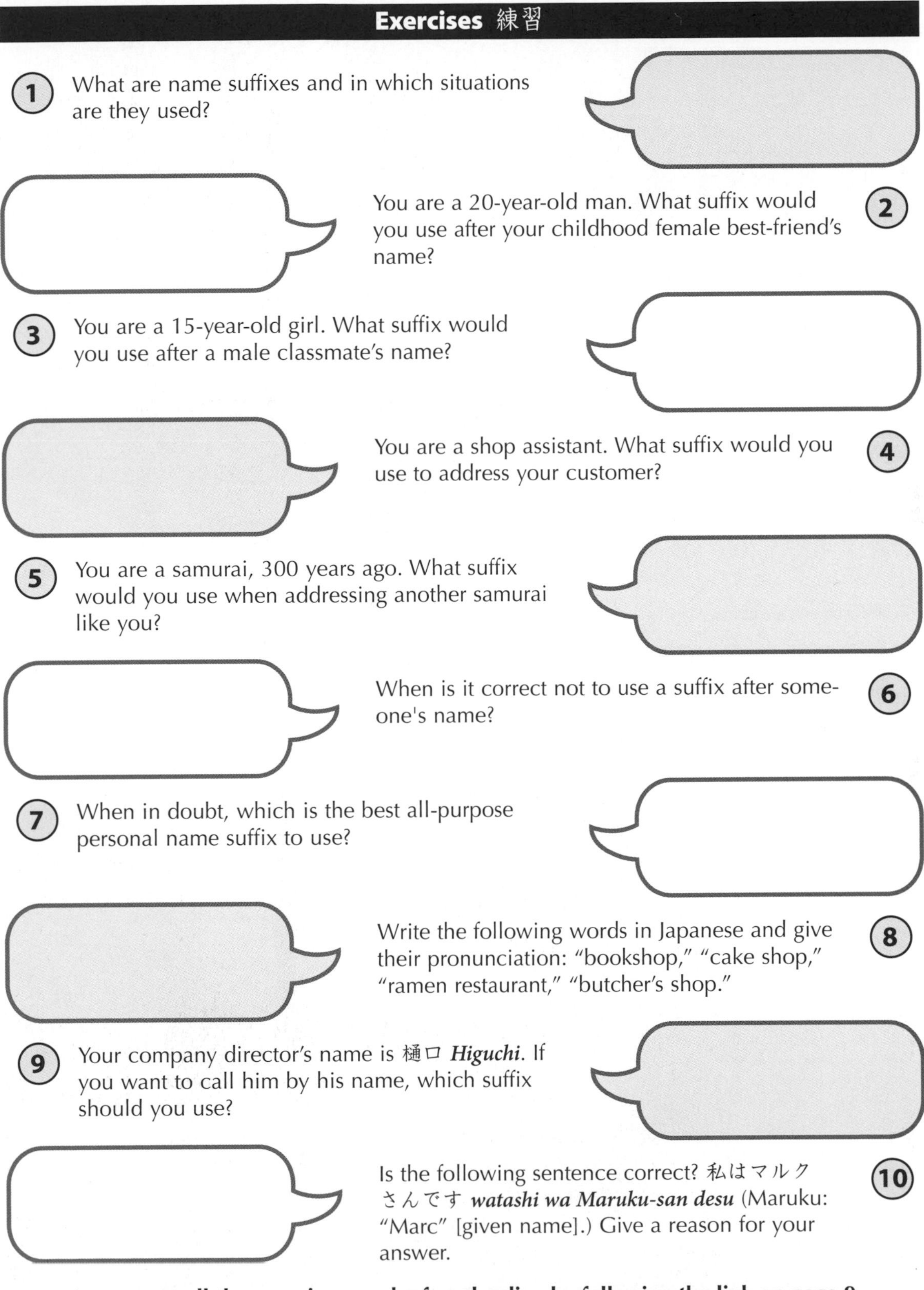

1. What are name suffixes and in which situations are they used?

2. You are a 20-year-old man. What suffix would you use after your childhood female best-friend's name?

3. You are a 15-year-old girl. What suffix would you use after a male classmate's name?

4. You are a shop assistant. What suffix would you use to address your customer?

5. You are a samurai, 300 years ago. What suffix would you use when addressing another samurai like you?

6. When is it correct not to use a suffix after someone's name?

7. When in doubt, which is the best all-purpose personal name suffix to use?

8. Write the following words in Japanese and give their pronunciation: "bookshop," "cake shop," "ramen restaurant," "butcher's shop."

9. Your company director's name is 樋口 ***Higuchi***. If you want to call him by his name, which suffix should you use?

10. Is the following sentence correct? 私はマルクさんです ***watashi wa Maruku-san desu*** (Maruku: "Marc" [given name].) Give a reason for your answer.

— Answers to all the exercises can be found online by following the link on page 9. —

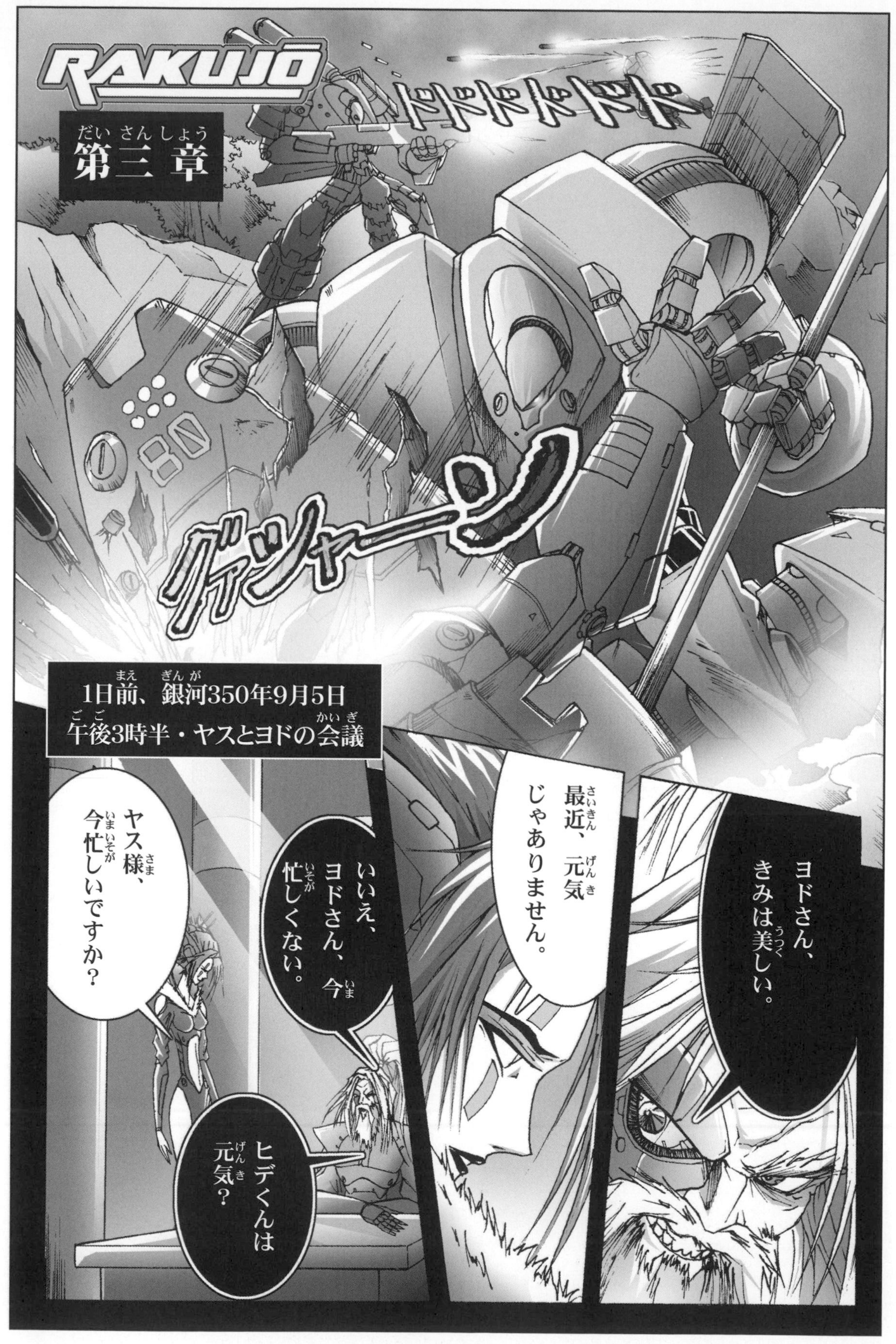
RAKUJŌ
第三章
ドドドドドド
グァシャーン
1日前、銀河350年9月5日
午後3時半・ヤスとヨドの会議
ヤス様、今忙しいですか？
いいえ、ヨドさん、今忙しくない。
ヒデくんは元気？
最近、元気じゃありません。
ヨドさん、きみは美しい。

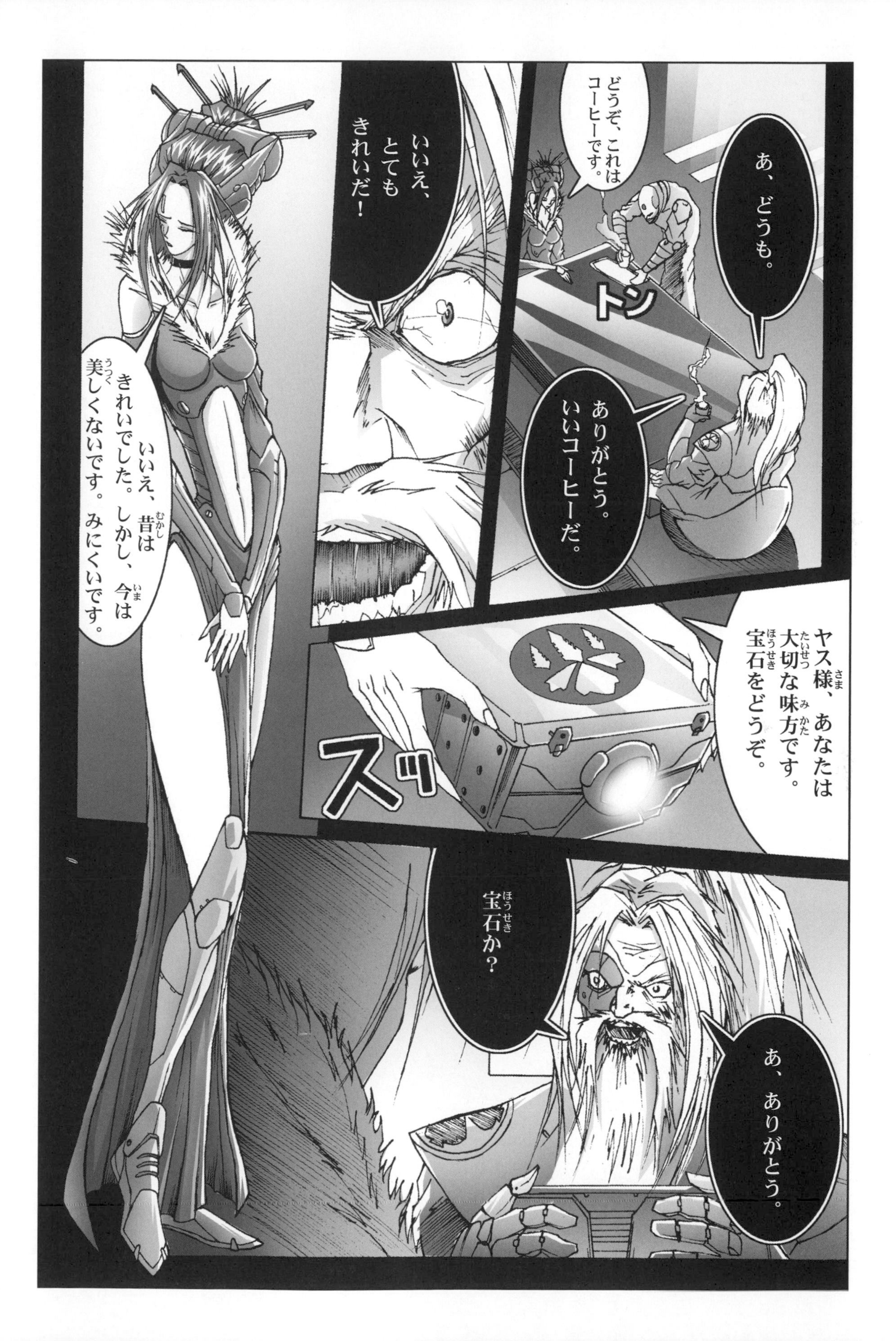
あ、どうも。
どうぞ、これはコーヒーです。
トン
ありがとう。いいコーヒーだ。
いいえ、とてもきれいだ！
いいえ、昔はきれいでした。しかし、今は美しくないです。みにくいです。
ヤス様、あなたは大切な味方です。宝石をどうぞ。
スッ
宝石か？
あ、ありがとう。

わしは大切じゃなかった!?五十個ください!!
何？宝石一個？
ザッ
50個？50個の宝石ですか!?無理な頼みです!!
あした、銀河350年9月6日、2時45分に来る！！
ビッ
じゃ。戦争だ!!!
ドン!!

今
パタパタ
ズジャッ
ゴッ
ドーーーン
大丈夫じゃない!! ヤスのアーミーは強い!!!
大丈夫ですか?

Review for Lessons 11–15

Answers to all the review exercises can be found online by following the link on page 9.

RAKUJŌ – New vocabulary 新しい単語

会議（かいぎ）	meeting	宝石（ほうせき）	precious stone, jewel
忙しい（いそが）	busy (-*i* adj.)	個（こ）	counter for small things
最近（さいきん）	lately	無理な（むり）	impossible (-*na* adj.)
昔（むかし）	long ago	頼み（たの）	request
みにくい	ugly (-*i* adj.)	戦争（せんそう）	war
とても	very	来る（く）	to come
味方（みかた）	ally	強い（つよ）	strong (-*i* adj.)

1. What name suffix does Yasu use when he talks to Yodo? Why does he use this one?

2. What name suffix does Yodo use toward Yasu? Why does she use this one? What are its connotations? What suffix does Yasu use when he talks about Hide? Why?

3. At what time does the meeting between Yodo and Yasu which opens the episode take place? Give the reading of this time and an alternative way of saying it. In addition, at what time does Yasu say he will return the next day? Give the reading and an alternative way of saying it.

4. Make a list of all the -*i* and -*na* adjectives that appear in this third episode of ***Rakujō***.

-*i* adjectives	-*na* adjectives
______________	______________
______________	______________
______________	______________
______________	______________
______________	______________

5. Change these two adjectives into the different forms indicated.

みにくいです	formal present affirmative	きれいです
______	simple present affirmative	______
______	formal past affirmative	______
______	simple past affirmative	______
______	formal present negative	______
______	simple present negative	______
______	formal past negative	______
______	simple past negative	______

6. Yodo, in one of her sentences, says 大切(たいせつ)な味方(みかた). Shortly after, Yasu adds 大切(たいせつ)じゃなかった. Why does the first sentence keep the な of the ***-na*** adjective, and the second sentence doesn't?

7. What is the misunderstanding about between Yodo and Yasu that makes Yasu so furious he decides to declare war?

8. What are counters and what do we use them for? Analyzing the context of the third episode, what do you think 個 ***ko*** means?

9. Circle the names of mammals in the box.

くま	あり	いちご	トマト	ライオン	馬(うま)	さる
へび	魚(さかな)	犬(いぬ)	鳥(とり)	豆(まめ)	きって	えいが
にく	ぞう	牛(うし)	みかん	もも	うさぎ	きのこ

10. Draw a line to link each store with the article it sells.

八百屋(やおや)	もも	魚屋(さかなや)	魚(さかな)
本屋(ほんや)	やさい	果物屋(くだものや)	カメラ
肉屋(にくや)	ざっし	電気屋(でんきや)	レタス
文房具屋(ぶんぼうぐや)	かみ	八百屋(やおや)	ごはん
果物屋(くだものや)	にく	レストラン	みかん

11. Complete the sentences by choosing he correct word from the box below.

a) バナナは____________です。
b) ____________ は赤(あか)いです。
c) あの犬(いぬ)は黒(くろ)くないです。____________ です。
d) ____________ は黄色(きいろ)いです。
e) 空(そら)は黄色(きいろ)くないです。____________ です。
f) ____________トマトが大好きです。

黄色(きいろ)い	青(あお)い	レモン	いちご	赤(あか)い	白い

12. In each sentence there is a word that is wrong. Find the word and correct it.

a) ももは~~やさい~~です。 [くだもの]
b) なしは果物(くだもの)ではありません
c) りんごは黒(くろ)いです。
d) ぞうは大(おお)きくないです。
e) 日本の夏は暑(あつ)くないです。
f) レモンは白(しろ)いです。

13. Write the clock times in Japanese and English. Remember there may be two ways to say certain times.

今、____________です

It's now____________.

今、____________です

It's now____________.

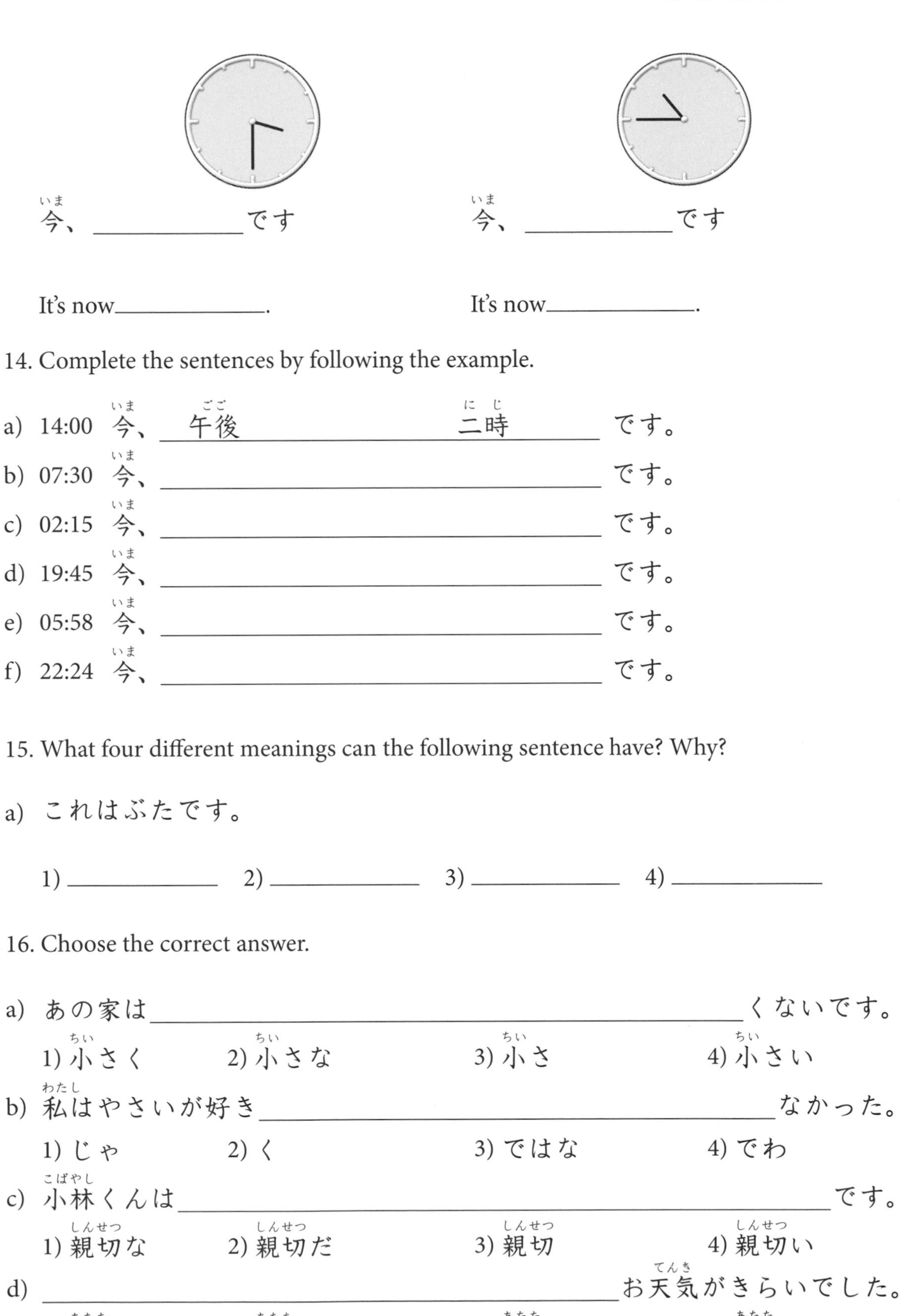

今(いま)、＿＿＿＿＿です　　　今(いま)、＿＿＿＿＿です

It's now＿＿＿＿＿.　　　It's now＿＿＿＿＿.

14. Complete the sentences by following the example.

a) 14:00 今(いま)、午後(ごご)二時(にじ)です。
b) 07:30 今(いま)、＿＿＿＿＿＿＿＿＿＿です。
c) 02:15 今(いま)、＿＿＿＿＿＿＿＿＿＿です。
d) 19:45 今(いま)、＿＿＿＿＿＿＿＿＿＿です。
e) 05:58 今(いま)、＿＿＿＿＿＿＿＿＿＿です。
f) 22:24 今(いま)、＿＿＿＿＿＿＿＿＿＿です。

15. What four different meanings can the following sentence have? Why?

a) これはぶたです。

1) ＿＿＿＿＿　2) ＿＿＿＿＿　3) ＿＿＿＿＿　4) ＿＿＿＿＿

16. Choose the correct answer.

a) あの家は＿＿＿＿＿＿＿＿＿＿くないです。
1) 小(ちい)さく　2) 小(ちい)さな　3) 小(ちい)さ　4) 小(ちい)さい

b) 私(わたし)はやさいが好き＿＿＿＿＿＿＿＿＿＿なかった。
1) じゃ　2) く　3) ではな　4) でわ

c) 小林(こばやし)くんは＿＿＿＿＿＿＿＿＿＿です。
1) 親切(しんせつ)な　2) 親切(しんせつ)だ　3) 親切(しんせつ)　4) 親切(しんせつ)い

d) ＿＿＿＿＿＿＿＿＿＿お天気(てんき)がきらいでした。
1) 暖(あたた)かいな　2) 暖(あたた)かいかった　3) 暖(あたた)かくなかい　4) 暖(あたた)かい

17. Write each adjective in the form indicated

a) この自転車は（赤い）＿＿＿＿＿＿＿＿＿＿＿＿。(formal past affirmative)

b) あのカメラは（高い）＿＿＿＿＿＿＿＿＿＿＿＿。(simple past negative)

c) キミコちゃんは（きれいな）＿＿＿＿＿＿＿＿。(formal present affirmative)

d) その山は（低い）＿＿＿＿＿＿＿＿＿＿＿＿＿。(formal present negative)

e) あのラーメン屋は（大きい）＿＿＿＿＿＿＿＿。(simple present affirmative)

f) 私は（静かな）＿＿＿＿＿＿＿＿＿庭が（好きな）＿＿＿＿＿＿＿＿＿。
(simple present affirmative)

f) 古い映画が（きらいな）＿＿＿＿＿＿＿＿＿＿＿。(formal past negative)

18. Rewrite each sentence with different words but the same meaning.

a) この家は新しいです。
この家は<u>古くないです</u>。

b) この試験はむずかしいです。
この試験は＿＿＿＿＿＿。

c) その馬は大きくなかった。
その馬は＿＿＿＿＿＿。

d) あのたてものは危険でした。
あのたてものは＿＿＿＿＿＿。

e) 神戸の肉は高かったです。
神戸の肉は＿＿＿＿＿＿。

f) 彼は魚が好きではない。
彼は魚が＿＿＿＿＿＿。

19. Make grammatically correct sentences using the following prompts:

a) 安い｜ボールペン｜これは｜です。 ＿＿＿＿＿＿＿＿＿＿＿＿

b) 上手（な）｜川田さんは｜でした。 ＿＿＿＿＿＿＿＿＿＿＿＿

c) 川本さんは｜人｜でした｜きれい（な）。 ＿＿＿＿＿＿＿＿＿＿＿＿

d) あの｜高かった｜りんごは｜です。 ＿＿＿＿＿＿＿＿＿＿＿＿

e) 女は｜その｜ではありません｜きれい（な）。 ＿＿＿＿＿＿＿＿＿＿＿＿

f) 山田さんは｜暗くない｜です｜家。 ＿＿＿＿＿＿＿＿＿＿＿＿

20. Correct any mistakes you find in the following sentences. One of them is correct!

a) あの車(くるま)は安いではないでした。

b) あれは有名(ゆうめい)おかしやだ。

c) 私(わたし)は暗(くら)いな教室(きょうしつ)がきらいでわありません。

d) 山田(やまだ)さんの家(いえ)は暗(くら)い家(いえ)ではない。

e) その安全(あんぜん)じゃないなレストランは大(おお)きいじゃないかった。

21. Complete the following sentences with the appropriate name suffix from the box below.

a) こんにちは、アキオ______。(talking to someone we don't know very well)

b) マリ______、元気(げんき)？(adult to a small girl)

c) 坂本(さかもと)______、忙(いそが)しいですか？(teacher to a student)

d) アキラ______、これは何(なに)？(young girl to her friend)

e) 新之助(しんのすけ)______は有名ですか？(one samurai to another)

f) 前田(まえだ)______、お元気(げんき)ですか？(shop assistant to a customer)

g) 大丈夫(だいじょうぶ)ですか、北山(きたやま)______？(company employee to the boss)

くん	先生(せんせい)	殿(どの)	社長(しゃちょう)	さん	ちゃん	様(さま)

Kanji

今 (57)	分 (53)	時 (59)	四 (90)	朝 (46)	昼 (47)	夜 (48)	午 (58)	前 (55)	後 (56)	好 (146)
白 (71)	赤 (72)	青 (73)	大 (49)	小 (50)	高 (83)	安 (84)	新 (104)	古 (105)	明 (159)	方 (65)

22. Practice writing the kanji below. Find the stroke order in the online Kanji Compilation section via the link on page 9.

高											
前											
赤											
時											
後											

23. Link each kanji with its most common reading (usually, the ***kun'yomi***).

昼	ふるい	高い	ちいさい
古い	やすい	大きい	たかい
青い	あさ	時	じ
朝	ひる	小さい	おおきい
夜	あおい	赤い	あかい
安い	よる	半	はん

24.Choose the correct kanji or kanji combination for each reading.

a) あかるい
1. 朋るい 2. 明るい 3. 朋い 4. 明い

b) ことし
1. 今年 2. 令年 3. 分年 4. 公年

c) しろい
1. 自い 2. 日い 3. 目い 4. 白い

d) あたらしい
1. 親しい 2. 新しい 3. 親い 4. 新い

25. Choose the correct reading for each kanji combination.

a) 古本
1) ふるぼん 2) ふるほん 3) こぼん 4) こほん

b) 好きな

1) あきな　2) こきな　3) きらきな　4) すきな

c) 午前

1) ごまえ　2) ごご　3) ごぜん　4) ごあと

26. Give the hiragana readings of the following words and their meaning.

古い	ふるい	old	五分	＿＿＿	＿＿＿
六分	＿＿＿	＿＿＿	三時半	＿＿＿	＿＿＿
高い	＿＿＿	＿＿＿	人前	＿＿＿	＿＿＿
前半	＿＿＿	＿＿＿	半分	＿＿＿	＿＿＿
青春	＿＿＿	＿＿＿	文明	＿＿＿	＿＿＿

27. Write the following words in kanji, and give their meaning.

あおい	青い	blue	やすい	＿＿＿	＿＿＿
あさ	＿＿＿	＿＿＿	かた	＿＿＿	＿＿＿
おおきい	＿＿＿	＿＿＿	いま	＿＿＿	＿＿＿
あかい	＿＿＿	＿＿＿	ごご	＿＿＿	＿＿＿
せいねん	＿＿＿	＿＿＿	せきじゅう字(じ)	＿＿＿	＿＿＿

Lesson 16 • 第16課

Particles

Japanese particles—the small markers that follow a word to indicate the function of a word within a sentence—can be tricky, but this lesson will help you quickly understand and master their correct usage.

What is a particle?

A particle is a small grammatical element (usually consisting of only one hiragana character) which has no meaning on its own: it is like a "marker" which follows a word, indicating the function that the word has in the sentence. These small elements are the sentence's true framework: there is no Japanese sentence without particles.

The table on page 144 lists the most important particles, with an explanation of their function and an example sentence. **Note:** Some particles are pronounced differently from the way they are written in hiragana. In the table on page 144, you will find three particles with special readings. For each, we give the correct pronunciation in italics in brackets underneath their "standard" reading. Thus, は is pronounced ***wa*** not ***ha***; を is ***o*** not ***wo***; and へ is ***e*** not ***he*** (but only when they function as particle, of course).

The particles

Let's study the particles, one by one. Refer the table on page 144 as you read the explanations. For now this is all you need to know about particles.

は ***wa*** This particle marks the topic of a sentence, "the thing we are talking about," or "the topic we want to emphasize." In the example, 私は学生です ***watashi wa gakusei desu***, we are talking about ***watashi***, "I." The translation would be "I am a student." Therefore, "I" is the topic, what is important in the sentence. Notice how, if we change the sentence slightly, obtaining 学生は私です ***gakusei wa watashi desu*** "I am the student," the topic (marked with the particle ***wa***) is now "student."

が ***ga*** This particle indicates "who" or "what" performs an action. In the table, the particle が ***ga*** indicates that the "stomach" (***onaka***) is what performs the action of "hurting" (***itai***). Be careful, because the topic particle は ***wa*** is easy to confuse with が ***ga***. Distinguishing the usage of ***wa*** from that of ***ga*** is one of the most difficult points for students of Japanese, even at advanced levels.

の ***no***: This is the possessive particle "whose." The word before の ***no*** "owns" the word after it. The example 私の本 ***watashi no hon*** would literally mean "I" (私 ***watashi***) own a "book" (本 ***hon***); in other words, "the book of me" or "my book."

に ***ni***: This particle has several functions:
a) Direct contact ("where," "in which place"), for example: 黒板に書く ***kokuban ni kaku***, "I write" (***kaku***) "on" (***ni***) the "blackboard" (***kokuban***).
b) Place ("where"). When the verb in the sentence means existence, such as ある ***aru***, いる ***iru*** ("there is / are," Lesson 18), or 住む ***sumu*** ("to live"), the に ***ni*** particle is used. If not, the particle で ***de*** should be used.
c) Indirect object marker ("to"). In the example in the chart overleaf, "Tarō" receives the book, so he is marked with に ***ni***.

で ***de***: This particle has two basic functions:
a) Place ("where an action occurs"). In the example, one studies (to study is an action verb) in the library, so the word 図書館 ***toshokan*** (library) must be marked with で ***de***. This particle is easy to confuse with に ***ni***.
b) Means of transport ("by"). For example, 電車で行く ***densha de iku***, "go by train," (***densha*** = "train"); 自転車で行く ***jitensha de iku***, "go by bicycle" (***jitensha*** = "bicycle"); バスで行く ***basu de iku***, "to go by bus" (***basu*** = "bus").

へ ***e***: The particle へ ***e*** indicates direction, that is, "to where" and it is only used with verbs like 行く ***iku*** (to go), 来る ***kuru*** (to come), and 帰る ***kaeru*** (to return). If, for example, you want to say you are going to Japan, the word 日本 ***nihon*** ("Japan") will be marked with へ ***e***.

を ***o***: The particle を ***o*** marks the direct object of a sentence, that is, "what" receives the verb's action. In the example, りんご ***ringo*** ("apple") is what receives the action of the verb 食べる ***taberu*** ("to eat"), therefore りんご ***ringo*** must be marked with を ***o***. Likewise, the sentence お茶を飲む ***ocha o nomu***, (お茶 ***ocha*** = "tea"; 飲む ***nomu*** = "to drink"), for example, means "to drink tea."

と ***to***: This is another multipurpose particle, with two different usages:
a) "And," "with." The particle と ***to*** is used for comprehensive lists (where all elements are given), for example, ペンと筆とゴム ***pen to fude to gomu***, "pen, pencil and eraser." This particle also means "in the company of," for example: 私と桂子 ***watashi to Keiko*** "Keiko and I."
b) To quote somebody else's words, for example,「愛している」と言う "***ai shite iru***" ***to iu***, which means someone literally "says" (***iu***) the words "I love you" (***ai shite iru***).

We have given you a lot of condensed information in these few pages, but don't despair: keep studying, and with practice you'll become able to use particles properly.

Grammatical particles			
は **ha** **(wa)**	Topic (what we are talking about)	私は学生です ***watashi wa gakusei desu*** I am a student.	私 ***watashi*** I 学生 ***gakusei*** student です ***desu*** to be
が **ga**	Subject	お腹が痛いです ***onaka ga itai desu*** My stomach hurts.	お腹 ***o-naka*** stomach 痛い ***itai*** painful
の **no**	Possessive	これは私の本です ***kore wa watashi no hon desu*** This is my book.	これ ***kore*** this 本 ***hon*** book
に **ni**	a) Direct contact b) Place (existence) c) Indirect object	a) 黒板に字を書く ***kokuban ni ji o kaku*** To write letters on the black-board. b) ここに犬がいる ***koko ni inu ga iru*** There is a dog here. c) 太郎に本をあげる ***tarō ni hon o ageru*** I give Tarō a book.	黒板 ***kokuban*** blackboard 字 ***ji*** letter 書く ***kaku*** to write ここ ***koko*** here 犬 ***inu*** dog いる ***iru*** to be あげる ***ageru*** to give
で **de**	a) Place (action) b) Means	a) 図書館で勉強する ***toshokan de benkyō suru*** To study in the library. b) 電車で行く ***densha de iku*** To go by train.	図書館 ***toshokan*** library 勉強する ***benkyō suru*** to study 電車 ***densha*** train 行く ***iku*** to go
へ **he** **(e)**	***Direction***	日本へ行く ***nihon e iku*** To go to Japan.	日本 ***nihon*** Japan
を **wo** **(o)**	Direct object	りんごを食べる ***ringo o taberu*** To eat an apple.	りんご ***ringo*** apple 食べる ***taberu*** to eat
と **to**	a) "with," "and" b) Quotation	a) 花子と太郎は結婚する ***Hanako to Tarō wa kekkon suru*** Hanako and Tarō get married. b)「愛している」という ***ai shite iru to iu*** To say "I love you."	結婚する ***kekkon suru*** to marry 愛する ***ai suru*** to love 言う ***iu*** to say

漫画例 Manga Examples

In the manga examples we will study several practical examples of the usage of particles. Refer to the Glossary of Abbreviations on page 9 to understand the abbreviations used here to describe the particles in each manga panel.

Manga Example 1: Topic particle *wa*

We have here two examples of the usage of the topic particle は ***wa***, possibly the most used particle in the Japanese language, and, owing to its similarity in use to が ***ga***, one of the most difficult to master for the student. As we mentioned a few pages earlier, the particle は ***wa*** indicates the previous word is the topic, that is, "what we are talking about." The particle は ***wa*** brings the conversation topic to the foreground.

In the first example, これはおそい ***kore wa osoi***, the topic in the sentence is the word before は ***wa***, that is これ ***kore*** ("this," Lesson 9). Therefore, Motohira tells us he is talking to us about "this" and, concerning it, he says that it is おそい ***osoi***, "slow."

In the second example, the topic of the sentence 犯人はクリスです ***hannin wa kurisu desu*** is 犯人 ***hannin*** ("criminal," although in this case we translate it as "murderer," for context reasons). Suppose we wanted to give importance to the name Chris and not ***hannin***. In that case, we could take the word "Chris" to the foreground by highlighting it as the topic of the sentence with は ***wa***, and say クリスは犯人です ***kurisu wa hannin desu*** ("Chris is the murderer").

J.M. Ken Niimura

Motohira: これはおそい!!
kore wa osoi!!
this TOP slow!!
This is slow!!

Studio Kōsen

Ryō: まさか 犯人はクリス...？
masaka hannin wa kurisu?
oh, no! criminal TOP Chris?
Impossible! Chris, the murderer?

Manga Example 2: Subject particle *ga*

This second example gives us an instance of the subject particle が ***ga***, used to mark the "the one who performs the action" as the subject of the sentence. In this case, the "telephone" (電話 ***denwa***) performs the action of "to ring" (なる ***naru***), therefore, we will place the subject particle が ***ga*** after it.

As we have already seen, it is very easy to confuse は ***wa*** and が ***ga***. For the moment, remember that は ***wa*** is used to mark information known beforehand, because it has previously appeared in the conversation, or because it is a unique and well known concept, such as "sky," "life," "happiness," and so on. In this panel, "telephone" appears for the first time in the conversation between Akira and Kumi, and that is why it is marked with が ***ga***.

Studio Kōsen

Akira: くみぃ！電話がなっているぞ〜！

Kumii! denwa ga natte iru zo!

Kumi! Telephone SP ring is EP!

Kumi! The telephone is ringing!

Manga Example 3: Possessive particle *no*

J.M. Ken Niimura

Takeshi: 桃の種…？

momo no tane...?

peach POP seed...?

A peach seed?

This simple example shows the usage of の ***no***. This particle is a noun modifier indicating possession and belonging to: the word tagged by の ***no*** "possesses" what comes before it.

The particle の ***no*** is always used between two nouns, and it gives additional information about the second one. This information is usually of the "possession" kind, as in 私の家 ***watashi no ie***, "my house" (lit: "the house of me"). Sometimes, its use does not indicate possession, but it provides extra, more detailed information about the second noun: here the word 種 ***tane*** ("seed") belongs to 桃 ***momo*** ("peach"), hence, the translation "peach seed."

Manga Example 4: Place particle *de*

In this panel we have a very clear example of the usage of the place particle で ***de***. This particle goes after the name of a place or adverb of place indicating "where" the action is performed. Remember that this particle cannot be used with verbs that indicate "existence," although you should not worry about this, since there are very few of these verbs. In this case, the verb 戦う ***tatakau*** ("to fight") is clearly a verb of action, not of existence, and therefore its adverb of place ここ ***koko*** ("here"), must be marked with で ***de***.

Guillermo March

Note: か ***ka*** is an end-of-sentence particle used to make questions (Lesson 17).

Zorg: ここで戦うか！？
koko de tatakau ka!?
here PP fight Q?!
Do we fight here?!

Manga Example 5: Place particle *ni*

Here we see Akiko looking desperately for her 手裏剣 ***shuriken*** ("ninja stars"). The particles used are the particle of place (existence) に ***ni***, the possessive particle の ***no*** and the subject particle が ***ga***. The particle に ***ni*** indicates that the previous word is the place where something is, and it is only used with verbs of existence, among which the most common by far are いる ***iru*** "to be," used for animate beings, and ある ***aru*** "to be," used for inanimate objects (Lesson 18). In this case "here" (ここ ***koko***) "are" (ある ***aru***) the "ninja stars" (手裏剣 ***shuriken***) of "me" (あたし ***atashi)***.

J.M. Ken Niimura

Note: The end-of-sentence particle の ***no*** has nothing to do with the possessive: it is a colloquial equivalent of か ***ka***, which we saw in the previous example, indicating a question. We will talk about these particles in the following lesson.

Akiko:	なあっ　なあっ！！	ここにあたしの手裏剣があるのっ！？
	naa naa!!	***koko ni atashi no shuriken ga aru no!?***
	hey, hey!	here PP I POP shuriken SP here is Q?!
	Hey, hey!!!	**Are my ninja stars here?!**

Manga Example 6: Direct object particle *o*

Here we have a very clear example of the usage of を ***o***. This particle indicates the previous word is a direct object, that is "the thing that receives the verb's action."

In this case, the verb is 貸す ***kasu*** ("to lend") and what is lent is これ ***kore*** ("this"). Therefore, the particle we must place after これ ***kore*** is を ***o*** because "this" is what receives the verb's action. This is one of the particles that gives rise to less confusion in its usage. **Notes:** The form 〜してあげる ***shite ageru*** is used in the sense of "doing something for somebody" (Lesson 28). When the verb ends in 〜よう ***-yō***, it means "to be going to do something."

Tomo: これをかしてあげよう。
kore o kashite ageyō
this DOP lend give
I'll lend you this.

Manga Example 7: Direction particle *e*

The last example in this lesson features two different particles. We already know the first one: it's の ***no*** and indicates possession or gives additional information about a noun. The second one, へ ***e***, indicates direction: "where" someone or something is going. The particle へ ***e*** is mainly used with the verbs 行く ***iku*** ("to go"), 来る ***kuru*** ("to come"), 帰る ***kaeru*** ("to return"), and a few more which are much less common. In this example, it is used with 帰る ***kaeru***.

Note: The form かもしれない ***kamo shirenai*** at the end of a sentence suggests doubt, something that is not certain, and it is usually translated as "might (do)," or "perhaps."

Pipy: さようなら、もう水の中へ帰らないかもしれない
sayōnara, mō mizu no naka e kaeranai kamo shirenai
goodbye any more water POP inside DP not return perhaps
Goodbye. I might never be able to return to the sea again.

Exercises 練習

1. What are particles, and what do we use them for?

2. For the hiragana characters は, へ and を give both their regular pronunciation and their pronunciation when they are used as particles.

3. When do we use the particle は? Construct a sentence with 私 using the words 私 ***watashi*** ("I") and 学生 ***gakusei*** ("student"). Translate it.

4. When do we use the particle に? Construct a sentence with に using the words バルセロナ ***baruserona*** ("Barcelona") and 住む ***sumu*** ("to live"). Translate it.

5. When do we use the particle の? Construct a sentence with の using the words 先生 ***sensei*** ("teacher") and 家 ***ie*** ("house"). Translate it.

6. When do we use the particle へ? Construct a sentence with へ using the words ソウル ***souru*** ("Seoul") and 行く ***iku*** ("to go"). Translate it.

7. Translate the sentence これはあなたの車です ***kore wa anata no kuruma desu*** into English. (***Kore***: "this," ***anata***: "you," ***kuruma***: "car.")

8. Translate the sentence "to give a flower to Hanako" into Japanese. (To give: あげる ***ageru***, flower: 花 ***hana***, Hanako: 花子.) Take a look at Lesson 15!

9. Translate the sentence 中国へ行く ***Chūgoku e iku*** into English. (***Chūgoku***: "China," ***iku***: "to go.")

10. Translate the sentence "to make a plastic model" into Japanese. (Plastic model: プラモデル ***pura-moderu***, to make: 作る ***tsukuru***.)

— Answers to all the exercises can be found online by following the link on page 9. —

Lesson 17 • 第17課

End-of-Sentence Particles

Continuing with the subject of particles, in this lesson we will take a close look at common particles that come at the end of a sentence. Knowing them will help you understand manga, anime and action movies.

What do we use end-of-sentence particles for?

As explained in Lesson 16, a particle is an element usually formed by one hiragana character, which equals a syllable in English. End-of-sentence particles are no different in this respect, as you can see in table on page 152. But don't confuse the "normal" particles we've studied in previous lesson, which have a grammatical role in the sentence, with end-of-sentence particles. The role of most end-of-sentence particles is usually to add nuance to the meaning of a sentence.

The particle ぞ ***zo***, for example (used by men) is used for emphasis, and to convey the confidence of the speaker. Remember these particles are almost exclusively used in spoken Japanese and, moreover, in rather informal situations. The only acceptable particles in formal spoken Japanese are か ***ka***, ね ***ne***, and, to a certain degree, よ ***yo*** and わ ***wa***.

In the Japanese language there is a heavy distinction between male and female speech, and this is also reflected in end-of-sentence particles: there are particles used only by men, and particles used only by women.

How to use end-of-sentence particles

Read the following definitions while referring to the explanatory table on page 152.

か ***ka***: This particle is more or less the equivalent of the English question mark. (The question mark is traditionally not used in Japanese documents but it is often used in manga for its expressive power.) The particle か ***ka*** turns a sentence into a question, for example:

君はすしが好きです ***kimi wa sushi ga suki desu*** You like sushi.
君はすしが好きですか ***kimi wa sushi ga suki desu ka***? Do you like sushi?

As you can see, both sentences are exactly the same but for the final か ***ka***, which turns the statement into a question. Making questions in Japanese is as easy as adding か ***ka*** at the end of the sentence, and giving the whole sentence a questioning intonation when you pronounce it.

ね ***ne***: This particle is also often used in Japanese. It has two functions:
a) It adds confirmation, equal to "isn't it?" or "you know..."
b) It can act as a "softener" at the end of a suggestion, like "okay...?" The word ね ***ne*** is the most common emphatic particle, and has many nuances, impossible to summarize in a few words. For now, get used to seeing it in context and use it sparingly. Foreigners with a modest level of Japanese tend to overuse ね ***ne***.

よ ***yo***: Just like ね ***ne***, よ ***yo*** is a very common particle, which we must also try to use sparingly. Among other nuances, it has two main functions:
a) To state, to give a degree of certainty, and to sound convincing.
b) At the end of a sentence which expresses an order or a wish, the particle よ ***yo*** has the function of insistence or pressure.

さ ***sa***: さ ***sa*** has a similar emphatic function to ね ***ne***, although its use is limited to the Tokyo area and its surroundings.

ぞ ***zo***: A particle used only by men in informal-vulgar language. Like the a) function of よ ***yo***, that is, it states and gives the sentence a strong sense of certainty or determination. Use cautiously: only if you are among close friends.

ぜ ***ze***: The functions of this particle are almost identical to よ ***yo*** and ぞ ***zo***, but with a "cooler" nuance. It tends to be used by younger men.

な ***na***: This particle implies the wish to do something which is theoretically very difficult to do, among other nuances. It is mainly used by men. **Note:** Don't mistake this particle for the "negative command" な ***na*** we will study in Lesson 30.

わ ***wa***: This is the female version of ぞ ***zo*** and ぜ ***ze*** with more or less the same functions as those two particles. In the Osaka area, men also use it.

の ***no***: The particle の ***no*** has two main functions:
a) Informal version of the particle か ***ka***, that is, it turns an affirmative or negative sentence into a question.
b) It gives an informative nuance to the sentence, and could be translated as "you know." It is generally used by women.

As you have seen, the end-of-sentence particles give important nuances to sentences, and are impossible to translate into English. Mastering the particles and their nuances can take time, so keep referring to this lesson until you get used to them.

End-of-sentence particles			
か ***ka***	Question	すしが好きですか ***sushi ga suki desu ka?*** Do you like sushi?	すし ***sushi*** sushi 好き ***suki*** to like です ***desu*** to be
ね ***ne***	a) Affirmation statement b) Softens a suggestion	a) この映画は長いですね ***kono eiga wa nagai desu ne*** This film is long, isn't it? b) あした、来てね ***ashita, kite ne*** Come tomorrow, okay?	この ***kono*** this 映画 ***eiga*** movie 長い ***nagai*** long あした ***ashita*** tomorrow 来て ***kite*** come (you)
よ ***yo***	a) Emphasis, statement b) Suggestion	a) 日本語はやさしいよ！ ***nihongo wa yasashii yo!*** Japanese is easy! b) 歌を歌ってよ！ ***uta o utatte yo!*** Sing a song, come on!	日本語 ***nihongo*** Japanese やさしい ***yasashii*** easy 歌 ***uta*** song 歌って ***utatte*** sing (you)
さ ***sa***	Emphasis, statement	ラーメンを食べたいさ ***raamen o tabetai sa*** I want to eat ramen, hey.	ラーメン ramen noodles 食べたい ***tabetai*** to want to eat
ぞ ***zo***	Emphasis, statement (♂, informal)	めっちゃ疲れたぞ！ ***meccha tsukareta zo!*** I'm so tired! / I'm exhausted!	めっちゃ ***meccha*** very much (informal) 疲れた ***tsukareta*** tired
ぜ ***ze***	a) Emphasis, statement (♂, informal) b) Suggestion (♂, informal)	a) あれは千円だぜ！ ***are wa sen en da ze!*** Hey, that's one thousand yen! b) いっぱい遊ぼうぜ！ ***ippai asobō ze!*** Let's have lots of good fun!	あれ ***are*** that 千円 ***sen en*** 1,000 yen だ ***da*** to be (informal) いっぱい ***ippai*** a lot 遊ぼう ***asobō*** let's have fun
な ***na***	Emphasis, statement, wish (♂) Negative command (♂)	中国へ行きたいな ***chūgoku e ikitai na*** I'd love to go to China! これを壊すな！ ***kore o kowasu na!*** Don't break it!	中国 ***chūgoku*** China 行きたい ***ikitai*** to want to go これ ***kore*** this 壊す ***kowasu*** to break
わ ***wa***	Emphatic statement (♀)	このお寺は感激するわ！ ***kono o-tera wa kangeki suru wa!*** This temple is impressive!	お寺 ***o-tera*** temple 感激する ***kangeki suru*** to be deeply impressed
の ***no***	a) Question (informal) b) Statement (♀)	a) あした来るの？ ***ashita kuru no?*** Will you come tomorrow? b) タイへ行くの ***tai e iku no*** I'm going to Thailand, you know.	あした ***ashita*** tomorrow 来る ***kuru*** to come タイ ***tai*** Thailand 行く ***iku*** to go

漫画例 Manga Examples

To help you remember what you've learned in this lesson, end-of-sentence particles are the main theme in the manga examples in this section. Let's take a look at how the most important ones function in a real context.

Manga Example 1: Informal question

The important particle in this panel is の ***no***. It is an informal version of か ***ka***, used to form questions in an informal or colloquial context. Be careful: in Lesson 16 we talked about "normal" particles, and the の ***no*** which indicates possession was among them. Take care not to confuse these two particles; they have nothing to do with each other. Here you can also see a set phrase (Lesson 27), ***o-daiji ni***, a farewell greeting aimed at sick people, meaning something like "take care."

Studio Kōsen

Mika:	じゃお大事に	**Tetsu:**	もう帰るの？
	ja o-daiji ni		***mō kaeru no?***
	well (set phrase)		already go home Q?
	Well, take care.		**Are you going already?**

Manga Example 2: Insistence, pressure

Here, a boy called Johan asks his sister to shoot him. The emphatic particle chosen by Johan is よ ***yo***, which indicates insistence or pressure at the end of a sentence where an order or a wish is expressed. Here, the order is further reinforced by adding よ ***yo*** at the end of the sentence ***boku o ute*** ("shoot me"). Our suggested translation is short, but conveys the sharpness of the Japanese original.

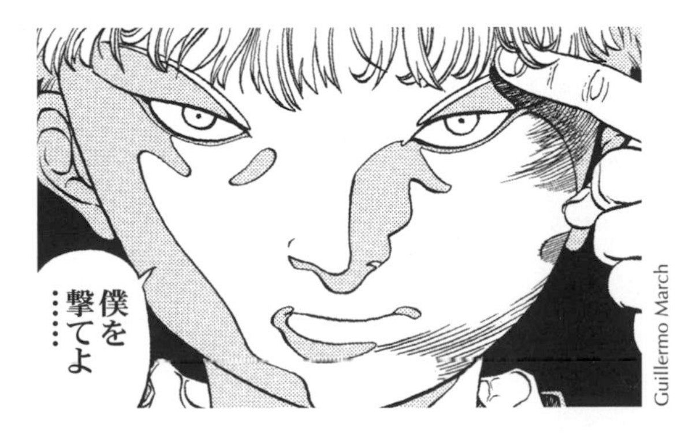

Guillermo March

Johan: 僕を撃てよ...
boku o ute yo...
me DOP shoot EP...
Shoot me...

Manga Example 3: Emphasis

The particle we will see here is ぜ ***ze***, used mainly by men in very informal situations, basically among friends. A sentence ending in ぜ ***ze*** has a nuance of insistence and assertion.

Notes: The dash after the word 行こ～ has the function of making the sound longer than usual. Also, make use of this example to review the grammatical particles は ***wa*** (topic), の ***no*** (possession), and へ ***e*** (direction), studied in Lesson 16.

Studio Kōsen

Shingō: 今度はお前の家へ行こ～ぜ！
kondo wa omae no ie e iko- ze!
next time TOP you POP home DP go EP!
Next time we'll go to your place!

Manga Example 4: Double use of end-of-sentence particles

This last panel will illustrate the use of two end-of-sentence particles together in the same sentence. Sometimes it seems one particle is not enough, and a combination of two (never more than two) is used to give the sentence a stronger emphatic tone, as you can see here.

You can also see the surprise or statement particle よ ***yo*** used together with the male confirmation particle な ***na***. Other common combinations are よね ***yo ne***, わね ***wa ne*** or わよ ***wa yo***. These last two combinations are mainly used in female language.

Guillermo March

We also have the frequent combination かな ***ka na***: used to indicate uncertainty or to wonder about something. Its meaning is similar to our "I wonder if..." A feminine alternative to かな ***ka na*** is かしら ***kashira***.

Schüle: 約束10時にあったよな
yakusoku jū ji ni atta yo na
promise 10 o'clock TP be EP EP
You had an appointment at 10, didn't you?

Exercises 練習

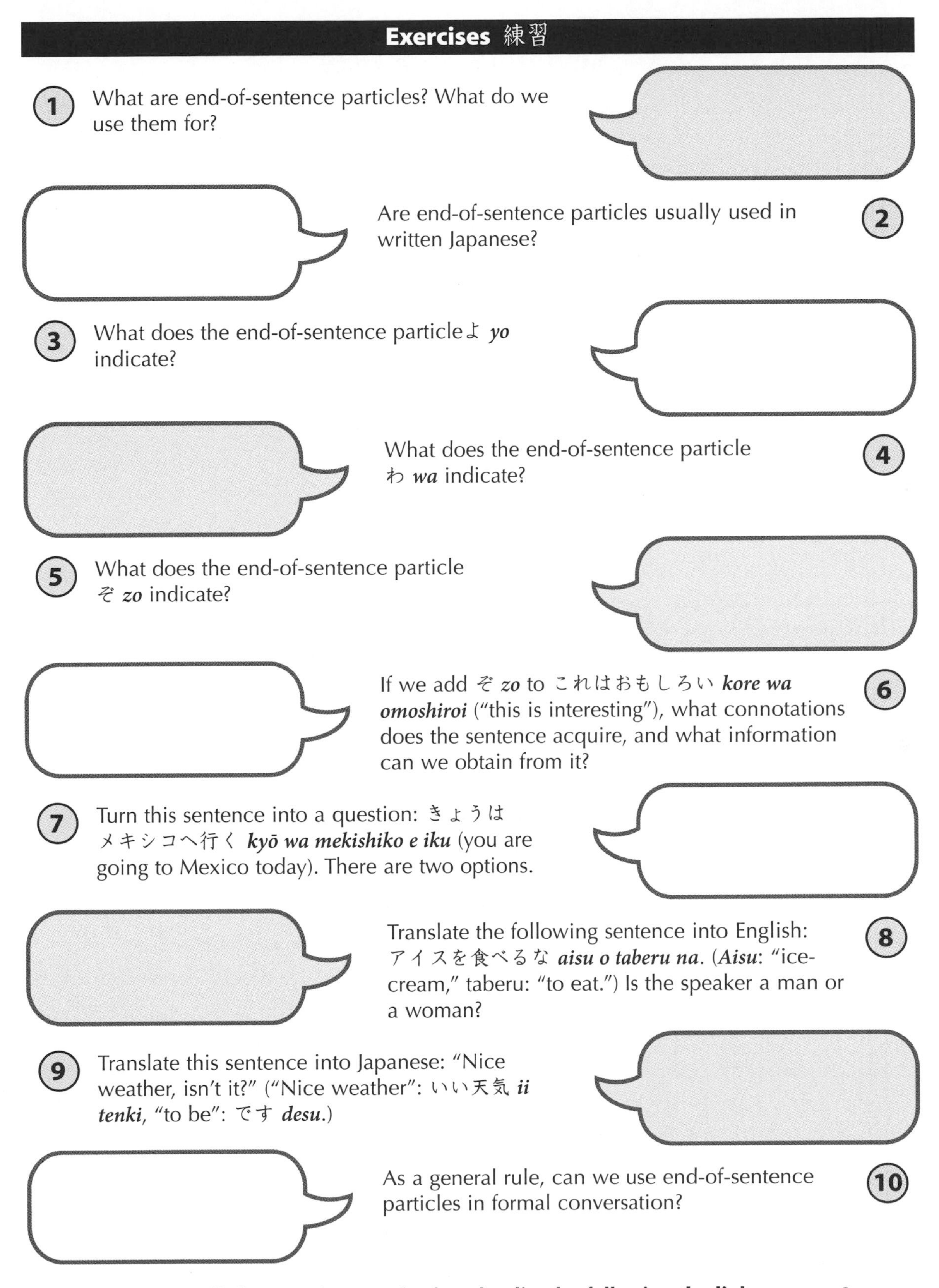

1. What are end-of-sentence particles? What do we use them for?

2. Are end-of-sentence particles usually used in written Japanese?

3. What does the end-of-sentence particle よ ***yo*** indicate?

4. What does the end-of-sentence particle わ ***wa*** indicate?

5. What does the end-of-sentence particle ぞ ***zo*** indicate?

6. If we add ぞ ***zo*** to これはおもしろい ***kore wa omoshiroi*** ("this is interesting"), what connotations does the sentence acquire, and what information can we obtain from it?

7. Turn this sentence into a question: きょうはメキシコへ行く ***kyō wa mekishiko e iku*** (you are going to Mexico today). There are two options.

8. Translate the following sentence into English: アイスを食べるな ***aisu o taberu na***. (***Aisu***: "ice-cream," taberu: "to eat.") Is the speaker a man or a woman?

9. Translate this sentence into Japanese: "Nice weather, isn't it?" ("Nice weather": いい天気 ***ii tenki***, "to be": です ***desu***.)

10. As a general rule, can we use end-of-sentence particles in formal conversation?

— Answers to all the exercises can be found online by following the link on page 9. —

Lesson 18 • 第18課

The Verbs Aru and Iru

In this lesson, as a prelude to Verbs 1 in Lesson 19, we will take some time to study two of the most basic verbs in Japanese: *aru* and *iru*.

Two verbs that have exactly the same meaning?

The verbs いる ***iru*** and ある ***aru*** both mean "there is / are" or "to be (somewhere)," but いる ***iru*** is used when the subject is a person or an animal (an animate being), and ある ***aru*** is used with inanimate things. Be sure to remember this difference, as it is essential.

As we said in Lesson 9, Japanese verbs always go at the end of the sentence: Japanese has an SOV / SAV structure (Subject + Object or Adverb + Verb), while English is SVO / A, as illustrated in the following examples:

English: I am in the library.
S V O

Japanese: ***Watashi wa toshokan ni iru*** (私は図書館にいる)
S O V

(私 ***watashi*** "I"; 図書館 ***toshokan*** = "library," いる ***iru*** = "to be")

Keep this order in mind when forming sentences. And don't forget about grammatical particles. Here, we have the topic particle は ***wa*** and the particle of place に ***ni***. Review Lesson 16 if you have any doubts about the usage of these particles.

Verb forms

The verbs いる ***iru*** and ある ***aru*** have the following forms: present, past, negative, and past negative. You can look up these forms in the table on the facing page.

The good news about Japanese verbs is that their form doesn't change depending on the person (e.g.: "I," "we," or "they"): the form is always the same. The only forms are present, past, negative and past negative (as shown in the table), as well as the ***-te*** form (Lesson 28), the command form (Lesson 30), and a few others.

What we do have is two different forms depending on the formality level. Let's look first at the ***-masu*** form, so called because all the present forms end in 〜ます ***-masu*** (います ***imasu*** and あります ***arimasu*** in the case of いる ***iru*** and ある ***aru***). The ***-masu*** form is also called the "formal form," because it is used in formal situations.

Inflections for the verbs *iru* and *aru*				
	Verb *iru* (animate)		Verb *aru* (inanimate)	
	Formal	Dict. form	Formal	Dict. form
Present (There is)	います ***imasu***	いる ***iru***	あります ***arimasu***	ある ***aru***
Past (There was)	いました ***imashita***	いた ***ita***	ありました ***arimashita***	あった ***atta***
Negative (There isn't)	いません ***imasen***	いない ***inai***	ありません ***arimasen***	ない ***nai***
Past negative (There wasn't)	いませんでした ***imasendeshita***	いなかった ***inakatta***	ありませんでした ***arimasendeshita***	なかった ***nakatta***

As this book is designed to teach you mainly spoken Japanese as found in manga, we must also explain the "simple form," also known as the "dictionary form" or the "casual form," used in informal and vulgar situations. It is called the "dictionary form" because it is in this form that verbs appear in dictionaries. It is by far the most commonly used in manga, anime, video games, and action movies, and that is why we are explaining it at this early stage—a conventional Japanese-study course would teach the dictionary form long after the ***-masu*** form).

Basic sentences

In this lesson we will show you how to form simple sentences using the verbs いる ***iru*** and ある ***aru***. You will need to have mastered the place pronouns ここ ***koko***, そこ ***soko***, あそこ ***asoko*** and どこ ***doko*** ("here," "there," "over there," "where"), taught in Lesson 9.

As we have mentioned, いる ***iru*** and ある ***aru*** have similar meanings, but いる ***iru*** is used for animate beings, whereas ある ***aru*** is used with inanimate things. Let's study these two different meanings.

Expressing "there is / are"

Read carefully these two sentences which follow the "place ***kosoado*** + ***ni*** + subject ***ga*** + ***aru*** / ***iru***" model. Sentences like these are easy to form, and you will find them very useful:

1. ここに亀がいる
koko ni kame ga iru
There is a turtle here.

2. そこに財布がありました
soko ni saifu ga arimashita
There was a wallet there.

As you can see, we have used the dictionary form of the verb いる ***iru*** in the present tense in the first example sentence. Notice that the subject is 亀 ***kame*** ("turtle"), that is, an animate being; therefore, the appropriate verb is いる ***iru***. In the second example, we have used the formal form in the past tense of the verb ある ***aru***. The subject is 財布 ***saifu*** ("wallet"), an inanimate object; thus, the appropriate verb is ある ***aru***.

Expressing "to be (somewhere)"

The two following sentences follow the "subject ***wa*** + adverb of place ***ni*** + ***aru*** / ***iru***" model. They are used to indicate that something or someone (marked with the topic particle は ***wa***) is at a particular place (marked with the place particle に ***ni***).

1. 佐藤さんは家にいませんでした
satō-san wa ie ni imasendeshita
Mr. Satō was not home.

2. めがねは机にない
megane wa tsukue ni nai
The glasses are not on the desk.

In the first sentence, when talking about a person (Mr. Satō), we have used the verb いる ***iru*** in its formal past negative form. In the second one, the subject being an object (glasses), we have used ある ***aru*** in its simple present negative form.

Expressing "to have"

Sometimes we can find the "subject ***wa*** + direct object ***ga*** + ***aru*** / ***iru***" construction that has a similar meaning to the English verb "to have." Take a look at the examples:

1. 僕は車がありません
boku wa kuruma ga arimasen
I don't have a car.

2. 里美ちゃんは犬がいるの？
satomi-chan wa inu ga iru no?
Does Satomi have a dog?

In these cases, it's better to use the verbs 持つ ***motsu*** "to have," "to own," or, for animals, 飼う ***kau*** "to keep," "to raise" instead of ある ***aru*** and いる ***iru***, respectively. Try constructing some of your own sentences using the words in the table below.

Animals and objects					
Japanese	**Rōmaji**	**Meaning**	**Japanese**	**Rōmaji**	**Meaning**
はえ	***hae***	fly	財布	***saifu***	wallet
蚊	***ka***	mosquito	めがね	***megane***	glasses
亀	***kame***	turtle	はし	***hashi***	chopsticks
ちょう	***chō***	butterfly	コップ	***koppu***	glass
さめ	***same***	shark	皿	***sara***	plate
かえる	***kaeru***	frog	フォーク	***fōku***	fork
くじら	***kujira***	whale	スプーン	***supūn***	spoon
からす	***karasu***	crow	ナイフ	***naifu***	knife

漫画例 Manga Examples

Let's now have a look at some examples taken from real manga of the verbs *iru* and *aru*, showing their different meanings of "there is / are," "to be somewhere," and "to have."

Manga Example 1: Aru "there is / are"

J.M. Ken Niimura

This first example illustrates the meaning of "there is" using the verb ある ***aru***. Remember the structure of this kind of sentence: "place particle ***ni*** + thing ***wa*** / ***ga*** + verb ***aru*** / ***iru***." Since the word スズ ***suzu*** is an inanimate object (bell), the chosen verb has to be ある ***aru***. In this case, the situation being an informal one, the speaker chooses the dictionary form.

Onimaru: ここにスズが2つある**...**
koko ni suzu ga futatsu aru...
here PP bell SP two there are
There are two bells here...

Manga Example 2: Iru "to be somewhere" (1)

Guillermo March

This frame gives an example of いる ***iru*** meaning "to be somewhere." Since we are talking about an animate being, ぼく ***boku*** (I), we use いる ***iru***. Notice the particle following the word for place is に ***ni*** (Lesson 16). **Note:** If you need to, you can review the usage of the end-of-sentence particle よ ***yo*** (Lesson 17).

Rabbit: ぼくはここにいるよ。
boku wa koko ni iru yo
I TOP here PP to be EP
I'm here!

Manga Example 3: Iru "to be somewhere" (2) — negative form

Studio Kōsen

We see here the two options for the present negative form of いる ***iru***. The teacher uses the dictionary or colloquial form (いない ***inai***, "not to be"), whereas the children, showing respect, use the formal form (いません ***imasen***). By the way, what they are looking for is the class hamster, and, consequently, they use the verb いる ***iru***, for living beings. Bearing in mind formality levels when you speak is very important: In Japan, you would not speak to your teacher the same way you would speak to your closest friend. In this book we teach both colloquial and formal expressions so that you don't have to address everyone using informal manga Japanese!

Teacher:	みんなの机の中にはいないな？	**Children:**	いませーん
	minna no tsukue no naka ni wa inai na?		***imaseeeen***
	everybody POP desk PP inside PP TOP not be EP		not be
	Isn't it inside any of your desks?		**Nooo!!**

Manga Example 4: Aru "there is / are" (2) — negative form

Finally, we see here the usage of the ***-masu*** form, or formal form, of the verb ある ***aru***. Mr. Mori uses its negative form, ありません ***arimasen*** ("there isn't"). Since the word 逃げ場 ***nigeba*** ("means of escape") is not a living being nor anything similar, but is in fact a concept, we will use the verb ある ***aru***, and not いる ***iru***. The ***-masu*** form is used when you don't know the person you are speaking to well, that is, in formal situations. It is roughly similar to the usage in English of adding "Mr.," "Mrs.," or "Ms." to a surname.

Guillermo March

Mio:	もう逃げ場はありませんよ。
	mō nigeba wa arimasen yo
	any more means of escape (TOP) there isn't (EP)
	You can't escape now!

Exercises 練習

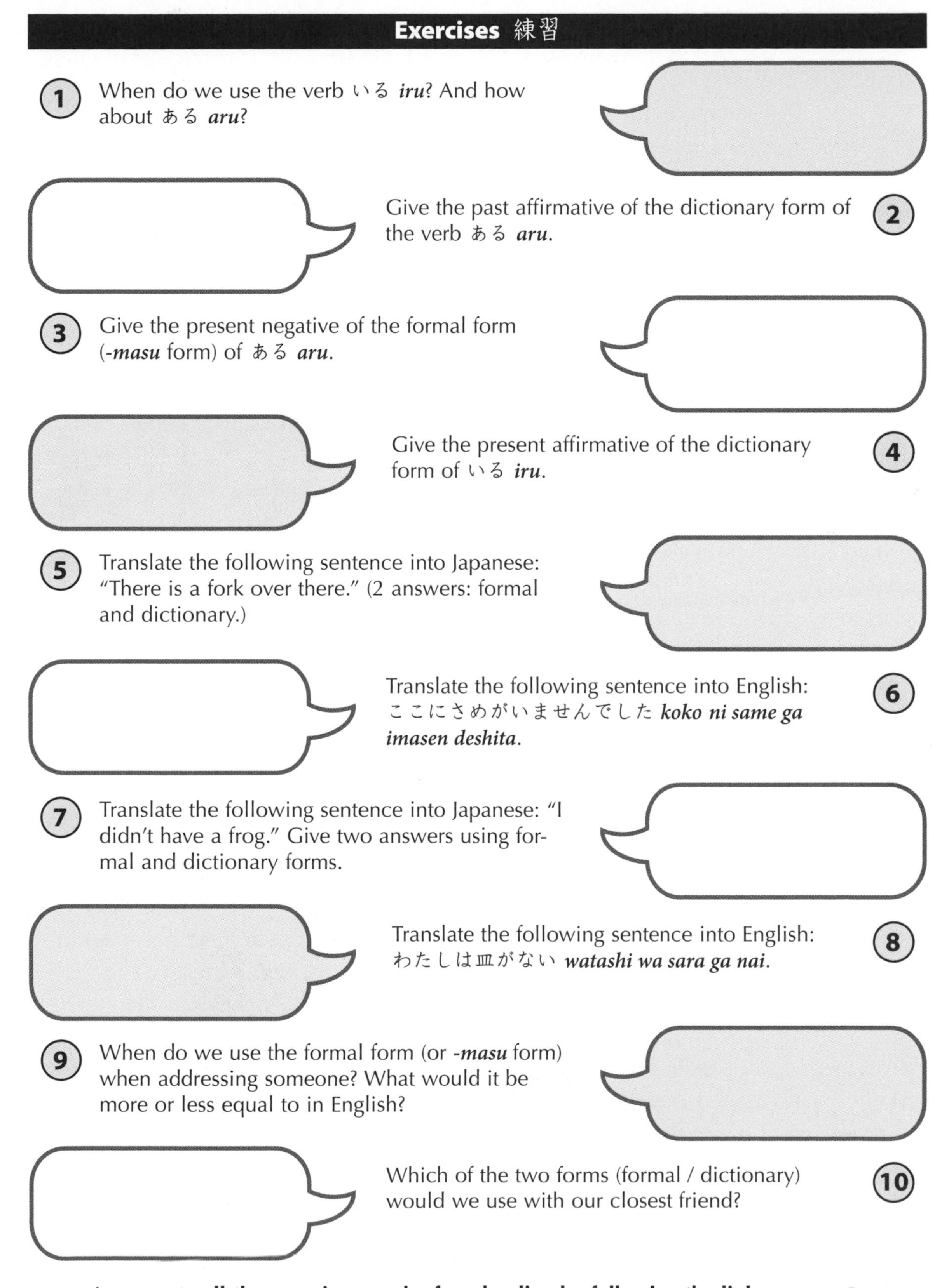

1. When do we use the verb いる ***iru***? And how about ある ***aru***?

2. Give the past affirmative of the dictionary form of the verb ある ***aru***.

3. Give the present negative of the formal form (-***masu*** form) of ある ***aru***.

4. Give the present affirmative of the dictionary form of いる ***iru***.

5. Translate the following sentence into Japanese: "There is a fork over there." (2 answers: formal and dictionary.)

6. Translate the following sentence into English: ここにさめがいませんでした ***koko ni same ga imasen deshita***.

7. Translate the following sentence into Japanese: "I didn't have a frog." Give two answers using formal and dictionary forms.

8. Translate the following sentence into English: わたしは皿がない ***watashi wa sara ga nai***.

9. When do we use the formal form (or -***masu*** form) when addressing someone? What would it be more or less equal to in English?

10. Which of the two forms (formal / dictionary) would we use with our closest friend?

— Answers to all the exercises can be found online by following the link on page 9. —

Lesson 19 • 第19課

Verbs (1): The -masu Form

As promised in the previous lesson, in this lesson we will take a closer look at how to deal with verbs. Japanese verb forms are very simple compared to other languages, they are even simpler than English verbs! However, unlike English, there are different verb forms for different degrees of formality.

The formal form

As we saw in Lesson 18, there are two different verb forms for different levels of formality: on the one hand we have the "simple form" or "dictionary form"; and on the other hand, we have the ***-masu*** form" or "formal form."

In the following lessons, we will study the different forms of Japanese verbs. In this lesson we will look at the formal form or the ***-masu*** form, and we will devote Lesson 20 to the informal or simple form. It may take a little time to master all the new concepts and verb forms introduced in these lessons, so we have provided extra manga examples in each lesson to help you along!

Sentence structure

We already mentioned in Lessons 9 and 18 that Japanese verbs always go at the end of the sentence: thus, to form a sentence we first have the subject, then the object or adverb, and finally the verb.

Remember we also need to add grammatical particles, which will function as "joints" between the different sentence parts (Lesson 16.) Here are some examples:

1. 私はパンを食べます
watashi wa pan o tabemasu
I TOP bread DOP eat
I eat bread.

2. 私はダンに本を貸しました
watashi wa dan ni hon o kashimashita
I TOP Dan IOP book DOP lend (past)
I lent Dan a book.

In example 1), は ***wa*** and を ***o*** are particles which indicate the previous words (私 ***watashi*** and パン ***pan***) are, respectively, the topic in the sentence and the direct object. In example 2), は ***wa*** and を ***o*** have the same function as in 1), while に ***ni*** is the marker for the indirect object, which is, as you can guess, ダン ***dan***. (Review Lesson 16 if you are not too sure about this.)

Verb forms

The formal ***-masu*** form of verbs is fairly easy. First, as with the verbs です ***desu*** ("to be," Lesson 9) and いる ***iru*** and ある ***aru*** ("to be [somewhere]," Lesson 18), you must bear in mind there are no different forms depending on person: whatever the subject, "I," "you," "he," "we," or "they," the verb form never changes. For example:

私は読みます ***watashi wa yomimasu*** "I read."
彼女は読みます ***kanojo wa yomimasu***. "She reads."

While in English the verb changes ("read" / "reads"), in Japanese it is always 読みます ***yomimasu***. If you don't remember the personal pronouns ("I," "you," "he," etc.), you can review Lesson 7, because it is essential that you know them.

Note: keep these pronunciation issues in mind:

1) In forms ending in ***-masu***, the final "u" is hardly pronounced. For example, 読みます ***yomimasu*** is pronounced something like "***yomimas***."

2) The "i" in the past tense ***-mashita*** ending, which we will now see, is hardly pronounced. For example, 読みました ***yomimashita*** is pronounced "***yomimashta***."

Verb groups

The verbs in the table on the next page are divided into Group 1 (Invariable), Group 2 (Variable), and Group 3 (Irregular). As mentioned in Lesson 18, verbs appear in dictionaries in the "simple form" (also called the "dictionary form"), which is similar to the infinitive form.

To obtain the ***-masu*** forms of verbs, we must know to which group they belong. In the first group we find verbs ending only in ***-iru*** or ***-eru,*** but there are also verbs ending in ***-iru*** and ***-eru*** in the second group, as you can see. Just knowing the simple form alone will not guarantee that you can tell whether a verb ending in ***-iru*** or ***-eru*** belongs to Group 1 or 2, so you will have to learn the tricky ones by heart. But mostly, when the simple form of a verb does not end in ***-iru*** or ***-eru***, it's safe to say that the verb belongs to the second group. The way to obtain the ***-masu*** form of a verb from its infinitive varies according to its group:

Group 1: Remove the る ***-ru*** of the infinitive and add ます ***-masu***, for example:
教える ***oshieru*** ⇒ 教えます ***oshiemasu*** ("to teach")

Group 2: The form changes according to the verb ending:
す ***su*** ⇒ します ***-shimasu***; つ ***tsu*** ⇒ ちます ***-chimasu***; う ***u*** ⇒ います ***-imasu***; る ***ru*** ⇒ ります ***-rimasu***; く ***ku*** ⇒ きます ***-kimasu***; ぐ ***gu*** ⇒ ぎます ***-gimasu***; ぶ ***bu*** ⇒ びます ***-bimasu***; む ***mu*** ⇒ みます ***-mimasu***; ぬ ***nu*** ⇒ にます ***-nimasu***.
Notice we generally replace the last ***u*** sound in the infinitive for ***-imasu***, for example:
書く ***kaku*** 書きます ***kakimasu*** ("to write").

Group 3: The ***-masu*** form is peculiar to these two verbs, and needs to be learned by heart.

	Simple f.	Meaning	-*masu* form	Past	Negative	Past negative
Group 1 Invariable	教える **oshieru**	to teach	教えます **oshiemasu**	教えました **oshiemashita**	教えません **oshiemasen**	教えませんでした **oshiemasendeshita**
	起きる **okiru**	to wake up	起きます **okimasu**	起きました **okimashita**	起きません **okimasen**	起きませんでした **okimasendeshita**
Group 2 Variable	貸す **kasu**	to lend	貸します **kashimasu**	貸しました **kashimashita**	貸しません **kashimasen**	貸しませんでした **kashimasendeshita**
	待つ **matsu**	to wait	待ちます **machimasu**	待ちました **machimashita**	待ちません **machimasen**	待ちませんでした **machimasendeshita**
	買う **kau**	to buy	買います **kaimasu**	買いました **kaimashita**	買いません **kaimasen**	買いませんでした **kaimasendeshita**
	帰る **kaeru**	to return	帰ります **kaerimasu**	帰りました **kaerimashita**	帰りません **kaerimasen**	帰りませんでした **kaerimasendeshita**
	書く **kaku**	to write	書きます **kakimasu**	書きました **kakimashita**	書きません **kakimasen**	書きませんでした **kakimasendeshita**
	急ぐ **isogu**	to hurry	急ぎます **isogimasu**	急ぎました **isogimashita**	急ぎません **isogimasen**	急ぎませんでした **isogimasendeshita**
	遊ぶ **asobu**	to play	遊びます **asobimasu**	遊びました **asobimashita**	遊びません **asobimasen**	遊びませんでした **asobimasendeshita**
	飲む **nomu**	to drink	飲みます **nomimasu**	飲みました **nomimashita**	飲みません **nomimasen**	飲みませんでした **nomimasendeshita**
	死ぬ **shinu**	to die	死にます **shinimasu**	死にました **shinimashita**	死にません **shinimasen**	死にませんでした **shinimasendeshita**
Group 3 Irregular	する **suru**	to do	します **shimasu**	しました **shimashita**	しません **shimasen**	しませんでした **shimasendeshita**
	来る **kuru**	to come	来ます **kimasu**	来ました **kimashita**	来ません **kimasen**	来ませんでした **kimasendeshita**

Past, negative, and past negative

Now we know how to form the ***-masu*** form, let's have a look at its inflections: past, negative, and past negative. It is extremely easy, and the three groups of verbs (including irregular verbs) work exactly the same way.

Past: Replace the す ***su*** part of the ***-masu*** form with した ***shita***. For example:
待ちます ***machimasu*** ("to wait") ⇒ (take off ***-su***) 待ちま ***machima***
⇒ (add ***-shita***) 待ちました ***machimashita*** ("I waited").

Negative: Replace the す ***su*** part of the ***-masu*** form with せん ***sen***. For example:
起きます ***okimasu*** ("to wake up") ⇒ (take off ***-su***) 起きま ***okima***
⇒ (add ***-sen***) 起きません ***okimasen*** ("I don't wake up").

Past negative: Replace the す ***su*** part of the ***-masu*** form with せんでした ***sendeshita***:
貸します ***kashimasu*** ("to lend") ⇒ (take off ***-su***) 貸しま ***kashima***
⇒ (add ***-sendeshita***) 貸しませんでした ***kashimasendeshita*** ("I didn't lend").

漫画例 Manga Examples

As usual, the manga examples in this section give us the opportunity to put into practice what was explained in the previous pages. This time we will see some different *-masu* forms of verbs.

Manga Example 1: Usage of the present tense (1)

We see here the present tense of the verb あげる ***ageru*** ("to give"), that is, あげます ***agemasu***, which belongs to Group 1. Japanese verbs don't have either number or gender, and therefore, as in this panel, when the subject is ***watashi*** ("I"), the verb in the present tense is ***agemasu***. When the subject is ***watashitachi*** ("we"), the present tense remains ***agemasu***, and the same happens with ***kanojo*** ("she"), ***anata*** ("you"), etc. We have chosen the future ("I will give") for the translation, as we thought it more appropriate. In Japanese there is also no specific future tense.

Note: The text in bubbles is usually written from top to bottom, and from left to right. In this case, we find the text written horizontally and from right to left. This is often used when a non-Japanese speaker appears in a manga, and we are offered a "translation" of what he or she is saying.

J.M. Ken Niimura

Fishbone: 私はミスター・ササキに命をあげます
watashi wa misutaa sasaki ni inochi o agemasu
I TOP mister Sasaki IOP life DOP give
I'll give my life for Mr. Sasaki.

Manga Example 2: Usage of the present tense (2)

Guillermo March

Here we have another example of the usage of the present tense. In this case the verb is 守る ***mamoru*** ("to protect"), a Group 2 verb, its ***-masu*** form being 守ります ***mamorimasu***. Thus, to conjugate it, we must replace the last ***-u*** sound with ***-imasu*** and ***mamoru*** becomes ***mamorimasu***. There are no doubts as to which group ***mamoru*** belongs, since it ends in ***-oru***. But it is impossible to know when a verb ending in ***-eru*** or ***-iru*** belongs to Group 1 or 2. In the online Vocabulary Index that you can access via the link on page 9, we indicate which groups verbs belong to when they end in ***-eru*** or ***-iru***.

Hirao:	小林先生、私が守ります!!	はい!
	Kobayashi-sensei, watashi ga mamorimasu!!	***hai!***
	Kobayashi professor, I SP *protect!!*	yes!
	I will protect you, Professor Kobayashi!!	**Yes!!**

Manga Example 3: Usage of the negative (1)

We see in this panel the negative form of the Group 1 verb 負ける ***makeru*** ("to lose") in its ***-masu*** form. The ***-masu*** form in the present tense of ***makeru*** is 負けます ***makemasu***. The negative is formed by replacing す ***su*** with せん ***sen***, no matter what group the verb belongs to. Thus: 負けます ***makemasu*** ⇒ 負けません ***makemasen*** ("not to lose").

The literal translation of this sentence would be "I don't lose," but we have used "going to," for a more natural-sounding translation. This panel also has a good example of the use of the end-of-sentence emphatic particle よ ***yo*** (Lesson 17).

Studio Kōsen

Sawada:	負けませんよ
	makemasen yo
	lose EP
	I'm not going to lose.

Manga Example 4: Usage of the negative (2)

Here is another example of the negative form. This time the verb is 知る ***shiru*** ("to know"), which belongs to Group 2, and, therefore, its ***-masu*** form in the present tense is 知ります ***shirimasu***. The negative we see here is 知りません ***shirimasen***. We already mentioned in the previous lesson that the ***-masu*** form is the formal or polite form, and if we look for an equivalent, the closest we get in English would be addressing somebody using either "Sir," or "Mr.," "Mrs." or "Ms." with their surname. We will seldom see this form in manga, since the dictionary form (which we will see in Lesson 20) is far more common.

Studio Kōsen

Ryōko: 何も知りません
nani mo shirimasen
nothing know
I know nothing.

Manga Example 5: Usage of the past tense

We have here an example of the past tense. The verb is 分かる ***wakaru*** ("to understand," "to know"), from Group 2, its ***-masu*** form being 分かります ***wakarimasu***. To form the past we replace the last ***-su*** with ***-shita***. Thus: 分かります ***wakarimasu*** ⇒ 分かりました ***wakarimashita*** ("I understood"). ***Wakarimashita*** is also often used to express phrases such as: "I see," "Fine," "OK," "Sure, I get you..."

J.M. Ken Niimura

Makie: わかりました...
wakarimashita...
understand...
I see...

Manga Example 6: Usage of the past negative

J.M. Ken Niimura

Johnson: 何も飲みませんでしたよ
nani mo nomimasendeshita yo
nothing drink EP
He didn't drink anything.

With this example of the past negative, we finish our journey through these manga examples of ***-masu*** forms. Here, we have the verb 飲む ***nomu*** ("to drink"), its ***-masu*** form in the present tense being 飲みます ***nomimasu***. As we saw at the start of this lesson, the past negative is formed by replacing the last ***-su*** with ***-sendeshita***. Thus: 飲みます ***nomimasu*** ⇒ 飲みませんでした ***nomimasendeshita***. Although 飲む ***nomu*** is a Group 2 verb, notice that the ***-masu*** forms are exactly the same for all the verbs regardless of group.

Manga Example 7: Usage of the past question form

Guillermo March

Akakage: 私を呼びましたか！？ 殿！？
watashi o yobimashita ka!? Tono!!
I DOP call Q?! Sir!!
Have you called me, sir?!

We will conclude this long lesson with a last example which will show us how to construct questions with all the verbs we have learned. Forming questions is very simple in Japanese: all you need to do is add か ***ka*** at the end of a sentence, and pronounce it with appropriate intonation (Lesson 17).

In this case, we have the verb 呼ぶ ***yobu*** ("to call"), its ***-masu*** form being 呼びます ***yobimasu***. To obtain the ***-masu*** form of a Group 2 verb, all you need to do is replace the last ***-u*** sound with ***-imasu***. The past of ***yobimasu*** is ***yobimashita*** (to obtain the past of a verb in the ***-masu*** form, we replace the last ***-su*** with ***-shita***). And, finally, the question form is made by adding か ***ka***: 呼びましたか ***yobimashita ka?*** "Have you called me?"

Exercises 練習

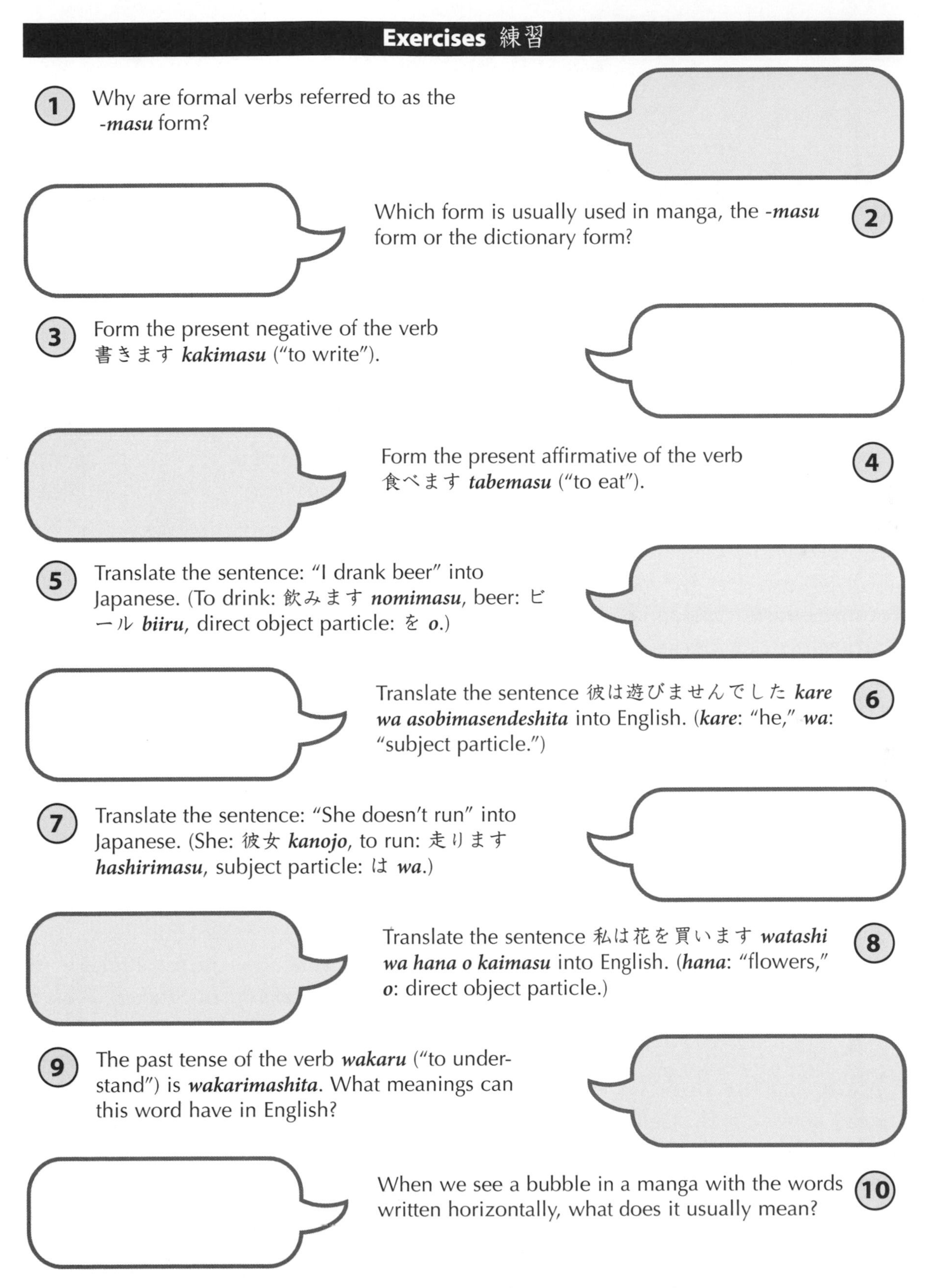

1. Why are formal verbs referred to as the *-masu* form?

2. Which form is usually used in manga, the *-masu* form or the dictionary form?

3. Form the present negative of the verb 書きます ***kakimasu*** ("to write").

4. Form the present affirmative of the verb 食べます ***tabemasu*** ("to eat").

5. Translate the sentence: "I drank beer" into Japanese. (To drink: 飲みます ***nomimasu***, beer: ビール ***biiru***, direct object particle: を ***o***.)

6. Translate the sentence 彼は遊びませんでした ***kare wa asobimasendeshita*** into English. (***kare***: "he," ***wa***: "subject particle.")

7. Translate the sentence: "She doesn't run" into Japanese. (She: 彼女 ***kanojo***, to run: 走ります ***hashirimasu***, subject particle: は ***wa***.)

8. Translate the sentence 私は花を買います ***watashi wa hana o kaimasu*** into English. (***hana***: "flowers," ***o***: direct object particle.)

9. The past tense of the verb ***wakaru*** ("to understand") is ***wakarimashita***. What meanings can this word have in English?

10. When we see a bubble in a manga with the words written horizontally, what does it usually mean?

— Answers to all the exercises can be found online by following the link on page 9. —

Lesson 20 • 第20課

Verbs (2): The Dictionary Form

In Lesson 19 we studied formal verb forms. In this lesson we will look at how to make the informal form of verbs, which is often referred to as the "simple form" or the "dictionary form."

Dictionary form

The "simple form" or "dictionary form" of a verb is used in informal situations, when we talk with friends or family. Because of its colloquial nature, it is the most common verb form in manga. As we have already mentioned, it is called the "dictionary form" because when looking up a verb in dictionaries, the verb will always appear in this form; it would be the equivalent to the infinitive in English.

The special characteristic of this form is that it always ends in ***-u*** (see table). Its past, negative and past negative forms are more complex than the ***-masu*** form, and need to be learned so that you can progress in your Japanese study: subsequent lessons will take for granted that you have completely mastered these verb forms.

The table on the facing page shows the simple forms of the different groups of verbs, as well as rules for forming the past, negative and past negative. Let's get ready to take a closer look.

The three groups

As we mentioned in the previous lesson, there are three groups of verbs:

Group 1: "Invariable" verbs; we will later see the reason for their name.

Group 2: "Variable" verbs. There are five subdivisions.

Group 3: Irregular verbs, which we should learn by heart, because the usual rules don't apply. There are only two irregular verbs in Japanese, する ***suru*** "to do" and 来る ***kuru*** "to come," plus the half-irregular 行く ***iku***, "to go."

A glance at the table

The first column of the table on the facing page shows the verb in the simple present form. Notice how all verbs, whatever their group, end in ***-u***. In Lesson 19 we studied how to obtain the ***-masu*** form of a verb from its infinitive form; you might need to thoroughly review these rules before carrying on.

Let's now study the different verb forms shown in the table, one by one, and at length.

The past tense

Group 1

Notice that verbs in Group 1 always end in ***-iru*** or ***-eru***. To form the past tense of a verb in this group, simply replace the last る ***-ru*** with た ***-ta***. The fact that this conjugation is so simple is why these verbs are known as "invariable": the verb stem doesn't change. For example: 起きる ***okiru*** ("to wake up") ⇒ 起きた ***okita*** ("I woke up," "I have woken up," etc.) Notice how the past form in Japanese (whether formal or informal) is equally equivalent to our past simple ("I woke up"), present perfect ("I have woken up"), and past perfect ("I had woken up"). The only way of deducing the exact meaning is through the context. Japanese verbs may be simple, but they are sometimes ambiguous!

		Simple f.	Meaning	Past	Rule	Negative	Rule	Past negative
Group 1 Invariable		教える ***oshieru***	to teach	教えた ***oshieta***	〜~~る~~た ***–~~ru~~ ta***	教えない ***oshienai***	〜~~る~~ない ***–~~ru~~ nai***	教えなかった ***oshienakatta***
		起きる ***okiru***	to wake up	起きた ***okita***		起きない ***okinai***		起きなかった ***okinakatta***
Group 2 Variable	A	貸す ***kasu***	to lend	貸した ***kashita***	〜~~す~~した ***–~~su~~ shita***	貸さない ***kasanai***	〜~~す~~さない ***–~~su~~ sanai***	貸さなかった ***kasanakatta***
	B	待つ ***matsu***	to wait	待った ***matta***	〜~~つ~~った ***–~~tsu~~ tta***	待たない ***matanai***	〜~~つ~~たない ***–~~tsu~~ tanai***	待たなかった ***matanakatta***
		買う ***kau***	to buy	買った ***katta***	〜~~う~~った ***–~~u~~ tta***	買わない ***kawanai***	〜~~う~~わない ***–~~u~~ wanai***	買わなかった ***kawanakatta***
		帰る ***kaeru***	to return	帰った ***kaetta***	〜~~る~~った ***–~~ru~~ tta***	帰らない ***kaeranai***	〜~~る~~らない ***–~~ru~~ ranai***	帰らなかった ***kaeranakatta***
	C	書く ***kaku***	to write	書いた ***kaita***	〜くいた ***–~~ku~~ ita***	書かない ***kakanai***	〜~~く~~かない ***–~~ku~~ kanai***	書かなかった ***kakanakatta***
	D	急ぐ ***isogu***	to hurry	急いだ ***isoida***	〜ぐいだ ***–~~gu~~ ida***	急がない ***isoganai***	〜~~ぐ~~がない ***–~~gu~~ ganai***	急がなかった ***isoganakatta***
	E	遊ぶ ***asobu***	to play	遊んだ ***asonda***	〜ぶんだ ***–~~bu~~ nda***	遊ばない ***asobanai***	〜~~ぶ~~ばない ***–~~bu~~ banai***	遊ばなかった ***asobanakatta***
		飲む ***nomu***	to drink	飲んだ ***nonda***	〜~~む~~んだ ***–~~mu~~ nda***	飲まない ***nomanai***	〜~~む~~まない ***–~~mu~~ manai***	飲まなかった ***nomanakatta***
		死ぬ ***shinu***	to die	死んだ ***shinda***	〜~~ぬ~~んだ ***–~~nu~~ nda***	死なない ***shinanai***	〜~~ぬ~~なない ***–~~nu~~ nanai***	死ななかった ***shinanakatta***
Group 3 Irregular		する ***suru***	to do	した ***shita***	Irregular verbs: there is no rule	しない ***shinai***	*Irregular verbs: there is no rule*	しなかった ***shinakatta***
		来る ***kuru***	to come	来た ***kita***		来ない ***konai***		来なかった ***konakatta***

Group 2

The conjugation of the verbs in this group depends on which of the five subdivisions they belong to, which is determined by their last syllable. Check the table for examples.

A) Verbs ending in す ***-su***. Replace ***-su*** with した ***-shita***.

B) Verbs ending in つ ***-tsu***, う ***-u*** or る ***-ru***. Always replace this last syllable with った ***-tta***. Be careful! As we mentioned in Lesson 19, there are verbs which end in ***-eru*** or ***-iru*** in both Groups 1 and 2, and this can cause confusion. You can only tell if a verb ending in ***-eru*** or ***-iru*** corresponds to Group 1 or 2 by committing it to memory or by looking it up in the online Vocabulary Index accessible via the link on page 9.

C) Verbs ending in く ***-ku***. Replace this last syllable with いた ***-ita***. Be careful! The past form of the verb 行く ***iku*** "to go" is 行った ***itta*** and not ***iita***. This is the only exception.

D) Verbs ending in ぐ ***-gu***. Replace this last syllable with いだ ***-ida***.

E) Verbs ending in ぶ ***-bu***, む ***-mu*** and ぬ ***-nu***. Replace the last syllable with んだ ***-nda***.

The negative

Group 1

To obtain the simple negative form of the verbs in Group 1, replace the last る ***-ru*** of the simple form with ない ***-nai***, for example:

食べる ***taberu*** ("to eat") ⇒ 食べない ("to not eat").

Group 2

As a general rule, replace the last ***u*** sound of the simple form with ***a*** and add ***-nai***, for example:

飲む ***nomu*** ("to drink") ⇒ 飲ま ***noma*** ⇒ 飲まない ***nomanai*** ("to not drink")

歩く ***aruku*** ("to walk") ⇒ 歩か ***aruka*** ⇒ 歩かない ***arukanai*** ("to not walk").

Pay attention to verbs ending in つ ***-tsu***, as they don't change into ***-tsanai*** but ***-tanai***, for example, 待つ ***matsu*** ("to wait") ⇒ 待たない ***matanai*** ("to not wait"). Pay attention also to verbs ending in う ***-u***, where ***-u*** is replaced with ***-wa***, for example, 洗う ***arau*** ("to wash") ⇒ 洗わない ***arawanai*** ("to not wash").

The past negative form

Finally, we will study the past negative form, the simplest of all, since there is no difference whatsoever among the groups. We just need to know the simple negative form of any verb, whatever the group, and we obtain the past negative by simply replacing the last い ***-i*** in the negative with かった ***-katta***, for example:

喜ぶ ***yorokobu*** "to be glad" ⇒ negative 喜ばない ***yorokobanai*** ("I'm not glad") ⇒ past negative 喜ばなかった ***yorokobanakatta*** ("I wasn't glad" / "I haven't been glad," etc.).

漫画例 Manga Examples

Let's now use some examples taken from real Japanese manga to see how Japanese verbs are conjugated in their dictionary form or simple form, the most common verb form to use when speaking with friends and family.

Manga Example 1: Usage of the present (1)

We start the manga examples with a panel that shows the present tense of the dictionary form of the verb 始まる ***hajimaru*** "to start." This verb belongs to Group 2 (variable), and, therefore, its ***-masu*** form (Lesson 19) is 始まります ***hajimarimasu***.

Notes: Notice how Mariko uses her own name to talk about herself: She says "Mariko's day starts now" and not "my day starts now," as one would expect. The usage of one's own name to refer to oneself is characteristic of the speech of small children and some young women (never men), and it gives the speaker a "childish" image that some people consider cute or lovable.

The sound さあさあ ***saa saa*** used by Mariko in the second bubble conveys an idea of haste or impatience, so its translation as "Here we go!" sounds appropriate.

Mariko:	まり子の今日は今からはじまるよ。	さあさあ
	Mariko no kyō wa ima kara hajimaru yo.	***saa saa***
	Mariko POP today TOP now from start EP	come now
	Mariko's day starts now!	**Here we go!**

Manga Example 2: Usage of the present (2)

Here we have a second example of the usage of a verb in the present simple form: 死ぬ ***shinu*** "to die," which belongs to Group 2. Its ***-masu*** form is 死にます ***shinimasu***. As you can see, we have translated Skunk's sentence using the form "are just about to...," which indicates a possible future. As we mentioned in Manga Example 1 in Lesson 19, the future tense doesn't exist in Japanese, and consequently, most of the time the present form of the verb is used to express it.

Note: Use this example as an opportunity to review the usage of the second person pronoun お前 ***omae*** ("you," Lesson 7) and the emphatic end-of-sentence particle ぞ ***zo*** (Lesson 17), both very characteristic of vulgar male language.

Skunk: これから死ぬぞ、お前
kore kara shinu zo, omae
this from die EP, you
You are just about to die!

Manga Example 3: Usage of the past tense (1)

We see here the verb 酔う ***you*** "to feel drunk" in the past tense of the dictionary form. Since the verb ends in う ***-u*** (Group 2, ***-masu*** form 酔います ***yoimasu***), the past is formed by replacing the last ***-u*** of the infinitive with った ***-tta***. Thus: 酔う ***you*** ⇒ 酔 ***yo*** ⇒ 酔った ***yotta*** ("I am drunk," "I have become drunk," or even "I'm gonna puke").

Freegh: どうしたの？ガルエール
dōshita no? Garueeru
what is the matter? Gharuel
What's wrong, Gharuel?

Gharuel: 酔った
yotta
feel drunk
I'm gonna puke.

Manga Example 4: Usage of the past tense (2)

In this panel you can see the past form of one of the two irregular verbs in Japanese: 来る ***kuru***, "to come." As you can see in the table on page 171 and in this example, the past tense of this verb is 来た ***kita***.

Guillermo March

Irregular verbs, just as their name implies, don't follow the usual rules and, therefore, we must learn their different forms by heart. Still, there are only two irregular verbs in Japanese, whereas in English there are lots more. Remember there is also a half-irregular verb, 行く ***iku*** "to go," its past tense being 行った ***itta*** and not ***iita*** (however, its other conjugations follow the rules, and, therefore, we can't consider it a fully irregular verb).

Rooster: トウモロコシ村に朝がきたぞーい！
tōmorokoshi mura ni asa ga kita zo-i!
corn village PP morning SP come EP
Morning has come to Corn Village!

Manga Example 5: Usage of the negative

This panel offers us the negative form of the verb 行く ***iku*** "to go," which, as we have just seen, has an irregular past form. Its negative form, though, follows the rules for Group 2 verbs, to which it belongs. Therefore, we just need to replace the last ***u*** sound of the infinitive form with ***a*** and add ***-nai***. In this case, 行く ***iku*** ⇒ 行か ***ika*** ⇒ 行かない ***ikanai*** ("to not go").

We have mentioned many times that the verb forms in Japanese are the same regardless of person and number. In this example, Rik says 行かない ***ikanai*** meaning "he doesn't go," but we would use exactly the same verb from to say "I don't go," "we don't go," etc.

Guillermo March

Rik: これであまり遠くへ行かない
kore de amari tooku e ikanai
this IOP not much far DOP go
With this, he won't go very far.

Manga Example 6: Usage of the past negative

Jūbei: 十郎にはできなかったぜ
Jūrō ni wa dekinakatta ze
Jūrō IOP top, be able to EP
Jūrō couldn't do it.

Here we have the past negative form of the verb できる ***dekiru***, "to be able to": できなかった ***dekinakatta***. To conjugate this form you have to replace the last ***i*** in the negative form with ***-katta***, like this: できる ***dekiru*** ⇒ negative できない ***dekinai*** ("I can't") ⇒ past negative できなかった ***dekinakatta*** ("I couldn't"). The conjugations of verbs in the simple form seem complex, but it is just a matter of getting used to them. You will soon find yourself handling verbs with great ease.

Note: We must remind you that verbs in their simple form are strictly used in colloquial or vulgar registers, so you must use them cautiously, always taking into account the status of the person you are talking to.

Manga Example 7: The negative as a question

竜次くん
いっしょに
入らない？
Studio Kōsen

Aya: 竜次くん いっしょに入らない？
Ryūji-kun isshoni hairanai?
Ryūji (SUF.) together enter?
Shall we bathe together, Ryūji?

We will conclude with an example of a negative usage of the verb that can cause misunderstandings. Sometimes, the negative in Japanese is used to make questions, just as we do when we say "Don't you feel like having a coffee?" Here, we have 入らない ***hairanai***, the negative of 入る ***hairu*** "to enter," "get into." In this context, they are talking about "getting into the bath," the word "bath" having been omitted. In English, a better translation would be "bathe." The literal translation of Aya's sentence is something like: "We don't enter together, Ryūji?" Be careful with these kinds of question negatives: it is easy to take them for denials, when they are really suggestions.

Exercises 練習

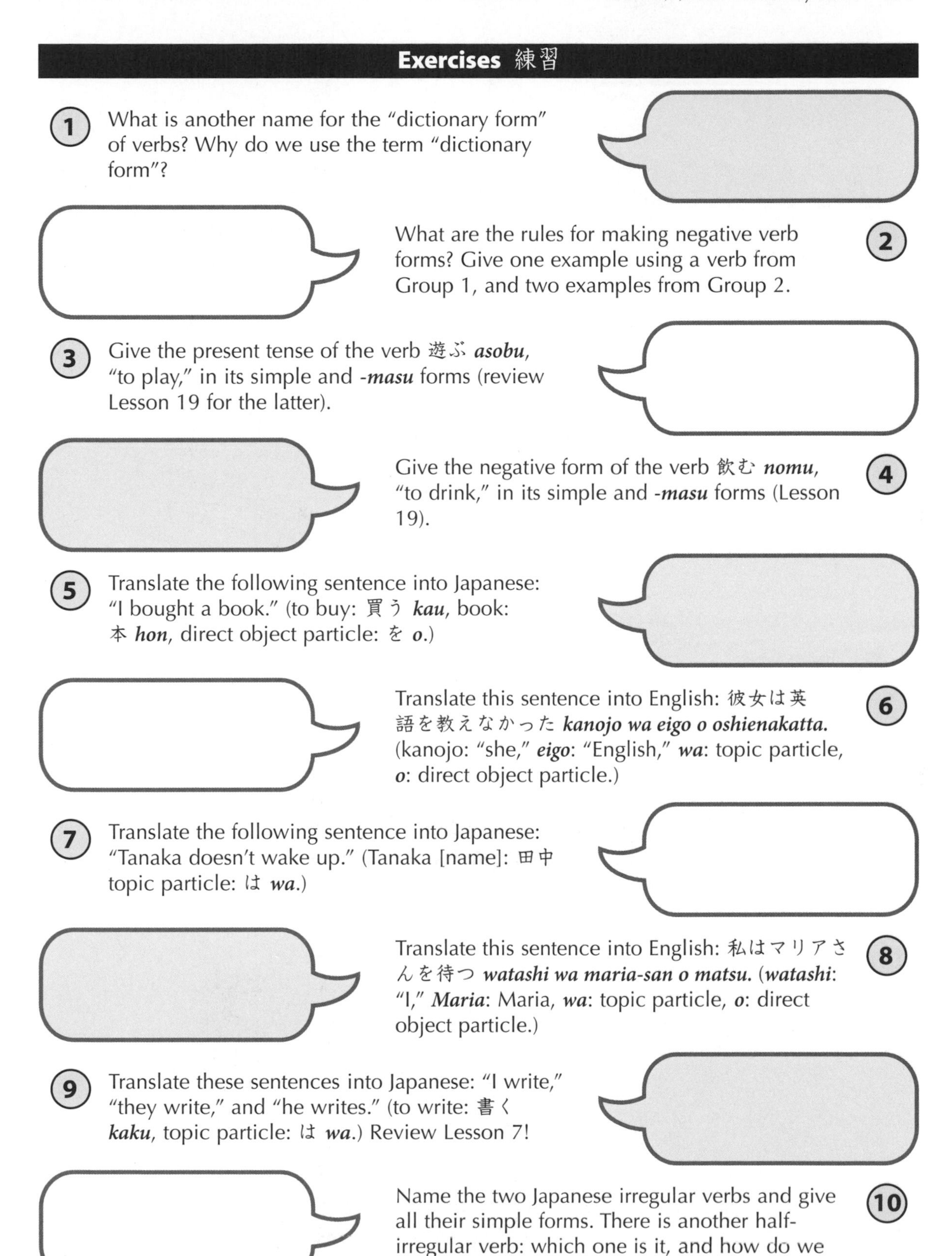

1. What is another name for the "dictionary form" of verbs? Why do we use the term "dictionary form"?

2. What are the rules for making negative verb forms? Give one example using a verb from Group 1, and two examples from Group 2.

3. Give the present tense of the verb 遊ぶ ***asobu***, "to play," in its simple and ***-masu*** forms (review Lesson 19 for the latter).

4. Give the negative form of the verb 飲む ***nomu***, "to drink," in its simple and ***-masu*** forms (Lesson 19).

5. Translate the following sentence into Japanese: "I bought a book." (to buy: 買う ***kau***, book: 本 ***hon***, direct object particle: を ***o***.)

6. Translate this sentence into English: 彼女は英語を教えなかった ***kanojo wa eigo o oshienakatta.*** (kanojo: "she," ***eigo***: "English," ***wa***: topic particle, ***o***: direct object particle.)

7. Translate the following sentence into Japanese: "Tanaka doesn't wake up." (Tanaka [name]: 田中 topic particle: は ***wa***.)

8. Translate this sentence into English: 私はマリアさんを待つ ***watashi wa maria-san o matsu.*** (***watashi***: "I," ***Maria***: Maria, ***wa***: topic particle, ***o***: direct object particle.)

9. Translate these sentences into Japanese: "I write," "they write," and "he writes." (to write: 書く ***kaku***, topic particle: は ***wa***.) Review Lesson 7!

10. Name the two Japanese irregular verbs and give all their simple forms. There is another half-irregular verb: which one is it, and how do we conjugate it?

— Answers to all the exercises can be found online by following the link on page 9. —

RAKUJŌ
第四章
ユキはどこにいるの？
ユキ様は「外へ出ます」と言いました。
スウ…
わかった。ありがとう。
そうですよ、ヨド様。
彼のアーミーはヤスのアーミーと基地の外で戦うか？
はい!!! 行くぜ!!
皆、勇気を出すよ！戦うぞ！
ガコッ
ガコンガコンガコン

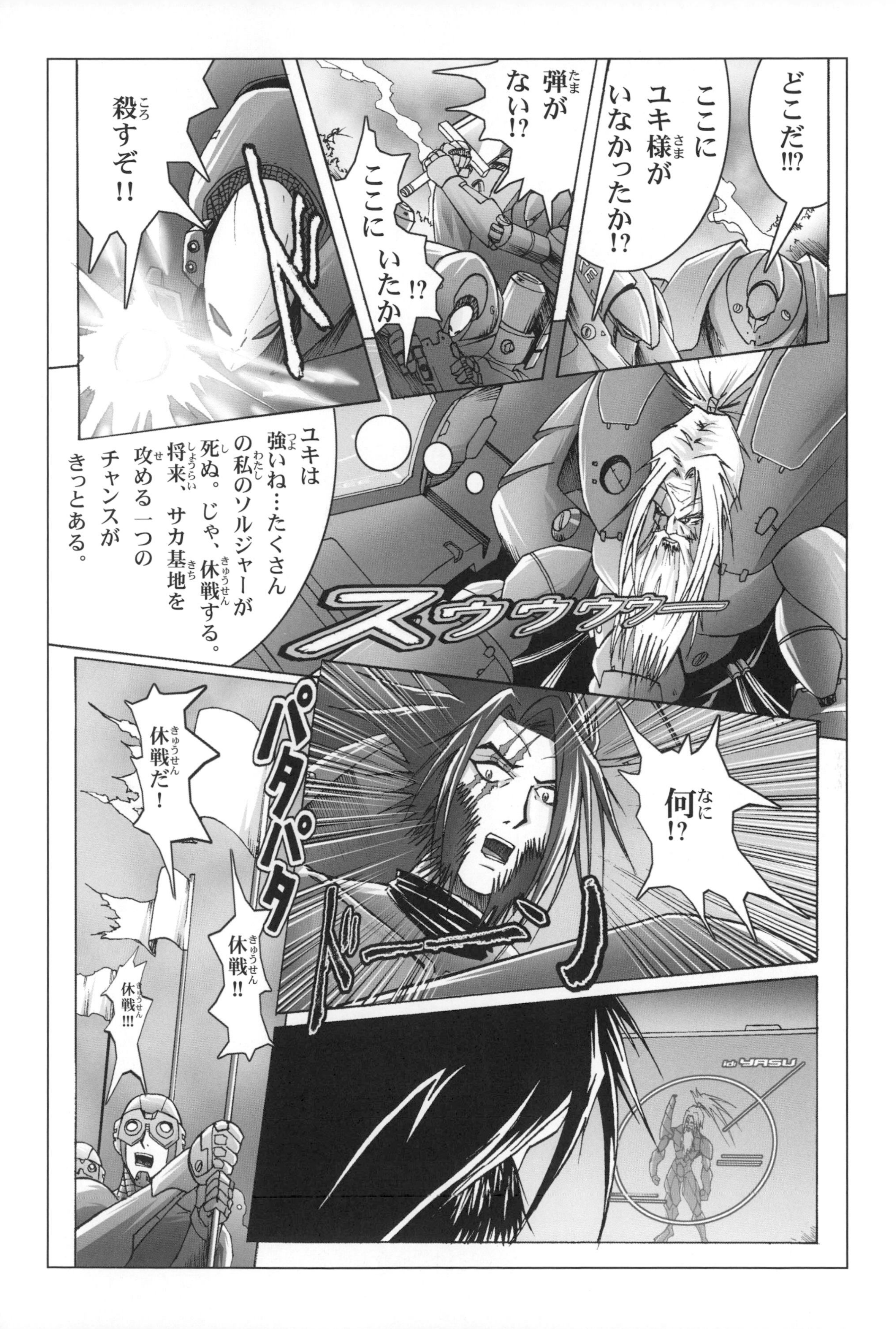
どこだ!!?
ここにユキ様がいなかったか!?
弾がない!?
ここにいたか!?
殺すぞ!!
ド
ユキは強いね…たくさんの私のソルジャーが死ぬ。じゃ、休戦する。将来、サカ基地を攻める一つのチャンスがきっとある。
スウウウウー
何!?
パタパタ
ドーーン
休戦だ!
休戦!!
休戦!!!
id: YASU

はい。
ヨドに会えるか？
話すわ
ヨド様！ヤス様がここにいます。彼と話しませんか？
ドンドン
ユキのアーミーはとても強いよ。感動した！あの男には勇気がある！
どうして戦争をやめましたの？
休戦の条件を伝えるぞ。聞かないか？
どうしてここに来ましたか？

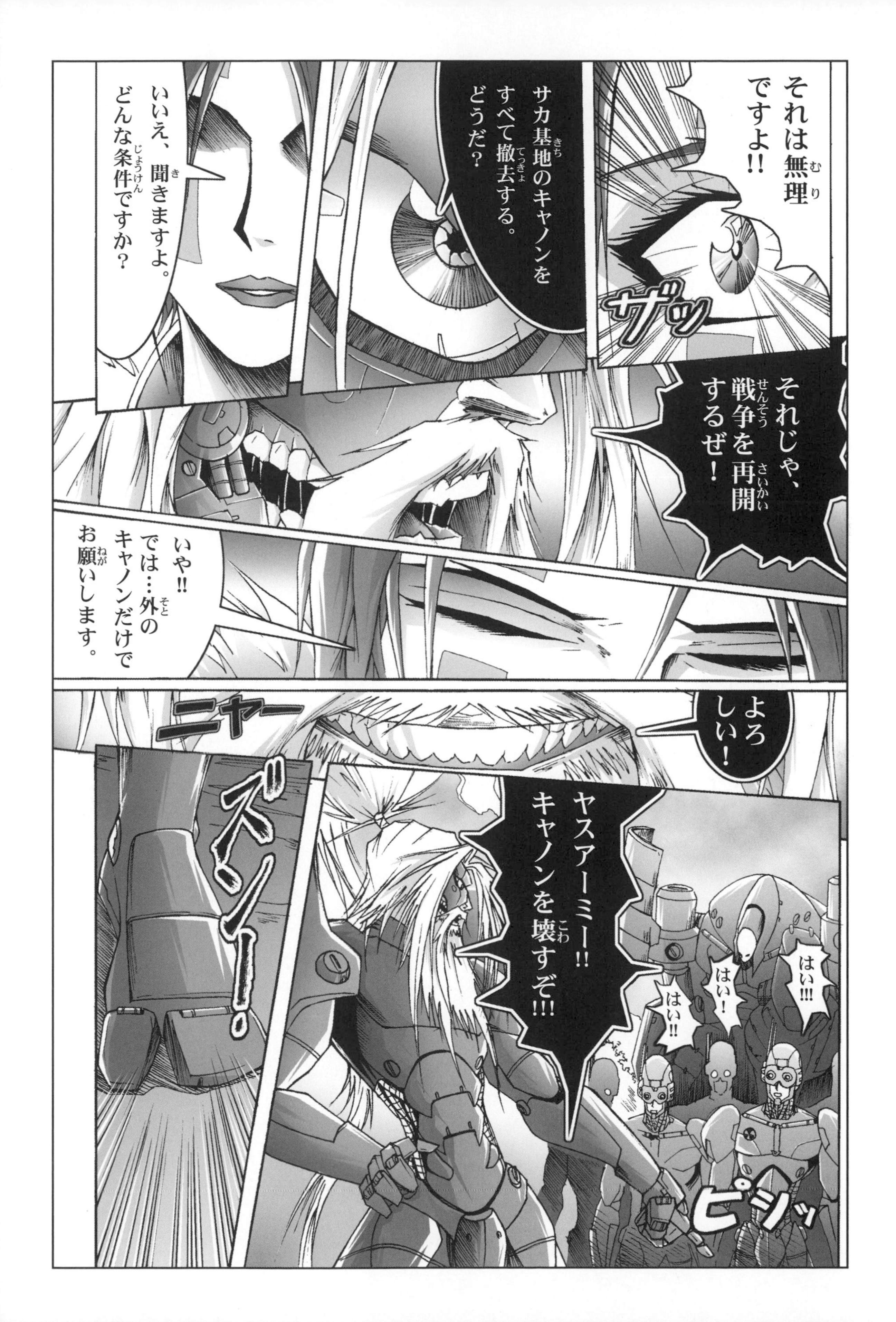
それは無理ですよ!!
ザッ
サカ基地のキャノンをすべて撤去する。どうだ？
いいえ、聞きますよ。どんな条件ですか？
それじゃ、戦争を再開するぜ！
いや!! では…外のキャノンだけでお願いします。
よろしい！
ニヤー
ヤスアーミー!! キャノンを壊すぞ!!!
はい!!!
はい！
はい!!
ズン！
ピシッ

Review for Lessons 16–20

Answers to all the review exercises can be found online by following the link on page 9.

RAKUJŌ – New vocabulary 新しい単語

どこ	where?	きっと	surely
出(で)る	to go out (Group 1)	会(あ)える	to be able to meet
戦(たたか)う	to fight	話(はな)す	to speak
そうです	that's right	どうして	why?
勇気(ゆうき)	courage, bravery	やめる	to stop, to abandon
出(だ)す	to take out	感動(かんどう)	to be impressed
弾(たま)	bullet	条件(じょうけん)	condition
ソルジャー	soldier	伝(つた)える	to convey (Group 1)
休戦(きゅうせん)	truce	聞(き)く	to listen
将来(しょうらい)	future	撤去(てっきょ)する	to dismantle
攻(せ)める	to attack	再開(さいかい)する	to resume
チャンス	chance	よろしい	good, all right (formal)

1. What verb form (simple or formal) does Yodo use when she speaks with Yasu? How about Yasu to Yodo? Why do you think they use these verb forms toward each other?

2. Explain why one of the fighting soldiers uses the verb いる in his sentence ここにいたか!? whereas another soldier uses the verb ある in his sentence 弾(たま)がない!

3. Change Yuki's sentence ヨド様(さま)!ヤス様はここにいます。ヤス様(さま)と話(はな)しませんか?into the simple form. Why does he use the formal form in this context?

4. Write the forms of the two verbs as indicated below:

話(はな)す	simple present affirmative	伝(つた)える
____________	simple past affirmative	____________
____________	simple present negative	____________

________________	simple past negative	________________
________________	formal present affirmative	________________
________________	formal past affirmative	________________
________________	formal present negative	________________
________________	formal past negative	________________

5. At the beginning of this episode, what does the particle の mean in Yodo's sentence ユキはどこにいるの?

6. 皆(みな)、勇気(ゆうき)を出(だ)すよ！戦(たたか)うぞ！What do the end-of-sentence particles よ and ぞ mean in these words uttered by Yuki before his soldiers?

7. Explain the function of の and を in the sentence 休戦(きゅうせん)の条件(じょうけん)を伝(つた)えるぞ.

8. ユキ様(さま)は「外(そと)へ出(で)ます」と言いました. Explain the function of the particles へ and と in this sentence.

9. Fill in the chart choosing words from the box below.

animals						
vegetables						
fruit						
stationery	ボールペン					
cutlery						
stores						
weather						

~~ボールペン~~	フォーク	もも	はえ	かぼちゃ	りんご	きり
からす	本屋(や)	八百屋(やおや)	雨(あめ)	はし	雪(ゆき)	皿(さら)
バナナ	くじら	たまねぎ	ナイフ	しか	くつ屋(や)	肉屋(にくや)
梅雨(ばいう)	ふで	ピーマン	パン屋(や)	馬(うま)	紙(かみ)	レタス
じゃがいも	コップ	あり	嵐(あらし)	切手(きって)	すいか	みかん

10. Draw a line to match each noun to a verb it could be used with.

ベッド	飲(の)む	日本語(ご)	教(おし)える
手紙(てがみ)	買(か)う	ご飯(はん)	呼(よ)ぶ
ボール	起(お)きる	本	食(た)べる
お茶(ちゃ)	書(か)く	人	帰(かえ)る
ケーキ屋(や)	遊(あそ)ぶ	家(いえ)	書(か)く

11. Which of the existence verbs, ある or いる is the most appropriate in the following sentences? What meaning (to be, there is/are, to have) do they have in each case?

a) 私は車(くるま)が ___ある___。 (meaning: to have)
b) 外(そと)にかえるが二匹(にひき) ________。 (meaning:)
c) ジョナサンくんは教室(きょうしつ)に ________。 (meaning:)
d) テーブルの上(うえ)にめがねが ________。 (meaning:)
e) トモコちゃん、えんぴつが ________ の？ (meaning:)
f) 庭(にわ)に木が四本 ________。 (meaning:)

12. Fill in the gaps by choosing an appropriate word from the box below.

a) 私は___家(いえ)___へ帰る。
b) アキラくんとマヤちゃんは山へ________。
c) 私はオレンジを________。
d) テレビの上(うえ)に ________ がいる。
e) 彼女(かのじょ)はコーヒーを ________。
f) ミツヒコさんは________で________を飲む。
g) 本田(ほんだ)さんは本を ________。
h) テレビの上に________がある。

読(よ)む	猫(ねこ)	行(い)く	飲(の)む	お金(かね)	スプーン	~~家(いえ)~~	スープ	食(た)べる

13. If the verb is incorrect in meaning, change it to a more appropriate one.

食べます

a) 彼はなしを~~飲みます~~。

b) 犬はあそこになかった。

c) 私はざっしを食べた。

d) 車で東京へ買った

e) あの山に川はいません。

f) さめは海にない

g) あなたはきれいな漢字を急いだ。

h) 先生は私に日本語を遊びます。

14. Indicate the level of formality of the following sentences (formal, colloquial, or vulgar), and say, as well, whether the speaker is a man, a woman, or whether it could be either.

a) あそこにとらがいたぞ！ (vulgar | man)

b) 青山さん、図書館へ行きますか？ ( )

c) そうなの？へー、おもしろいわ。 ( )

d) すみません、あれはオレの車だよ。 ( )

e) ここでは日本語を教えますね。 ( )

f) すしを食べなかったぜ！ ( )

15. Fill in the gaps with the correct grammatical particle.

a) これ＿＿私＿＿自転車です。

1. を 2. は 3. の 4. で
1. の 2. に 3. を 4. へ

b) アキオさんは明日アメリカ＿＿行く＿＿言いました。

1. で 2. は 3. と 4. へ
1. に 2. と 3. は 4. を

c) マリコちゃんは家＿＿紙＿＿漢字＿＿書いた。

1. へ 2. に 3. で 4. が
1. へ 2. に 3. で 4. が
1. を 2. と 3. に 4. の

16. Complete the following sentences with the correct particles.

a) 先生____きれいな教室____いました。
b) 今、僕____頭____いたいです。
c) 先生____学生____スペイン語____教えました。
d) 今日は病院____自転車____行く。
e) テーブルの上____えんぴつ____ボールペンがあります。
f) 三時間前、私は彼女____手紙____読んだ。
g) だれ____本____あげましたか？｜高田さん____あげたよ。
h) 「君、家____トモくん____遊ぶの？」____彼は言った。

17. Correct any grammatical particle mistakes in the following sentences.

a) 私と名前はジョナサンです。
b) 彼女は家でいる。しかし、教室に勉強する。
c) フミコさんは電車にここを来ますよ。
d) 私はレストランがケーキの食べる。

18. Make grammatically correct sentences using the following prompts:

a) ここ｜います｜が｜あり｜に ______________________
b) です｜車｜青い｜は｜の｜私 ______________________
c) 庭｜遊んだ｜先生｜で｜と｜は｜私 ______________________
d) りんご｜を｜あなた｜食べました｜か｜は ______________________
e) 私｜で｜へ｜電車｜帰る｜家｜は ______________________
f) 彼｜家｜か｜しずか（な）｜の｜は｜です ______________________

19. Complete the table by following the example in the first two lines.

います	いました	いる	いた
いません	いませんでした	いない	いなかった
あります		ある	あった
	ありませんでした		
	食(た)べました		食(た)べた
食(た)べません		食(た)べない	
呼(よ)びます		呼(よ)ぶ	
	呼(よ)びませんでした		
			持(も)った
持(も)ちません		持(も)たない	
		守(まも)る	

20. Correct any errors in the verb forms in the following sentences.

a) あの鳥(とり)はケーキを食(た)べないかった。

b) 二時間前(にじかんまえ)、彼女(かのじょ)の家(いえ)へ行きます。

c) ここでやさいを買(か)あない。

d) 明日(あした)、社長(しゃちょう)とコーヒーを飲(の)まなかった。

Kanji

見 (131)	行 (100)	来 (101)	帰 (123)	買 (117)	売 (118)	教 (134)	食 (150)	飲 (151)	持 (115)	待 (116)
思 (132)	出 (69)	入 (70)	上 (60)	下 (61)	右 (62)	左 (63)	中 (64)	外 (145)	間 (91)	石 (45)

21. Practice writing the kanji below. Find the stroke order in the online Kanji Compilation section via the link on page 9.

来										
買										
食										
右										
待										

22. Link each kanji with its most common reading (usually, the ***kun'yomi***).

見る	みぎ	外	おもう
右	みる	思う	くる
売る	はいる	買う	なか
入る	いし	来る	そと
石	うる	出る	でる
左	ひだり	中	かう

23. Choose the correct kanji or kanji combination for each reading.

a) かえる
1. 掃える　2. 帰る　3. 帰える　4. 掃る

b) ばいしゅん
1. 買春　2. 買秋　3. 売秋　4. 売春

c) もつ
1. 待つ　2. 特つ　3. 持つ　4. 時つ

d) いんしょく
1. 食飯　2. 飲食　3. 食飯　4. 食飲

24. Choose the correct reading for each kanji or kanji combination.

a) 来月、わたしの家(いえ)へ来ますか？

来月：1. らいげつ　2. らいがつ　3. くるつき　4. くつき

来ます：1. いきます　2. きます　3. くます　4. かえります

b) あの金持ちは大きい教室(きょうしつ)に入った。

金持ち：1. かねまち　2. きんまち　3. かねもち　4. きんもち

入る：1. はった　2. いった　3. でった　4. はいった

c) 今、時間がない。後でその見本を読(よ)みますよ。

時間：1. じかん　2. しかん　3. じがん　4. しがん

見本：1. みき　2. けんき　3. みほん　4. けんほん

25. Give the hiragana readings of the following words and their meaning. (**Note:** The words marked with an asterisk appear in kanji tables studied in previous lessons.)

出る	________	________	右	________	________
石	________	________	教える	________	________
行う	________	________	下がる	________	________
*人間	________	________	*朝食	________	________

26. Write the following words in kanji, and give their meanings.

うえ	________	________	なか	________	________
いく	________	________	あいだ	________	________
がいじん	________	________	おもう	________	________
*ちゅうねん	________	________	*やかん	________	________

Lesson 21 • 第21課

The Family

In this lesson we will take a breather by slowing down on the grammar and theory, and focusing on some useful vocabulary to do with the family. The Japanese language has some special characteristics as far as family relationships are concerned, so study this lesson carefully.

My family

We have drawn two family trees to help you understand the vocabulary of family relationships. The one below is entitled "My family" and the one on the facing page "Tanaka-san's family." This is because Japanese uses two different names for each relative, depending on whether they belong to one's own family or to someone else's. Generally, words used to talk about one's own relatives are shorter. You should know both by heart; it is very important.

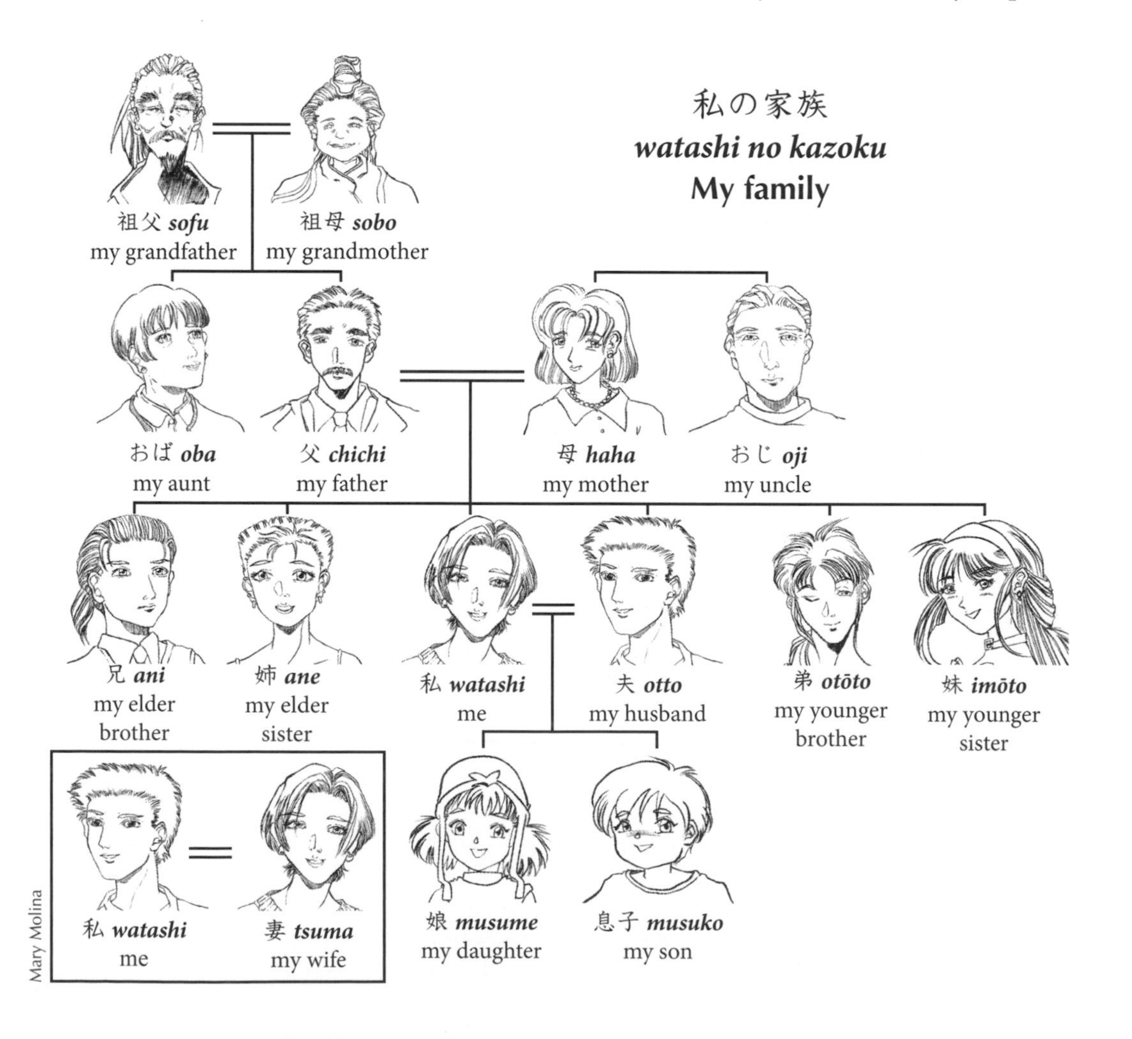

Starting with one's own family, thoroughly study the words in the family tree. The only peculiarity here is that Japanese has a different word for each brother and sister. We have 兄 ***ani***, "elder brother," 姉 ***ane***, "elder sister," 弟 ***otōto***, "younger brother," and 妹 ***imōto***, "younger sister."

Somebody else's family

In the family tree below we have the words we use when talking about somebody else's family: all of these words are imbued with respect, relating to the extreme respect Japanese have for other people, and, consequently, for their families. Using the words meant for one's own family when talking about someone else's family is a serious mistake in Japanese and shows a lack of respect. Generally speaking, the words for the members of someone else's family are longer and they have the suffix for respect, さん ***-san*** (Lesson 15).

The exceptions, which don't appear in the table, are いとこ ***itoko*** ("cousin"), おい ***oi*** ("nephew"), and めい ***mei*** ("niece"), which, curiously enough, are exactly the same, whether we are talking about our own family or someone else's.

An example

Have a look at these two sample sentences:

(私の)弟は先生です	(彼の)弟さんは先生です
(watashi no) otōto wa sensei desu	***(kare no) otōtosan wa sensei desu***
My younger brother is a teacher.	**His younger brother is a teacher.**

As you can see, we have used the word ***otōto*** in the first example and the word ***otōtosan*** in the second one. They both mean "younger brother": The difference lies in that the first example refers to my brother, whereas the second one refers to someone else's brother.

Generally it is clear from the context whose family member we are talking about, which is why we have placed the possessive 私の ***watashi no***, "my," and 彼の ***kare no***, "his," in brackets. In natural Japanese we don't usually specify this information.

However...

In modern Japanese, there is a tendency to use those words meant for somebody else's family to refer to members of one's own family who are older than the speaker. Thus, hearing お父さんは警察官だ ***otōsan wa keisatsukan da***, "My father is a policeman" instead of 父は警察官だ ***chichi wa keisatsukan da*** is very normal, although both forms are valid. Be careful, because the same doesn't happen when referring to younger relatives: one will never say 娘さんは学生だ ***musumesan wa gakusei da***, but 娘は学生だ ***musume wa gakusei da*** "My daughter is a student."

Some speakers, especially children, change the さん ***-san*** suffix for ちゃん ***-chan*** (Lesson 15) to make it more familiar, and sometimes they even leave out the honorific prefix お ***o-***. Thus, we have お母ちゃん ***okaachan*** or 母ちゃん ***kaachan*** for "mommy," お父ちゃん ***otōchan*** or 父ちゃん ***tōchan*** for "daddy"; おじいちゃん ***ojiichan*** or じいちゃん ***jiichan*** for "grandpa"; and おばあちゃん ***obaachan*** or ばあちゃん ***baachan*** for "grandma," among others.

Mothers-in-law, fathers-in-law, husbands and wives

The family trees in this lesson don't feature the "in-laws." Words for these family members are seldom used. Usually, the son-in-law and the daughter-in-law call their mother-in-law お母さん ***okaasan*** ("mother") and their father-in-law お父さん ***otōsan*** ("father") or, sometimes, when they are very close, they even call them by their first name plus ***-san***. The father or mother in law will usually call their sons or daughters-in-law by their first name plus ***-san***. Finally, there are several words used to refer to one's own husband or wife. To refer to one's husband we have旦那 ***danna***, 主人 ***shujin*** and 夫 ***otto***. ***Shujin*** literally means "the main person," so many women prefer using ***otto*** or ***danna***. For one's own wife, we have 家内 ***kanai*** ("inside home"), 女房 ***nyōbō*** ("woman in the room"), and 妻 ***tsuma***. In this case, the most politically correct option seems to be ***tsuma***.

漫画例 Manga Examples

In Japanese, the words used to name family members are not always straightforward. Let's see some examples taken from real manga panels to illustrate what you have learned in this lesson and offer up some other possibilities.

Manga Example 1: When talking about someone else's family

Guillermo March

We can see here how to refer to somebody else's relatives with the words you can find in the family tree on page 191. Also, this panel introduces two new words: ***okosan*** and ***omagosan***. The first can be translated as "son," "daughter," or "child," and the second as "grandson," "granddaughter," or "grandchild." When talking about one's own grandchild we use 孫 ***mago***.

Teru: お子さん…いや、お孫さんですか？
okosan... iya, omagosan desu ka?
child... no, grandchild be Q?
Your son? No... Your grandson?

Manga Example 2: Addressing relatives affectionately

Here is a sample of the tendency in colloquial Japanese to address one's older relatives with respectful terms usually used for someone else's family. Changing the suffix ***-san*** for ***-chan*** is quite frequent, as shown here with the word お兄ちゃん ***oniichan***, "elder brother," especially when the speaker is a child or a young girl.

J.M. Ken Niimura

Rie: お兄ちゃんに狙いをつけたの
oniichan ni nerai o tsuketa no
elder brother IOP aim DOP take EP
I took aim at my brother...

Manga Example 3: Alternative words

In some cases there several different words that can be used to talk about one's closest family members, as in the names for "husband" and "wife" we saw earlier in this lesson. We have here the word おふくろ ***ofukuro***, used by men to talk about their mothers; the equivalent word to talk about fathers is 親父 ***oyaji***. Also very common are 父親 ***chichioya***, "father" and 母親 ***hahaoya***, "mother," which have rather formal connotations. The words パパ ***papa*** and ママ ***mama*** are also used in Japanese, meaning "mommy" and "daddy."

J.M. Ken Niimura

In this panel there is also the word 叔母さん ***obasan*** "aunt." Curiously enough, depending on the kanji used to write it, this word can mean "father / mother's younger sister" (叔母さん) or "father/mother's elder sister" (伯母さん).

Kazu: おふくろと叔母さんのことか？
ofukuro to obasan no koto ka?
mother and aunt POP about Q?
Is it about my mother and my aunt?

Manga Example 4: When talking to or about a stranger

Words like "elder sister" are often used to refer to young women whose name we don't know, as in this example. The younger girl, Aiko, addresses the girl who is older than her as お姉さん ***oneesan***, even though she isn't actually her sister. Other words used with the same intention, that is, to refer to people whose name we don't know, are お兄さん ***oniisan*** (for a young man), おじさん ***ojisan*** (for a 40–50 year-old man), ***obasan*** (for a 40–50 year-old woman), おじいさん ***ojiisan*** (for an old man), or おばあさん ***obaasan*** (for an old woman).

Studio Kōsen

Aiko: あ…お姉さん 大丈夫？
a... oneesan daijōbu?
oh... elder sister be well?
Ah... are you okay?

Exercises 練習

1. Why are different words used in Japanese to refer to one's own family members and to somebody else's?

2. What's the name for one's own wife? And somebody else's wife? How about the equivalent name for the husband in both cases?

3. English only distinguishes between "brother" and "sister." How about Japanese? What are the eight words we can use?

4. What word do we use to talk about one's own uncle? And somebody else's uncle?

5. What word do we use to talk about one's own cousin? And somebody else's cousin?

6. How do we translate the word めい ***mei*** into English? Is this one's own relative or somebody else's?

7. Translate into formal Japanese: "My father is a doctor." (I: 私 ***watashi***, doctor: 医者 ***isha***, to be: です ***desu***, possessive particle: の ***no***.)

8. Translate the following sentence into formal Japanese: "Kumi's father is a doctor." (Kumi: 久美 girl's name.)

9. Name at least three words we can use to refer to one's own father.

10. What three meanings can the word お姉さん ***oneesan*** have?

— Answers to all the exercises can be found online by following the link on page 9. —

Lesson 22 • 第22課

Adverbs

Having seen pronouns (Lesson 7), nouns (Lesson 11), adjectives (Lessons 13 and 14), grammatical particles (Lesson 16), and verbs (Lessons 18, 19 and 20), we are now going to study another part of speech: adverbs.

What are adverbs?

As you probably know, adverbs are words which modify the meaning of verbs or adjectives. Words such as "today," "extremely," or "very" belong to this category of parts of speech.

Adverbs in Japanese, can be a little tricky to use correctly as there are many adverbs of many kinds, although at this stage you only need to master the most basic ones. But make sure you study this lesson well, because adverbs are widely used in all varieties of Japanese, both written and spoken, both colloquial and formal.

In this lesson we provide a vocabulary table (below) and a grammar table (opposite). In the vocabulary table you will find a list of adverbs; they are probably the most commonly used in Japanese, and it is worthwhile committing them to memory. For ease of reference, we have divided them into the following order: time adverbs (from 今日 ***kyō***, "today," to いつ ***itsu***, "when"); place adverbs (from 下に ***shita ni***, "under," to 後ろに ***ushiro ni***, "be-

Adverbs					
Japanese	**Rōmaji**	**Meaning**	**Japanese**	**Rōmaji**	**Meaning**
今	***ima***	now	ゆっくり	***yukkuri***	slowly
今日	***kyō***	today	よく	***yoku***	much, well
昨日	***kinō***	yesterday	どんなに	***donna ni***	how
明日	***ashita***	tomorrow	何	***nani***	what
まだ	***mada***	still, yet	いくら	***ikura***	how much
もう	***mō***	already	とても	***totemo***	very
いつ	***itsu***	when	大変	***taihen***	very / serious
下に	***shita ni***	under	たくさん	***takusan***	a lot, many
上に	***ue ni***	on, over	十分	***jūbun***	enough
そばに	***soba ni***	beside	だけ	***dake***	only
前に	***mae ni***	in front of	少し	***sukoshi***	a little, some
後ろに	***ushiro ni***	behind	ちょっと	***chotto***	a little; rather
きっと	***kitto***	certainly	もっと	***motto***	more

Making adverbs from adjectives					
	Adjective	Meaning	Rule	Adverb	Meaning
-i adjectives	新しい ***atarashii***	new	～~~い~~く ***–~~i~~ ku***	新しく ***atarashiku***	newly
	強い ***tsuyoi***	strong		強く ***tsuyoku***	strongly
	大きい ***ookii***	big		大きく ***ookiku***	in a large way
-na adjectives	便利な ***benri-na***	convenient	～~~な~~に ***–~~na~~ ni***	便利に ***benri ni***	conveniently
	静かな ***shizuka-na***	quiet, calm		静かに ***shizuka ni***	quietly, calmly
	簡単な ***kantan-na***	easy		簡単に ***kantan ni***	easily

hind"); adverbs of manner (from きっと ***kitto***, "certainly," to どんなに ***donna ni***, "how"); and adverbs of quantity (from いくら ***ikura***, "how much" to もっと ***motto***, "more").

How to make adverbs

It is very easy to make adverbs from adjectives in English. In most cases all you have to do is add "ly" to the adjective to obtain an adverb. Thus: "easy" ⇒ "easily," "high" ⇒ "highly," "noisy" ⇒ "noisily."

In Japanese, there is a very similar way of forming adverbs from adjectives. As you probably remember, there are two kinds of adjectives in Japanese, ***-i*** adjectives (Lesson 13) and ***-na*** adjectives (Lesson 14). The rule for the formation of adverbs changes depending on the type of adjective, as we can see in the grammar table above. For **-*i* adjectives**, we replace the final い ***i*** with く ***ku***, for example:

新しい ***atarashii***, "new" ⇒ 新しく ***atarashiku***, "newly."

For **-*na* adjectives**, we replace the final な ***na*** with に ***ni***, for example:

簡単な ***kantan-na***, "easy" ⇒ 簡単に ***kantan ni***, "easily."

You can practice this by trying to make your own adverbs from the adjective vocabulary you learned in Lessons 13 and 14.

Other adverb forms

There are also other ways of making adverbs in Japanese:.

a) Adding the suffix 的に ***teki ni***, for example:

具体 ***gutai***, "concrete" ⇒ 具体的に ***gutaiteki ni***, "concretely"

b) The ***-te*** form (which we will study in Lesson 24) of some verbs can occasionally be used as an **adverb, for example**:

喜んで ***yorokonde***, "gladly" (from 喜ぶ ***yorokobu***, "to be glad")
はじめて ***hajimete***, "for the first time" (from はじめる ***hajimeru***, "to start")

c) Some adverbs are formed by repeating a word or a sound, for example:
しばしば ***shibashiba***, "often"
いちいち ***ichiichi***, "one by one"
時々 ***tokidoki***, "sometimes"
(**Note:** The character 々 is used to indicate repetition of the same kanji).

Example sentences

In Japanese, adverbs are usually placed before the verb or adjective they modify. For example, in たくさん食べる ***takusan taberu***, "to eat a lot," the adverb たくさん ***takusan*** ("a lot") goes before the verb 食べる ***taberu*** ("to eat"), whereas in English it is the other way round. Let's now look at some full-sentence examples:

a) 前に ***mae ni***, "in front of"
私はテレビをテーブルの前に置く
watashi wa terebi o teeburu no mae ni oku
I put the television in front of the table.

b) ゆっくり ***yukkuri***, "slowly"
私はゆっくり歩きます
watashi wa yukkuri arukimasu
I walk slowly.

c) ちょっと ***chotto***, "a little"
ちょっと待ってください
chotto matte kudasai
Wait a moment, please.

d) 静かに ***shizuka ni***, "quietly"
彼は静かに勉強します
kare wa shizuka ni benkyō shimasu
He studies quietly.

Untranslatable adverbs

Some adverbs have special nuances, or don't have a clear translation into English. To conclude this section, let's see four common ones:

a) やっぱり ***yappari***. This is the colloquial form of やはり ***yahari***, an adverb used with the meaning of "just as I thought," "just as was to be expected," or "after all." **Example:** 彼はやっぱりアメリカ人ですね ***kare wa yappari amerika-jin desu ne***. "(Just as I thought / it's obvious that / after all) he's American, isn't he?"
b) まさか ***masaka***. This adverb has a more or less similar meaning to "Don't tell me!," "Impossible!," "You're kidding!" You have an example of its use in Manga Example 1 in Lesson 16. It has negative connotations.
c) さすがに ***sasuga ni***. This adverb has the approximate meaning of "as may be expected," "it is only natural," "indeed." **Example:** さすがに彼は速く走る ***sasuga ni kare wa hayaku hashiru,*** "(As might be expected) he runs fast." It has positive connotations.
d) とにかく ***tonikaku***. "Anyway," "at any rate," "all in all," "somehow or other." **Example:** とにかく家へ帰る ***tonikaku ie e kaeru***, "Anyway, I'm going back home."

漫画例 Manga Examples

As usual, this part of the lesson is devoted to examples taken from real Japanese manga to further illustrate the language that has been taught so far. Let's look at some manga panels that show adverb usage.

Manga Example 1: Quickly

This panel gives us a good example of an adverb derived from an ***-i*** adjective. It is the adverb 早く ***hayaku*** ("quickly" "right now"), derived from the adjective 早い ***hayai*** ("quick"). Remember, to form adverbs from ***-i*** adjectives, all we need to do is replace the last い ***i*** in the adjective with く ***ku***.

The adjective ***hayai*** has two slightly different meanings, depending on the kanji used to write it: 早い ***hayai*** is "quick (in time)," or "early"; 速い ***hayai*** means "fast (in speed)."

Guillermo March

Yuki: 何してるんだ？早く入れ！
nani shiteru n da? hayaku haire!
what do be? quickly get in!
What are you doing? Get in, quickly!

Manga Example 2: Neatly

J.M. Ken Niimura

In Example 1 we saw an adverb formed from an ***-i*** adjective. Here, we see an adverb derived from a ***-na*** adjective. As you saw in the table on page 197, ***-na*** adjectives replace な ***na*** with に ***ni*** to form an adverb. Therefore: きれいな ***kirei-na*** ("clean," "beautiful") becomes the adverb きれいに ***kirei ni*** ("neatly," "beautifully").

Spectators: きれいに抜いた！？
kirei ni nuita!?
neat (adv) pass?!
Did it pass neatly?!

Manga Example 3: Hypothetically and completely

There are many more adverbs in Japanese which are not derived from adjectives, but are true adverbs, like those found in the vocabulary table on page 196.

Actually, adverbs are probably some of the most difficult words to master in Japanese, because they usually give a very important nuance, which color sentences with deeper meaning. In this sentence we have two adverbs, 仮に ***kari ni*** ("hypothetically," "supposing that") and まったく ***mattaku*** ("completely," "entirely"), with very important nuances, essential to obtaining a deeper understanding of what Sugita is saying...

Studio Kōsen

Sugita: 仮に 敵の力がまったく未知のものだったら**...**
kari ni teki no chikara ga mattaku michi no mono dattara...
supposing enemy POP strength SP completely unknown POP thing be
Supposing the enemy's strength is completely unknown...

Manga Example 4: For the first time

Besides true adverbs and those derived from adjectives, there are adverbs formed using other strategies. A very common way to form adverbs is by adding the suffix 的に ***teki ni*** to certain nouns. Another way is using the ***-te*** form (Lesson 24) of certain verbs, like in this panel, where we have the adverb はじめて ***hajimete*** ("for the first time"), ***-te*** form of the verb はじめる ***hajimeru*** ("to start").

Note: The word 酒 ***sake*** has two meanings. The first one is the famous Japanese liquor made from rice, called sake. The second one, used much more often in everyday life, covers any kind of alcoholic drink (beer, whisky, whatever).

J.M. Ken Niimura

Kyōsuke: はじめて飲んだお酒の味は**...**
hajimete nonda o-sake no aji wa...
for the first time drink sake POP taste TOP
The taste of the first time I drank liquor...

Exercises 練習

1. What does the adverb そばに *soba* ni mean? What kind of adverb is it (time, manner...)? How about まだ *mada*?

2. What is the rule of formation for adverbs derived from *-i* adjectives?

3. Form adverbs from the adjectives すごい *sugoi*, "amazing"; 低い *hikui*, "low"; 熱い *atsui*, "hot." What do these newly formed adverbs mean?

4. What is the rule for the formation of adverbs from *-na* adjectives?

5. Form adverbs from the adjectives 貧乏な *binbō-na*, "poor"; 複雑な *fukuzatsu-na*, "complicated"; 必要な *hitsuyō-na*, "necessary" and give their translation.

6. Translate into English: この試験は大変難しいです *kono shiken wa taihen muzukashii desu* (shiken: "exam," *muzukashii*: "difficult.")

7. Translate this sentence into Japanese: "It's raining a little" (2 valid options). (to rain: 雨が降る *ame ga furu*, Lesson 10.)

8. Translate this sentence into English: 漢字を小さく書く *kanji o chiisaku kaku* (*kanji*: "kanji," *chiisai*: "small," *kaku*: "to write.")

9. What two words can be pronounced *hayai*? How do we write them and what do they mean?

10. What are the two meanings for 酒 *sake*? Which is most commonly used?

— Answers to all the exercises can be found online by following the link on page 9. —

Lesson 23 • 第23課

Swear Words and Insults

You #%@*er! Yes, we will be dealing with insults and swear words in this lesson, an essential subject if you wish to be able to fully understand what is said in manga, anime, and movies. And also to have a little fun . . . Come on, you know you've been waiting for this! By the way, the word up top is "winner." What were you thinking?

An important warning

Insults are actually hardly ever used in Japanese society, so you're not likely to pick them up naturally if you're spending time in Japan. The Japanese DON'T usually use these kind of words. However, when you open a manga, or you watch an anime or action movie, you'll probably come across many swear words. As the aim of this book is to teach you Japanese through the medium of manga, and because we imagine that if you've bought this book you're a manga fan, we feel obliged to teach you some of the swear words you'll come across in your manga reading.

As usual, we have a vocabulary table in this lesson, on the facing page, which offers 22 insulting terms. However, many of them are not often used. The most common swear words by far are: 馬鹿 ***baka*** (and derivatives), 阿呆 ***ahō***, and 糞 ***kuso***. The other swear words in the list have a rather limited usage and we seldom see them.

What would you say if your bike was stolen?

We took it upon ourselves to perform an experiment in Japan which was related to insults. The experiment consisted of asking several people what they would say if they got to the place they had left their bike and found out it had been stolen. This is a typical case where a Westerner might let fly with a string of insults and swear words.

Well, the almost unanimous answer to the question was 信じられない！ ***shinjirare-nai***! ("I can't believe it!"). At most, there were some who said クソ！ ***kuso!*** ("shit!").

This experiment proves the Japanese don't use swear words in the same arbitrary way as Westerners do, and they seldom insult other people. Losing one's control is a sign of bad manners, and it is something people frown upon: the accepted thing is to keep a poker face, remaining impassive, very often with a false smile, even though the person might be cursing quietly on the inside.

Main swear words

Let's now review the contents of the vocabulary table. We must warn you that although the table always gives the kanji writing for the corresponding swear word, these are usually written in the katakana syllabary in manga, due to its visual impact. It's quite rare to see swear words written in kanji.

The most commonly used swear word in Japan is バカ ***baka***. This word has numerous possible translations and many derivatives, such as バカ者 ***bakamono*** or バカ野郎 ***bakayarō***. Next, we have the word 阿呆 ***ahō***, which most times we will find in katakana and with a short "o": アホ ***aho***. Dictionaries usually consider the words ***baka*** and ***aho*** synonymous, although in the Osaka area ***aho*** is a rather non-offensive word, even friendly and funny, whereas ***baka*** is a strong insult. In Tokyo and its surroundings, we find exactly the opposite: ***baka*** is the "friendly" word (depending on the intonation used, of course), whereas ***aho*** denotes greater aggressiveness. You must be careful, because there are many stories about terrible misunderstandings that have ended badly due to this regional difference.

An interesting fact is that the words ***baka*** and ***kuso*** can work as pejorative suffixes before certain nouns, in a similar way to our "damn," or "fucking." Examples: クソ警官 ***kuso-keikan*** ("damn policeman"), バカ先生 ***baka-sensei*** ("fucking teacher"), etc... Of course, we absolutely don't recommend using any of these words.

Main insults and swear words			
馬鹿 ***baka***	fool, ass, dunce, idiot, stupid	気持ち悪い ***kimochiwarui***	disgusting (person/thing)
馬鹿者 ***bakamono***	⇒ ***baka***	気色悪い ***kishokuwarui***	⇒ ***kimochiwarui***
馬鹿野郎 ***bakayarō***	fool, stupid, son of a bitch	くず ***kuzu***	rubbish, scum, dregs, junk
馬鹿にする ***baka ni suru***	to make fun of, make a fool of	畜生 ***chikushō***	beast, brute, damn it!
馬鹿を言う ***baka o iu***	to talk nonsense	糞 ***kuso***	shit, damn it!
馬鹿馬鹿しい ***bakabakashii***	absurd, ridiculous, ludicrous	くそったれ ***kusottare***	swine, son of a bitch
阿呆 ***ahō***	⇒ ***baka***	糞食らえ ***kusokurae***	go to hell!, eat shit!
ドジ ***doji***	(to make a) mess (of it)	下手糞 ***hetakuso***	good-for-nothing, awful
ブス ***busu***	ugly woman, plain-looking	化け物 ***bakemono***	spook, monster, goblin
タコ ***tako***	yellow-belly, octopus, coward	ボケ ***boke***	airhead, ditz, out of touch
間抜け ***manuke***	half-wit, fool, moron	変態 ***hentai***	pervert, slob, sex maniac

"You . . . !"

Sometimes, you will be surprised to see or hear someone insulting someone else in a manga or a movie with the words きさま ***kisama***, てめえ ***temee*** or おのれ ***onore***, especially when you look them up in the dictionary. The translation given for the first of those two words is "you," and, for the last word, "I." However, 90 percent of the time, these words are used as insults. The most appropriate translation in these cases would be "bastard," "damned," "I'm going to beat you to a pulp," "You're a dead man," or something similar. It is also curious how この野郎 ***kono yarō***, which literally means "this guy," has, nevertheless, the same meaning as ***kisama***, ***temee*** or ***onore***. Finally, こら ***kora*** indicates a threat, with a similar meaning to "beware," "watch what you do / say," or even "you'll get what's coming to you."

Yakuza jargon

Some of the most abundant characters in Japanese cinema are gangsters, the famous ヤクザ ***yakuza*** (also called 極道 ***gokudō***), with their chivalrous values (任侠 ***ninkyō***) and their sense of honor and duty (仁義 ***jingi***). Apart from the fact that their customs and mentality seem peculiar to us, such as their love of 入れ墨 ***irezumi***, "tattoos," or the 指詰め ***yubizume*** ritual, which entails cutting one's little finger off to express repentance due to a failure, the organization of their gangs (組 ***kumi***) is also complex. The absolute leader is called 組長 ***kumichō***, the bosses of the various subgroups are the 親分 ***oyabun*** (literally "like a father") and the subordinates are the 子分 ***kobun*** (literally "like a son"). Moreover, the youngest members call their mentors 兄貴 ***aniki*** ("elder brother"). The table below gives some typical yakuza jargon which may help you better understand yakuza movies!

Yakuza jargon					
Japanese	**Rōmaji**	**Meaning**	**Japanese**	**Rōmaji**	**Meaning**
組	***kumi***	yakuza gang	斬る	***kiru***	to kill
組長	***kumichō***	gang leader	任侠	***ninkyō***	code of values
親分	***oyabun***	boss	仁義	***jingi***	duty, justice
子分	***kobun***	subordinate	サツ	***satsu***	police(man)
兄貴	***aniki***	veteran	チャカ	***chaka***	gun
チンピラ	***chinpira***	baby hooligan	ハジキ	***hajiki***	gun
しま	***shima***	territory	ブツ	***butsu***	drugs
入れ墨	***irezumi***	tattoo	シャブ	***shabu***	drugs
指詰め	***yubizume***	to cut off the pinkie	ダチ	***dachi***	friend

漫画例 Manga Examples

Let's now have a look at some examples of swearing and insults in the context of real manga! Again, we can't stress strongly enough that we don't recommend that you use any of these expressions yourself!

Manga Example 1: *Baka*

This is a good example of the usage of the top swear word in Japanese: バカ ***baka***. Here Ryō is a little confused and insults the fighting cow calling it "horse-deer" (the 馬 ***ba*** in ***baka*** (馬鹿) is the kanji for "horse," whereas 鹿 ***ka*** is the kanji for "deer"). Leaving aside this tremendously bad joke, you can use this example to see how this swear word has a similar meaning to our "idiot," "stupid," "moron," "nerd," etc.

J.M. Ken Niimura

Ryō: ば ばか 苦しいっ どけ！
ba baka kurushii doke!
i... idiot painful move off
You... idiot! It hurts! Move off!

Manga Example 2: *Urusai / busu*

Here we have two rude expressions in one example. The first is うるさい ***urusai***, which literally means "noisy," but most times it is used to make somebody be quiet: it is like our "shut up," "shut your mouth," or "you're a pain." The second expression is ブス ***busu***, and, although it is literally translated as "ugly," this is the most offensive expression you can say to a woman: a word to avoid. Be careful: don't mistake ブス ***busu*** for バス ***basu*** ("bus")!

Guillermo March

Kazu: うるさい ブス！
urusai busu!
noisy ugly
Shut up, you frights!

Manga Example 3: *Kuso*

We have here an example of what was mentioned earlier in the lesson: sometimes, words such as クソ ***kuso*** ("shit") or バカ ***baka*** ("fool") are used as a pejorative prefix before certain nouns. This usage is very similar to our "fucking," or "damn." Here we have クソネコ ***kuso-neko***, that is, "damn cat." Notice the word こら ***kora***, at the end of the sentence. This word doesn't have any specific meaning, but it indicates a threat: we have tentatively translated it here as "beware" or "you'll get what's coming to you." In vulgar Japanese, especially among criminals and the yakuza, the "r" is rolled, like the double "rr" sound in Spanish. A threat such as こら！この野郎 ***kora, kono yarō***, would be something like ***korrrra, kono yarrrrō***!

Sōun: このクソネコ またおまえか、こら！
kono kuso-neko mata omae ka, kora!
this shit cat again you Q? hey
You again, damn cat?! Beware!

Manga Example 4: *Chikushō*

ちくしょう ***chikushō*** is quite a strange word. Originally, ***chikushō*** refers to "wild animal" or "beast." Oddly enough, the sense in which it is most often used nowadays is similar "damn it," or "God." That is, this expression is used when something doesn't go right, when there is a setback or a reversal of fortune.

To conclude this lesson, we remind you again that insults are seldom used in Japan. The most obvious proof of this is the limited number of insults in Japanese compared to the richness of swear words in English. But hey! They are worth knowing, just in case, right?

Yamazaki: ちくしょう！
chikushō!
Damn it!

Exercises 練習

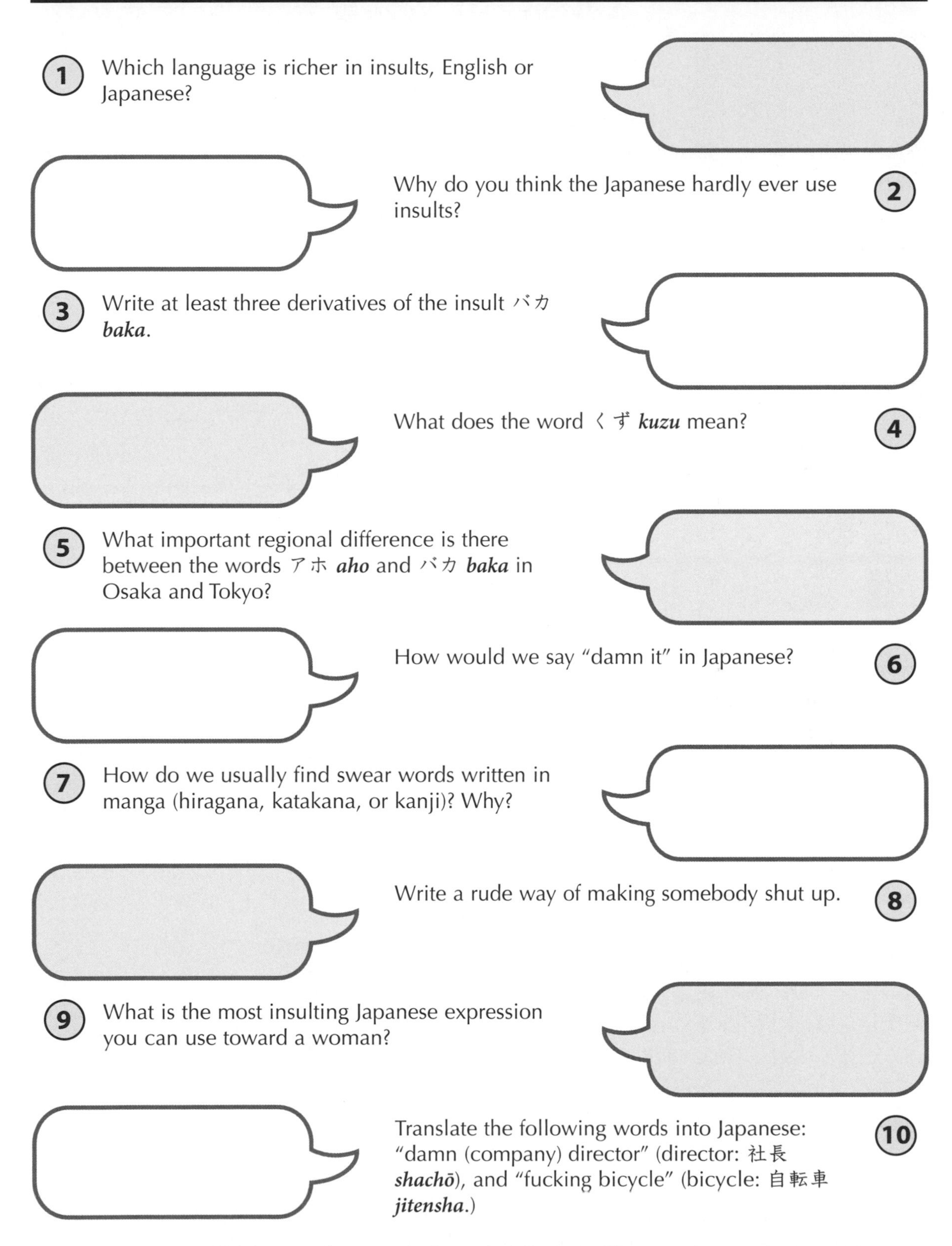

1. Which language is richer in insults, English or Japanese?
2. Why do you think the Japanese hardly ever use insults?
3. Write at least three derivatives of the insult バカ ***baka***.
4. What does the word くず ***kuzu*** mean?
5. What important regional difference is there between the words アホ ***aho*** and バカ ***baka*** in Osaka and Tokyo?
6. How would we say "damn it" in Japanese?
7. How do we usually find swear words written in manga (hiragana, katakana, or kanji)? Why?
8. Write a rude way of making somebody shut up.
9. What is the most insulting Japanese expression you can use toward a woman?
10. Translate the following words into Japanese: "damn (company) director" (director: 社長 ***shachō***), and "fucking bicycle" (bicycle: 自転車 ***jitensha***.)

— Answers to all the exercises can be found online by following the link on page 9. —

Lesson 24 • 第24課

Verbs (3): The -te Form

The *-te* form of the Japanese verb is essential in the formation of many basic grammatical expressions. The well-known expression *ganbatte* ("hang in there!"), which is common not just in manga but in everyday life, is the *-te* form of the verb *ganbaru* ("to persist in").

Formation

In this lesson we will see two of the most basic grammatical expressions formed with the ***-te*** form: The -ing form (also known as the gerund) and the request form. However, you should know that the ***-te*** form is used for many more things, and mastering the ***-te*** conjugation is therefore essential; it is one of the mainstays of Japanese grammar. The good news is that the ***-te*** form is extremely easy to learn, because it is almost identical to the past tense form, which we saw in Lesson 20. So, ***ganbatte***!

Having studied Lesson 20 well, you shouldn't have any problem in learning the ***-te*** form. The only difference between the ***-te*** form and the past tense is that all た ***-ta*** and だ ***-da*** past tense endings will be replaced with て ***-te*** and で ***-de***, respectively. Thus, if the past of 書く ***kaku*** ("to write") is 書いた ***kaita***, its ***-te*** form will be 書いて ***kaite***. And, in the case of 遊ぶ ***asobu*** ("to play"), the past is 遊んだ ***asonda***, and the ***-te*** form 遊んで ***asonde***.

For more information, you can check the table on this page, where the different forms of each type of verb are specified, as well as their respective formation rules.

Group		Simple f.	Meaning	*-te* form	Rule
Group 1 Invariable		教える ***oshieru***	to teach	教えて ***oshiete***	～~~る~~て **-~~ru~~ te**
		起きる ***okiru***	to wake up	起きて ***okite***	
Group 2 Variable	A	貸す ***kasu***	to lend	貸して ***kashite***	～~~す~~して **-~~su~~ shite**
	B	待つ ***matsu***	to wait	待って ***matte***	～~~つ~~って **-~~tsu~~ tte**
		買う ***kau***	to buy	買って ***katte***	～~~う~~って **-~~u~~ tte**
		帰る ***kaeru***	to return	帰って ***kaette***	～~~る~~って **-~~ru~~ tte**
	C	書く ***kaku***	to write	書いて ***kaite***	～~~く~~いて **-~~ku~~ ite**
	D	急ぐ ***isogu***	to hurry	急いで ***isoide***	～~~ぐ~~いで **-~~gu~~ ide**
	E	遊ぶ ***asobu***	to play	遊んで ***asonde***	～~~ぶ~~んで **-~~bu~~ nde**
		飲む ***nomu***	to drink	飲んで ***nonde***	～~~む~~んで **-~~mu~~ nde**
		死ぬ ***shinu***	to die	死んで ***shinde***	～~~ぬ~~んで **-~~nu~~ nde**
Group 3 Irregular		する ***suru***	to do	して ***shite***	Irregular verbs: there is no rule
		来る ***kuru***	to come	来て ***kite***	

What do we use the -te form for?

Having seen that verbs in the -te form always end in て *-te* (except for those whose dictionary form ends in ぐ *-gu*, ぶ *-bu*, む *-mu*, and ぬ *-nu*, which end in で *-de*), it is no wonder this form is called the "*-te* form." But, what do we use this form for?

A verb in the *-te* form doesn't actually have any important function on its own: it is just a kind of "prop" used for several essential grammatical forms, such as the -ing form or the request form 〜てください *-te kudasai*.

The -ing form

The only indispensable condition for the formation of the -ing form (or the present continuous form) is mastering the *-te* form. As we can see in the grammar summary-table on this page, the -ing form is created by adding いる *iru* (Lesson 18) to a verb in the *-te* form. Thus, we will be able to form sentences such as: "I'm doing x."

Remember the great advantage of Japanese is that verbs don't have different forms depending on gender or number, which means that the same form can go with any subject. Thus, the sentence 教えている *oshiete iru* can mean either "I am teaching," "they are teaching," or "she is teaching," et cetera.

To obtain the corresponding forms of the past, negative, and past negative, as well as to obtain more formal versions, all we need to do is conjugate the verb いる *iru*, just as you learned in Lesson 18. Take a look at these examples:

私は歩いている ***watashi wa aruite iru*** I'm walking. (simple present affirmative)	マリアは待っていない ***Maria wa matte inai*** Maria is not waiting. (simple present negative)	彼らは食べていました ***karera wa tabete imashita*** They were eating. (formal past affirmative)

Grammatical structures derived from the *-te* form			
Gerund (to be doing)	〜て+いる ***-te + iru***	待っている ***matte iru*** 遊んでいる ***asonde iru*** 教えている ***oshiete iru***	to be waiting to be playing to be teaching
Request (Please do...)	〜て+ください ***-te + kudasai***	待ってください ***matte kudasai*** 遊んでください ***asonde kudasai*** 教えてください ***oshiete kudasai***	please wait please play please teach

Requests

A second use for the ***-te*** form is the forming of requests: "please do x." Forming a request is very simple, all you need to do is add ください ***kudasai*** after a verb in the ***-te*** form.

In the table on the previous page you have some examples of the usage of this extremely common request form in Japanese, which is used both in written and spoken language, as well as in formal and informal situations, and is therefore essential to master. Here you have some extra examples:

食べてください	急いでください	来てください
tabete kudasai	***isoide kudasai***	***kite kudasai***
Please eat.	Please hurry.	Please come.

In everyday spoken Japanese, (as well as in manga, anime, and movies), ***kudasai*** can be omitted when making requests, so that we are left with the verb in the ***-te*** form alone. That is why, in this lesson's introduction, we said がんばって ***ganbatte*** just like that. The full expression is actually がんばってください ***ganbatte kudasai***, but since we were talking in an informal and friendly way, we did without the ***kudasai*** part.

がんばって ***ganbatte*** comes from がんばる ***ganbaru***, a verb in Group 2 (type B, see page 171) which means "persevere," "persist in," "hold out." The expression ***ganbatte kudasai*** (or just ***ganbatte***) is popular among the Japanese and you will hear it very often if you go to Japan. A more appropriate translation of this expression, used to wish somebody good luck or to encourage somebody, would be "stick to it," "show your nerve," or "come on."

-suru verbs

Now we will change subject, briefly moving away from the ***-te*** form to talk about ***suru*** verbs. These verbs are originally nouns, but once we add the verb する ***suru*** ("to do," one of the two irregular verbs in Japanese) they become verbs. For example, from the noun 勉強 ***benkyō***, "study," we obtain the verb 勉強する ***benkyō suru***, "to study."

With these verbs the formation is extremely simple, all we need to do is conjugate する ***suru*** in any of the forms we have studied so far and in those we will study from now on. It goes without saying that we must know the different forms of the verb する ***suru*** perfectly well. Here are some more examples with the verb 勉強する ***benkyō suru***:

Simple past tense: 勉強した ***benkyō shita*** ("I studied," "I had studied," etc.)
Formal negative form: 勉強しません ***benkyō shimasen*** ("I don't study")
-te form + ***kudasai***: 勉強してください ***benkyō shite kudasai*** ("Please study"), etc.

Other common ***-suru*** verbs include 運転する ***unten suru*** ("to drive"), 結婚する ***kekkon suru*** ("to marry"), 質問する ***shitsumon suru*** ("to ask"), and many more.

漫画例 Manga Examples

The manga examples in this section will illustrate the three grammatical points explained in this lesson: the formation of the -ing form, the formation of requests and -*suru* verbs.

Manga Example 1: The -ing form / gerund

J.M. Ken Niimura

We have a clear example of the usage of the -ing form in Japanese in this manga panel. The -ing form is also known as the gerund or the present/past continuous tense in English, and the formation of the equivalent tense in Japanese is "***-te*** form + conjugated verb ***iru***."

The main verb here is 残る ***nokoru*** ("to remain," "to be left"). To conjugate the ***-te*** form, we have to check the group it belongs to, which is 2. Therefore, following the formation rules of that table, the ***-te*** form of this verb is 残って ***nokotte***. Adding the verb いる ***iru***, we obtain the gerund: 残っている ***nokotte iru*** ("remaining"). Remember, as well, that you can obtain the past tense, negative form, and past negative form of the -ing form (in both their formal and informal versions) just by conjugating the verb ***iru*** (Lesson 18). In this panel, for example, we have an instance of the gerund in the formal present affirmative: 残っています ***nokotte imasu*** ("remaining").

Hayashida: この「証拠」がこの会場に残っています！！
kono "shōko" ga kono kaijō ni nokotte imasu!!
this "proof" SP this assembly hall PP remain GER!!
The proof is still in this assembly hall!

Manga Example 2: Informal present affirmative gerund

This second example will help us illustrate a common feature: in the formation of the -ing form using the ***-te*** form + conjugated verb ***iru***, the い ***i*** in the verb いる ***iru*** is very often removed. Just like all languages, spoken Japanese is actually quite different from written Japanese; and manga, in spite of being a written medium, is a reflection of spoken language. Therefore, finding colloquial language, contractions, and even dialect forms in manga is quite common. Here, the gerund of the verb 動く ***ugoku*** "to move," from Group 2 (type C, see page 171), would be 動いている ***ugoite iru***, but in spoken Japanese we usually drop the い ***i*** of いる ***iru*** thus obtaining 動いてる ***ugoiteru*** ("to be moving").

J.M. Ken Niimura

Veena: サトミ まだ動いてるよ！
satomi mada ugoiteru yo
Satomi still move GER EP
Satomi! It's still moving!

Manga Example 3: Informal past negative gerund

Here we see the past negative continuous form of the verb 言う ***iu***, "to say," from Group 2 (type B, see page 171). It is made using the ***-te*** form of the main verb (言って ***itte***) plus いる ***iru*** in its past negative form (いなかった ***inakatta***). Here, however, just as in Example 2 above, the い ***i*** of いる ***iru*** is dropped (as this is informal language), giving us 言ってなかった ***ittenakatta***, "I wasn't saying."

The ***-te*** form + ***iru*** in Japanese expresses continuity of an action or state. The verb 言う ***iu*** on its own simply means "to say," but its gerund, 言っている ***itte iru***, indicates that the action of "saying" is continuous, dynamic.

Studio Kōsen

Imamura: オレは何も言ってなかったんだ！！
ore wa nani mo itte nakatta n da!!
I TOP nothing say GER be!!
I said nothing!!

Manga Example 4: Request form

Another of the main usages of the ***-te*** form is to make a request (with the meaning of "Please do x"). This request formation is very simple: ***-te*** form + ***kudasai***.

In this example, the main verb is 抱きしめる ***dakishimeru*** "to hug," which belongs to Group 1, its ***-te*** form being 抱きしめて ***dakishimete***. Just by adding ください ***kudasai***, we obtain the request form 抱きしめてください ***dakishimete kudasai***: "hug me, please." Try practicing this request form using other verbs you know.

Kotomi: 抱きしめてください。
dakishimete kudasai.
hug please
Hug me, please.

Manga Example 5: *-suru* verb

Hiroshi: 僕は彼女と結婚する！
boku wa kanojo to kekkon suru!
I TOP her with marry do!
I'll marry her!

Here is a very simple example of a ***-suru*** verb. The word 結婚 ***kekkon*** on its own means "wedding," "marriage." Just by adding the verb する ***suru*** ("to do"), we will obtain a verb which works just like all other verbs: 結婚する ***kekkon suru***, "to marry."

These verbs are formed by conjugating the verb する ***suru*** and leaving the main word untouched. In this panel you have a simple present form, 結婚する ***kekkon suru*** ("I marry"). Its other forms include 結婚します ***kekkon shimasu*** ("I marry"); the simple past tense 結婚した ***kekkon shita*** ("I married"); the formal negative 結婚しません ***kekkon shimasen*** ("I don't marry"), and so on. What are the other possible forms that you know for this verb?

Manga Example 6: *-suru* verb + request form

This panel is a sort of summary of the lesson, since here we can see a ***-suru*** verb in the request form ***-te*** + ***kudasai***. The ***-suru*** verb we are dealing with here is 約束する ***yakusoku suru***. On its own, the noun 約束 ***yakusoku*** means "promise" but, after becoming a ***-suru*** verb, it means "to promise." To make its request form, we must first conjugate する ***suru*** in its ***-te*** form: since it is an irregular verb, you must remember that its ***-te*** form is して ***shite***. Once you have obtained this ***-te*** form, you only need to finish the job by adding ください ***kudasai***, thus obtaining the request form 約束してください ***yakusoku shite kudasai***, "promise me, please."

Yamamoto: 約束してくださいよ！
yakusoku shite kudasai yo!
promise do please EP!
Promise me, please!

Manga Example 7: *Ganbatte!*

The request form ***-te*** + ***kudasai*** can be simplified in spoken Japanese by removing the word ください ***kudasai***, as in this example.

What Chiyo actually wants to say is がんばってください ***ganbatte kudasai***, but removing ***kudasai*** and leaving ***ganbatte*** ("hang in there") alone is much more informal and friendly. This simplified request form in spoken language and, by extension, in manga, is very common, although you should only use it with close friends.

Having said this, we say goodbye to this lesson with a loud がんばって ***ganbatte*** for your study of the ***-te*** form!

Chiyo: ロドニーさん がんばって！
rodonii san ganbatte!
Rodney (SUF.) hold out GER
Come on, Rodney!

Exercises 練習

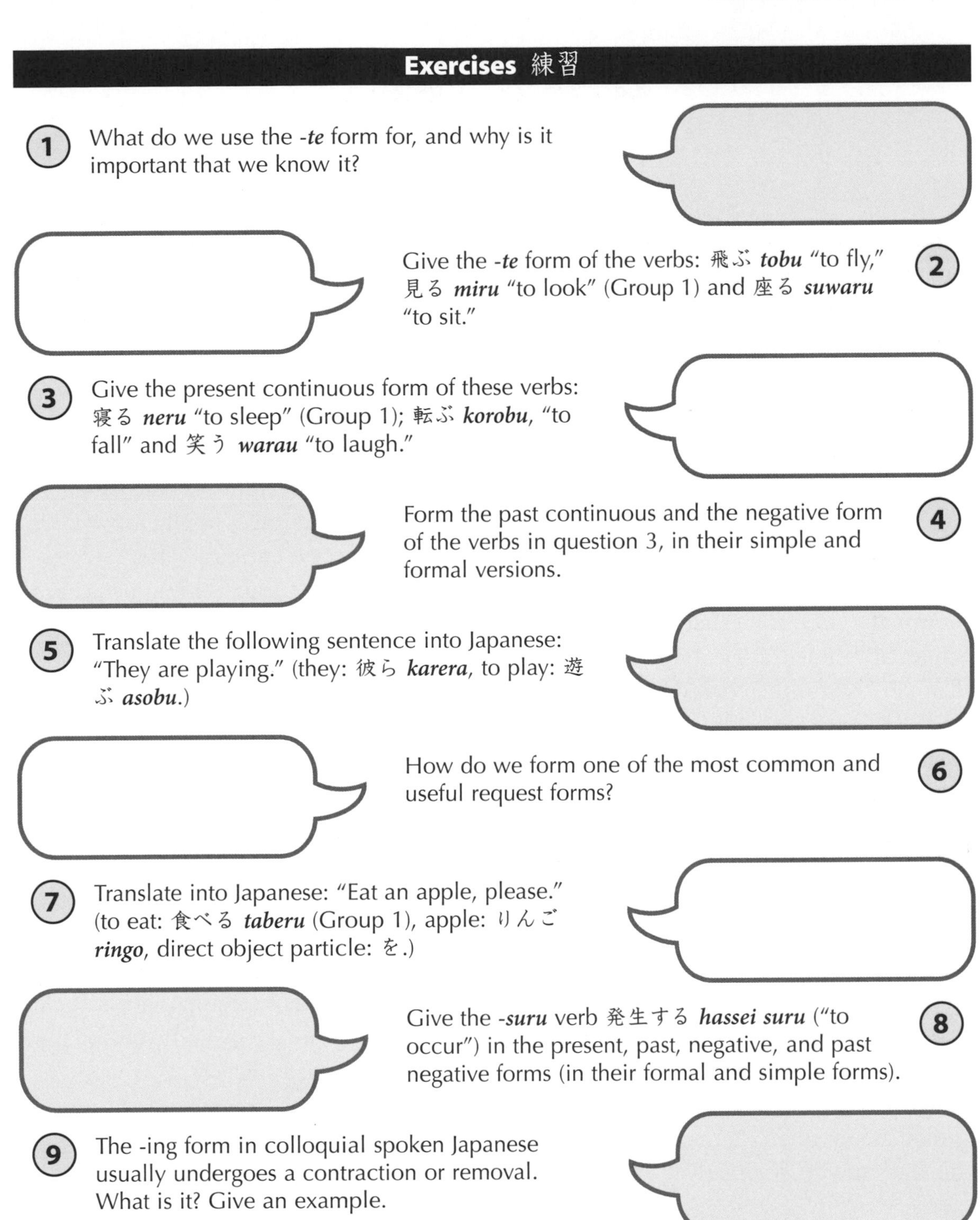

1. What do we use the *-te* form for, and why is it important that we know it?

2. Give the *-te* form of the verbs: 飛ぶ ***tobu*** "to fly," 見る ***miru*** "to look" (Group 1) and 座る ***suwaru*** "to sit."

3. Give the present continuous form of these verbs: 寝る ***neru*** "to sleep" (Group 1); 転ぶ ***korobu***, "to fall" and 笑う ***warau*** "to laugh."

4. Form the past continuous and the negative form of the verbs in question 3, in their simple and formal versions.

5. Translate the following sentence into Japanese: "They are playing." (they: 彼ら ***karera***, to play: 遊ぶ ***asobu***.)

6. How do we form one of the most common and useful request forms?

7. Translate into Japanese: "Eat an apple, please." (to eat: 食べる ***taberu*** (Group 1), apple: りんご ***ringo***, direct object particle: を.)

8. Give the ***-suru*** verb 発生する ***hassei suru*** ("to occur") in the present, past, negative, and past negative forms (in their formal and simple forms).

9. The -ing form in colloquial spoken Japanese usually undergoes a contraction or removal. What is it? Give an example.

10. The ***-te*** + ***kudasai*** form in colloquial spoken Japanese usually undergoes a contraction or removal. What is it? Give an example.

— Answers to all the exercises can be found online by following the link on page 9. —

Lesson 25 • 第25課

Counters

In this lesson we will see one of the special characteristics of the Japanese language: the so-called "counters." Although, at first glance, it may seem a minor subject on which you don't need to dwell too much, it is worth taking the time to study this area thoroughly.

When do we use counters?

As we have mentioned many times throughout the book, Japanese doesn't distinguish between male, female, singular, or plural in nouns. We commented on the male-female problem at length in Lesson 11 (nouns), and we also mentioned counters briefly as well. Our intention here is to broaden our knowledge on the usage of these curious words.

"Counters" are words combined with one or more nouns that indicate number, that is, "how many" things there are of something. In English we say, for example, "I want five apples." To indicate "how many" apples we want, all we do is add the corresponding number, "five" in this case. In Japanese, however, we must add a suffix to this number. This suffix is called a "counter," and depending on the noun or nouns we want to count we will choose from several counters. The choice will depend on the physical characteristics of the noun we want to count: for example, if it is something long, we will use 本 ***hon***, if it is a person, we will choose 人 ***nin***, if it is a machine, it will then be 台 ***dai***, etc.

Pronouncing counters

In the table on the facing page you will find the most common counters, as well as a breakdown of their pronunciation. Be careful, because quite a few of these readings are irregular. Generally, only certain readings for numbers 1, 3, 6, 8, and 10 are irregular. If you still have problems remembering the numerals, it is highly recommended that you thoroughly review Lesson 5 (numerals) and Lesson 6 (days and months) before carrying on.

After the number 10, there are no changes in the reading of a number. For instance, 47 plus the counter 冊 ***satsu*** will be 四十七冊 ***yon jū nana satsu***.

I want five apples

The sentence we saw above, "I want five apples," easy as it may be in English, does not have a direct translation into Japanese. The sentence りんごを五ください ***ringo o go kudasai*** (***ringo***: "apple," ***o***: DOP, ***go***: "five," ***kudasai***: "please") is incorrect. A counter must be added to the number 五 ***go*** (five) for the sentence to be correct.

First of all, let's analyze an apple: It is a small round object. The most convenient counter for it is 個 ***ko***, because we use it to count small round things. So the correct sentence would be: りんごを五個ください ***ringo o go ko kudasai***.

Note: In case we wanted to ask for not five, but six apples, the sentence would be りんごを六個ください ***ringo o rokko kudasai***. Although 六 (6) is usually pronounced ***roku***, when it is used together with the counter 個 ***ko*** thus forming the compound 六個, this is pronounced ***rokko*** and not ***roku ko*** for phonetic reasons (see the table below).

Nevertheless, if you find this difficult, you don't need to worry; there is a kind of counter that can be used to count anything without fear of being wrong, your secret "trump card": this very practical counter is つ ***tsu***.

However, as you can see in the table, all the readings in the ***tsu*** line are irregular and they must be learned by heart. Still, no matter how practical つ ***tsu*** may be, it is much better knowing how to use the right counter on each occasion, so try not to automatically resort to つ ***tsu***.

A complete set of counters

	つ ***tsu***	人 ***nin***	枚 ***mai***	台 ***dai***	本 ***hon***	匹 ***hiki***	冊 ***satsu***	階 ***kai***	個 ***ko***
1	一つ ***hitotsu***	一人 ***hitori***	一枚 ***ichi mai***	一台 ***ichi dai***	一本 ***ippon***	一匹 ***ippiki***	一冊 ***issatsu***	一階 ***ikkai***	一個 ***ikko***
2	二つ ***futatsu***	二人 ***futari***	二枚 ***ni mai***	二台 ***ni dai***	二本 ***ni hon***	二匹 ***ni hiki***	二冊 ***ni satsu***	二階 ***ni kai***	二個 ***ni ko***
3	三つ ***mittsu***	三人 ***san nin***	三枚 ***san mai***	三台 ***san dai***	三本 ***san bon***	三匹 ***san biki***	三冊 ***san satsu***	三階 ***san gai***	三個 ***san ko***
4	四つ ***yottsu***	四人 ***yo nin***	四枚 ***yon mai***	四台 ***yon dai***	四本 ***yon hon***	四匹 ***yon hiki***	四冊 ***yon satsu***	四階 ***yon kai***	四個 ***yon ko***
5	五つ ***itsutsu***	五人 ***go nin***	五枚 ***go mai***	五台 ***go dai***	五本 ***go hon***	五匹 ***go hiki***	五冊 ***go satsu***	五階 ***go kai***	五個 ***go ko***
6	六つ ***muttsu***	六人 ***roku nin***	六枚 ***roku mai***	六台 ***roku dai***	六本 ***roppon***	六匹 ***roppiki***	六冊 ***roku satsu***	六階 ***rokkai***	六個 ***rokko***
7	七つ ***nanatsu***	七人 ***nana nin***	七枚 ***nana mai***	七台 ***nana dai***	七本 ***nana hon***	七匹 ***nana hiki***	七冊 ***nana satsu***	七階 ***nana kai***	七個 ***nana ko***
8	八つ ***yattsu***	八人 ***hachi nin***	八枚 ***hachi mai***	八台 ***hachi dai***	八本 ***happon***	八匹 ***happiki***	八冊 ***hassatsu***	八階 ***hakkai***	八個 ***hakko***
9	九つ ***kokonotsu***	九人 ***kyū nin***	九枚 ***kyū mai***	九台 ***kyū dai***	九本 ***kyū hon***	九匹 ***kyū hiki***	九冊 ***kyū satsu***	九階 ***kyū kai***	九個 ***kyū ko***
10	十 ***too***	十人 ***jū nin***	十枚 ***jū mai***	十台 ***jū dai***	十本 ***juppon***	十匹 ***juppiki***	十冊 ***jussatsu***	十階 ***jukkai***	十個 ***jukko***
?	いくつ ***ikutsu?***	何人 ***nan nin?***	何枚 ***nan mai?***	何台 ***nan dai?***	何本 ***nan bon?***	何匹 ***nan biki?***	何冊 ***nan satsu?***	何階 ***nan gai?***	何個 ***nan ko?***

Main counters

つ ***tsu***:	Universal counter. It can always be helpful when in trouble, because it can be used to count anything.
人 ***nin***:	To count people. Watch out for the special readings 一人 ***hitori*** ("one person") and 二人 ***futari*** ("two people"), which are very much used.
枚 ***mai***:	This counter is used to count papers and flat things in general (such as blankets, tickets, etc.)
台 ***dai***:	For machines in general (cars, computers, televisions, etc.)
本 ***hon***:	For long and slender things (pencils, ballpoint pens, trees, etc.) Curiously enough, it is also used for telephone calls.
匹 ***hiki***:	Small animals (mice, cats, dogs, etc.) Large animals (horses, cows, etc.) are counted with 頭 ***tō***, while small animals which "hop," such as birds and rabbits, are counted with 羽 ***wa***.
冊 ***satsu***:	Books, magazines, as well as printed and bound material in general.
階 ***kai***:	Building floors. **Note:** 一階 ***ikkai***, the Japanese "first floor" is equivalent to the American "first floor" and British "ground floor."
個 ***ko***:	Small things, and generally, round or compact things (apples, stones, etc.)

Example sentences

Let's finish this lesson with some example sentences, so you can see a few uses of counters. The best formula you can use with these words is "noun + が ***ga*** + numeral + counter."

ここにえんぴつが三本あります ***koko ni enpitsu ga san bon arimasu***
There are three pencils here. (***enpitsu***: "pencil" | counter: 本 ***hon***.)

本を五冊ください ***hon o go satsu kudasai***
Give me five books, please. (***hon***: "book" | counter: 冊 ***satsu***.)
(Don't confuse 本 ***hon*** ("book") with the counter for long slender things 本 ***hon***, both written and pronounced the same way.)

家の前に子どもが二人います ***ie no mae ni kodomo ga futari imasu***
There are two children in front of the house.
(***kodomo***: "child" | counter: 人 ***nin*** [***futari*** is an irregular reading].)

桃を三つください ***momo o mittsu kudasai***
Give me three peaches, please. (***momo***: "peach.")

In this last sentence, the most appropriate counter is 個 ***ko*** (small round things), but, as an example, we have used つ ***tsu***, the universal counter, which can be used with anything.

漫画例 Manga Examples

Let's start counting! But remember counting things in Japanese is a lot more complex than in English, since we must know first how to use the different varieties of "counters." Let's have a look at some examples.

Manga Example 1: Counter for people and counter for long things

In this manga example we can see two counters at work. The first is 四人 ***yo nin*** (4 + counter for people), and the second one is 一本 ***ippon*** (1 + counter for long and slender things). Be careful, because both counters have irregular readings: the first one is not ***shi nin*** or ***yon nin***, and the second one is not ***ichi hon***, as should be expected (Lesson 5).

This time, we have chosen to offer a literal translation, which will help you better understand the structure of the original sentence, as well as a more fluent translation.

As for the counters, the usage of the counter in the first case, 人 ***nin***, is obvious, since we are counting people, four team members to be precise. In the second case, the words to be counted are "arm" and "leg" (to say "take an arm or a leg each"). Arms and legs are long, slender things, therefore, the counter is, undoubtedly, 本 ***hon***.

Leader: 四人が一度にロボトンの手と足を一本ずつねらえ！
yonin ga ichido ni roboton no te to ashi o ippon zutsu nerae!
4 people SP Roboton POP hand and leg DOP one by one aim
Literal: You four, take one of Roboton's arms and legs each!
Final: Between the four of you, take one of Roboton's arms and legs each!

Manga Example 2: Counter for spoonfuls

Here we have a very clear example of the counter 杯 ***hai***, which is used to count cups (tea, coffee, etc.), glasses (milk, water, wine, whisky, etc.), and spoonfuls, as in this example.

J.M. Ken Niimura

The complete breakdown for this counter from 1 to 10 is 一杯 ***ippai***, 二杯 ***ni hai***, 三杯 ***san bai***, 四杯 ***yon hai***, 五杯 ***go hai***, 六杯 ***roppai***, 七杯 ***nana hai***, 八杯 ***happai***, 九杯 ***kyū hai*** and 十杯 ***juppai***. Take note of the special readings for 1, 3, 6, 8, and 10.

Sabin:	そして砂糖をいれたんだ。	一杯、二杯...	三杯、四杯...
	soshite satō o ireta n da.	***ippai, ni hai...***	***san bai, yon hai...***
	then sugar DOP put in be.	one, two...	three, four...
	Then he put the sugar in.	**One, two...**	**Three, four spoonfuls...**

Manga Example 3: Universal counter

Let's now see an instance of the universal counter, つ ***tsu***, which we can use to count anything. In this example, Yoshi is referring to one of his 歯 ***ha***, "teeth," and he uses this counter. He probably does it because from the tooth's shape and size we can't clearly tell which counter would be the most appropriate (a possibility could be 個 ***ko***, because it is small in size). To avoid headaches, he uses つ ***tsu***.

J.M. Ken Niimura

Yoshi:	歯が一つ折れちゃった	**Maeda:**	何？
	ha ga hitotsu orechatta		***nani?***
	tooth SP one break		what?
	I've broken one tooth.		**What?**

Manga Example 4: Counter for people (2)

Studio Kōsen

This panel gives a good example of the counter for people, 人 ***nin***. It is a widely used counter in Japanese, but it has a very peculiar feature: two of its readings are completely irregular.

一人 is not read ***ichi nin***, the most obvious reading, but ***hitori***; and 二人, which appears in this panel, is not read ***ni nin*** but ***futari***.

The remaining usages of this counter are completely regular: you can check the table on page 217.

Tao-jun:	なんなの それは…！？	何故二人とも動かない…！？
	nan na no sore wa...!?	***naze futari to mo ugokanai...!?***
	what what this top...?!	why two both move...?!
	But, what's going on?!	**Why isn't either of them moving?!**

Manga Example 5: Counter for plates and counter for glasses

In this example ere we have two different counters: 皿 ***sara***, to count plates, and 杯 ***hai***, which, as we saw in Manga Example 2, is used to count cups, glasses, etc.

Guillermo March

Here, the client does not specify what kind of drink he wants, but the use of the word 一杯 ***ippai*** on its own, in a context like this, usually means "a glass" of an alcoholic drink, possibly beer.

As for 皿 ***sara***, since the word itself means "plate," it is no wonder that it is used to count plates of food. The kanji for 一皿, "one plate," has an irregular reading: It isn't ***ichi sara***, but ***hito sara***.

Chef:	はい、目玉を一皿ね！	**Client:**	一杯飲みたいな！
	hai, medama o hitosara ne!		***ippai nomitai na!***
	yes, eye DOP one plate EP!		one glass drink EP!
	Here you are, a plate of eyes!		**I feel like a drink!**

Manga Example 6: Counter for small animals

Here we have an example of the counter 匹 ***hiki*** (the reading 一匹 ***ippiki*** is irregular), used to count small animals such as rats, cats, worms, etc.

Studio Kōsen

But this counter is used here with an untranslatable pejorative nuance. Yoshimura has actually defeated a person, but uses the counter 匹 ***hiki*** to humiliate and belittle the defeated opponent, in a usage which brings to mind the fact of calling an enemy "chicken," "worm," or "rat" in English. These puns using counters are frequently found in manga.

Yoshimura:	くくくくっ	一匹おわり！
	ku ku ku ku	***ippiki owari!***
	(sound of laugh)	one (counter for small animals) finish!
	He, he, he, he!	**One down!**

Manga Example 7: Counter for tatami

We would not want to end this lesson without warning you that there are many more counters besides those we have studied. Some are used to count the most unlikely things. For instance, we have in this panel the counter 畳 ***jō***, which is used to count ***tatami*** (straw mats used to cover the floor in a house). Japanese houses are measured in tatami. One ***tatami*** mat is about 6 feet (1.8m) long x 3 feet (0.9m) wide.

Guillermo March

Nana:	大好きだったな あのアパート…	小さい6畳の部屋に…
	daisuki datta na ano apaato...	***chiisai roku jō no heya ni...***
	be very fond of EP that apartment...	small 6 tatami POP room PP...
	I was very fond of that apartment...	**In that small 10 m² room...**

Exercises 練習

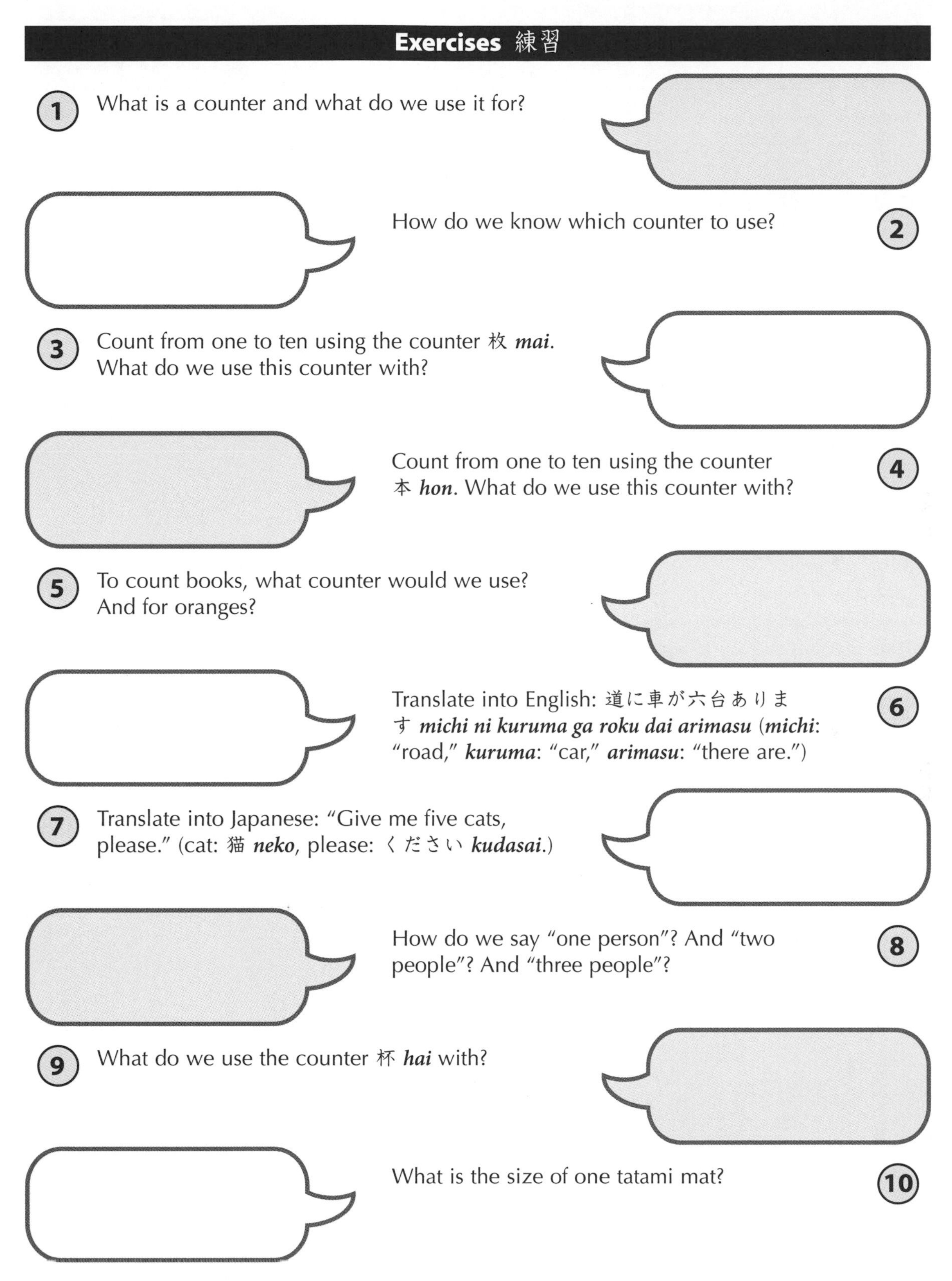

1. What is a counter and what do we use it for?

2. How do we know which counter to use?

3. Count from one to ten using the counter 枚 ***mai***. What do we use this counter with?

4. Count from one to ten using the counter 本 ***hon***. What do we use this counter with?

5. To count books, what counter would we use? And for oranges?

6. Translate into English: 道に車が六台あります ***michi ni kuruma ga roku dai arimasu*** (***michi***: "road," ***kuruma***: "car," ***arimasu***: "there are.")

7. Translate into Japanese: "Give me five cats, please." (cat: 猫 ***neko***, please: ください ***kudasai***.)

8. How do we say "one person"? And "two people"? And "three people"?

9. What do we use the counter 杯 ***hai*** with?

10. What is the size of one tatami mat?

— Answers to all the exercises can be found online by following the link on page 9. —

RAKUJŌ
三日後
第五章
だいごしょう
そうね、ヒデ。
しかし、あのじいさんは
やっぱり頑固だ…私たちは
とても弱くなった。
お母さん、
これはひどいよ…
ブーン
大変です！ヤスのアーミー
は中のキャノンも撤去
していますよ!!!
何!?まさか…
カッ
カッ

やめてください！何をしている、バカもの‼
外のキャノンだけを撤去すると約束したわ‼
ドーン
誰の命令ですか⁉
僕は知りませんよ。僕は命令に従うだけです。
ブーン
はい、お母さん。
パタパタ
ちくしょう！行くわよ、ヒデ‼
もちろん、ヤス様の命令ですよ。

カッカッ
カッカッ
ヤス様！
どうして中の
キャノンも
壊しました!?
ビシッ
中の
キャノン？
知らないよ！
外に十台が
あった。中に
六台があった。
少し間違った
だけだよ。
ごめんなさい。
バカを言え!!
このクソ親父！
静かにして
くださいよ。今はもう
遅い。わしはもう
謝った！
もっと深く
考えてください！
これは
ひどいわ!!
はっ

ビッッ
君ら、この女と彼女の息子を外へ出してください。
ハハハ！サカ基地はもうわし一人の物だ！
ギロッ
くそ～!!!
はい、ヤス様!!
はい、ヤス様！
カッ
カッ
ドカッ!!
はい、お母さん。
ヒデ、もう負けたよ。

Review for Lessons 21–25

Answers to all the review exercises can be found online by following the link on page 9.

RAKUJŌ – New vocabulary 新しい単語

ひどい	terrible, cruel	もちろん	of course
頑固(がんこ)な	stubborn	深(ふか)い	deep
なる	to become	考(かんが)える	to think (Group 1)
命令(めいれい)	command	謝(あやま)る	to apologize (Group 2)
従(したが)う	to follow, to obey	物(もの)	thing (tangible)

1. Based on what you have read in episode 5 of ***Rakujō***, why does Yodo get so angry with Yasu that she insults him? Make a list of the insults and swear words she uses.

2. What does the word おじいさん? literally mean? And, in the context where it appears in ***Rakujō***, uttered by Yodo before Yasu, what meaning do you think it acquires?

3. How many cannons (inside and outside) were there at the Saka base before they were dismantled? What counter do we use to count these cannons? And, if they were trees instead of cannons, what counter would we use? And what if they were pigeons?

4. In this episode find three adverbs derived from adjectives. Identify the adjectives.

5. Make these adjectives in to adverbs: ひどい , 頑固(がんこ)な and 遅(おそ)い .

6. What do the following adverbs mean: もう , だけ , 少(すこ)し and とても ?

7. Find four verbs in the ***-te*** form, give their simple form, ***-masu*** form, and their meaning.

8. Write each of the verbs below in the form indicated

   謝(あやま)る (simple gerund):
   従(したが)う (request):
   負(ま)ける (formal negative gerund):
   壊(こわ)す (simple past gerund):

9. In this episode find two ***-suru*** verbs and give their dictionary form (simple form), ***-masu*** form, ***-te*** form, and their meaning.

10. What word does Hide use to address his mother? Why doesn't he use 母(はは)?

11. Place each word from the box below next to its corresponding counter.

人(にん)	兄				
枚(まい)					
台(だい)					
本(ほん)					
匹(ひき)					
頭(とう)					
冊(さつ)					
個(こ)					

~~兄(あに)~~	電車(でんしゃ)	先生(せんせい)	かえる	車(くるま)	へび	マンガ
いちご	紙(かみ)	羊(ひつじ)	カメラ	くま	男	手紙(てがみ)
足	えんぴつ	本	ディスク	妻(つま)	オレンジ	ぶた
バナナ	パソコン	あり	ふで	コンピュータ	自転車(じてんしゃ)	ライオン
猫	雑誌(ざっし)	たこ	警察官(けいさつかん)	新聞(しんぶん)	さる	馬(うま)
ボール	ゴム	おじいさん	木	もも	切手(きって)	みかん
とら	母親(ははおや)	象(ぞう)	すし	バス	写真(しゃしん)	ボールペン

12. Complete the following sentences with the most appropriate counter, and add the reading of the “counter + number” combination. Indicate their 〜つ equivalent, as well.

a) あの人の家(いえ)には車(くるま)が (3) <u>三台(さんだい)</u> あります。 (三(みっ)つ)
b) なしを (9) ________________ ください。 (　　　)
c) この建物(たてもの)は (8) ____________ あります。
　(何(なん)) ________________ に行きますか？ (　　　)(　　　)
d) あなたは子供(こども)が (2) _______ いますか？ (　　　)
e) 道(みち)には大きい牛が (4) _______ いるぜ！ (　　　)
f) この (6) ___________ の本を読(よ)んだか？ (　　　)
g) 今日(きょう)はビデオを (3) ______ 見ましたよ。 (　　　)
h) あそこに犬が (1) ____ いたと思います。 (　　　)

13. Draw a line to match each of the following words with its most suitable counterpart.

おかあさん	おねえさん	パパ	とうちゃん
おっと	だんなさん	おふくろ	つま
かない	はは	おばさん	おばあさん
むすめさん	おじいちゃん	あに	おば
あね	むすめ	にょうぼう	おにいさん
そふ	おくさん	そぼ	ははおや

14. Correct the use of vocabulary in the following sentences when necessary. (Bear in mind social positions.)

a) アキラの~~父(ちち)~~ お父(とう)さん はラーメン屋(や)さんだ。
b) あたしの妹(いもうと)さんはとてもバカだよ。
c) 私のお母(かあ)さんは昨日(きのう)、ケーキを三つ食べたよ。
d) あなたの妻(つま)はたいへん美(うつく)しいですね。
e) 石川(いしかわ)さんのいとこは本を買いました。

15. Choose the most appropriate answer in each case.

a) _____、私は映画館(えいがかん)へ行きました。

1. まだ　2. あさって　3. 明日　4. 昨日

b) サオリちゃんの雑誌(ざっし)はつくえの _____ あると思うよ。

1. とても　2. 上に　3. ゆっくり　4. やっぱり

c) このなすとかぼちゃを _____ 売ってくださいよ、八百屋さん！

1. 安(やす)く　2. 低(ひく)く　3. 小(ちい)さく　4. むずかしく

d) 中田先生(なかたせんせい)は _____ 教室(きょうしつ)にいますよ。

1. そばに　2. もっと　3. きっと　4. いくら

e) あの人は _____ 漢字(かんじ)を書いている。

1. 危険(きけん)に　2. きらいに　3. ひまに　4. 上手(じょうず)に

16. Fill in the table, which continues overleaf, following the first example. To check which group a verb belongs to, check the online Vocabulary Index via the link on page 9).

洗(あら)う	洗(あら)って	to wash	座(すわ)る		
見る					to buy
		to sleep		抱(だ)きしめて	
	急(いそ)いで		行く		
	貸(か)して		作(つく)る		
		to play	ある		
呼(よ)ぶ					to read
疲(つか)れる				来て	

	して		走(はし)る		
飲む					to die
		to teach	歩(ある)く		
歌(うた)う			知(し)る		

17. Complete the following sentences with the verb form indicated.

a) 今、彼(かれ)の写真(しゃしん)を 見ていました。(見る | formal past gerund)

b) いいえ、映画(えいが)はまだ ________________。(終(お)わる | informal negative gerund)

c) おもしろくないですか？ __________________________ よ！(笑(わら)う | request)

d) 青木(あおき)くん！先生(せんせい)が __________________ よ。(呼(よ)ぶ | informal present gerund)

e) 明日(あした)、広島(ひろしま)へ ____。(行く | request)

f) いいえ、私はあのかえるを ______________。(殺(ころ)す | formal negative gerund)

g) 西田先輩(にしだせんぱい)は今たばこを ________________ か？(吸(す)う | formal present gerund)

h) あなたが大嫌(だいきら)いだ！家へ ____________________________。(帰(かえ)る | request)

i) 私？ ________________________ よ、酒(さけ)。(飲(の)む | formal past negative gerund)

18. Fill each gap with a missing adverb, choosing from the box below, and changing adjectives into adverbs as necessary.

a) あなた！うるさいですよ！ 静(しず)かに 食べてくださいね。

b) A: 妹(いもうと)はどこにいるの？| B: テレビの __________ 座(すわ)っているよ！

c) 明日(あした)、もっと __________ 来てください！わかったか？

d) __________、彼(かれ)は来なかった。しかし、__________ は来ると思うよ。

e) 彼女(かのじょ)は __________ 来ますよ。__________ 待ってくださいね。

f) トモコちゃん！この字(じ)は大きいよ！ __________ 書(か)いてね。

g) あの人は __________ 歌(うた)いました。

昨日(きのう)	前(まえ)に	小(ちい)さい	きっと	~~静(しず)かな~~	早(はや)い	上手(じょうず)な	ちょっと	明日(あした)

19. Fill each gap with the ***-suru*** verb form of the noun in brackets.

a) アサミさんにこれをすると<u>約束(やくそく)した</u>。(約束(やくそく) | informal past)

b) あの女は山本(やまもと)さんと ____________ よ。(結婚(けっこん) | formal past gerund)

c) ユズヒコ！テレビを見るな！ ____________ よ！(勉強(べんきょう) | request)

d) オサムくんは車(くるま)を ____________。(運転(うんてん) | formal gerund)

e) バスはまだ ____________。(出発(しゅっぱつ) | informal past negative)

20. Complete the following sentences with the correct particles.

a) モモコさん____自転車(じてんしゃ)は大学(だいがく)の前____ある____思います。

b) A: 学校(がっこう)____バス____来ますか？ B: いいえ、電車(でんしゃ)____来ますよ。

c) 彼女(かのじょ)____教室(きょうしつ)____お母(かあ)さん____ケーキ____食べているか？

d) 姉(あね)____弟(おとうと)は私に映画(えいが)____好(す)きだ____言(い)っている。

e) ここ____は私____本____２冊(さつ)あります。本田(ほんだ)さん____あげてください。

Kanji

父	母	弟	四	姉	妹	多	少	休	体	力
(36)	(37)	(38)	(39)	(40)	(41)	(51)	(52)	(124)	(125)	(108)
名	元	気	家	会	社	近	遠	広	強	弱
(102)	(66)	(67)	(160)	(80)	(81)	(96)	(97)	(111)	(106)	(107)

21. Practice writing the kanji below. Find the stroke order in the online Kanji Compilation section via the link on page 9.

弟										
姉										

気										
弱										
家										

22. Link each kanji with its most common reading (usually, the ***kun'yomi***).

父	いもうと	体	からだ
妹	おとうと	弱い	つよい
近い	おおい	強い	よわい
遠い	ちかい	家	いえ
弟	とおい	兄	あね
多い	ちち	姉	あに

23. Choose the correct kanji or kanji combination for each reading.

a) ひろい
1. 広い　2. 遠い　3. 多い　4. 弱い

b) あね
1. 兄　2. 弟　3. 姉　4. 妹

c) かいしゃ
1. 今社　2. 社今　3. 社会　4. 会社

d) ふぼ
1. 父母　2. 祖父　3. 母父　4. 祖母

24. Choose the correct reading for each kanji or kanji combination.

a) あの少年の名前はなんですか？
少年：1. しょうとし　2. しょうねん　3. しゅうねん　4. しゅうとし
名前：1. めいぜん　2. まなえ　3. めいまえ　4. なまえ

b) お父さんはバルセロナと神戸(こうべ)が姉妹都市(とし)だと言(い)いました。
父：1. ちち　2. かあ　3. はは　4. とう
姉妹：1. あねいもうと　2. いもうとあね　3. しまい　4. まいし

c) オレのバカ弟は元気にマンガ家になりたいと言(い)っているぞ！

弟：1. おとうと　2. いもうと　3. あね　4. あに

元気：1.きげん　2.もとき　3.げんき　4.きもと

家：1.か　2.け　3.いえ　4.うち

25. Give the reading in ***furigana*** of the underlined kanji.

a) 会社へ行く前に、彼女(かのじょ)に会いました。

b) 昨日(きのう)は天気がよかったですね。ちょっと家を出て、遠くへ行った。

c) おい！「社会の窓(まど)」が開(あ)いてるよ、お兄さん！

d) 体力がないね ... 私の体は少し弱いと思う ... 休むな！

26. Write the following words in kanji, and give their meaning. (**Note:** The words marked with an asterisk appear in kanji tables studied in previous lessons.)

はは	________	________	ちから	________	________
ひろい	________	________	つよい	________	________
きゅうじつ	________	________	たぶん	________	________
*にんき	________	________	*きもち	________	________

Lesson 26 • 第26課

The Body

After a few grammar lessons, taking time to stock up on vocabulary is always useful. In this lesson, we'll take a break from grammar to look at some vocabulary relating to parts of the body, basing the explanations on three pictures full of new words.

The body

The Japanese word for "body" is 体 ***karada***. In the illustration on this page we can see the names in Japanese for the main parts of the body. Each word is given in kanji or hiragana, followed by a transcription in ***rōmaji***, and, finally, the English translation.

Even though the picture gives you a quite comprehensive list of terms, you don't actually need to know absolutely all of them. In the first stage of learning, the main ones should be enough. Therefore, try at least to learn the following: 顔 ***kao***, 首 ***kubi***, 髪の毛 ***kaminoke***, 頭 ***atama***, 胸 ***mune***, 背中 ***senaka***, 腕 ***ude***, 手 ***te***, お腹 ***o-naka*** and 脚 / 足 ***ashi***. Later on, when you have perfectly mastered these terms, you can study the rest.

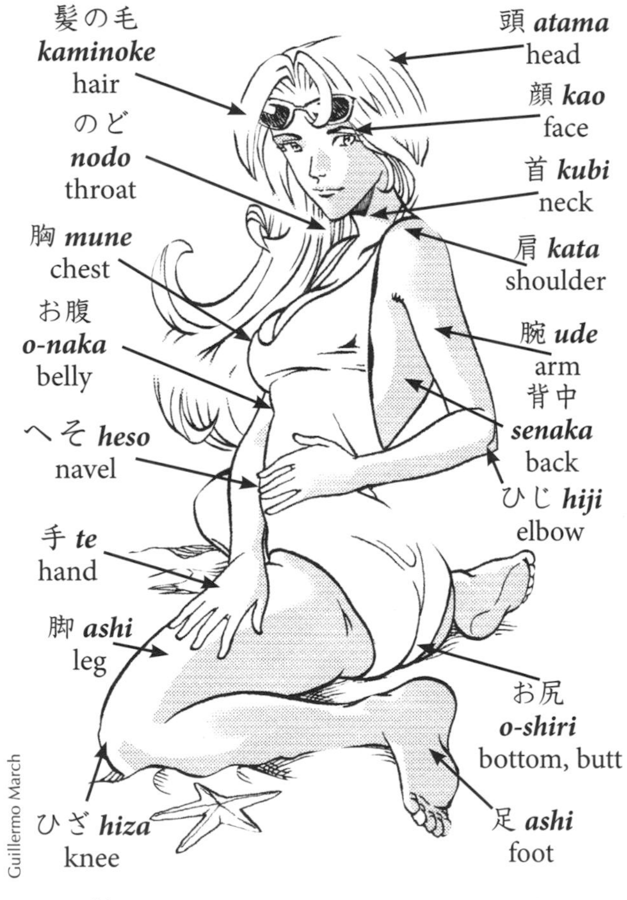

The inside of the body

The illustration on this page provides a lot of useful vocabulary, but all the words belong to the outside parts of the body. To supplement this, we will provide you with a list of names for some of the interior parts of the body that you might find useful to know: 頭脳 ***zunō***, "brain"; 心臓 ***shinzō***, "heart"; 血管 ***kekkan***, "vein" or "artery"; 肺臓 ***haizō***, "lungs"; 肝臓 ***kanzō***, "liver"; 腎臓 ***jinzō***, "kidneys"; 胃 ***i***, "stomach"; 腸 ***chō***, "intestines"; 生殖器官 ***seishoku kikan***, "reproductive organs."

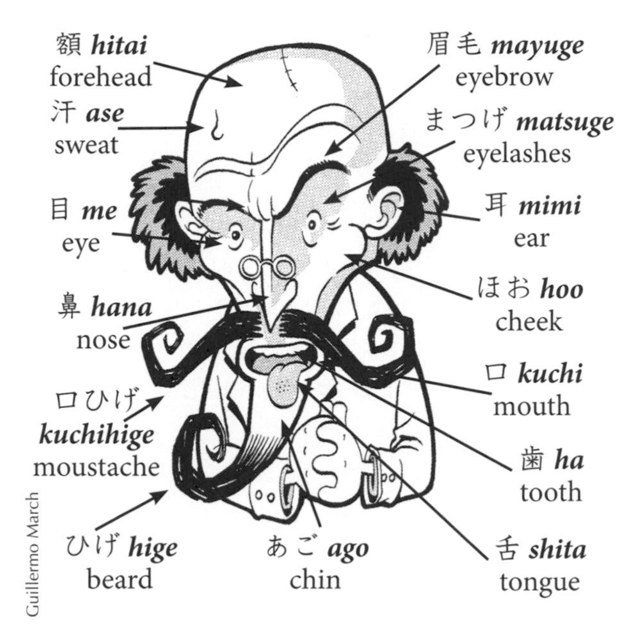

Guillermo March

Face and hand

The illustration on the left shows the words for parts of the face and the head. "Face" is 顔 ***kao*** in Japanese, which you have already learned in the first picture. Other key vocabulary to retain this time includes 目 ***me***, 口 ***kuchi***, 鼻 ***hana***, 耳 ***mimi***, 舌 ***shita***, 歯 ***ha*** and ひげ ***hige***.

Finally, in the illustration below, we can see a manga illustration of the hand of somebody who has passed away. "Hand" is 手 ***te***, and the essential words that you should retain here are 指 ***yubi***, 爪 ***tsume*** and 手の平 ***tenohira***."

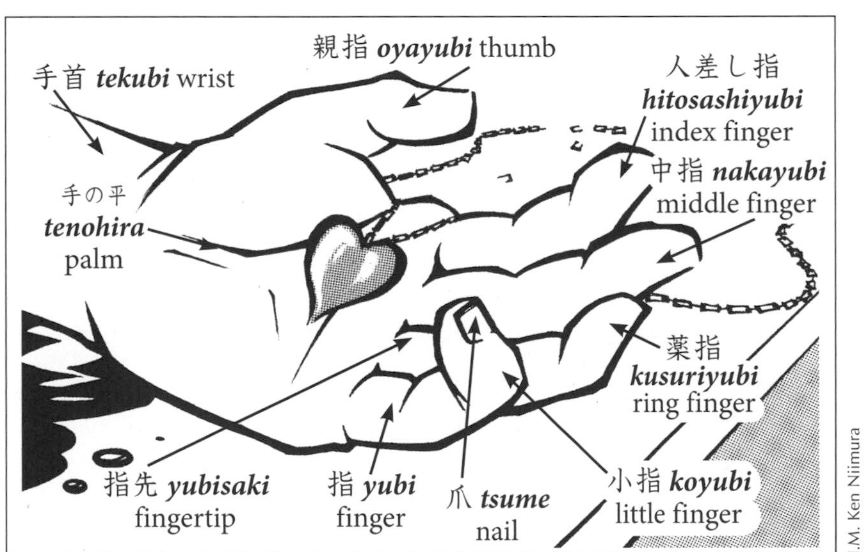

J.M. Ken Niimura

Feeling pain

Something very useful and which can get you out of trouble in any language is knowing how to say "x hurts." Forming this sentence in Japanese is quite simple if we know the names for the different parts of the body. All we need to do is follow the structure ***x ga itai desu*** (" x SP painful be"). Take a look at these examples:

頭が痛いです	お腹が痛いです	胸が痛いです
atama ga itai desu	***o-naka ga itai desu***	***mune ga itai desu***
I have a headache.	I have stomach pains.	My chest hurts.

Expressions with parts of the body

Japanese has many more expressions related to parts of the body than we have in English. Here are some useful ones:

- 頭がいい/悪い ***atama ga ii/warui*** (Lit. "good / bad head"). To be intelligent / dumb.
- 頭を下げる ***atama o sageru*** (Lit. "to lower one's head"). To excuse oneself in a more or less humiliating way (lowering one's head in a bow, in sign of repentance).
- 頭にくる ***atama ni kuru*** (Lit. "to come to one's head"). To get angry, to get furious.
- 顔が広い ***kao ga hiroi*** (Lit. "broad face"). To be well-known, to have many contacts.
- 顔を売る ***kao o uru*** (Lit. "to sell one's face"). To make oneself known, advertise oneself.
- 目が高い ***me ga takai*** (Lit. "high eyes"). To be an expert, to know something very well.
- 耳が痛い ***mimi ga itai*** (Lit. "to have an earache"). To be ashamed to hear.
- 耳が遠い ***mimi ga tooi*** (Lit. "distant ear"). To be hard of hearing, to be a little deaf.
- 口が軽い ***kuchi ga karui*** (Lit. "light mouth"). To not be able to keep a secret.
- 口が堅い ***kuchi ga katai*** (Lit. "hard mouth"). To be able to keep a secret.
- 口が悪い ***kuchi ga warui*** (Lit. "bad mouth"). To be foulmouthed.
- 鼻が高い ***hana ga takai*** (Lit. "high nose"). To be proud of something.
- 首になる ***kubi ni naru*** (Lit. "to turn into a neck"). To be fired from a job.
- 胸を張る ***mune o haru*** (Lit. "to extend one's chest"). To pluck up courage.
- 腕がいい ***ude ga ii*** (Lit. "good arm"). To be good at something.
- 手を上げる ***te o ageru*** (Lit. "to raise one's hand"). To give up, to resign oneself.
- 手を貸す ***te o kasu*** (Lit. "to lend a hand"). To lend a hand, to help.
- 手を出す ***te o dasu*** (Lit. "to take one's hand out"). To have a hand in some affair.
- 手も足も出ない ***te mo ashi mo denai*** (Lit. "neither hand nor foot come out"). To not know what to do, to see no solution to something, to find oneself helpless.
- 腹が立つ ***hara ga tatsu*** (Lit. "the stomach rises"). To get furious, to get angry.
- 尻が重い ***shiri ga omoi*** (Lit. "heavy bottom"). To be slow, to be lazy.
- 尻をぬぐう ***shiri o nuguu*** (Lit. "to clean one's bottom"). To solve somebody else's error.
- 足を洗う ***ashi o arau*** (Lit. "to wash one's feet"). To wash one's hands of a murky affair

Although it isn't part of the human body, the expression 羽を伸ばす ***hane o nobasu*** (Lit. "to spread one's wings") is interesting. Although it uses the same words as the English expression "to spread one's wings," it means "to take it easy."

Finally, a couple of extra sayings to do with the body. The first is 口はわざわいのもと ***kuchi wa wazawai no moto***, literally "the mouth is the origin of misfortune," its meaning being quite clear. The second is the Japanese version of the famous biblical saying "an eye for an eye and a tooth for a tooth": 目には目を、歯には歯 を ***me ni wa me o, ha ni wa ha o***.

漫画例 Manga Examples

The only way to master about the vocabulary of the body is to sit down and memorize it. But these examples of body-related language from real manga might also help, as well as expanding on what you know already.

Manga Example 1: Body and soul

Studio Kōsen

Here, apart from the word 体 ***karada*** ("body"), with which we are already familiar, we have the word 心 ***kokoro*** meaning "heart," but a spiritual kind of heart: it is the mind, the soul, the thing that makes us human. That is why we have translated the sentence as "in flesh and spirit." Remember the word "heart," the physical organ which pumps the body's blood is called 心臓 ***shinzō***. Don't confuse both words.

Title: PART 6 心も体も
paato roku kokoro mo karada mo
part 6 heart too body too
Part Six: In flesh and spirit.

Manga Example 2: Something slightly more vulgar...

Studio Kōsen

Just like in any other language, in Japanese there are vulgar words to refer to some parts of the body. Here, for example, we see オッパイ ***oppai***, a word with the same sense and connotations as the English word "boobs," instead of 胸 ***mune*** ("breast"). Likewise, ケツ ***ketsu*** is the vulgar word for "ass."

Robot: オッパイ ミサイル
oppai misairu
boobs missile
Booby missile!

Manga Example 3: Medical vocabulary

Just as in English, there are literally thousands of words that refer to the human body, most of them used only in medical fields; Japanese is no exception. In this lesson we have seen some of the most common words related to the body, but this manga panel is interesting because it uses a few specialized terms. For example, the brain 脳 ***nō*** is divided into 大脳 ***dainō***, "brain"; 小脳 ***shōnō***, "cerebellum"; and 間脳 ***kannō***, "diencephalon." We are told in this panel about a brain's artery, the center brain artery to be precise, and its literal translation would be "brain artery, center-left area."

Guillermo March

Doctor: 銃弾が左中大脳動脈をかすめている。
jūdan ga sachū dainō dōmyaku o kasumete iru.
bullet SP center-left brain artery DOP graze
The bullet is grazing the center brain artery.

Manga Example 4: Feeling pain

Earlier in this lesson, on page 237, we saw how to make sentences of the "x hurts" variety. In English we have different expressions for pain, where we use verbs such as "to hurt" or "to ache," or nouns such as "pain" or "ache." In Japanese, however, we use ***itai*** ("painful") which is an ***-i*** adjective. Therefore, its past tense will be 痛かった ***itakatta*** ("was painful," "had been painful," etc.), its negative 痛くない ***itakunai*** ("it's not painful"), and its past negative 痛くなかった ***itakunakatta*** ("it wasn't painful," "it has not been painful," etc.)

J.M. Ken Niimura

Toshio: 俺はいま頭が痛いんだ...
ore wa ima atama ga itai n da...
I TOP now head SP painful be
I have a headache now...

Exercises 練習

1. What is the Japanese word for "face"? And for "hand"? Write the basic vocabulary for the parts of the face and hand, giving their ***rōmaji*** reading as well.

2. How do you say the following words in Japanese: "brain," "lungs," "stomach"?

3. Translate into Japanese: "Your eyes are beautiful." (your: 君の ***kimi no***, beautiful: きれいな ***kirei-na***.) Review Lesson 14 if necessary.

4. Translate into English: 彼の腕は強いです ***kare no ude wa tsuyoi desu*** (***kare***: "he," ***no***: pop, ***tsuyoi***: "strong," ***desu***: "to be" (Lesson 19).

5. Translate the following sentence into Japanese: "My thumb hurts."

6. Translate the following sentence into English: 肩が痛いです ***kata ga itai desu***.

7. Translate the following sentence into English: この人は鼻が高いです ***kono hito wa hana ga takai desu*** (***kono***: "this," ***hito***: "person.")

8. Which expression would a Japanese gangster use if he wanted to leave his 組 ***kumi*** (yakuza group)?

9. What two Japanese words can be translated as "heart" and what are their different meanings?

10. Which is the vulgar equivalent of the word お尻 ***o-shiri***? What about 胸 ***mune***?

— Answers to all the exercises can be found online by following the link on page 9. —

Lesson 27 • 第27課

Everyday Expressions

In this lesson we will get a deeper insight into a subject we first looked at in Lesson 4: expresssions that are used in our everyday interactions.

Good morning!

In the vocabulary table on the facing page we can find a list of everyday expressions in the Japanese language. However, we have intentionally omitted the most common greetings, as we studied them in depth in Lesson 4. Anyway, let's have a quick reminder:

おはようございます ***ohayō gozaimasu*** good morning
こんにちは ***konnichi wa*** hello
こんばんは ***konban wa*** good evening
おやすみなさい ***o-yasumi nasai*** good night (when somebody goes to bed)
お元気ですか ***o-genki desu ka?*** how are you?
はい、元気です ***hai, genki desu*** I'm fine [thank you]
さようなら ***sayōnara*** good bye
またね ***mata ne*** see you later
ありがとう ***arigatō*** thank you
どういたしまして ***dō itashimashite*** you're welcome

Beyond konnichi wa

However, to be able to go beyond ***konnichi wa***, there are several common expressions you need to learn. These daily expressions, which are hard to translate literally, can become an obstacle, unless you learn them in context with an explanation about their meaning and their most common sphere of usage. Some of the trickiest expressions are those used when entering or leaving a house or a place. These can be divided into two groups:

Group 1. These are expressions used when we enter or leave our own home. These are: ただいま ***tadaima*** (said by the person coming into his or her home); お帰りなさい ***o-kaeri nasai*** (said by the person inside his or her home in answer to the first person's ***tadaima***, and very often contracted to お帰り ***o-kaeri***); 行ってきます ***itte kimasu*** (said by the person leaving his or her home); and 行ってらっしゃい ***itte rasshai*** (said by the person who stays home in answer to the first person's ***itte kimasu***).

Group 2. These are expressions used when entering or leaving somebody else's home or when leaving or entering the workplace. We have お邪魔します ***o-jama shimasu*** (said by the person entering); いらっしゃい ***irasshai*** (said by the person inside his or her home as an expression of welcome to the visitor); and 失礼します ***shitsurei shimasu*** (said by the person leaving). Memorize this complex set of expressions, because you may find them very useful.

Key everyday expressions		
Expression	**Explanation**	**Translation**
失礼します ***shitsurei shimasu***	Used when entering or exiting	Excuse me. | I'm leaving now.
ただいま ***tadaima***	Used when entering one's home	I'm home.
お帰りなさい ***o-kaeri nasai***	Answer to ***tadaima***	Welcome home.
行ってきます ***itte kimasu***	Used when leaving one's own home / work place	• I'm leaving. • I'll be back soon.
行ってらっしゃい ***itte rasshai***	Answer to ***itte kimasu***	• Don't be long. • See you soon.
お邪魔します ***o-jama shimasu***	Used when entering somebody else's home	May I come in? Lit. "I'm being rude"
いらっしゃい ***irasshai***	Answer to ***o-jama shimasu***	• Come in. • Welcome.
ごめんください ***gomen kudasai***	Calling for attention when you enter someone's home	Is anyone home?
いらっしゃいませ ***irasshaimase***	Greeting from shop assistant to customer (which you don't answer)	Welcome! May I help you?
ごめんなさい ***gomen nasai***	Apology, asking to be forgiven	I'm sorry. | Excuse me.
すみません ***sumimasen***	a) Apology b) To get someone's attention	a) Sorry, excuse me. b) Excuse me.
いただきます ***itadakimasu***	At the start of a meal	Bon appetit. Lit. "I accept," "I receive"
ごちそうさま ***gochisō-sama***	At the end of a meal, expression of gratitude	• It was very good. • Thank you for the meal.
お疲れ様 ***o-tsukare-sama***	When finishing a job or any other activity	Good job. Lit. "Thanks for getting tired."
ご苦労様 ***gokurō-sama***	Similar to ***o-tsukare-sama*** (but usually from superiors to subordinates)	Good job. Lit. "Thanks for getting tired."
おめでとうございます ***omedetō gozaimasu***	Expression of congratulations	Congratulations.
よろしくお願いします ***yoroshiku o-negai shimasu***	After asking for a favor or asking so. to do sth. for the speaker	• Please. • Pleased to meet you. • It's in your hands now.

Expressions and culture

The Japanese culture is obviously very different from the Western one, and has many peculiar features. Language reflects the character and the mentality of the people who use it, and Japanese is not an exception. Why are we explaining all this? Well, the point is that the characteristic features of Japanese mentality are reflected much more in their daily expressions than those in Western languages.

One of the clearest cases is the extremely common expression よろしくお願いします ***yoroshiku o-negai shimasu*** (see table), which you will hear over and over again if you visit Japan. This expression is used after having asked a favor of somebody, when we have just met somebody or when we leave some task in the hands of another person.

The most literal translation of this expression would be something like "I humbly ask for your favorable consideration," which is a phrase that says a lot about the Japanese mentality: asking for a favor means placing responsibility on another person, which is not perceived as "honorable." Thus, we need to apologize when asking someone to do something for us, and we must be very humble about it.

Another interesting example is the usage of すみません ***sumimasen*** (Lesson 4), an expression which originally means "excuse me" or "sorry," but which is very often used meaning "thank you," rather than "sorry." For example, X drops a coin on the ground, and Y picks it up and returns it to X. In this case, instead of ありがとう ***arigatō***, X will most probably thank Y's gesture with a すみません ***sumimasen***. This way of "thanking" implies something like "I'm sorry to have made you take the trouble to do me this favor (and I thank you for it)."

I know it's something insignificant, but...

When a Japanese person gives a present to somebody, he or she will tend to reduce the importance of what he or she is giving, as an act of humility. The traditional expression used when giving a present (only in very formal occasions) is: つまらない物ですけれど、どうぞ ***tsumaranai mono desu keredo, dōzo...*** Its literal translation would be "I know it's something insignificant, but please (take it)." In fact, this "insignificant" present could very well be something very valuable or even really expensive.

There is another interesting traditional expression which is used in formal situations by someone who invites a visitor to enter his or her house: 汚いところですけれど、どうぞ上がってください ***kitanai tokoro desu keredo, dōzo agatte kudasai*** (literally "this is a dirty place, but please come in"). The funny thing is that, in most cases, this "dirty place" is a beautiful and immaculate house, as clean as a hospital.

Mastering Japanese does not only mean mastering the written and spoken language, it also means understanding the culture behind it and being able to adapt oneself to it (since the culture will not adapt itself to us), which is maybe the most challenging aspect.

漫画例 Manga Examples

Even if we look for everyday expressions in our dictionary, the definition we find is not always good enough. Since they say a picture is worth a thousand words, let's have a look at some manga examples.

Manga Example 1: Entering and leaving a place

J.M. Ken Niimura

Earlier in the lesson we studied in detail the set of expressions used when entering or leaving a house.

Here we have an example taken from a manga. In the panel, Marc has just arrived at his own home or office and Ken just leaving. Marc's expression, ***tadaima***, is used to greet the people inside the building, and their answer should be ***o-kaeri nasai***. In Ken's case, he is leaving with the words ***itte kimasu***, so the people staying in the building should say goodbye to him with ***itte rasshai***.

Marc:	ただいま！	Ken:	行ってきます！
	tadaima!		***Itte kimasu!***
	I'm home!		I'm off!

Manga Example 2: I'm hungry

Another useful expression is "I'm hungry" or "I'm thirsty." There are many ways of saying it depending on the speaker. To say "I'm hungry," ***hara ga hetta*** is a quite vulgar expression used by men, ***onaka ga suita*** is the standard form, and ***onaka ga peko peko*** is rather childish. To say "I'm thirsty," ***nodo ga kawaita*** is the standard form, and ***nodo ga karakara*** is the colloquial one.

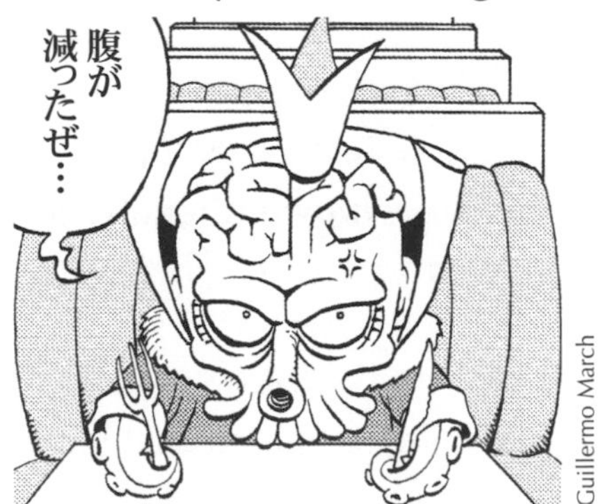

Guillermo March

Slime:	腹が減ったぜ...
	hara ga hetta ze...
	stomach SP decrease EP
	I'm hungry...

Manga Example 3: Happy New Year!

In this manga panel we have an expression we have not seen yet: the New Year's greeting 明けましておめでとうございます ***akemashite omedetō gozaimasu***. It literally means "congratulations on the opening (of the New Year)," in other words,"Happy New Year." The greeting is usually followed by the expression: 今年もよろしくお願いします ***kotoshi mo yoroshiku o-negai shimasu***.

Kotoshi mo means "this year too." To remind yourself of the usage of ***yoroshiku o-negai shimasu***, see page 244. ***Omedetō gozaimasu***, on its own, means "congratulations" and is used for birthdays, successes, celebrations, and so on.

Maria: 明けましておめでとうございます。
akemashite omedetō gozaimasu
Happy New Year.

Manga Example 4: It's been a long time (since we last met)

The world of daily expressions is quite large. For example, there are several greetings that can be used when meeting someone, such as the well-known ***konnichi wa, konban wa***, etc. ***O-hisashiburi desu*** (or simply ***hisashiburi***) could also be classified in this category, and its approximate meaning is "it's been a long time (since we last met)."

Besides these, there are several fixed expressions with similar meanings or variations, such as the different ways of thanking someone (***arigatō, dōmo, arigatō gozaimasu***, etc.), or of saying goodbye (***sayōnara***, ***mata ne, bai bai,*** etc.). These expressions were introduced in Lesson 4. Likewise, to apologize, apart from the well-known ***sumimasen*** and ***gomen nasai***, we have the informal ***gomen ne,*** or the more formal 申し訳ない ***mōshiwake nai*** or 申し訳ありません ***mōshiwake arimasen***.

Sanada: お久しぶりです、バッハ先生
o-hisashiburi desu, bahha sensei
long time be, Bach-professor
It's been a long time, Dr. Bach...

Exercises 練習

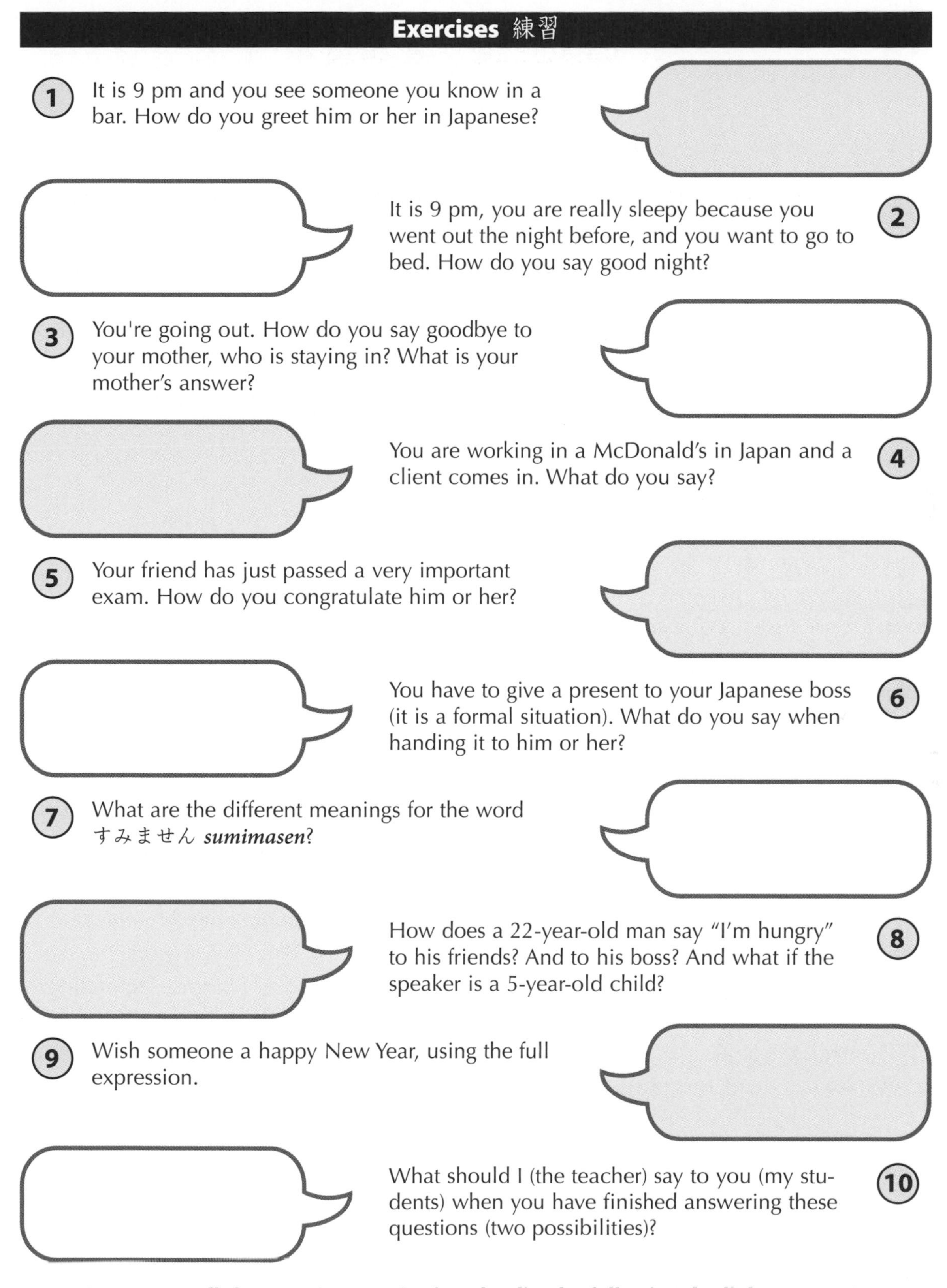

1. It is 9 pm and you see someone you know in a bar. How do you greet him or her in Japanese?

2. It is 9 pm, you are really sleepy because you went out the night before, and you want to go to bed. How do you say good night?

3. You're going out. How do you say goodbye to your mother, who is staying in? What is your mother's answer?

4. You are working in a McDonald's in Japan and a client comes in. What do you say?

5. Your friend has just passed a very important exam. How do you congratulate him or her?

6. You have to give a present to your Japanese boss (it is a formal situation). What do you say when handing it to him or her?

7. What are the different meanings for the word すみません ***sumimasen***?

8. How does a 22-year-old man say "I'm hungry" to his friends? And to his boss? And what if the speaker is a 5-year-old child?

9. Wish someone a happy New Year, using the full expression.

10. What should I (the teacher) say to you (my students) when you have finished answering these questions (two possibilities)?

— Answers to all the exercises can be found online by following the link on page 9. —

Lesson 28 • 第28課

Verbs (4): The Verb Naru

The time has come to study hard, because, even though we have named this lesson "the verb naru," we are really going to study a lot more than just that. We will assume you have studied and memorized the contents of Lessons 13, 14, 16, 19, 20, 22 and 24.

The verb naru

One of the most frequent verbs in Japanese is なる ***naru***. It has no exact translation in English, although it can be paraphrased as "to have suffered some change," "to grow into," or, probably the closest in meaning, "to become."

Usage of *naru*		
Noun	+になる + ***ni naru***	先生になる ***sensei ni naru*** to become a teacher
-*i* adjective	~~い~~+くなる ***i + ku naru***	強くなる ***tsuyoku naru*** to get strong
-*na* adjective	~~な~~+になる ~~***na***~~ + ***ni naru***	静かになる ***shizuka ni naru*** to grow quiet
suru verb	~~する~~+になる ~~***suru***~~+ ***ni naru***	勉強になる ***benkyō ni naru*** to prove educational

In the table of the verb なる ***naru*** we see the different inflections this verb asks of the word before it. For example, when this word is an -***i*** adjective (Lesson 13), we will replace the last い ***i*** with く ***ku.*** Thus, 難しい ***muzukashii*** ("difficult") ⇒ 難しくなる ***muzukashiku naru*** ("to become / get difficult"). With -***na*** adjectives (Lesson 14), な ***na*** will be replaced with に ***ni*** . Thus, 乱暴な ***ranbō-na*** ("violent") ⇒ 乱暴になる ***ranbō ni naru*** ("to become / grow violent"). With nouns, になる ***ni naru*** must be added. Thus, 社長 ***shachō*** ("[company] director") ⇒ 社長になる ***shachō ni naru*** ("to become [company] director").

The verb なる ***naru*** is extremely common in any register and situation in Japanese, and its forms are as follows: present tense, なる ***naru***; past tense, なった ***natta***; negative, ならない ***naranai***; past negative, ならなかった ***naranakatta***; -***masu*** form なります ***narimasu*** (see Lesson 19 for -***masu*** form conjugations). For example:

彼女はとてもやさしくなった
kanojo wa totemo yasashiku natta
She has become very kind.

アキは先生になりません
Aki wa sensei ni narimasen
Aki does not become a teacher.

To go to...

<table>
<tr><th colspan="3">“To go to...” / “To come to...” structures</th></tr>
<tr><td>V<s>ます</s>+に行く
V <s>masu</s> + ni iku</td><td>買いに行く
kai ni iku
to go to buy</td><td>見に行く
mi ni iku
to go to see</td></tr>
<tr><td>V<s>ます</s>+に来る
V <s>masu</s> + ni kuru</td><td>遊びに来る
asobi ni kuru
to come to play</td><td>書きに来る
kaki ni kuru
to come to write</td></tr>
<tr><td colspan="3">買う kau: to buy | 見る miru: to see
遊ぶ asobu: to play | 書く kaku: to write</td></tr>
</table>

In Lesson 19 we learned that all verbs have a ます ***-masu*** form. If we conjugate a verb in its ***-masu*** form, remove the last ます ***masu***, and replace it with the particle に ***ni*** and the verb 行く ***iku*** (“to go”), we will form sentences with the structure “to go to...”

Let’s look at the verb 買う ***kau*** (“to buy”). The ***-masu*** form is 買います ***kaimasu***. If we remove ます ***masu***, we have 買い ***kai***. Adding に行く ***ni iku***, we obtain the form 買いに行く ***kai ni iku***, which means “to go to buy.” Conjugating the verb 行く ***iku***, we can obtain the past, negative, and past negative forms. Take a look at the examples:

次郎さんは肉を買いに行く
jirō-san wa niku o kai ni iku
Jirō (SUF.) TOP meat DOP buy go to
Jirō goes to buy meat.

彼と食べに行きません
kare to tabe ni ikimasen
he with eat go to
I don’t go to eat with him.

Using くる ***kuru*** (“to come”) instead of 行く ***iku***, creates the structure “to come to”:

広美さんはテレビを見に来る
hiromi-san wa terebi o mi ni kuru
Hiromi (SUF.) TOP television DOP watch come to
Hiromi comes to watch television.

彼は遊びに来なかった
kare wa asobi ni konakatta
he TOP play come to
He didn’t come to play.

Giving and receiving

The table on the next page shows the usage of the verbs あげる ***ageru*** (“to give”), もらう ***morau*** (“to receive”) and くれる ***kureru*** (“to give [to me]”). Here are their forms:

あげる | Past: ***ageta***; Neg.: ***agenai***; Past neg.: ***agenakatta***; ***-masu*** form: ***agemasu***
もらう | Past: ***moratta***; Neg.: ***morawanai***; Past neg.: ***morawanakatta***; ***-masu*** form: ***moraimasu***
くれる | Past: ***kureta***; Neg.: ***kurenai***; Past neg.: ***kurenakatta***; ***-masu*** form: ***kuremasu***

To be use these verbs correctly, you need to confirm who performs the action, who receives the action, and which particle corresponds to each. ***Ageru*** and ***morau*** are straightforward, as they closely correspond to the English "to give" and "to receive." But you must look closely at the usage of particles!

私は鳥にパンをあげる
watashi wa tori ni pan o ageru
I TOP bird IOP bread DOP give
I give bread to the bird.

彼女はヒデに雑誌をもらわない
kanojo wa hide ni zasshi o morawanai
she TOP Hide IOP magazine DOP receive
She does not receive a magazine from Hide.

The verb くれる ***kureru*** is trickier. It is used when someone "gives" something to either "me" or to "someone close to me" (family member, classmate, colleague, etc.)

彼は私に雑誌をくれる
kare wa watashi ni zasshi o kureru
he TOP me IOP magazine DOP give
He gives me a magazine.

ヨシオ君は母にえんぴつをくれました
Yoshio-kun wa haha ni enpitsu o kuremashita
Yoshio (SUF.) TOP mother IOP pencil DOP give
Yoshio gave a pencil to my mother.

Therefore, we will never use あげる ***ageru*** to indicate "someone gives something to me or to someone close to me": instead, we must use くれる ***kureru***.

There is also a grammatical structure made with the ***-te*** form (Lesson 24) plus these three verbs, which has a similar meaning to "to perform an action which gives or receives a favor." Look at this sentence:

私は彼女に花を買ってあげた
watashi wa kanojo ni hana o katte ageta
I TOP she IOP flowers DOP buy (give)
I bought her flowers (doing her a favor).

Basic usage of *ageru, morau* and *kureru*		
あげる ***ageru*** **"to give"**	**XはYにZをあげる** ***x wa y ni z o ageru*** Mr. x gives z to Mr. y **(x: gives | y: receives)**	太郎さんはマリアさんに本をあげる ***Tarō-san wa Maria-san ni hon o ageru*** **Tarō (SUF.) TOP Maria (SUF.) IOP book DOP give** Tarō gives a book to Maria.
もらう ***morau*** **"to receive"**	**XはYにZをもらう** ***x wa y ni z o morau*** Mr. x receives z from Mr. y **(x: receives | y: gives)**	山田さんは伊藤さんにたばこをもらう ***Yamada-san wa Itō-san ni tabako o morau*** **Yamada (SUF.) TOP Itō (SUF.) IOP tobacco DOP receive** Mr. Yamada receives tobacco from Mr. Itō.
くれる ***kureru*** **"to give"**	**Xは私にZをくれる** ***x wa watashi ni z o kureru*** Mr. x gives z to me **(x: gives | io: receives)**	鈴木君は私にワインをくれる ***Suzuki-kun wa watashi ni wain o kureru*** **Suzuki (SUF.) TOP I IOP wine DOP give** Suzuki gives me wine.

漫画例 Manga Examples

This time we provide four pages of manga examples to help you reinforce and consolidate the large amount of information relating to the three main grammatical structures we've introduced in this lesson.

Manga Example 1: *-i* adjective + *naru* | *-te* form + *morau*

In this panel we can see two of the three grammatical structures we have studied in this lesson: the verb なる ***naru***, and the use of the ***-te*** form + もらう ***morau*** ("to receive").

First, we have the combination of the ***-i*** adjective 大きい ***ookii*** ("big") with ***naru***. Remember that, to combine them, we need to replace the last い ***i*** with く ***ku***. In this panel you can see the words 大きくなる ***ookiku naru*** ("to get big," "to grow").

Secondly, notice さわってもらう ***sawatte morau***, a combination of the verb さわる ***sawaru*** ("to touch") and もらう ***morau*** ("to receive"). ***Sawatte morau*** has the connotation of "receiving the fact of being touched." Thus, Maya perceives the fact of "being touched" as a favor she receives from our reluctant magician.

Note: Notice the usage of the word お兄さん ***oniisan***. As you know, this word means "brother," but it is sometimes used to indicate the idea of a "young man whose name we don't know," like here. Review Manga Example 4 in Lesson 21 for more information.

Guillermo March

Maya: 私のペチャパイもお兄さんにさわってもらうと大きくなるかも
watashi no pechapai mo oniisan ni sawatte morau to ookiku naru kamo
I POP flat breast also brother IOP touch would receive big become maybe
Maybe, if you touched them, my small breasts might grow.

Manga Example 2: Noun + *naru*

Having seen the combination of an ***-i*** adjective with なる ***naru*** in the previous example, we will now see a noun with this verb. With nouns, we must add the particle に ***ni*** before なる ***naru***. Here we have チンピラになる ***chinpira ni naru***. ***Chinpira*** means "hooligan" (or rather, some kind of apprentice yakuza, Lesson 23), therefore ***chinpira ni naru*** will be "to become a hooligan," "to turn into a hooligan," "to grow to be a hooligan," etc. Generally speaking, なる ***naru*** has the meaning of "something or somebody that has changed regarding a previous state or position."

J.M. Ken Niimura

Nobu: チンピラになったな...
chinpira ni natta na...
hooligan becom EP...
I've become a hooligan...

Manga Example 3: To come to...

Here is a good example of a sentence with the compound verb structure ***-masu*** form verb + ***ni kuru*** meaning of "to come to...."

Let's review how to make this structure using the same verb as Takashi: 殺す ***korosu*** ("to kill"). The ***-masu*** form of this verb is 殺します ***koroshimasu***. After removing the ます ***masu*** part, we get the root 殺し ***koroshi***. Finally, we add the particle に ***ni*** and the verb 来る ***kuru*** ("to come") and thus we obtain 殺しに来る ***koroshi ni kuru*** ("to come to kill").

If we change the verb 来る ***kuru*** for the verb 行く ***iku*** ("to go"), the sentence 殺しに行く ***koroshi ni iku*** will mean "to go to kill." The "***-masu*** verb + ***ni*** + ***iku / kuru***" construction is very useful.

Studio Kōsen

Takashi: マサオを殺しに来たんだろう?
Masao o koroshi ni kita n darō?
Masao DOP kill come to right?
You've come to kill Masao, haven't you?

Manga Example 4: *Ageru* ("to give")

Let's now move onto the verbs meaning to give and to receive. This example shows how to use あげる ***ageru*** ("to give"). The usage of this verb is probably the easiest in the trio formed by ***ageru***, ***morau***, and ***kureru***, because it means purely "to give": The speaker is usually the one performing the action of giving and the other person is the one receiving it. It is different with ***morau*** and ***kureru***, because there are many variations, and they can get to be very complex. The best thing is for you to memorize the table on page 250; with time you will get used to handling them.

J.M. Ken Niimura

Nami: 全部あげるわっ！！
zenbu ageru wa!!
everything give EP!!!
I'll give you everything!!

Manga Example 5: *Kureru* ("to give [to me]")

Here the main verb is くれる ***kureru***, which means "to give," with the peculiarity that the person receiving the action is either "me" or someone psychologically close to "me." It is probably the most difficult verb to master in the trio ***ageru***, ***morau***, and ***kureru***. In this sentence, for example, the subject is お前 ***o-mae***, "you" (Lesson 7), who gives an object (指輪 ***yubiwa***, "a ring") to 娘 ***musume***, "my daughter." The word 娘 ***musume*** is used for a person who is psychologically close to the speaker, and, consequently, the use of ***kureru*** is justified. The subject is marked with the topic particle は ***wa***, and the person receiving the action ("me" or "someone close to me") is marked with に ***ni***.

Studio Kōsen

Muneo: お前は娘に指輪をくれたな...
omae wa musume ni yubiwa o kureta na...
you TOP daughter IOP ring DOP give EP...
You have given my daughter a ring, haven't you?

Manga Example 6: *-te ageru*

This manga provides a good example of the usage of a verb in the ***-te*** form with ***ageru***. The verb 教える ***oshieru*** means "to teach" (or simply "to say," "to tell," "to explain"), but if we conjugate it in the ***-te*** form (教えて ***oshiete***) and add あげる ***ageru*** (thus obtaining 教えてあげる ***oshiete ageru***), then we have a construction with the nuance "to teach / to explain doing a favor" (which, unfortunately, is lost in translation).

J.M. Ken Niimura

Likewise, if we used the other two verbs in the trio instead of ***ageru***, we would have the following: 教えてもらう ***oshiete morau*** "to receive a lesson" and 教えてくれる ***oshiete kureru*** "someone teaches something to me or to someone close to me."

Karin: わからないの！？ それじゃ、教えてあげるわ！
wakaranai no!? sore ja, oshiete ageru wa
understand Q??! then teach give EP
You don't understand? I'll tell you then!

Manga Example 7: Command

A derivative of the ***-te*** form plus ***ageru / morau / kureru*** is the construction "***-te*** form + ***kure***" (***kure*** is the command form of ***kureru***). This construction is often found in manga and is used to give commands in quite a direct way. In this panel, for instance, we have got 死んでくれ ***shinde kure***. ***Shinde*** is the ***-te*** form of the verb 死ぬ ***shinu*** ("to die"), and adding くれ ***kure*** it becomes a command (死んでくれ ***shinde kure***, "die"). We will see more about this form and about the command form in general in Lesson 30.

Guillermo March

Joey: 死んでくれ！
shinde kure!
die (receive)
Die!

Exercises 練習

1 What does the verb なる ***naru*** mean? Give the present, past, negative and past negative of なる ***naru*** in its simple form.

2 How do we conjugate -***i*** adjectives with the verb ***naru***? How about -***na*** adjectives? And nouns?

3 Add なる ***naru*** to the words やさしい ***yasashii*** ("easy"), 便利な ***benri-na*** ("convenient"), and 学生 ***gakusei*** "student." Give the meaning of each.

4 Translate into English: 彼は映画を見に行く ***kare wa eiga o mi ni iku***. (***kare***: "he," ***eiga***: "movie," ***miru***: "to see.")

5 Translate the following sentence into Japanese: "He comes to write a novel." (he: 彼 ***kare***, to write: 書く ***kaku***, novel: 小説 ***shōsetsu***.)

6 What do the verbs あげる ***ageru*** and もらう ***morau*** mean? What is the difference between あげる ***ageru*** and くれる ***kureru***?

7 Translate: フランクは道子に本をあげた ***Furanku wa Michiko ni hon o ageta***. (***Furanku***: "Frank," ***Michiko***: "Michiko" [girl's name], ***hon***: "book.")

8 Translate into Japanese: "Mr. Smith receives a document from Mr. Brown." (Smith: スミス ***sumisu***, document: 書類 ***shorui***, Brown: ブラウン ***buraun***.)

9 Translate: 私は生徒に日本語を教えてある ***watashi wa seito ni nihongo o oshiete ageru***. (***watashi***: "I," ***seito***: "pupil/s," ***nihongo***: "Japanese," ***oshieru***: "to teach.")

10 Order someone to drink up their milk using the -***te*** form + ***kure***. (milk: 牛乳 ***gyūnyū***, to drink: 飲む ***nomu***.)

— Answers to all the exercises can be found online by following the link on page 9. —

Lesson 29 • 第29課

Onomatopoeia

In this lesson we will study another of the idiomatic peculiarities of the Japanese language. We are talking about onomatopoeia, which can be classified into two large groups. It may surprise you to learn that this subject is very important in the study of Japanese, so read carefully.

Onomatopoeia

If you usually read manga, you will know that onomatopoeia abounds on each and every page. Many describe sounds like "boom," "crash," or "knock-knock" in English), but some have no English equivalent because they don't represent sounds but states. This lesson, together with the online Glossary of Onomatopoeia accessible via the link on page 9, has been designed to help you better understand this "language."

Most of the words we call onomatopoeia work very often as adverbs (Lesson 22). They can be divided into two groups: sound-imitating words (***giongo***) and words that "describe" a state of mind or a physical condition with no sound (***gitaigo***). This definition may be difficult to understand at first, but it will become clear very soon if you keep on reading.

Giongo

The word 擬音 ***gion*** means "to imitate a sound," and 語 ***go*** is "word." Therefore, 擬音語 ***giongo*** are "sound imitating words." The concept is very similar to our onomatopoeia. For example, the sound of a beating heart in Japanese is どきどき ***dokidoki*** and its meaning is "to be nervous" or "to be excited" (because heartbeats are faster at such times).

Other examples of ***giongo*** are ドカン ***dokan*** (explosion, "booom"), げらげら ***geragera*** (boisterous laugh, "haw, haw, haw"), or ぺこぺこ ***pekopeko*** (the sound the stomach makes when we are hungry, which in English would be something like "growl").

Some *giongo*	
ぺらぺら ***perapera***	(to talk) fluently
しくしく ***shikushiku***	(to weep) silently
どきどき ***dokidoki***	to be nervous (***doki***: sound of heartbeat)
げらげら ***geragera***	(to laugh) boisterously
ぺこぺこ ***pekopeko***	hungry (***peko***: noise of stomach)
ぱくぱく ***pakupaku***	(to eat) with relish
がらがら ***garagara***	slide open (a door)

Gitaigo

The word 擬態 ***gitai*** means "to imitate a state," and 語 ***go*** is "word" (as you know). Therefore, 擬態語 ***gitaigo*** means "state-imitating words." Unlike ***gion-***

go, which imitate sounds that can be heard, ***gitaigo*** do not imitate any sound, they are completely conceptual words. Within the ***gitaigo*** there are two groups: those which describe a physical condition and those which describe a state of mind.

In the first ***gitaigo*** group, relating to physical conditions, we find words such as からから ***karakara***, which means something is dry or, by extension, that we are very thirsty (since our throat is dry). Also, we find the word ぴかぴか ***pikapika***, which means something is very bright, dazzling.

In the second group, ***gitaigo*** that refer to a state of mind, we find for example くたくた ***kutakuta***, which indicates "tiredness" or "exhaustion"; and いらいら ***iraira***, which indicates "irritation" or "bad temper."

Some *gitaigo*			
いらいら ***iraira***	fretful, irritated	ぐっと ***gutto***	(to come out) by surprise, suddenly
くたくた ***kutakuta***	tired, exhausted	ぐるぐる ***guruguru***	(to go) round and round
からから ***karakara***	dry / very thirsty	びっしょり ***bisshori***	soaked
しっかり ***shikkari***	resolute / firm	ぴかぴか ***pikapika***	shiny, sparkling, glittering
じっと ***jitto***	staring	きらきら ***kirakira***	glittering, dazzling
めちゃくちゃ ***mechakucha***	a mess	ほっと ***hotto***	relieved
すっきり ***sukkiri***	refreshed / relieved	わくわく ***wakuwaku***	nervous, excited

Real usage

A student's first reaction on seeing these apparently "not very serious" words is to think that they are hardly ever used, or if so, that they belong to the language used by very young children. That's not the case. All Japanese, children and adults, use ***giongo*** and ***gitaigo*** in real life, both in written and spoken language. Any student of Japanese who is serious about his or her studies should master the most basic ones at least (which you can find in the two tables provided in this lesson).

These words are usually placed before a verb, since they very often work as adverbs, as we pointed out before (and, as you know, adverbs modify verbs).

Giongo and ***gitaigo*** can be written in hiragana or katakana but never in kanji: the choice of hiragana or katakana will depend on the author's personal taste, and the emphasis he or she wants to give. Here, we have chosen to present all of them in hiragana.

Onomatopoeia and its usage

There are some ***giongo*** and ***gitaigo*** that take particular verbs. For example, ぐるぐる ***guruguru*** almost always goes with the verb 回る ***mawaru***, "to turn round" as in ぐるぐる回る ***guruguru mawaru***: "to go round and round." In most cases, ぱくぱく ***pakupaku*** goes with the verb 食べる ***taberu***, "to eat" as in ぱくぱく食べる ***pakupaku taberu***: "to munch," "to eat with relish"). You might find the particle と to between the onomatopoeia and the verb, as in げらげらと笑う ***geragera to warau***, "to laugh boisterously."

Some ***giongo*** and ***gitaigo*** take the verb する ***suru*** ("to do"), for example いらいらする ***iraira suru*** ("to be irritated") or どきどきする ***dokidoki suru*** ("to be nervous," "to be excited"). Others take the verb だ ***da*** ("to be," Lesson 9), for example くたくただ ***kutakuta da*** ("to be exhausted") or からからだ ***karakara da*** ("to be dry" or "to be very thirsty"). There is no rule saying which word precedes one verb or another; you just have to memorize them. Bear in mind that studying these words can be quite tough, because they all sound much alike and it is easy to get them mixed up. Take a look at these examples:

水をがぶがぶ飲むな！
mizu o gabugabu nomu na!
water DOP (gulp-gulp) drink no!
Don't gulp down water!

あなたは日本語がぺらぺらですね
anata wa nihongo ga perapera desu ne
you TOP Japanese SP (bla-bla) be EP
You speak Japanese very fluently, don't you?

きょうはぐっすり寝た
kyō wa gussuri neta
today TOP (very well) sleep
Today I slept like a log.

あのカップル、いちゃいちゃしているね
ano kappuru, ichaicha shite iru ne
that couple (to grope) do EP
That couple are making out, aren't they?

"tto" onomatopoeia

Some onomatopoeia end in an abrupt sound, written in manga as ぴたっ ***pita*** ("to stop suddenly") or ぼけっ ***boke*** ("to be out of touch"). When we use these onomatopoeia in everyday conversation, we usually add と ***to*** to make them easier to pronounce, as in the sentence 彼はぴたっと止まった ***kare wa pitatto tomatta*** "He stopped suddenly."

In the online Glossary of Onomatopoeia via the link on page 9, we will indicate onomatopoeia with the と ***to*** included, but you will likely find them in manga without the と ***to***.

Animal sounds

Finally, let's look at the incredible difference between animal sounds in English and Japanese. For example, an English dog barks "bow wow," but in Japanese it barks わんわん ***wanwan***. A cat mews にゃんにゃん ***nyan-nyan***, a frog croaks けろけろ ***kerokero***, and a pig oinks ぶうぶう ***bū-bū***.

漫画例 Manga Examples

We will now illustrate the very curious world of onomatopoeia via examples taken from real manga panels. You'll see a wide range of words which imitate sounds and describe states of mind and physical conditions.

Manga Example 1: *Bikkuri*

Studio Kōsen

In our first example we will introduce a new ***gitaigo***, which, although not seen earlier in the lesson, is one of the most common in Japanese.

It is びっくり ***bikkuri***, which, together with the verb する ***suru*** ("to do"), means "to be surprised." You will hear this phrase a lot if you go to Japan, so it is definitely worth memorizing.

> **Hiromi:** びっくりさせてやろっと
> ***bikkuri sasete yaro tto***
> surprise make somebody do give
> **I'll surprise him.**

Manga Example 2: *Sukkiri*

Guillermo March

Here is an example of the ***gitaigo*** すっきり ***sukkiri***, which is also used with する ***suru***. ***Sukkiri suru*** means "to be refreshed," "to feel relieved." It is used, for instance, when we can at last quench our thirst, or in other situations of relief, such as the one shown here!

> **Slime:** あースッキリしちゃった！！
> ***aa sukkiri shichatta!!***
> oooh relieve do (complete)!!
> **Oooh! What a relief!**

Manga Example 3: *Dokidoki*

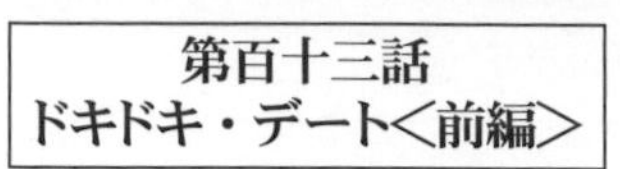

J.M. Ken Niimura

In this manga example, we can see the ***giongo***, どきどき ***dokidoki*** (which represents the sound of a heartbeat). ***Dokidoki***, with the implicit meaning of "nervousness" and "excitement," is used in this panel as an adjective for the noun デート ***deeto*** ("date"). Thus, the literal translation of this title would be something like "nervous date" or "exciting date" or "waiting for a date which is exciting."

Notice that in this panel どきどき ***dokidoki*** is written in katakana (ドキドキ): there is no rule specifying how onomatopoeia must be written, therefore, the author can choose the syllabary he or she wants.

Title:	第百十三話	ドキドキ・デート＜前編＞
	dai hyaku jū san wa	***dokidoki deeto <zenpen>***
	number 113 chapter	*nervousness date <first part>*
	Chapter 113:	**Nervous about a date <first part>**

Manga Example 4: *Wan wan*

We will conclude the lesson seeing how a Japanese dog barks. Unlike English-speaking dogs, who say "bow wow," Japanese dogs say わんわん ***wanwan***. Some Japanese (specially children and women) call dogs ワンちゃん ***wan-chan*** instead of 犬 ***inu.*** As you know from Lesson 15, ちゃん ***-chan*** is an affectionate suffix.

Guillermo March

Dog:	ワンワンワンワン	**Master:**	まてまて 静かに！
	wan wan wan wan		***mate mate shizuka ni!***
	(sound of dog barking)		wait wait calm (adv.)!
	Bow wow bow wow!		**Just a minute! Hush...**

Exercises 練習

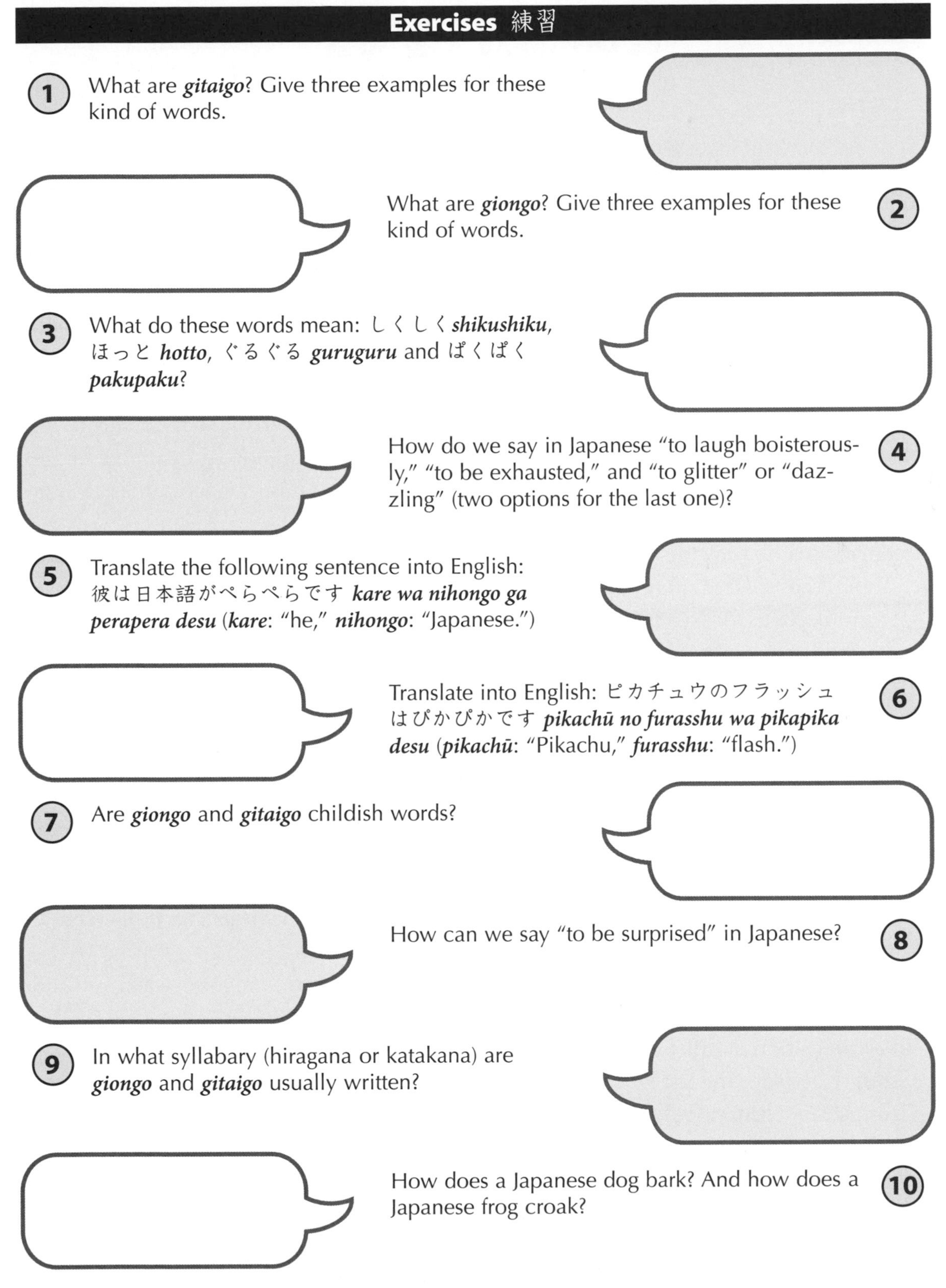

1. What are ***gitaigo***? Give three examples for these kind of words.

2. What are ***giongo***? Give three examples for these kind of words.

3. What do these words mean: しくしく ***shikushiku***, ほっと ***hotto***, ぐるぐる ***guruguru*** and ぱくぱく ***pakupaku***?

4. How do we say in Japanese "to laugh boisterously," "to be exhausted," and "to glitter" or "dazzling" (two options for the last one)?

5. Translate the following sentence into English: 彼は日本語がぺらぺらです ***kare wa nihongo ga perapera desu*** (***kare***: "he," ***nihongo***: "Japanese.")

6. Translate into English: ピカチュウのフラッシュはぴかぴかです ***pikachū no furasshu wa pikapika desu*** (***pikachū***: "Pikachu," ***furasshu***: "flash.")

7. Are ***giongo*** and ***gitaigo*** childish words?

8. How can we say "to be surprised" in Japanese?

9. In what syllabary (hiragana or katakana) are ***giongo*** and ***gitaigo*** usually written?

10. How does a Japanese dog bark? And how does a Japanese frog croak?

— Answers to all the exercises can be found online by following the link on page 9. —

Lesson 30 • 第30課

Commands

In this lesson we will take a close look at commands and orders in Japanese, a somewhat knotty subject, as you will see as we progress, but certainly interesting!

Commands

In most Japanese-language courses commands and orders (also referred to as the imperative form) are usually not studied at beginner level.

However, our book is not a "conventional" course, but one which aims to teach Japanese from a basically colloquial and spoken perspective (while also referring to more formal and orthodox grammar). The main aim of this course is to bring you, the student, to a level of Japanese that allows you to understand what is said in manga, anime, video games, or movies in their original Japanese version.

In Japanese everyday life, commands are hardly ever used: giving orders in a normal conversation is considered quite rude. Instead, the request form ***-te*** + ***kudasai***, seen in Lesson 24, is profusely used. This is not so different from English: it is considered more polite to say "could you bring me a pencil, please?" rather than giving the order "bring me a pencil."

Nevertheless, commands are extremely frequent when it comes to manga, anime, video games, and movies, where colloquial and sometimes vulgar language prevails. For that reason we will devote this lesson to the study of commands and orders.

Formation

In the grammar table on the facing page, you have, as usual, the verbs arranged in three groups, which we already explained in Lessons 19, 20 and 24. The first and third columns correspond to the simple or "dictionary" form (Lesson 20) and the ***-masu*** form (Lesson 19) respectively; the second column gives the meaning of each verb.

In the fourth column we give the command form, in its most straightforward and rude form. (**Note:** Women virtually NEVER use this form.)

The conjugation of this form is very simple (the rules are in the fifth column):

Group 1. Replace the last 〜る ***-ru*** of the dictionary form of the verb with 〜ろ ***-ro.***

Group 2. As a general rule, replace the last ***-u*** in the dictionary form with ***-e***. For example:

帰る ***kaeru*** ("to return") ⇒ 帰れ ***kaere*** ("return")
買う ***kau*** ("to buy") ⇒ 買え ***kae*** ("buy")
飲む ***nomu*** ("to drink") ⇒ 飲め ***nome*** ("drink").

But be careful with verbs ending in 〜つ ***-tsu***, which is replaced with 〜て ***-te*** and not ***-tse*** (which is a nonexistent syllable in Japanese). For example:

待つ ***matsu*** ("to wait") ⇒ 待て ***mate*** ("wait")
勝つ ***katsu*** ("to win") ⇒ 勝て ***kate*** ("win").

Group 3. As you know, these two verbs are irregular, so we must learn their forms by heart.

The negative command form

The negative command form is so simple, there is no need to go into much depth concerning its formation: as we saw in Lesson 17, we only need to add な ***na*** after a verb in the dictionary form to give a negative order. For example:

パンを食べるな ***pan o taberu na***, "Don't eat the bread."

	Dictionary form	Meaning	*-masu* form	Command form	Rule	"Gentle" command	Rule
Group 1 Invariable	教える ***oshieru***	to teach	教えます ***oshiemasu***	教えろ ***oshiero***	～~~る~~ろ **–~~ru~~ ro**	教えなさい ***oshienasai***	～~~ます~~なさい ***–~~masu~~ nasai***
	起きる ***okiru***	to wake up	起きます ***okimasu***	起きろ ***okiro***		起きなさい ***okinasai***	
Group 2 Variable	貸す ***kasu***	to lend	貸します ***kashimasu***	貸せ ***kase***	～~~す~~せ **–~~su~~ se**	貸しなさい ***kashinasai***	
	待つ ***matsu***	to wait	待ちます ***machimasu***	待て ***mate***	～~~つ~~て **–~~tsu~~ te**	待ちなさい ***machinasai***	
	買う ***kau***	to buy	買います ***kaimasu***	買え ***kae***	～~~う~~え **–~~u~~ e**	買いなさい ***kainasai***	
	帰る ***kaeru***	to return	帰ります ***kaerimasu***	帰れ ***kaere***	～~~る~~れ **–~~ru~~ re**	帰りなさい ***kaerinasai***	
	書く ***kaku***	to write	書きます ***kakimasu***	書け ***kake***	～~~く~~け **–~~ku~~ ke**	書きなさい ***kakinasai***	
	急ぐ ***isogu***	to hurry	急ぎます ***isogimasu***	急げ ***isoge***	～~~ぐ~~げ **–~~gu~~ ge**	急ぎなさい ***isoginasai***	
	遊ぶ ***asobu***	to play	遊びます ***asobimasu***	遊べ ***asobe***	～~~ぶ~~べ **–~~bu~~ be**	遊びなさい ***asobinasai***	
	飲む ***nomu***	to drink	飲みます ***nomimasu***	飲め ***nome***	～~~む~~め **–~~mu~~ me**	飲みなさい ***nominasai***	
	死ぬ ***shinu***	to die	死にます ***shinimasu***	死ね ***shine***	～~~ぬ~~ね **–~~nu~~ ne**	死になさい ***shininasai***	
Group 3 Irregular	する ***suru***	to do	します ***shimasu***	しろ ***shiro***	Irregular verbs: there is no rule	しなさい ***shinasai***	
	来る ***kuru***	to come	来ます ***kimasu***	来い ***koi***		来なさい ***kinasai***	

The "gentle" command

There is another command form which is softer and less rude. This is the ～なさい ***-na-sai*** form, which is mainly used by adults when giving orders or commands to children. It means something like "please (do it)."

We mentioned earlier that women rarely use the command form shown in the middle of the table on page 263. When a woman wants to give a command she will tend to use the ***-nasai*** form if she is familiar with the person who receives the command, her child or her husband, for example. This form can also be used by a teacher with a pupil, and in situations where the speaker is or feels in a higher position than the person he or she is addressing.

The formation is simple and has no exceptions, not even with irregular verbs. Just remove the ～ます ***-masu*** ending of any verb and add ～なさい ***-nasai***. For example:

書く ***kaku*** ("to write") ⇒ ***-masu*** form 書きます ***kakimasu*** ⇒ remove ***-masu*** 書き ***kaki*** ⇒ add ***-nasai*** 書きなさい ***kakinasai*** ("Please write.").

手紙を書きなさい ***tegami o kakinasai***, "Please write a letter."

The -tamae form

There is a third command form, seldom used but which may appear occasionally in manga: It is the ***-tamae*** form. In the old days, this command form was used with deep respect, but nowadays it is usually used by a speaker who is or feels superior to the person they are addressing (in superior-subordinate, teacher-pupil and similar relationships). This form is perceived as authoritarian and arrogant.

It is formed exactly the same way as the ***-nasai*** form: We remove the ～ます ***-masu*** of a verb conjugated in the ***-masu*** form, and we add たまえ ***-tamae***. For example:

遊ぶ ***asobu*** ("to play") ⇒ ***-masu*** form 遊びます ***asobimasu*** ⇒ remove ***-masu*** 遊び ***asobi*** ⇒ add ***-tamae*** 遊びたまえ ***asobitamae*** ("Come on, play").

子どもと遊びたまえ ***kodomo to asobitamae***, "(Come on), play with the boy."

The -te kure form

As we glimpsed in Lesson 28, there is a structure ***-te*** + ***kureru*** based on the giving verb くれる ***kureru*** (which, as you may remember, means "to give," but with the meaning of "someone gives something to me or to someone close to me"). Well, this structure has a variation, ～てくれ ***-te kure***, which, as we saw in Manga Example 7 in Lesson 28, has the meaning of a straightforward order. The form くれ ***kure*** is the (irregular) command form of the verb くれる ***kureru***, therefore ～てくれ ***-te kure*** has the meaning "do me the favor of," for example:

この本を読んでくれ ***kono hon o yonde kure***, "Read this book, (come on)."

漫画例 Manga Examples

Commands are hardly ever used in "real" Japanese, that is, in the Japanese that is used in everyday life. However, they are profusely used in manga. Let's have a look at some examples.

Manga Example 1: Die!

J.M. Ken Niimura

In this panel we the see the violent Klangor in mid-attack. Since this is a fight scene, Klangor doesn't care about tactfulness or good manners, and he allows himself to use the rudest command form. The verb used here is 死ぬ ***shinu*** ("to die"), which is a Group 2 verb, so the last ***-u*** sound is replaced with an ***-e*** sound. Thus, 死ぬ ***shinu*** ("to die") ⇒ 死ね ***shine*** ("die").

Klangor: 死ねーっ！！！
shineeee!!!
die!!!
Dieee!!!

Manga Example 2: "Gentle" command, *-nasai*

Here is an example of the "gentle" command form, ***-nasai***. The speaker is a girl, and that is why she doesn't use the straightforward command form. To conjugate this gentle form, we will replace the 〜ます***-masu*** ending of the verb with ***-nasai***: 降りる ***oriru*** ("to come down") ⇒ 降ります ***orimasu*** (***-masu*** form) ⇒ 降りなさい ***orinasai*** ("Please come down,").

Studio Kōsen

Girl: おりなさい！さぁさぁ
orinasai! saa saa
come down, come on
Come down. Come on, now.

Manga Example 3: *-te kure* command

In this panel, we have an example of a command formed by a verb in the ***-te*** form (Lesson 24) plus くれ ***kure***, the irregular command form of the verb くれる ***kureru*** (Lesson 28). Even though this kind of command is frequently used in manga, it is quite rude and we don't recommend using it in real life. This goes for all the command forms introduced in this lesson. Instead you should use the request form ***-te kudasai*** (Lesson 24).

J.M. Ken Niimura

Frolaine: 待ってくれ！
matte kure!
wait (give)!
Wait!

Manga Example 4: *-tamae*

Here we have the command form ***-tamae***. This form is seldom used, but now and then we will come across it in manga. Its conjugation is identical to the ***-nasai*** form, and the speaker who uses it usually is or feels superior to the person they are speaking to. In this case, Yoshi wants to impress the girl and he invites her into his car using the ***-tamae*** form. The verb used is 乗る ***noru*** ("to get in," "to ride") ⇒ 乗ります ***norimasu*** (***-masu*** form) ⇒ 乗りたまえ ***noritamae*** ("Come on, get in").

We should mention as well the usage of お待たせ ***o-matase***, a short version of ***o-matase shimashita*** ("Sorry I kept you waiting").

Guillermo March

Yoshi: おまたせ　乗りたまえ
o-matase noritamae
kept waiting get in
Sorry I'm late. Come on, get in...

Exercises 練習

1. Is the command form commonly used in Japanese?

2. Name four command forms and the difference between them. How does the negative command form work?

3. Give the regular command form of 見る ***miru*** ("to see," Group 1), 聞く ***kiku*** ("to hear"), 乗る ***noru*** ("to ride"), and 洗う ***arau*** ("to wash").

4. Give the "gentle" comand or ***-nasai*** form of the verbs in question 3.

5. Give the ***-te kure*** form of the verbs in question 3.

6. Why would a woman never use the straightforward command form? What form would she use instead?

7. Translate the following into English: 日本語講座を読め ***nihongo kōza o yome*** (***nihongo***: "Japanese language," ***kōza***: "course.")

8. Translate the following sentence into Japanese using the straightforward command form: "Buy the newspaper." (newspaper: 新聞 ***shinbun***.)

9. Translate the following sentence into Japanese using the ***-nasai*** command form: "Sit on the chair." (to sit: 座る ***suwaru***, chair: いす ***isu***.)

10. When is the ***-tamae*** form used? Is it a very commonly used form?

— Answers to all the exercises can be found online by following the link on page 9. —

RAKUJŌ
第六章
お帰りなさい、ヨド様、ヒデ様。
ただいま…
よろっ
お母さん、気持ちは分かります。しかし、ヤスは頭がいいです。ユキさんを呼びましたか?
はい、ヨド様。すみません。
ヌッ
ビクッ
頭が痛いよ。くたくたただ!! だまってくれ。
ヒデ!! 待ちなさい!
あの人はとても腕がいいですよ! 僕は彼を呼びに行きます!!
呼ばなかったわよ!!

そうですか？
すぐ行きます!!
ユキ、母と話しに
行ってあげてください。
とても悲しくなったよ。
行ってくれる？
くすん
はい、
ヒデ様!!
ぎゅっ
ありがとう
ございます！
ご苦労様！
元気では
ないわ！
いらいらだ!!
来い!!!
ガッ
お邪魔
します。ヨド様、
お元気ですか？
ヤスのやろうは
中のキャノンも
壊したよ。
そっ
はい、しかし
しっかりしてくだ
さいよ、ヨド様。

何!?これは許しません!どうしますか!?
ギョッ
そうか?私も頭にきた!!じゃ、戦え!!!
はい、ヨド様!
ヤスにサカ基地をあげる前に戦いますよ!
知らない…もう終わりだ…
へへへ!バカもの!この戦争はわしが勝ったぞ!!!来いよ、負け犬たち!ハハハハハ!!
ばっ
皆に戦ってもらうぞ!ヤスアーミーと合戦するぜ!!
ギュッ
カッ

ヤスを殺せ!!!
死ね!!
戦え!
ゴー
ドンドーンドーン
サカ基地、バンザイ!!!!!
バンザイ
ガ
バンザイバンザイ
銀河350年9月6日に、サカ基地が落城した。
ユキ、ヨドとヒデのアーミーが全滅した。ヤスは銀河の独裁者になった。
しかし、サカ基地のソルジャーの勇気は今も皆覚えている。

Review for Lessons 26–30

Answers to all the review exercises can be found online by following the link on page 9.

🎧 ***RAKUJŌ*** – New vocabulary 新しい単語

だまる	to be quiet	やろう	guy, fellow
気(き)持(も)ち	feeling	負(ま)け犬(いぬ)	loser, underdog
悲(かな)しい	sad	落城(らくじょう)する	to fall (a castle)
すぐ	at once	全滅(ぜんめつ)する	to be annihilated
許(ゆる)す	to forgive, to allow	独裁者(どくさいしゃ)	dictator
合戦(かっせん)する	to battle	覚(おぼ)える	to remember (Group 1)

1. Why does Hide say ただいま in the first panel? How does the soldier inside reply?

2. What expression would Hide use if he entered Yasu's house? How would Yasu (being at home) reply to him?

3. According to Yodo, what part of her body is hurting? Write the sentences "My back hurts," "I have an earache," and "My knee hurts" in Japanese.

4. In this episode there are three onomatopoeic expressions used in the dialogue. Find them and specify in each case whether they are ***giongo*** or ***gitaigo***.

5. What does the expression 悲(かな)しくなる ***kanashiku naru*** mean? Use the verb なる with the words 便利(べんり)な ***benri na***, 深(ふか)い ***fukai*** and リーダー and give the meaning of the resulting expression.

6. In Hide's sentence「ユキ、母と話(はな)しに行ってあげてください。とても悲(かな)しくなったよ。行ってくれる？」, what nuance do the verbs あげる and くれる add?

7. Give the following verbs in the command forms indicated:

	"Rough" command	*-nasai* command
呼(よ)ぶ	__________	__________
だまる	__________	__________
許(ゆる)す	__________	__________
待つ	__________	__________
覚(おぼ)える	__________	__________

8. In the text we find the sentence 呼びにいきます. What is its meaning? Change the verbs in the previous exercise into this 〜にいきます form.

9. What is the meaning of the set phrases 頭(あたま)がいい and 腕(うで)がいい？

10. Fill in the chart choosing words from the box below.

Head	ひたい						
Torso							
Limbs							
Hand							

~~ひたい~~	ひじ	目(め)	中指(なかゆび)	人差し指(ひとさしゆび)	爪(つめ)	舌(した)
手首(てくび)	足(あし)	ひげ	手の平(てのひら)	脚(あし)	かみの毛(け)	小指(こゆび)
頭(あたま)	指(ゆび)	おなか	のど	口(くち)	まつげ	あご
ほお		ひざ	胸(むね)	顔(かお)	背中(せなか)	肩(かた)
へそ	首(くび)	歯(は)	耳(みみ)	鼻(はな)	うで	親指(おやゆび)

11. Draw a line to match the situations on the left with a suitable expression on the right.

1. 誕生日(たんじょうび)	a. 明(あ)けましておめでとうございます！
2. 私は私の家に入る	b. いらっしゃいませ！
3. 本屋(や)さんに入る。店(みせ)の人はこう言う	c. ごちそうさまでした
4. 私の家を出る。母はこう言(い)う	d. 申(もう)し訳(わけ)ありません
5. ご飯(はん)を食べる前	e. 誕生日(たんじょうび)おめでとうございます！
6. 私は先生(せんせい)の家に入る	f. お疲(つか)れ様(さま)です
7. １月１日	g. いってらっしゃい
8. ごめんなさい	h. おめでとうございます！
9. ご飯(はん)を食べた後	i. ただいま
10. 試験(しけん)に合格した！	j. お邪魔(じゃま)します
11. 仕事(しごと)が終わった。課長(かちょう)はこう言う	k. いただきます！

Extra vocabulary: 誕生日(たんじょうび) : birthday | 店(みせ) : store | こう : thus, so | 合格(ごうかく)する : to pass an exam

12. Fill in the gaps with the correct word.

a) ヒデキさんは＿＿＿＿＿＿＿＿＿＿＿＿＿＿と笑(わら)いましたよ。
1. くたくた　2. げらげら　3. ぴかぴか　4. わくわく

b) 今日(きょう)は彼女(かのじょ)のお母さんとお父さんに会う。＿＿＿＿＿＿＿＿するね！
1. げらげら　2. しくしく　3. ぱくぱく　4. どきどき

c) ああ！トイレにいった！＿＿＿＿＿＿＿＿＿＿＿＿＿＿したぞ！
1. すっきり　2. しっかり　3. ぐるぐる　4. いらいら

d) お腹(なか)が＿＿＿＿＿＿だ。レストランへ行って、＿＿＿＿＿＿食べるぞ！
1. ぺこぺこ　2. ぺらぺら　3. ぱくぱく　4. いらいら

13. Fill in the gaps choosing words from the box below.

a) 私の名前はフォスターです。＿＿＿＿＿＿。

b) 彼女(かのじょ)の黒(くろ)い ＿＿＿＿＿＿ はとても長(なが)いです。

c) マキコちゃんは ＿＿＿＿＿＿ 泣(な)いている。

d) 私のお父さんの兄は私の＿＿＿＿＿＿です。

e) 家の前に ＿＿＿＿＿＿ が一頭(いっとう)いますよ！

f) あたしの＿＿＿＿＿＿はとてもかっこいいですわ！ほほほ！

g) トムさんは＿＿＿＿＿＿が青いですね。

h) ツネオのお父さんの母はツネオの＿＿＿＿＿＿です。

i) ノボル：ただいま！｜お母さん：あ、ノボル、 ＿＿＿＿＿＿ ！

j) 家の前に＿＿＿＿＿＿が一匹いますよ！

k) ＿＿＿＿＿＿がすいたよ！

l) 私の母の母は私の＿＿＿＿＿＿です。

m) 指輪(ゆびわ)をもらったので、 ＿＿＿＿＿＿ にはめた。

n) あの人は、日本語(ご)が ＿＿＿＿＿＿ ですね！すごいわ！

おじ	祖母(そぼ)	よろしくお願(ねが)いします	ぺらぺら	さる	おばあさん		
薬指(くすりゆび)	かみの毛(け)	だんな	馬(うま)	おかえりなさい	お腹(なか)	しくしく	目(め)

14. Complete the table following the example. If you don't know which group a verb belongs to, check the online Vocabulary Index via the link on page 9.

食(た)べろ	食(た)べなさい	食(た)べてくれ	食(た)べるな	to eat
行け				
	回(まわ)りなさい			

読め				
		貸してくれ		
			触るな	
洗え				
	教えなさい			
		呼んでくれ		
			狙うな	
	死になさい			
			走るな	
急げ				

15. Specify in the table who gives and who receives the objects or actions exchanged in the following sentences.

a) 私はエリカさんにボールペンをあげた。
b) アケミさんは私にパソコンをくれました。
c) 弟はお母さんに手紙を書いてあげた。
d) クミちゃんはテツさんに自転車をもらいます。
e) 山本くん、これをモモコさんにあげてください。
f) 私は学生に本屋さんに行ってもらった。
g) 兄は山田さんにおもしろい雑誌をもらいました。

Gives	Receives
私	エリカ

16. Place the word in brackets into the sentence, making necessary grammatical changes.

a) 川田さんは二年前＿＿＿先生に＿＿＿なった。 （先生）
b) 昨日、課長の家へ＿＿＿＿＿＿に行きました。 （遊ぶ）
c) 私はすしがとても＿＿＿＿＿＿なった。 （好きな）
d) あの人はとても腕が＿＿＿＿＿＿なりましたね。 （いい）
e) 本田くん、これを＿＿＿＿＿＿来てくれますか？ （読む）

17. Fill in the gaps with the most appropriate answer.

a) キヨコ！皿(さら)を____________よ！

1. 洗い　2. 洗(あら)いさい　3. 洗(あら)え　4. 洗(あら)お

b) ヒロシ！魚屋(さかなや)さんへ魚(さかな)を____________に行ってくれますか？

1. 買い　2. 買え　3. 買う　4. 買って

c) あの人は「あそこへ電車(でんしゃ)____________行ってくれ」と言(い)ったよ。

1. に　2. と　3. は　4. で

d) 金田(かねだ)さんは私にＣＤを____________。

1. もらえ　2. あげなさい　3. くれました　4. あげた

e) ヨーコ！ここへ____________よ！

1. 来(こ)なさい　2. 来(く)なさい　3. 来(き)なさい　4. 来(か)なさい

f) ____________お風呂(ふろ)に入りなさいよ！

1. 早(はや)い　2. 速(はや)い　3. 早(はや)く　4. 速(はや)く

g) アキラ！ここへ____________！

1. 来(こ)い　2. 来(く)い　3. 来(き)い　4. 来(か)い

h) 今日は耳____________とても痛(いた)いぞ！

1. と　2. が　3. は　4. を

i) おい、君！オレの彼女(かのじょ)をじっと____________！殺(ころ)すぞ！

1. 見なさい　2. 見ろ　3. 見てください　4. 見るな

Kanji

口	目	手	足	心	耳	店	学	校	先	生
(23)	(24)	(25)	(26)	(27)	(28)	(75)	(76)	(77)	(78)	(79)
楽	変	国	語	言	立	道	車	自	友	文
(157)	(147)	(152)	(153)	(126)	(109)	(92)	(93)	(94)	(103)	(68)

18. Practice wrwiting the kanji below. Find the stroke order in the online Kanji Compilation section via the link on page 9.

足										
学										
先										
国										
車										

19. Link each kanji with its most common reading (usually, the ***kun'yomi***).

国	くち	目	なま
口	みみ	変	め
心	こころ	生	みせ
足	くに	道	て
車	くるま	手	みち
耳	あし	店	へん

20. Choose the correct kanji or kanji combination for each reading.

a) たのしい
1. 楽しい 2. 薬しい 3. 楽い 4. 薬い

b) がくせい
1. 先生 2. 学生 3. 生先 4. 生学

c) がっこう
1. 学年 2. 学国 3. 学校 4. 学生

d) がいこく
1. 入国 2. 国入 3. 外国 4. 国外

21. Choose the correct reading for each kanji or kanji combination.

a) 今日(きょう)、大学へ行った。友だちと先生に会った。

大学：1. だいかく　2. たいかく　3. だいがく　4. たいがく
友だち：1. どもだち　2. ゆだち　3. ゆうだち　4. ともだち
先生：1. せいせん　2. せえせん　3. せんせい　4. せんせえ

b) あなたは中国語ができますか？よかった、安心しましたよ。

中国語：1. ちゅこくご　2. ちゅうごくこ　3. ちゅごくご　4. ちゅうごくご
安心：1. やすごころ　2. あんしん　3. やすこころ　4. あんじん

c) A: あの高校生を殺(ころ)したか？ | B: いいえ、まだ生きているぞ！

高校生：1. こうこうせい　2. ここせい　3. こうこせい　4. ここうせい
生きている：1. なまきている　2. いきている　3. うきている　4. せいきている

22. Give the reading in ***furigana*** of the underlined kanji.

a) 先月の遠足は楽しかったね！
b) 出口の売店へ先に行ってください。その前の道に車があります。
c) お前はあの私立学校の中学生を殺したの？早く自白してくれ！
d) 赤道へ行く楽な近道を言ってください。

23. Write the following words in kanji, and give their meaning. (**Note:** The words marked with an asterisk appear in kanji tables studied in previous lessons.)

くち	______	________	みみ	______	________
あし	______	________	じんせい	______	________
たのしい	______	________	にほんご	______	________
*ぼこく	______	________	*ぶんめい	______	________

Lesson 31 • 第31課

Expressing Wants

To express that we want to do something in Japanese, there are some special points to be aware of. First of all, in Japanese you distinguish between "wanting to do something" and "wanting something," and there is also a big difference in the subtlety level when talking about your own wishes and when talking about what other people want, as we will now see.

To want to do something

The form "to want to do something" is quite easily constructed adding the 〜たい ***-tai*** ending to the root of a verb. First, we need to conjugate the verb we wish to use into the 〜ます ***-masu*** form (Lesson 19). Next, we remove the ending 〜ます so we now have the root of the verb, and we add 〜たい; with a little bit of practice you will easily pick this up. The root form of the verb is the basis for many grammatical constructions in Japanese, verb root will appear several times further on, so it is highly recommended that you study it carefully, using the table on the facing page.

A verb in the 〜たい form (such as 買いたい ***kaitai***, "want to buy") is no longer grammatically considered a verb and it becomes to all purposes an ***-i*** adjective. Therefore, all its forms (negative, past and past negative) will function just as we saw in Lesson 13 with ***-i*** adjectives. Have a look at this table:

		Affirmative	Negative
Present	General rule	〜い	〜~~い~~くない
	Example	行(い)きたい	行(い)きたくない
	Translation	I want to go	I don't want to go
Past	General rule	〜~~い~~かった	〜~~い~~くなかった
	Example	行(い)きたかった	行(い)きたくなかった
	Translation	I wanted to go	I didn't want to go

The direct object in 〜たい sentences is marked either with the particle を or the particle が. There is only a difference of usage: using が implies a stronger wish than を. Compare the two examples テレビを見たい and テレビが見たい ***terebi o/ga mitai***. Both sentences mean "(I) want to watch television." In the second case, with が, the wish is a burning one.

	Simple f.	Meaning	Rule	*-masu* f.	Root	Rule	*-tai* form
Group 1 Invariable	教える	to teach	〜~~る~~ます	教えます	教え	Root+〜たい	教えたい
	起きる	to wake up	〜~~る~~ます	起きます	起き		起きたい
Group 2 Variable	貸す	to lend	〜~~す~~します	貸します	貸し		貸したい
	待つ	to wait	〜~~つ~~ちます	待ちます	待ち		待ちたい
	買う	to buy	〜~~う~~います	買います	買い		買いたい
	帰る	to return	〜~~る~~ります	帰ります	帰り		帰りたい
	書く	to write	〜~~く~~きます	書きます	書き		書きたい
	急ぐ	to hurry	〜~~ぐ~~ぎます	急ぎます	急ぎ		急ぎたい
	遊ぶ	to play	〜~~ぶ~~びます	遊びます	遊び		遊びたい
	飲む	to drink	〜~~む~~みます	飲みます	飲み		飲みたい
	死ぬ	to die	〜~~ぬ~~にます	死にます	死に		死にたい
Group 3 Irregular	する	to do	Irregular verbs: no rule	します	し		したい
	来る	to come		来ます	来		来たい

Finally, we will point out that if we add the verb です ***desu*** after 〜たい we obtain a formal sentence, for example テレビを見たいです.

The structure of this kind of sentences is usually Subject は Direct object を (が) Verb in 〜たい form (+ optional です). See the following examples:

- メタリカの新発売(しんはつばい)のアルバムを買(か)いたかった。I wanted to buy Metallica's latest album.
- 私(わたし)はあの本(ほん)を読(よ)みたくない。I don't want to read that book.
- 僕(ぼく)は弁護士(べんごし)になりたいです。I want to become a lawyer. (formal)

Note: The verb なる ***naru,*** "to become," always comes with the particle に (Lesson 28).

To want something

To indicate we want a particular thing, we will not use 〜たい, which is used when we want to carry out an action, but ほしい. After the direct object we will always have the が particle or, sometimes, は (we never use を in this case), for example マンガが欲しい ***manga ga hoshii,*** "I want a manga." Remember that by adding です at the end of the sentence, we obtain a formal sentence: マンガが欲しいです "I want a manga."

It is important to bear in mind that, just like 〜たい, ほしい functions the same way as *-i* adjectives, and therefore it is has the same forms: ほしい, ほしくない (neg.), ほしかった (past), ほしくなかった (neg. past.) Study the examples below:

- 新(あたら)しい彼女(かのじょ)が欲(ほ)しい I want a new girlfriend.
- 私(わたし)はパソコンが欲(ほ)しいです I want a computer. (formal)
- コーヒーは欲(ほ)しくない。コーラが欲(ほ)しい I don't want a coffee. I want a cola.
- りんごは欲(ほ)しくなかったです I didn't want an apple.

Another usage of ほしい, explained in the table below, is in sentences expressing "I want someone to do something." Take care if you use this type of sentence, since it implies the speaker is, or at least feels, superior in hierarchy to the person they are addressing.

These command sentences are formed with the *-te* form verb (Lesson 24) plus ほしい. We will add です at the end to give the sentence a more formal tone.

- この文章(ぶんしょう)を生徒達(せいとたち)にわかってほしい
  I want the students to understand this sentence.
- この映画(えいが)をあなたに見(み)てほしいです I want you to see this movie.
- この人(ひと)を愛(あい)してほしい I want you to love this person.

Usages of *hoshii*	
A: I want something Subject は Thing が欲(ほ)しい(です) 私(わたし)は辞書(じしょ)が欲(ほ)しい(です) I want a dictionary.	私(わたし): I 辞書(じしょ): dictionary 田中(たなか): Tanaka 買(か)う: to buy
B: I want someone (inferior to me) to do something Subject は Someone に Thing を *-te* form + 欲(ほ)しい(です) 私(わたし)は田中(たなか)さんに辞書(じしょ)を買(か)って欲(ほ)しい(です) I want Tanaka-san to buy (or "to buy me") a dictionary.	

Another person

No one can truly know what other people want to do. You can guess or have a strong idea, but you can never be certain. This point of view may help you understand why the 〜たい and ほしい forms are never used in Japanese when referring to the third person: she, he or they.

There are, of course, strategies to overcome this hindrance, for example, the 〜がる form. With 〜がる a sentence takes the meaning of "it looks like the other person wants to do x." To use this expression you only need to replace the last い in 〜たい or in ほしい with 〜がる. Thus, 彼は新しい車 を欲しがっている ***kare wa atarashii kuruma o hoshigatte iru*** could be translated as "It looks like he wants a new car." An important point is that this form can only be used in the -***te*** form (Lesson 24). This sentence 彼は眠たがる ***kare wa nemutagaru,*** "It looks like he wants to sleep" is wrong; you must use the -***te*** form: 彼は眠たがっている. Here are some further examples:

- あの男は子どもと遊びたがっている It looks like that man wants to play with the child.
- 彼は新しい彼女を欲しがっている It looks like he wants a new girlfriend.
- 三井さんはパソコンを欲しがっていました It looks like Mr. Mitsui wanted a computer.

The negative form of sentences with 〜がる is an exception to this rule, because both the normal negative form and the negative -***te*** form are allowed:

- 彼は学校に行きたがらない It looks like he doesn't want to go to school.

Alternative strategies

However, it is possible to make sentences with the 〜たい and the ほしい forms with another person as the subject. We won't go into detail here, but we will have a look at some examples.

I think; he says

Using と思う ***to omou*** "I think" or と言う ***to iu*** "s/he says" at the end of a sentence make the sentence slightly more impersonal because, instead of a categorical statement, we are giving a hypothesis (with と思う) or a quotation of somebody else's words (with と 言う), for example:

- あなたは韓国へ行きたくなかったと思います I think you didn't want to go to Korea.

It seems, apparently

We can use forms such as みたい, ようだ or らしい at the end of the sentence, expressions with the general meaning of "apparently."

- 彼女は結婚したいらしい Apparently, she wants to get married.

I intend to…

The word つもり, meaning "I intend to" is another way of expressing what we want to do. The usage of this construction is very easy: you only need to add つもり after the simple form of the verb (Lesson 20), then the verb "to be" at the end. Remember the verb "to be" is だ in its colloquial form and です in its formal one (Lesson 9). See the following examples:

- 新(あたら)しいパソコンを買(か)うつもりだ I intend to buy a new computer.
- 来年(らいねん)、日本(にほん)へ行(い)くつもりです Next year, I intend (I want) to go to Japan.
- 美穂(みほ)と結婚(けっこん)するつもりです I intend / I am going to marry Miho.

We should stress that つもり is never conjugated; what we conjugate is the verb before or after it. Notice what happens when we place the verb before つもり:

- 俺(おれ)は戦(たたか)わないつもりだ I intend not to fight.
- 美穂(みほ)と結婚(けっこん)しないつもりです I intend not to marry Miho.

Notice what happens if we place the negative after つもり. It is a rather strong negative:

- 君(きみ)と結婚(けっこん)するつもりはありません I have no intention of marrying you.
- 中国人(ちゅうごくじん)と交渉(こうしょう)するつもりはない I have no intention of negotiating with the Chinese.

More about "I intend to…"

It is important to state that, just as with 〜たい and ほしい the expression つもり cannot be used to state the intentions of other people. You must use the alternative strategies we looked at on page 283: I think, he says, it seems, apparently. Note that the 〜がる form cannot be used with つもり.

However, つもり is not only used to mean "I intend to." Very often, depending on the context, it is used to express "being convinced that" or "believing that."

- 母(はは)は元気(げんき)なつもりです My mother is convinced she is healthy [*although I think otherwise*].

  Note: When つもり functions with a ***-na*** adjective, that adjective keeps the な; it doesn't lose it as in other cases (Lesson 14).
- 僕(ぼく)は偉(えら)い人(ひと)のつもりではない I don't believe I am an important person.

  Note: With nouns, we must use the particle の before つもり.

漫画例 Manga Examples

We have reached the manga examples section. Let's take a look at some manga panels that illustrate the use of the expressions of wanting and intending that we have learned so far in the lesson.

Manga Example 1: I want to

Our first example shows usage of the 〜たい form to indicate one's own wish. The root verb, in this case, is the irregular する to do, whose 〜たい form is したい.

We almost always use the particle を between the direct object (in this case 話 ***hanashi, talk***) and the verb (in this caseする here), but in this manga example が is used. The reason for this, as we discussed earlier, is that using が gives more emphasis, a stronger urge. To conclude, we will comment that Masao must know the person he is speaking to well (or, either, he treats him as an inferior) because he doesn't add the verb です after 〜たい. By adding です, the speaker would have formed a politer sentence.

あなたと
話がしたい。
J.M. Ken Niimura

Masao: あなたと話(はなし)がしたい。
you CP conversation SP want to do
I want to talk to you.

Manga Example 2: I don't want to

Ueda has hurt himself badly playing rugby and comes out with this sentence when his teammates try to cheer him up. The verb 聞きたくない ***kikitakunai*** "I don't want to hear" comes from 聞く, "to hear." As we saw

うるさいったら!
ラグビーのことなんか
聞きたくない!
二度と口に
出すな!
Xian Nu Studio

Ueda: うるさいったら！
ラグビーのことなんか聞(き)きたくない！
noisy I say! Rugby POP not even want to hear
Shut up! I don't want to hear anything about rugby!
二度(にど)と口(くち)に出(だ)すな！
twice mouth PP take out (prohibition)
Don't mention it again!

in the verb table on page 281, the ～たい form of verbs ending in ～く is Root + きたい, which makes 聞きたい "I want to hear." The negative is formed in same way as the negative of *-i* adjectives, so we will replace the last ～い with ～くない. Thus we get 聞きたくない.

In Lesson 17 we studied the end-of-sentence particles and we glanced at the particle な. As we see here, な after a verb in its simple form, at the end of a sentence, functions as a negative command, that is, we use it to give orders such as "don't do x." A very clear example would be: 日本語を勉強するな！ ***Nihongo o benkyō suru na!*** "Don't study Japanese!"

Manga Example 3: I want something

We find here the typical structure: direct object + が + ほしい but with reversed sentence order, something very common in spoken Japanese.

The nucleus of this sentence would be 証拠が欲しい ***shokō ga hoshii*** "I want proof."Everything else just embellishes the sentence with nuances. The やっぱり is an adverb with no clear translation, that we have translated as "of course," but in other contexts it can also mean "too," "still" or "after all."

Xian Nu Studio

Teru: やっぱり欲(ほ)しいな… 決定的(けっていてき)な証拠(しょうこ)が…
of course I want EP… conclusive proof SP...
Of course I want… to find conclusive proof...

Manga Example 4: I want you to do something

J.M. Ken Niimura

Even though Shimane is talking to a stranger, in a rather formal way, he has to collect the taxes owed by the taxpayers. Therefore, although he is using formal Japanese, he uses the expression て+ほしい, which, as we saw earlier, is a type of command, as well as implying that the speaker feels superior to the person he is

Shimane: で、金子(かねこ)さん、滞納(たいのう)している税金(ぜいきん)を払(はら)ってほしいんですが。
well, Kaneko (SUF.) fail to pay tax DOP pay want to be but
Well, Mr. Kaneko, I want you to pay the taxes you owe us.
自動車税(じどうしゃぜい)、12万3千円(じゅうにまんさんぜんえん)
car tax 12 "man" three thousand yen
The automobile tax is 123,000 yen.

speaking to. Shimane's linguistic strategy is to speak in a polite but firm and commanding way so that the person he is speaking to feels embarrassed and pays up.

Manga Example 5: It looks like he wants

When talking about somebody else's wishes, you cannot use the 〜たい or ほしい forms directly, because it is impossible to know for certain if someone wants something or if it only looks like he does. Therefore, we use the 〜がる form, which has the connotation "it looks as if." This form is obtained replacing the last い of 〜たい and ほしい with 〜がる (〜たがる, ほしがる). The resultant verb is then used in the *-te* form. In this panel we have the expression 会いたがっていました ***aitagatte imashita*** "Apparently he wanted to meet [someone]." 会いたがっていました is nothing but the ***-te + iru*** form, Lesson 24) of 会いたがる, which comes from 会いたい "I want to meet," which in turn comes from the verb 会う "to meet."

あなたに会いたがっていましたよ。

Studio Kōsen

Kyōko: あなたに会(あ)いたがっていましたよ。
you IOP meet apparently EP
Apparently, he wanted to meet you...

Manga Example 6: I intend to...

Here is a good example of つもり, which we use to say "I intend to." The negative is usually constructed by adding つもり after the negative form of the verb, but here, to obtain a flatter refusal, the form つもりはない is used. In this example, then, the speaker's intentions are very clear.

Note also the particle か in 知るか ***shiru ka***, which is a more colloquial and shorter form of ものですか. The meaning expressed by 知るか is "How do you expect me to know?" or "What do I know?" Don't mistake this か for the question particle か (Lesson 17).

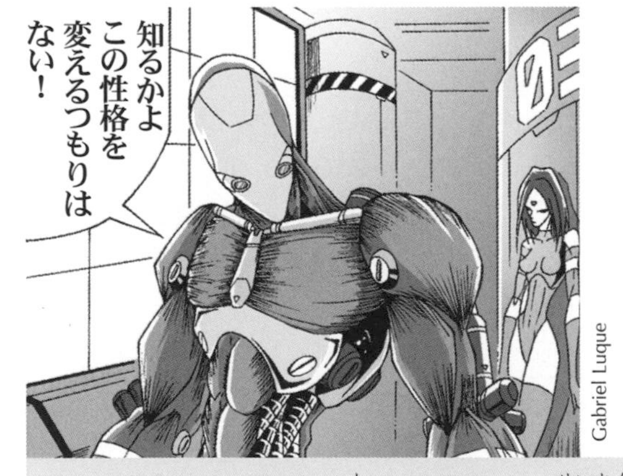

知るかよ この性格を変えるつもりはない!

Gabriel Luque

Bailey: 知(し)るかよ　この性格(せいかく)を変(か)えるつもりはない!
know Q? EP this character change intend there isn't
What do I know? I'm not going to change my character!!

Manga Example 7: I'm convinced that...

In this last example, we will see a different connotation of the つもり form. We saw earlier that つもり had the implicit meaning of "I intend to," but in other contexts the expression can mean "I'm convinced that" or "I believe that." In this case, Sonia asks Jan to walk properly, that she's had enough of his halfhearted way of walking. Jan's answer is, literally, "I believe I walk normally." That is, the speaker really believes his way of walking is correct, even though it isn't from Sonia's point of view.

Studio Kōsen

Jan: 普通(ふつう)に歩(ある)いてるつもりですがね。
normally walk I believe to be EP
I believe I walk normally.

Exercises 練習

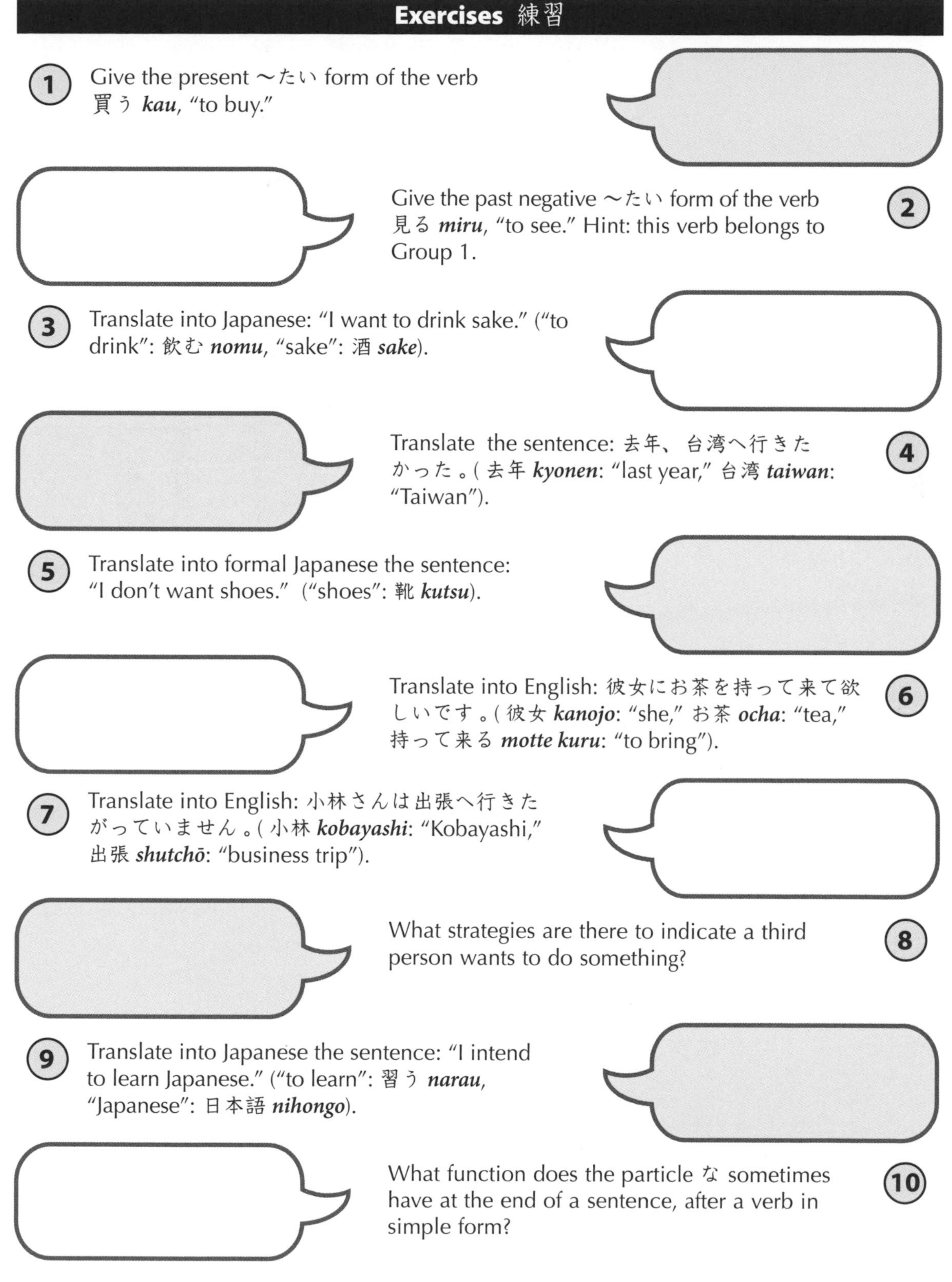

1. Give the present 〜たい form of the verb 買う ***kau***, "to buy."

2. Give the past negative 〜たい form of the verb 見る ***miru***, "to see." Hint: this verb belongs to Group 1.

3. Translate into Japanese: "I want to drink sake." ("to drink": 飲む ***nomu***, "sake": 酒 ***sake***).

4. Translate the sentence: 去年、台湾へ行きたかった。(去年 ***kyonen***: "last year," 台湾 ***taiwan***: "Taiwan").

5. Translate into formal Japanese the sentence: "I don't want shoes." ("shoes": 靴 ***kutsu***).

6. Translate into English: 彼女にお茶を持って来て欲しいです。(彼女 ***kanojo***: "she," お茶 ***ocha***: "tea," 持って来る ***motte kuru***: "to bring").

7. Translate into English: 小林さんは出張へ行きたがっていません。(小林 ***kobayashi***: "Kobayashi," 出張 ***shutchō***: "business trip").

8. What strategies are there to indicate a third person wants to do something?

9. Translate into Japanese the sentence: "I intend to learn Japanese." ("to learn": 習う ***narau***, "Japanese": 日本語 ***nihongo***).

10. What function does the particle な sometimes have at the end of a sentence, after a verb in simple form?

— Answers to all the exercises can be found online by following the link on page 9. —

Lesson 32 • 第32課

Can and Must

In this lesson we will study the potential and obligation forms in Japanese, in other words, we will learn how to form sentences that express what you can do and what you must do.

The simplest structure

We will now see how to form sentences such as "I can do x." Without a doubt, the simplest way to construct this kind of sentence is by using the pattern "sentence + ことができる" (which can be translated as "to be able to" or "can").

The formation is as simple as making a normal sentence (with the verb in the simple form) and adding ことができる.

- 私(わたし)はピーマンを食(た)べる I eat green peppers.
- 私(わたし)はピーマンを食(た)べることができる I can eat green peppers.

The formal form, the past, and the negative are obtained by conjugating the verb in the same way we have already seen: past できた, negative できない, past negative できなかった. Very often we will find this verb written in kanji as 出来る or 出来ます:

- 俺達(おれたち)は歌舞伎(かぶき)を楽(たの)しむ We enjoy kabuki.
- 俺達(おれたち)は歌舞伎(かぶき)を楽(たの)しむことが出来(でき)ない We can't enjoy kabuki.
- ここでおいしいパンを食(た)べることができる You can eat good bread here.

With ***suru*** verbs (Lesson 24) the verb する is left out and we just add できる.

- 彼女(かのじょ)は飛行機(ひこうき)を操縦(そうじゅう)する She flies a plane.
- 彼女(かのじょ)は飛行機(ひこうき)を操縦(そうじゅう)できた She could / knew how to fly a plane.

There are also some cases where you can express what someone can do just using the following structure: noun + が + できる.

- 里美(さとみ)さんはスワヒリ語(ご)ができます Satomi can (speak) Swahili.
- 僕(ぼく)はギターができない I can't (play) the guitar.

A more complicated structure

The structure "sentence + ことができる" is slightly formal. However, it is very practical for beginners, because all that is required to expresses ability to do something is to add ことができる to the sentence.

Another way to talk about ability is to use the potential form of the verb. As usual, forming the potential form is relatively easy, but not obvious, so you should study the following table carefully. Let's have a look at the rules:

- **Group 1 Verbs** (Lesson 20): Replace the final 〜る with 〜られる, for example 見る ***miru,*** "*to see*" ⇒ 見られる "*can see.*"
- **Group 2 Verbs**: Replace the last -***u*** with -***e*** and add -***ru***. Thus, ***kau*** ⇒ ***ka***- ⇒ ***kae***- ⇒ ***kaeru*** ,***asobu*** ⇒ ***asob***- ⇒ ***asobe***- ⇒ ***asoberu***, etc. The only special conjugation is that of verbs ending in -***tsu***, which become -***teru*** and not -***tseru***.
- **Irregular verbs:** As usual, these must be learned by heart. Note the potential of する,"to do" is できる,"can." Are you beginning to see how it goes?

	Simple f.	Meaning	Rule	Potential	Negative	Cond. negative
Group 1 Invariable	教(おし)える	to teach	〜~~る~~られる	教えられる	教えない	教えなければ
	起(お)きる	to wake up		起きられる	起きない	起きなければ
Group 2 Variable	貸(か)す	to lend	〜~~す~~せる	貸せる	貸さない	貸さなければ
	待(ま)つ	to wait	〜~~つ~~てる	待てる	待たない	待たなければ
	買(か)う	to buy	〜~~う~~える	買える	買わない	買わなければ
	帰(かえ)る	to return	〜~~る~~れる	帰れる	帰らない	帰らなければ
	書(か)く	to write	〜~~く~~ける	書ける	書かない	書かなければ
	急(いそ)ぐ	to hurry	〜~~ぐ~~げる	急げる	急がない	急がなければ
	遊(あそ)ぶ	to play	〜~~ぶ~~べる	遊べる	遊ばない	遊ばなければ
	飲(の)む	to drink	〜~~む~~める	飲める	飲まない	飲まなければ
	死(し)ぬ	to die	〜~~ぬ~~ねる	死ねる	死なない	死ななければ
Group 3 Irregular	する	to do	*Irregular verbs: no rule*	できる	しない	しなければ
	来(く)る	to come		来(こ)られる	来(こ)ない	来(こ)なければ

The use of the potential form

Let's have a look at some examples of this new grammatical form. So that we can get a clearer idea, we will try to transform the sentences seen in the first section

The verb in the first example sentence on page 290, 私はピーマンを食べる, is 食べる. Since this verb belongs to Group 1, we must leave out the last ～る and replace it with ～られる, making 私はピーマンを食べられる *"I can eat green peppers."*

In the second example sentence, 俺達は歌舞伎を楽しむ, the verb 楽しむ belongs to Group 2, therefore, we must replace the last -***u*** with an -***e***, and add ～る. Thus: 俺達は歌舞伎を楽しめない *"We can't enjoy kabuki."* We have taken the potential form of the verb, 楽しめる, and made it negative. Remember that the resultant verb is, to all purposes, a normal verb (be careful, as it always belongs to Group 1), and can be conjugated as such.

Note: The only difficulty in this potential form lies in knowing when a verb ending in -***eru*** or -***iru*** belongs to Group 1 or 2 (for example, 食べる ***taberu*** belongs to Group 1, but 帰る ***kaeru*** belongs to Group 2). Being aware of this will allow you to form the verbs correctly. If you are not sure, you can use "sentence + ことができる" to be on the safe side. Study the examples below:

- 友達は論文を書けない My friend can't write a thesis.
- 悟くんは 60 キロを走れる Satoshi can run 60 kilometers (Group 2).
- 私は6時に起きられません I can't wake up at 6 o'clock (Group 1).

On particles

In the example sentences above, you can see that を, the direct object particle, remains unchanged. However in sentences that express ability or potential you can use either が or を after the DOP. That is, the above sentences could also be written 私はピーマンが食べられる and 俺達は歌舞伎が楽しめない.

There are small nuance differences between the use of one particle over another, but they are so subtle and subjective that we won't go into it here. Therefore, we can state to a certain degree that it makes no difference, at this stage in your study of Japanese whether you use the particle が or を in this kind of sentence.

Need or obligation

The second kind of sentence we will learn to construct are sentences of need or obligation (*I must do* x).

There are many ways to construct this kind of sentence, most of which are illustrated in the adjoining table, ordered according to their degree of formality. The most basic and useful is ～ければなりません with its casual form ～ければならない.

Need or obligation		
	Structure	Example: I must sleep
Formal	～ければなりません	寝(ね)なければなりません
	～くてはなりません	寝なくてはなりません
	～ければいけません	寝なければいけません
Informal	～ければならない	寝なければならない
	～くてはならない	寝なくてはならない
	～ければいけない	寝なければいけない
	～ければだめだ	寝なければだめだ
Colloquial	～きゃならない	寝なきゃならない
	～きゃいけない	寝なきゃいけない
	～きゃだめだ	寝なきゃだめだ
Vulgar	～ければ	寝なければ
	～きゃ	寝なきゃ

To form sentences of this kind you must change the verb into the negative form and replace the last ～い with any of the forms illustrated in the table on the right. Here are some example sentences using this structure:

- 夫(おっと)は料理(りょうり)を作(つく)らなければなりません My husband has to cook.
- 本(ほん)を読(よ)まなければだめだ I (you, we, etc.) must read a book.
- 猫(ねこ)にえさをあげなきゃいけない We (I, you, etc.) must feed the cat.
- 部屋(へや)をかたづけなきゃ！ The room must be tidied up!

Permission and prohibition

Now let's take a look at how to make sentences giving permission and sentences that forbid something. Both types of sentence are constructed with the help of verbs in their -***te*** form, which we studied in Lesson 24 and which you should review carefully to be able to make the most of this lesson. First, let's see how permission sentences are constructed.

Permission

To give or ask for permission in Japanese we will add も to the -*te* form, followed by any of the following expressions: よろしいです, かまいません or いいです. Take a look at the table on the right to see the different forms of these expressions. The basic form is 〜てもいい, followed by the verb です if we want to create a formal sentence. To turn the sentence into a question, that is, to make a request, we only have to add か after the sentence and give that か an questioning intonation, a very easy construction studied in Lesson 17. Let's go over some examples:

Permission		
	Structure	Example: You can make it
Formal	〜てもよろしいです	作(つく)ってもよろしいです
	〜てもかまいません	作ってもかまいません
	〜てもいいです	作ってもいいです
Informal	〜てもかまわない	作ってもかまわない
	〜てもいい	作ってもいい
Col.	〜ていい	作っていい

- ここに座(すわ)ってもいいです You (I/we, etc.) can sit here.
- このケーキを食(た)べてもよろしいですか？ Can I eat this cake?
- 辞書(じしょ)を使(つか)ってもいい You can use the dictionary.

Prohibition

To conclude this lesson, we will take a close look at sentences that express prohibition. These are also based on verbs in the -*te* form, to which は (being a particle, pronounced ***wa*** here, not ***ha***) and one of the forms in the table on the right are added. The most basic forms are 〜てはいけない and 〜てはだめだ. Watch out for the colloquial contraction of the ては form into ちゃ; it is very common.

Prohibition		
	Structure	Example: You can't make it
Formal	〜てはなりません	作(つく)ってはなりません
	〜てはいけません	作ってはいけません
Informal	〜てはならない	作ってはならない
	〜てはいけない	作ってはいけない
	〜てはだめだ	作ってはだめだ
Col.	〜ちゃだめ	作っちゃだめ

- このケーキを食(た)べてはいけません You must not eat this cake.
- 辞書(じしょ)を使(つか)ってはだめだ You mustn't use the dictionary.

漫画例 Manga Examples

Expressions of potential, need, permission and prohibition in Japanese are not difficult to learn due to the relative simplicity of the verb forms. The manga examples here will help us consolidate what we have learned.

Manga Example 1: Can (verbs in Group 1)

In this example, typical of one of the many typical cooking mangas, we have the hero sitting at the counter of a ramen noodle restaurant. As he sits there he declares that this ramen "can't be eaten" anywhere else, so he uses the negative potential form of the verb to eat, 食べる ***taberu***. Take a look at the first table in this lesson to check how this verb is conjugated (it belongs to Group 1): you remove the last 〜る and add 〜られる, therefore, the verb should be 食べられる "can eat," the negative form being 食べられない "can eat."

But . . . have you noticed something strange in the manga example? Indeed, the hero says 食べれない instead of the correct form 食べられない. In fact, this form is a relatively new phenomenon, but increasingly widespread: very often, especially among the younger generation, the ら is omitted in the potential form of the verb, giving us verbs such as 見れる "can see," 起きれる "can wake up," or 考えれる "can think," whose normal forms are 見られる, 起きられる and 考えられる respectively.

Xian Nu Studio

Client: コクがあってとてもよそでは食(た)べれないよ
body/taste SP have absolutely other place PP SP eat EP
They are very tasty, you can't have them anywhere else.

Manga Example 2: Can (verbs in Group 2)

We will now see an example of the potential form of a Group 2 verb. As we saw in the table on page 292, the potential form of Group 2 verbs is created by replacing the last -***u*** of the verb in the simple form with -***e*** and adding 〜る. With the verb we have here, 会う ***au*** "to meet," the process would be ***au*** ⇒ ***a***- ⇒ ***ae***- ⇒ ***aeru***, 会える "can meet"). Once you get used to it, learning how to make the potential form isn't difficult. The best way to learn it is to practice putting all the verbs we've been studying throughout the course into their potential form, referring to the table on page 291.

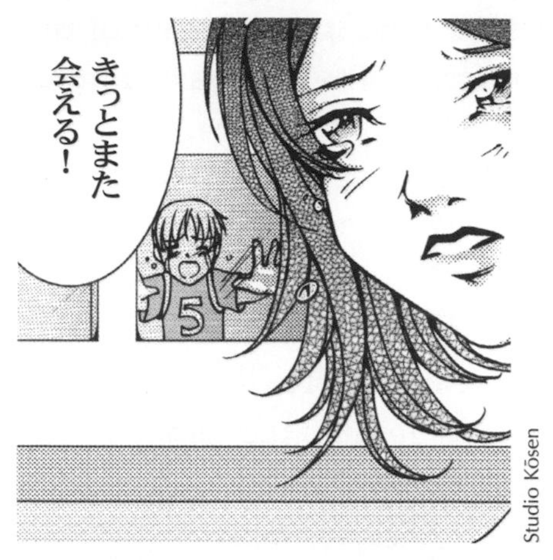

Studio Kōsen

Yōko: きっとまた会(あ)える！
sure again meet!
I'm sure we'll meet again!

Manga Example 3: *Koto ga dekiru*

The main sentence in this manga example is [あなたは] 断言する ***[anata wa] dan-gen suru***, which has been turned into a potential sentence via the useful expression ことができる. Notice how こと is written in kanji here (事). In fact, the expression we are now studying can be entirely written in kanji (事が出来る), although its use depends on one's own preferences.

What would be the potential form of the verb 断言する? As it is a ***suru*** verb (Lesson 24), we would only need to conjugate the する part. In the table on page 291 we see that the potential form of する is できる. Therefore, the potential form would be 断言できる "can affirm."

J.M. Ken Niimura

Tanaka: 彼(かれ)らの人生(じんせい)は幸(しあわ)せだと断言(だんげん)する事(こと)ができますか…？
they POP life SP happy be SBP affirm do can Q?…?
Can you affirm that theirs is a happy life?

Manga Example 4: a special case: *kikoeru* and *mieru*

The potential form of the verbs 見る ***miru*** "to see," and 聞く ***kiku*** "to hear," is noteworthy because the Japanese make a distinction between what one can see or hear unconsciously or passively and what one can see or hear because one specifically wants to. In the first case (what we see or hear unconsciously) the verbs 見える and 聞こえる are used and the particle が is compulsory. In the second case (what we see or hear consciously) the normal potential forms 見られる and 聞ける are used with が or を. However, both are translated as "can see" and "can hear."

Title: 波(なみ)が聞(き)こえる
wave SP hear
I can hear the waves.

In this panel, for example, we don't hear the waves (波 ***nami***) because we want to, but because the sound is there and it reaches our ears. Thus, we use 聞こえる. On the other hand, if we "can hear" a record because that is what we want, we will say レコードが聞ける.

Manga Example 5: Must

We will now see an example of expressing need or obligation. As we saw earlier in the lesson, there are many ways to construct these types of sentences, from formal expressions to colloquial and vulgar ones. The most basic one is, without a doubt, 〜ければならない.

Kim: 佐藤君(さとうくん)　助(たす)けなきゃっ　ねえっ
Satō (SUF.) help EP
We must save Sato! OK?!

In this case, we have one of the most colloquial formations, the ending 〜きゃ. The base of this ending is 〜ければならない, but the first part, ければ, has been contracted into きゃ, and the last part, ならない has been left out. The verb in this case is 助ける ***tasukeru*** "to save." To create the standard need-obligation form we must conjugate the verb in the negative (助けない), remove the last 〜い and add 〜ければならない, thus obtaining 助けなければならない "must save." Just as we see in the example, the colloquial form is 助けなきゃ.

Manga Example 6: Permission

Here is an example of how to request something politely. Remember you must use the -*te* form of the verb and then add もいい, followed by です when creating a formal sentence. When requesting permission, you must add the question particle か at the end. In this case, we have the verb 壊す ***kowasu*** "to break," its -*te* form being 壊して, to which we add ～もいいですか to form a request sentence: 壊してもいいですか "Can I break . . ./Do you mind if I break . . . ?"

J.M. Ken Niimura

Mario: あの壁(かべ)…壊(こわ)してもいいですか？
that wall… break can Q?
Do you mind if I break that wall?

Manga Example 7: Prohibition

This last example illustrates an expression of prohibition. As we saw earlier in the lesson, expressions of prohibition are also formed with the -*te* form of the verb plus ～はいけない, as in ほれる "to fall in love" ⇒ -*te* form ほれて ⇒ prohibition form ほれてはいけない "you must not fall in love." In the colloquial register, contracting the ては part and turning it into a simple ちゃ, as in this example, is very common. Let's use this form to forbid Mario in the previous example, from breaking the wall: 壊す ***kowasu*** ⇒ -*te* form 壊して ⇒ formal prohibition form (he made his request formally, so the answer should be formal) 壊してはいけません or 壊しちゃいけません if we contract the ては part into ちゃ.

Xian Nu Studio

Ken'ichi: まゆこ、オレにほれちゃいけないぜ。
Mayuko, me IOP fall in love no must EP
Mayuko, you mustn't fall in love with me.

Exercises 練習

1 Give the potential forms of うばう ***ubau***,"to steal"; おどる ***odoru***, "to dance"; (Group 2), 泳ぐ ***oyogu***, "to swim"; and 考える ***kangaeru***, "to think" (Group 1).

2 If we are not sure whether 見る ***miru***,"to see" and 切る ***kiru***,"to cut" are Group 1 or Group 2 verbs, how can we form the potential?

3 Translate into Japanese:
"You can't fly." ("to fly": 飛ぶ ***tobu***).

4 Translate into English: ソニアさんは英語を話すことができますか？ (英語 ***eigo***: "English," 話す ***hanasu***: "to speak").

5 Translate into informal Japanese: "I must go to school." ("school": 学校 ***gakkō***, "to go": 行く ***iku***).

6 Translate into English: 彼女はスパゲッティを食べなきゃいけない。(彼女 ***kanojo***: "she", スパゲッティ ***supagetti***: "spaghetti", 食べる ***taberu***: "to eat").

7 Translate into formal Japanese: "Can he read the newspaper?" ("he": 彼 ***kare***, "to read": 読む ***yomu***, "newspaper": 新聞 ***shinbun***).

8 Translate into informal Japanese: "Don't read the newspaper."

9 Translate into English: 黒板に書いちゃだめ！(黒板 ***kokuban***: blackboard, 書く ***kaku***: "to write"). What is this ちゃ？

10 Translate "You can see Mt. Fuji from here" and give an argument for the verb you have chosen. ("Mt. Fuji": 富士山 ***fujisan***,"from here": ここから).

— Answers to all the exercises can be found online by following the link on page 9. —

Lesson 33 • 第33課

At the Airport

Now we will start a new kind of lesson, where we will choose a situation and develop possible conversational strategies. You can use these lessons to learn different ways of expressing yourself when talking, to practice structures already seen, and finally, to learn a little bit about Japanese culture.

Some basic sentences

To be honest, airports and airplanes, even if they are Japanese, are the most "linguistically safe" places in the world, because almost everybody can speak English fluently and expects us (if our features are non-Japanese, of course) to speak in English, as well. But you will still find some useful language in this lesson, especially if you are traveling in Japan.

Airport vocabulary					
airport	空港 (くうこう)	check in	チェックイン	passenger	乗客 (じょうきゃく)
aisle	通路 (つうろ)	counter	カウンター	pillow	まくら
arrival	到着 (とうちゃく)	delay	遅刻 (ちこく)	plane	飛行機 (ひこうき)
baggage	荷物 (にもつ)	departure	出発 (しゅっぱつ)	plane connection	乗り継ぎ (の つ)
boarding	搭乗 (とうじょう)	economy class	エコノミークラス	plane ticket	航空券 (こうくうけん)
boarding gate	搭乗口 (とうじょうぐち)	emergency exit	非常口 (ひじょうぐち)	seat	座席 (ざせき) | シート
boarding pass	搭乗券 (とうじょうけん)	excess baggage	超過重量 (ちょうかじゅうりょう)	seat belt	シートベルト
boarding time	搭乗時刻 (とうじょうじこく)	first class	ファーストクラス	takeoff	離陸 (りりく)
booking	予約 (よやく)	flight attendant	客室乗務員 (きゃくしつじょうむいん)	time difference	時差 (じさ)
business class	ビジネスクラス	landing	着陸 (ちゃくりく)	toilet	トイレ
captain	機長 (きちょう)	number x	X番 (ばん)	window	窓 (まど)

So let's make the most of this lesson to review some grammatical structures and learn a lot of new vocabulary. As a rule, in this lesson we will only use those grammatical expressions we already know from previous lessons, so you can take the opportunity to review as you study. Let's start with the simplest and most useful sentences:

Question words	
how?	どう
how much?	いくら｜どれほど
what?	何 / 何
when?	いつ
where?	どこ
who?	誰
why?	どうして

- 日本語が分かりません
  I don't understand Japanese.
- 日本語をあまり話せません
  I don't speak much Japanese.
- 英語で話してください Could you please speak in English?
- 英語ができますか？ Do you speak English?
- 私はアメリカから来ました I come from the US.

In the above examples, some interesting things have appeared, such as a verb in the negative potential form (Lesson 32), 話せません, a request using the -***te*** form + ください (Lesson 24), and the verb できる (Lesson 32). There are a few new things, such as the word あまり which means "not much" when it comes with a verb in the negative, and the word から which means "from."

In the last sentence you can change the word "US" for the name of your own country using the list overleaf.

Check in

Let's start our journey by safely checking in our baggage in Japanese:

- チェックインをしたいんですが I would like to check in. (Lesson 32)
- 窓側の席をお願いします A window seat, please.
- お荷物はいくつですか？ How many bags do you have? (Lesson 25)
- 搭乗時間は何時ですか？When is boarding time? (Lesson 12)
- 搭乗ゲートは何番ですか？ What number is my boarding gate? (Lesson 5)
- 6番ゲートはどこですか？ Where is Gate 6?

Countries in the world	
Argentina	アルゼンチン
Australia	オーストラリア
Brazil	ブラジル
Canada	カナダ
China	中国（ちゅうごく）
Chile	チリ
Costa Rica	コスタリカ
Cuba	キューバ
Cyprus	キプロス
France	フランス
Germany	ドイツ
India	インド
Ireland	アイルランド
Israel	イスラエル
Italy	イタリア
Jamaica	ジャマイカ
Kenya	ケニア
Malaysia	マレーシア
Mexico	メキシコ
New Zealand	ニュージーランド
Nigeria	ナイジェリア
Pakistan	パキスタン
Portugal	ポルトガル
Russia	ロシア
Singapore	シンガポール
South Africa	南（みなみ）アフリカ
South Korea	韓国（かんこく）
Spain	スペイン
UK	イギリス
United States	アメリカ
Zambia	ザンビア

On the plane

Now we are on the plane and it is probably full of Japanese passengers, so one of these sentences could come in useful before, during or after the journey. Some essential phrases, taught in Lesson 4 are ありがとう "thank you," どういたしまして "you're welcome," ごめんなさい "I'm sorry," and すみません "I'm sorry/excuse me." Other useful sentences composed of grammatical structures you have already studied include the following:

- はじめまして、Xです
  How do you do, my name is x. (Lesson 4)
- X番（ばん）の席（せき）はどこですか？ Could you tell me where seat number x is? (Lesson 9)
- 席（せき）を替（か）わってください Could you please change my seat? (Lesson 24)
- この荷物（にもつ）をここに置（お）いてもいいですか？ Can I put my bag here? (Lesson 32)
- シートを倒（たお）してもいいですか？
  Do you mind if I lean my seat back? (Lesson 32)
- すみません、トイレに行（い）きたいんですが
  Excuse me, I need to go to the toilet. (Lesson 31)
- すみません、通（とお）してください
  Excuse me, could you let me through, please? (Lesson 24)

Another very common situation when you're on board a plane is interaction with flight attendants, who, even though they always speak English, will often be surprised or amused if we speak to them in Japanese. At this stage, expressions with "please" (Xをください and Xをお願いします***X o onegaishimasu***) which we glanced at in Lesson 4, will be very useful:

Airplane food	
apple juice	りんごジュース
beer	ビール
chicken	鶏肉
coffee	コーヒー
fish	魚
ice	氷
meat	肉
milk	牛乳
orange juice	オレンジジュース
snack	おつまみ
sugar	砂糖
tea	お茶｜ティー
tomato juice	トマトジュース
vegetables	野菜
whisky	ウイスキー
wine	ワイン

- シートベルトを締めてください
  Fasten your seat belt, please.
- お食事は何にしますか？
  What would you like to eat?
- どんな飲み物がありますか？
  What sort of drinks do you have? (Lesson 18)
- ワインをお願いします Wine, please.
- コーヒーのおかわりをください
  More coffee, please.
- まくらと毛布をください
  A pillow and a blanket, please.
- 大阪に何時に到着しますか？
  What time do we arrive in Osaka? (Lesson 12)
- 次の乗り継ぎに間に合いますか？
  Will we get there in time for the next flight connection?
- 気分が悪いので薬をお願いします
  I don't feel well, could I have some medicine, please?

Flight connections and baggage claim

If we ever need to make a flight connection in a Japanese airport, this section should be helpful. We have also included sentences that may come in handy at baggage claim.

- ＪＬ724便に乗り継ぎたいんですが
  I want to make a connection with flight JL724 (Lesson 31)
- 乗り換えカウンターはどこですか？
  Where is the counter for flight connections?
- 乗り継ぎ便に間に合いませんでした
  I have missed my flight connection.
- 荷物の受け取り所はどこですか？
  Where is the baggage claim?
- カートはどこにありますか？
  Where are the trolleys?
- 私の荷物が見つかりません
  I can't find my bags.

Passport control and changing money

Finally, let's go through passport control and then change some money. Then, we will leave the sterile environment of the airport and breathe the air of our destination, Japan!

- パスポートを見(み)せてください
  Can I see your passport, please.
- 滞在予定(たいざいよてい)は何日(なんにち)ですか？
  How many days are you planning to stay?
- １５日間(じゅうごにちかん)です 15 days.
- 滞在(たいざい)の目的(もくてき)は何(なん)ですか？
  What is the purpose of your visit?
- 観光(かんこう)です Tourism.
- 申告(しんこく)するものはありますか？
  Anything to declare?
- あります / ありません Yes. / No.
- 両替所(りょうがえじょ)はどこですか？
  Where is the money exchange counter?
- 両替(りょうがえ) をしたいんですが
  I would like to change some money
- これを円(えん)に替(かえ)えてください
  Change this into yen, please.
- 手数料(てすうりょう)はいくらですか？
  What commission do you charge?

Customs	
business	ビジネス
customs	税関(ぜいかん)
declaration	申告(しんこく)
entry card	入国(にゅうこく) カード
nationality	国籍(こくせき)
passport	パスポート
passport control	入国(にゅうこく) 審査(しんさ)
stay	滞在(たいざい)
studies	留学(りゅうがく)
tourism	観光(かんこう)
visa	ビザ

Changing money	
bank	銀行(ぎんこう)
bank note	紙幣(しへい)
cash	現金(げんきん)
exchange rate	為替(かわせ)レート
coin	硬貨(こうか) | コイン
commission	手数料(てすうりょう)
dollars	ドル
euros	ユーロ
money change	両替(りょうがえ)
yen	円(えん)

漫画例 Manga Examples

We have already mentioned that airports and airplanes won't give us many chances to practice our Japanese, but there's no harm in seeing some typical and useful situations and sentences. We will now do this using the manga examples.

Manga Example 1: Buying a ticket

We start with a sentence full of specific airport vocabulary: this is what someone says when going to buy a plane ticket. In the sentence, our client specifies the departure time 15時00分, ***jugoji zero fun*** "15:00 hours," adding the suffix 発 ***hatsu***, which means "leaving at." He also gives the flight number, JAL 105, plus the suffix 便 ***bin***, which in this context has the meaning of "flight." He also mentions the destination Osaka (大阪), followed by the word 行き ***yuki***, which could be translated as "destination," or, literally, "going to."

As you can see, there is a lot of information in just one sentence. You don't need to learn it all by heart, but hopefully this manga example will help you review some of the vocabulary and grammar points we have already studied, such as the 〜たい form to express wanting (Lesson 31). Note the tag んですが, common in spoken language and used to soften a sentence. Here, it makes the expression of wanting something sound more polite.

J.M. Ken Niimura

Client: 15時00分発JAL105便大阪行きに乗りたいんですが…
(じゅうごじ ぜろ ふんはつ ジャル いちぜろごびん おおさか ゆ の)
15:00 hours departure JAL105 number Osaka destination PP get on want be but…
I would like to get on flight JAL 105 going to Osaka, leaving at 3 pm.

Manga Example 2: Checking in the baggage

This ground attendant seems to be quite angry! The truth is that the Japanese are extremely kind when talking to customers. Someone must have done something terrible to this woman for her to act in this way and to speak in such a short and colloquial manner to her customer! In the panel we see how she is brusquely giving Hideo his boarding pass (搭乗券 ***tōjōken*** or 搭乗カード ***tōjō kaado***) and asking him if he wants to check in any bags (荷物***nimotsu***). She uses the verb あずける which means "entrust/hand in." Take note of the word はい a very versatile word which doesn't simply mean "yes" (the meaning we have seen until now), but also "as well/let's see/here you are," or as a word to attract someone's attention.

Xian Nu Studio

Woman: はい 搭乗券（とうじょうけん）！あずける荷物（にもつ）は？
here boarding pass! hand in bag SP?
Here is your boarding pass!
Any bags to check in?

Hideo: これです。すみません...
this be. Excuse me...
This is it. Excuse me...

Manga Example 3: The boarding pass

Studio Kōsen

The ground attendant gives the customer his flight number (JAL 107 便 ***jaru ichi maru nana bin***) and says 気をつけて ***ki o tsukete***, which we saw in Lesson 4. It means "take care," but here it is basically "goodbye," and, in this context, it means "Have a good trip." Here, the attendant uses the most formal form of this expression (and the longest) お気をつけていってらっしゃいませ, because she is speaking to a customer, and in Japan "the customer is king," or, in their own words, "god."

Woman: JAL １０７便（ジャル いちまるななびん）です。お気をつけていってらっしゃいませ。
JAL107 flight be. take care (formal)
It's flight number JAL107. Have a good trip.

Manga Example 4: Everything ready to board

Xian Nu Studio

Here is another sentence full of airport terminology. The first part is very similar to what we saw in the first manga example. Key words are 出発 ***shuppatsu*** "departure," ただ今 ***tadaima*** (which means "now," in a formal context), the omnipresent 搭乗 ***tōjō*** "boarding," and手続き ***tetsuzuki*** which means "procedure."

Note the form 〜ております, which means exactly the same as 〜ています (Lesson 24). However, おります is used to lower the speaker's status, thus raising the status of the customer and showing "humbleness." This is the treatment a customer deserves as the "god" he is.

じゅうよじ ゼロ ふんはつタイペイ ゆ ゼロいちななびん しゅっぱつ かた
Voice: 14時00分発台北行き017便で 出発 の方は
14:00 hours departure Taipei destination 017 flight PP, departure POP person SP
Passengers to Taipei on flight 017, with departure time of 14:00 hours...
いまとうじょうてつづ おこな
ただ今 搭乗 手続きを 行 っております。
now board procedure DOP make (humble)
...are now proceeding to board.

Manga Example 5: Cabin service

Once on the airplane, flight attendants will start offering us everything we need for the trip, ranging from magazines to food to headphones. In Japan, the most common sentence used is exactly the same as the one in the manga example, 〜はいかがですか (in the example the particle は is omitted). The word いかが belongs to the formal register and means "Do you feel like...?" or "How about...?" In colloquial register we use the word どう to express the same, like in the sentence ビールはどうですか? "How about a beer?"By the way, the air hostess in the example is holding 週刊誌 ***shūkanshi***, that is, "weekly magazines."

J.M. Ken Niimura

しんぶん ざっし
Attendant: 新聞・雑誌いかがですか？
newspaper magazine how about be Q?
Would you like to read a newspaper or a magazine?

Manga Example 6: Message from the captain

This is a typical message from the captain to the passengers. How many times have we heard the phrase "fasten your seat belts"? Well, in Japanese we say シートベルトを締めてください ***shiitoberuto o shimete kudasai***, whereas the very formal version is as shown in the manga panel: シートベルトをお締めになってください. The construction お + verb root + になる is an example of very formal Japanese usage.

まもなく
着陸
致します。
シート
ベルトを
お締めに
なって下さい。

Gabriel Luque

Although we see that 下さい ***kudasai,*** "please," can be written in kanji, we often find that it is written in hiragana. In the first part of the sentence, we see the word 着陸 ***chakuriku,*** "landing," and the verb 致します ***itashimasu***, which is the most formal version of the omnipresent verb する "to do." So adding する to 着陸 gives us the verb 着陸する "to land."

Captain: まもなく 着陸(ちゃくりく) 致(いた)します。シートベルトをお締(し)めになって下(くだ)さい。
soon landing do (formal). Seat belt DOP fasten (formal) please
We will be landing shortly. Fasten your seat belts, please.

Manga Example 7: Information sign

Our last example has not been taken from a manga, it is a real photograph taken at a Japanese airport. In the photo we see the words 出発 ***shuppatsu,*** "departure," as well as 到着 ***tōchaku,*** "arrival," and many words in katakana which show the great influence English has on Japanese: ターミナル "terminal," デッキ "deck," ロビー "lobby" or チェックイン "check in." The other words you can see on the sign are 南 ***minami***, "south" and 展望 ***tenbō***, "observation."

南ターミナル
South Terminal
4F 展望デッキ Obs. Deck
3F 出発ロビー Departure Lobby
1F チェックインロビー Check-in Lobby
1F 到着ロビー Arrival Lobby

Foto: Marc Bernabé

In an airport we will never have any orientation or comprehension problems, because signs are almost always in English. Remember, though, that once we step outside the airport, it's a whole other world!

Exercises 練習

1 Write the following words in Japanese: "booking," "departure," "toilet" and "airplane."

Translate the following words into English: 通路 ***tsūro***, 空港 ***kūkō***, シートベルト and 到着 ***tōchaku***.

3 Write the following sentence in Japanese: "Can you speak English?"

日本語(にほんご)が分(わ)かりません. Translate this sentence into English.

5 Give at least five names of foreign countries in Japanese.

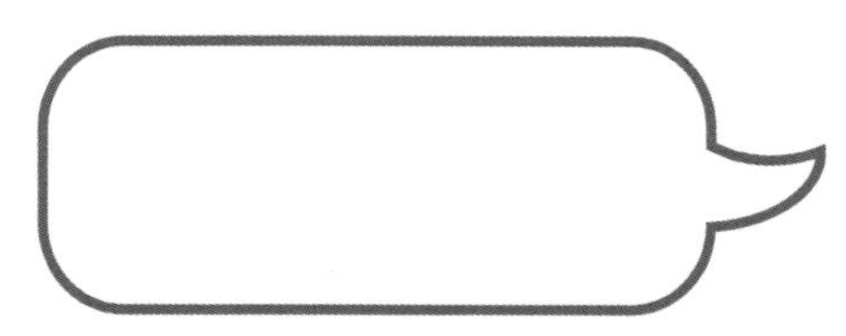

You need to go to the toilet while on a plane, but you have a window seat and can't get out. What do you say?

7 You would like some more orange juice (you already had some before). What do you say to the flight attendant?

滞在(たいざい)の目的(もくてき)は何(なん)ですか? How would you answer this question asked at passport control?

9 観光(かんこう), 銀行(ぎんこう), ユーロ, ビザ and 国籍(こくせき). Translate these words into English.

How do we say in Japanese: "Fasten your seat belts, please"? 10

— Answers to all the exercises can be found online by following the link on page 9. —

Lesson 34 • 第34課

Question Words and the Future

We have already studied the past and present forms of the verb thoroughly, including how to make the question form of the verb. In this lesson we will look at the question words that are often used when asking for information as well as how to convey the future tense in Japanese.

The question form

We have already seen how to make the question form in Japanese, as well as some common question words such as 何 ***nani*** "what," どこ "where" andいくら "how much?" In this lesson we will look at a wider range of question words, which will give your questions in Japanese a much wider dimension.

You will remember that the basic question form consists of adding the particle か at the end of a sentence, and pronouncing the sentence with a rising intonation. In informal speech, the particle の is sometimes used instead. It is also possible to do without particles altogether and simply pronounce the sentence using a questioning intonation. Study the following sentences:

- 横浜(よこはま)は近(ちか)いです
  Yokohama is close. (formal statement)
- 横浜(よこはま)は近(ちか)いですか？
  Is Yokohama close? (formal interrogation)
- 横浜(よこはま)は近(ちか)いの？ Is Yokohama close? (informal interrogation)
- 横浜(よこはま)は近(ちか)い？ Yokohama is close? (colloquial interrogation)

Question words	
何(なに)｜何(なん)	what?
いつ	when?
いくら	how much?
いくつ	how many?
誰(だれ)	who?
どうして	why?
どう	how?
どこ	where?
どの	which?
どれ	which?
どんな	what kind of?
どれくらい	how much?

What, when, where, who?

Let's start with "what?", useful when asking all sort of things. All we need to do is replace the direct object with 何 ***nani***, very often pronounced ***nan*** for phonetic reasons, and remember to add か at the end of the sentence. Study these examples:

- ここに何(なに)がいるか？｜ここに亀(かめ)がいる What is there here? | There is a turtle here.
- 何(なに)を食(た)べたいの？｜魚(さかな)が食(た)べたい What do you want to eat? | I want to eat fish.
- それは何(なん)ですか？｜それはチーズです What is that? | That is cheese.

For “when?”, “where?” and “who?”, the usage is the same: we only need to replace the relevant object. We will use いつ for “when?”, どこ for “where?” and 誰 ***dare*** for “who?”:

- いつハワイへ行(い)った？| 去年(きょねん)、ハワイへ行(い)った
  When did you go to Hawaii? | I went to Hawaii last year.
- 下着(したぎ)はどこにありますか？| 下着(したぎ)はソファにあります
  Where is my underwear? | Your underwear is on the sofa.
- 誰(だれ)がビールを飲(の)んだの？| 美穂(みほ)ちゃんがビールを飲(の)んだ
  Who drank the beer? | Miho drank the beer.

How much?

There are several ways to ask this question. The two most basic expressions are いくら (when talking about a price), and どれくらい (to ask about distance, weight, etc.):

- このキャベツはいくらですか？| このキャベツは200円(にひゃくえん)です
  How much is this cabbage? | This cabbage is 200 yen.
- 新宿(しんじゅく)はどれくらい遠(とお)いですか？| 何(なん)キロも遠(とお)いです
  How far is Shinjuku? | It’s many kilometers away.

The other way to express how much is related to “counters,” which we studied in Lesson 25, so you may need to review that lesson before going on:

- 本(ほん)を何冊(なんさつ)買(か)いますか？| 四冊(よんさつ)です
  How many books are you buying? | Four.
- パソコンを何台(なんだい)持(も)っている？| 三台(さんだい)だ
  How many computers do you have? | Three.

Don’t forget the very useful ～つ counter, whose question form is いくつ. This general counter can be used when we don’t remember the correct counter for a noun:

- 柿(かき)をいくつ食(た)べますか？| 三(みっ)つです
  How many persimmons will you eat? | Three.

Why?

The word どうして means “why?” To answer, simply add から “because,” to your reply:

- どうしてフランスに行(い)きたいの？| フランス語(ご)を勉強(べんきょう)したいから
  Why do you want to go to France? | Because I want to study French.

The kosoado group

In Lesson 9 we learned that ***kosoado*** is a collective term for pronouns that have the prefixes ***ko***- (close to the speaker), ***so***- (close to the hearer), ***a***- (far from both), and ***do***- (question), for example: これ "this," それ "that," あれ "that over there" and どれ "which?" Using ***kosoado*** to make questions is extremely useful and simple: all you need to do is use the appropriate question word.

The *kosoado* group			
Close		**Half-way**	
ここ	here	そこ	there
こちら	this way	そちら	that way
この	this	その	that
これ	this one	それ	that one
こんな	this kind of	そんな	that kind of
こう	like this	そう	like that
Far		**Question**	
あそこ	there	どこ	where?
あちら	that way	どちら	which way?
あの	that	どの	which?
あれ	that one	どれ	which one?
あんな	that kind of	どんな	what kind of?
ああ	like that	どう	how?

- 君(きみ)のペンはどれですか？| これです
  Which is your pen? |This one.
- 彼(かれ)はどこですか？| あそこです
  Where is he? | Over there.
- どんな音楽(おんがく)が好(す)き？| ヘビーメタルだよ What music do you like? | Heavy metal.

Japanese has no fixed future tense

Japanese has no specific future tense: there are other strategies to express the future. Often, forming sentences in the present and getting the idea of the future from the context is enough, or, we can add "time" adverbs as shown in the table. In the third example below, the use of つもり (Lesson 31) add weight to what is being said:

Time adverbs	
後(あと)で	afterward
これから	from now on
今度(こんど)	next time
～後(ご)	...in xx time
明日(あした)	tomorrow
あさって	the day after tomorrow
来週(らいしゅう)	next week
来月(らいげつ)	next month
来年(らいねん)	next year
ある日(ひ)	some day
将来(しょうらい)	in the future
今後(こんご)	after this

- 青森(あおもり)に行(い)きます | 明日(あした)、青森(あおもり)に行(い)きます I go to Aomori. | I will go to Aomori tomorrow.
- 医学(いがく)を勉強(べんきょう)する | 来年(らいねん)、医学(いがく)を勉強(べんきょう)する I study medicine. | I will study medicine next year.
- 来年(らいねん)、医学(いがく)を勉強(べんきょう)するつもりです
  I intend to study medicine next year.

🎧 Deciding on something

One of the example sentences in a previous lesson went like this: お食事は何にしますか？ ***O shokuji wa nan ni shimasu ka?*** "*What would you like to eat?*" What exactly does the expression にします (or にする in its simple form) mean? This expression is used when deciding on something, that is, to form sentences such as: "I choose x" or "I'm inclined to go for x." Using にする usage is very simple, because we always use it after a noun or a nominalized sentence. Later we will see in more detail how a sentence is nominalized, but for the time being, adding こと should be all you need to know. For example: 日本へ行く ***Nihon e iku*** "to go to Japan" | 日本へ行くこと "the fact of going to Japan." Study these examples:

- A: お食事は何にしますか？ What would you like to eat?
  B: から揚げとラーメンにします I'll have (choose) fried chicken and ramen.
- A: どんなセーターを買うことにしたの？ What sort of sweater did you end up buying?
  B: 大きなセーターにしたよ I chose (bought) a large one.
- A: 来年、何を勉強するつもりですか？ What are you going to study next year?
  B: う〜ん ... 経済にしようかな？ Hmm... I might decide on economics.

🎧 Let's

Even though it isn't directly related to the future, let's look at a verb form that expresses invitation as well as wanting (but in a subtler way than with the 〜たい, 欲しい and つもり forms in Lesson 31). We are talking about the expressions "let's" for invitation, and "I'm going to / I mean to" to express one's will. This is how the verb form is made:

- **Group 1:** Replace the last 〜る with 〜よう, for example: 見る ***miru*** "I see" ⇒ 見よう "let's see."
- **Group 2:** Replace the last -***u*** with -***ō***, for example: 急ぐ ***isogu*** "to hurry" ⇒ 急ごう "let's hurry"; 遊ぶ **asobu** "to play" ⇒ 遊ぼう "let's play." **Note:** Be careful with verbs ending in -***tsu***, which are conjugated -***tō*** and not -***tsō***.
- **Irregular verbs:** As usual, we must learn these by heart.

If using the formal -***masu*** form of the verb, all we need to do is replace the last 〜す with 〜しょう, no matter what group the verb belongs to: 行きます ***ikimasu*** "to go"⇒ 行きましょう "let's go." When the -***ō*** form is used to express intention, we will sometimes need the help of と思う ***to omou,*** "I think / I believe," to clearly express this idea, except in exclamations or sentences with a lot of "feeling" as in the third of the examples on the following page. Notice in the last three examples, when we use the form for invitation, we can use the conjugated verb alone.

	Simple f.	Meaning	Rule	Let's...	*-masu* f.	Let's... (formal)
Group 1 Invariable	教(おし)える	to teach	～~~る~~よう	教えよう	教えます	教えましょう
	起(お)きる	to wake up		起きよう	起きます	起きましょう
Group 2 Variable	貸(か)す	to lend	～~~す~~そう	貸そう	貸します	貸しましょう
	待(ま)つ	to wait	～~~つ~~とう	待とう	待ちます	待ちましょう
	買(か)う	to buy	～~~う~~おう	買おう	買います	買いましょう
	帰(かえ)る	to return	～~~る~~ろう	帰ろう	帰ります	帰りましょう
	書(か)く	to write	～~~く~~こう	書こう	書きます	書きましょう
	急(いそ)ぐ	to hurry	～~~ぐ~~ごう	急ごう	急ぎます	急ぎましょう
	遊(あそ)ぶ	to play	～~~ぶ~~ぼう	遊ぼう	遊びます	遊びましょう
	飲(の)む	to drink	～~~む~~もう	飲もう	飲みます	飲みましょう
	死(し)ぬ	to die	～~~ぬ~~のう	死のう	死にます	死にましょう
Group 3 Irregular	する	to do	*Irregular verbs: no rule*	しよう	します	しましょう
	来(く)る	to come		来(こ)よう	来(き)ます	来(き)ましょう

- 食(た)べる (to eat) ⇒ うどんをたくさん食(た)べようと思(おも)う
  I will eat a lot of udon.
- あげる (to give) ⇒ 哲(てつ)さんにこれをあげようと思(おも)います
  I mean to give this to Tetsu.
- 読(よ)む (to read) ⇒ 今日(きょう)は本(ほん)を全部(ぜんぶ)読(よ)もうぜ！
  I will read the whole book today!
- 踊(おど)る (to dance) ⇒ 一緒(いっしょ)にサンバを踊(おど)ろうか？
  Shall we dance the samba together?
- 行(い)く (to go) ⇒ 今度(こんど)、一緒(いっしょ)にカナダへ行(い)こう
  Let's go to Canada soon.
- 誘(さそ)う (to invite) ⇒ 先生(せんせい)をパーティに誘(さそ)いましょう
  Let's invite the teacher to the party.

漫画例 Manga Examples

The manga panels in this section will help you reflect on all the grammar points we've covered in this lesson. Let's take a look at some "real" examples of question words and references to the future.

Manga Example 1: Who?

Just a few pages earlier we saw that to ask *who?* we use 誰 ***dare***. Then, what is that どなた Keisuke is using, which apparently means the same?

We have already mentioned that Japanese is a hierarchical society and that "politeness" must be reflected in words and phrases that have been carefully selected. So どなた is the polite way of saying 誰 and we use it when asking a stranger "who is it?" in a formal situation. Likewise, there are formal and informal versions of other adverbs and pronouns used in questions. For instance, as we saw in Manga Example 5 in Lesson 33, the formal version of どう (meaning "how about?") is いかが.

Xian Nu Studio

In the case of どうして "why?" we have a formal version (なぜ) and even a colloquial version (なんで). Finally, the word どんな "what kind of ?" is a contraction of どのような, a version which is used in formal situations.

Keisuke:	どなたですか？ who be Q? **Who is it?**
Maiko:	あんたのママのお友達(ともだち)、マイコおねえさんだよ you POP mommy POP friend, Maiko sister be EP **It's Maiko, your mommy's friend.**

Manga Example 2: Where?

In this lesson we looked at ***kosoado*** words, which indicate closeness or distance. In this manga panel, we have two ***kosoado*** words: indicating place: ここ "here" and どこ "where?". The two other forms of this word are そこ "there" and あそこ "over there." Remember this last one is slightly irregular. Mastering ***kosoado*** is essential if you want your Japanese to sound natural.

どこだ？
ここは…

Gabriel Luque

Kōji: どこだ？ここは...
where be? here SP...
Where is... Here...?

Manga Example 3: When?

Let's use this manga example to practice forming a question from an answer we already know. What should we ask Emi, so that she gives us this answer? Since she replies with "when," we should obviously ask her "when?" using いつ. For example, いつ私に会ったか？ ***itsu watashi ni atta ka?*** "When did you meet me?" The answer is in the manga.

We can see Emi's sentence has the word ときに (usually written in kanji as 時に). The word 時 means "time," but before a subordinate sentence like this one, its function is to indicate "when" or "at that moment"; that is, a perfect answer when we are asked when something happened. The particle に after 時 is optional. Let's look at some examples:

ひとりで、
生きてきて
………
…全てを
失ったときに、
あなたに会った
のですもの。

Studio Kōsen

- いつ日本語(にほんご)を学(まな)びましたか？
  When did you learn Japanese?
- 京都(きょうと)にいた時(とき)、日本語(にほんご)を学(まな)びました
  I learned Japanese when I was in Kyoto.
- いつお風呂(ふろ)に入(はい)るの？ When do you have a bath?
- 汚(きたな)い時(とき)にお風呂(ふろ)に入(はい)る I have a bath when I'm dirty.

Emi: ひとりで、生(い)きてきて… 全(すべ)てを失(うしな)ったときに、あなたに会(あ)ったのですもの。
alone, live come, everything DOP loose when TP, you IOP meet be then
I had always lived alone... I met you when I had lost everything.

Manga Example 4: Why?

Here is an example of a conversation where someone asks "why?" and the other person answers. The word どうして "why?" is easy to use: just add it at the start of your question. To answer, just add から "because" at the end of the reply, for example:

- どうして日本語は難しいのですか？ Why is Japanese difficult?
- 漢字があるからです Because it has kanji.
- どうして目が大きいのですか？ Why are your eyes big?
- 君を見たいから Because I want to see you.
- どうして口が大きいの？ Why is your mouth big?
- 君を食べたいから！ Because I want to eat you!

Boy: どうしてかえるの？
why go back Q?
Why are you going?

Taku: あまりにもくだらないからだ！
too much nonsense because be!
Because this is absolute nonsense!

Manga Example 5: Intention

We use the verb ending ***-ō*** to express the idea of intention, or to invite or suggest something. In the manga example here, the idea expressed is clearly the first one: the old man "had the intention" of giving the ball to the person he is speaking to. When intention is expressed, we often use the tag と思う ***to omou,*** "I think that..." to strengthen the idea. In this case, the verb is in the past continuous tense: と思ってた "I was thinking." Another example is: 車を買おうと思う "I think I'm going to buy a car." Without と思う, the sentence would have been ambiguous: 車を買おう could be translated as "Lets's buy a car" (suggestion) or "I'm going to buy a car" (intention).

Man: おまえに渡そうと思ってたんだ...
you IOP give SBP think be...
I was going to give it to you...

Manga Example 6: Deciding on

To express deciding on something, we have a useful and easy structure: にする. In this case, the man in the example is deciding which sushi dish he is going to eat from the conveyor belt of the 回転寿司 ***kaiten zushi*** or "revolving sushi" restaurant and the expression he uses is にする .

次はどれにしようかなァ。
Xian Nu Studio

Man: 次(つぎ)はどれにしようかなァ。
next SP which "choose" (doubt)
Which one shall I choose now?

Curiously enough, this example is a mixture of what we have seen in this lesson, since the にする is conjugated in the -*ō* form (にしよう) and there is even an question word of the ***kosoado*** kind (どれ "which") We must stress the fact that the sentence どれにしようかな is very common when one has several options and doesn't know which to choose. The かな in the end is a combination of the question particle か, which we already know, and the emphatic particle な, which in this case has a connotation of doubt. Here's another example: 彼は漫画家かな？ ***kare wa manga ka kana?*** *Could he be a comic artist?*

Exercises 練習

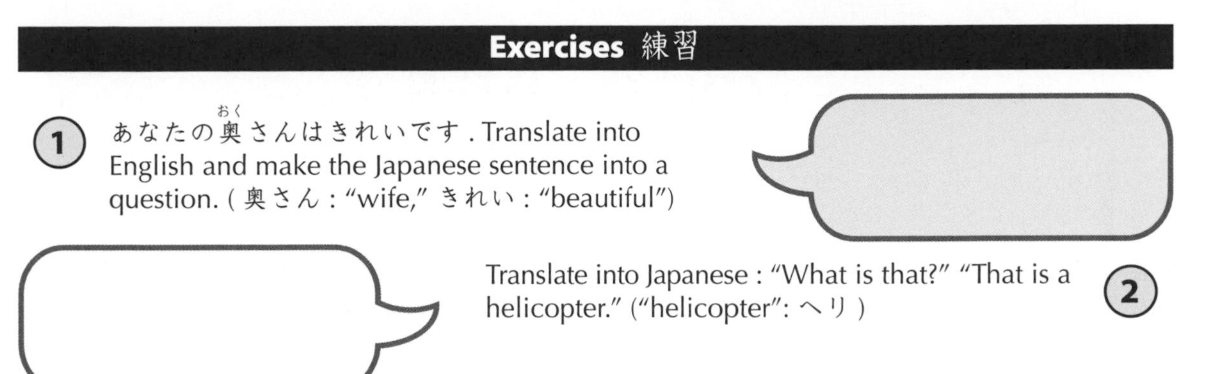

1. あなたの奥(おく)さんはきれいです. Translate into English and make the Japanese sentence into a question. (奥さん : "wife," きれい : "beautiful")

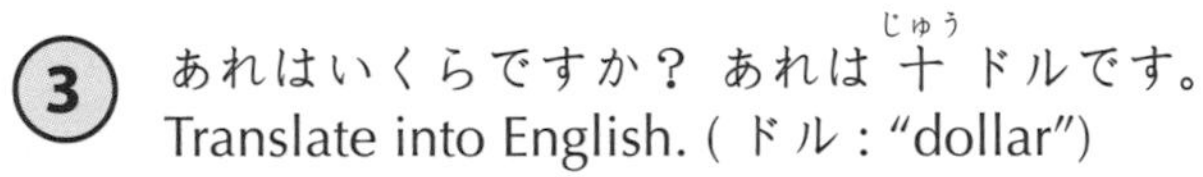

2. Translate into Japanese : "What is that?" "That is a helicopter." ("helicopter": ヘリ)

3. あれはいくらですか？ あれは十(じゅう)ドルです。 Translate into English. (ドル : "dollar")

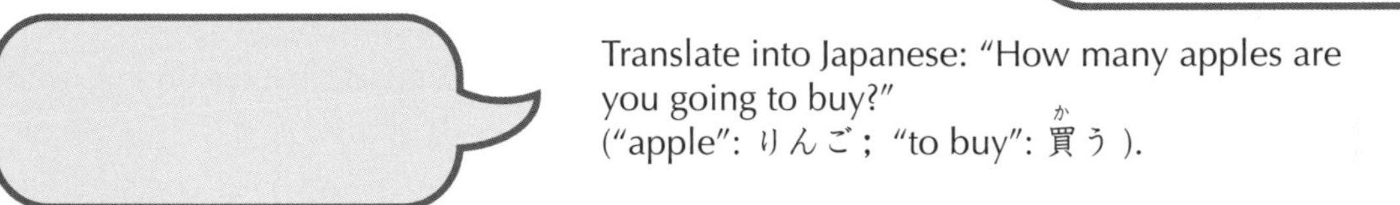

4. Translate into Japanese: "How many apples are you going to buy?" ("apple": りんご; "to buy": 買(か)う).

5. なんでテレビを見(み)たくないの？ 面白(おもしろ)くないから。(テレビ : "television," 面白い : "interesting"). Translate into English.

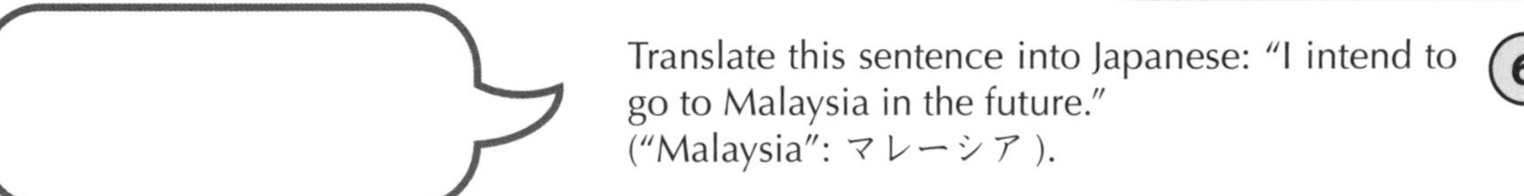

6. Translate this sentence into Japanese: "I intend to go to Malaysia in the future." ("Malaysia": マレーシア).

7. Give the simple -ō form of 拝む ***ogamu***,"to pray" and 壊す ***kowasu***, "to break" (Group 1); 行く ***iku***, "to go" and 走る ***hashiru***,"to run"(Group 2).

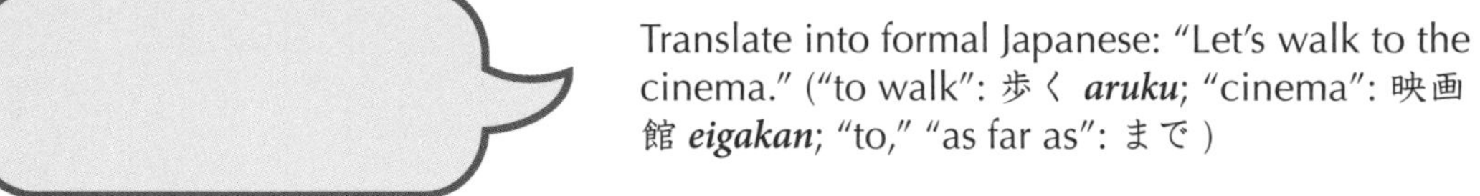

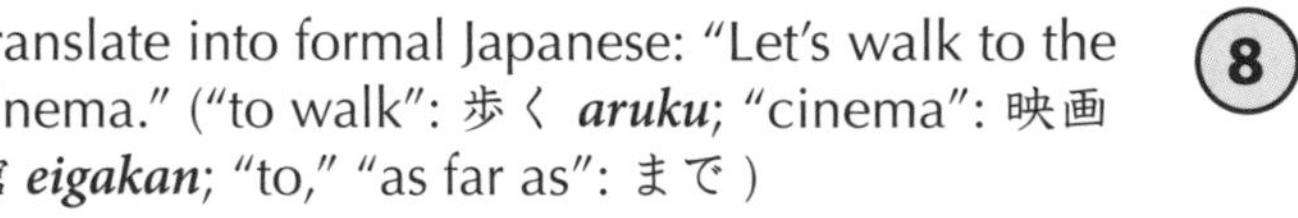

8. Translate into formal Japanese: "Let's walk to the cinema." ("to walk": 歩く ***aruku***; "cinema": 映画館 ***eigakan***; "to," "as far as": まで)

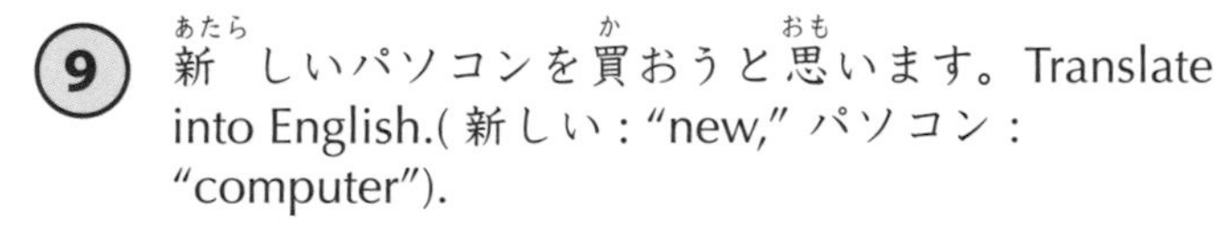

9. 新(あたら)しいパソコンを買(か)おうと思(おも)います。Translate into English.(新しい : "new," パソコン : "computer").

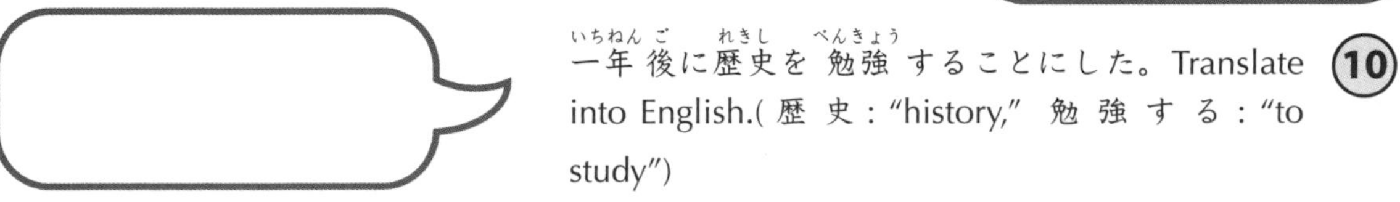

10. 一年後(いちねんご)に歴史(れきし)を勉強(べんきょう)することにした。Translate into English.(歴史 : "history," 勉強する : "to study")

— Answers to all the exercises can be found online by following the link on page 9. —

Lesson 35 • 第35課

-te Form Special

We have already studied the *-te* form in Lesson 24, and saw that it could be used when forming many different expressions. We are now going to devote this lesson to studying it in depth. Obviously, we recommend reviewing Lesson 24 before going on.

Formation

In Lesson 24 we saw how the *-te* form of several verbs was constructed, depending on their infinitive (dictionary form). If you take a look at the table, you will realize there is a new feature: the negative *-te* form, obtained just by adding で to the simple negative form of the verb (Lesson 20). You can also see the negative *-te* form, which is made by replacing the last ～い of the verb's negative with ～くて.

		Simple form	Meaning	Rule	*-te* form	Simple negative	Negative *-te* form	*-te* form of negative
Group 1 Invariable		教える	to teach	～~~る~~て	教えて	教えない	教えないで	教えなくて
		起きる	to wake up		起きて	起きない	起きないで	起きなくて
Group 2 Variable	A	貸す	to lend	～~~す~~して	貸して	貸さない	貸さないで	貸さなくて
	B	待つ	to wait	～~~つ~~って	待って	待たない	待たないで	待たなくて
		買う	to buy	～~~う~~って	買って	買わない	買わないで	買わなくて
		帰る	to return	～~~る~~って	帰って	帰らない	帰らないで	帰らなくて
	C	書く	to write	～~~く~~いて	書いて	書かない	書かないで	書かなくて
	D	急ぐ	to hurry	～~~ぐ~~いで	急いで	急がない	急がないで	急がなくて
	E	遊ぶ	to play	～~~ぶ~~んで	遊んで	遊ばない	遊ばないで	遊ばなくて
		飲む	to drink	～~~む~~んで	飲んで	飲まない	飲まないで	飲まなくて
		死ぬ	to die	～~~ぬ~~んで	死んで	死なない	死なないで	死ななくて
Group 3 Irregular		する	to do	Irregular verbs: no rule	して	しない	しないで	しなくて
		来る	to come		来て	来ない	来ないで	来なくて

A brief review

So far, we have studied several expressions where the *-te* form is used. Let's review them briefly. If there is anything you're not sure about, go back to the corresponding lesson:

- Continuous form of the verb (Lesson 24): 本を読んでいます I'm reading a book.
- "Please" (Lesson 24): 本を読まないでください Don't read a book, please.
- Wish / order (Lesson 31): 本を読んで欲しいです I want you to read a book.
- Prohibition (Lesson 32): 本を読んではいけません You must not read books.
- Permission (Lesson 32): 本を読んでもいいです It's ok if you read books.

The combination of ～てもいい and the negative *-te* form will allow us to construct sentences such as: "you don't have to," that is, expressing a lack of obligation. For example: 読む ***yomu*** "to read" ⇒ negative: 読まない ⇒ *-te* form: 読まなくて ⇒ sentence: 本を読まなくてもいいです ***hon o yomanakute ii desu*** "you don't have to read this book." As you can see, the negative form of a verb is considered as an *-i* adjective and its *-te* form is conjugated as such. Here's one more sentence: 行かなくてもいいです ***ikanakute ii desu*** "you don't have to go."

- Give / receive (Lesson 28): 本を読んでもらいます Someone reads me a book.

In Lesson 28 we briefly saw the usage of the *-te* form plus the verbs あげる "to give," もらう "to receive" and くれる "to receive." We will go over this subject in depth in Volume 2.

Connecting sentences

The *-te* form can be used to join two or more phrases together, enabling us to add a higher level of complexity to our sentences in Japanese.

	Infinitive	Meaning	Rule	*-te* form
-i adj.	高い	tall	~~い~~くて	高くて
-na adj.	静かな	silent	~~な~~で	静かで
Noun	先生	teacher	で	先生で

- 彼女は掃除して、洗濯する She does the cleaning and (then) the washing.
- 私 は遊んで、本を読みます I play (have fun) and (then) read a book.

We will see this way of connecting sentences again in Volume 2, but for now it is worth knowing that adjectives and nouns can also be connected using the *-te* form. Check the table above for their forms, which are very simple.

- ***-i* adj:** この本は安くておもしろいです This book is cheap and interesting.
- ***-na* adj:** その電車は便利で速いです That train is convenient and fast.
- **Noun:** 父はサラリーマンで、友隆と言います
  My father is an office worker and his name is Tomotaka.

Finished action

Now we will study some very useful structures which are based on the **-*te*** form, allowing us to create many new types of expressions.

The first expression we will see is ～てある, which has the connotations of "a finished action" and "something has been done, and the consequence of this action remains unchanged."

- 料理は作ってある The meal is ready.
- 盆栽はテーブルに置いてある
  The bonsai has been put on the table (and it is still there).
- パソコンはつけてある The personal computer has been turned on (and it is still on).

Going and coming

Other common structures are ～ていく and ～てくる. The first one, ～ていく, has the connotation of "going" or "doing something (progressing)." It comes from 行く ***iku*** "to go".

- **To take:** 明日、マンガを持っていく I'll take the comic book tomorrow.
- **To go:** 駅まで走っていきます I'm running to the station.
- **To do something (constant):** 僕は経済を勉強していく I study (and continue to study) economics.

The second, ～てくる, has several possible meanings, although all of them imply the idea of "coming." It is based on the verb 来る ***kuru***, "to come".

- **To bring:** 明日、マンガを持ってくる I'll bring the comic book tomorrow.
- **To come:** 先生は歩いてきます The teacher comes walking.
- **To go (and then come back):** メキシコへ行ってきたよ
  I went to Mexico (and came back).
- **To come back:** ワインを買ってきた I've bought wine (and have come back).

There are many connotations here, so it may be slightly confusing. Advice: Think about the equations いく = to go and くる = to come, and it will be clearer.

After doing something

In the previous lesson we saw the lack of a future tense in Japanese and several strategies to express the idea of future. The ～てから form can also help us in this context, since it means "after doing...," very useful when expressing future actions.

- テレビを見てからご飯を食べる I eat (I'll eat) after watching TV.
- 一杯飲んでから寝ましょう I'll go to sleep after having a drink.
- 死んでから天国へ行くよ After dying, you go to heaven.

To try

The expression 〜てみる (very common) has the connotations of "to try to do something" and "to do something just to try." These examples will help you understand:

- この本を翻訳してみます I'll try to translate this book.
- 刺身を食べてみたい I'd like to try and eat sashimi.
- カラオケへ行ってみよう I'll try and go to karaoke.

Note: Most of the expressions we are now seeing are compatible with other structures we have previously seen. For instance, example #2 combines 〜てみる with the ending meaning "want," 〜たい (Lesson 31) and #3 combines 〜てみる with the ***-ō*** form (Lesson 34).

Leave something done

The expression 〜ておく, which comes from the verb 置く ***oku*** "to place/put/leave (something)" has the connotation of doing something beforehand (so it is useful later).

- ビールを買っておいたよ I've bought beer [for later].
- この本を読んでおこう I'm going to read this book [in case it is necessary later].
- 日本語を勉強しておかなければなりません I must study Japanese [it might be useful later on].

Note: In the second example we have also used the ***-ō*** form (Lesson 34) and in the third example, the form for need or obligation (Lesson 32). In spoken language, 〜ておく can be contracted into 〜とく（言っておく ***itte oku*** ⇒ 言っとく "I tell you"）or into 〜どく（読んでおく ***yonde oku*** ⇒ 読んどく "I read it").

Finish doing / regret doing

The expression 〜てしまう has two very different connotations. The first one is "to finish doing something completely," "to get through something," and the second (very common) is "having done something one regrets," or "doing something with consequences."

- 一週間で教科書を読んでしまった I read the textbook through in a week.
- 日本語を全部 忘れてしまった I have completely forgotten my Japanese.
- 彼に「バカ」と言ってしまった I called him an idiot [and now I regret it].
- 僕は彼の不倫を見てしまった I saw his [illicit] affair [and this could have consequences].

Obviously, if we don't know the context, we could encounter ambiguous sentences:

- 私(わたし)はケーキを食(た)べてしまった I ate [all of? / by mistake?] the cake.

Note: 〜てしまう can be contracted into 〜ちゃう (言ってしまう ***itte shimau***⇒ 言っちゃう "I tell / blurt it out") or into 〜じゃう (読んでしまう ***yonde shimau*** ⇒ 読んじゃう "I'll read it through").

To be dying to

The last expression we will look at, 〜てたまらない (formal version: 〜てたまりません), is used to indicate the intensity of something, the feeling of something being unbearable, or that we have a very strong desire. It is exclusively used with the ***-te*** form of ***-i*** or ***-na*** adjectives, as well as with verb forms that function as an ***-i*** adjective (like the〜たい form).

- 今日(きょう)は寒(さむ)くてたまらないよ！ I can't stand the cold today!
- あの女性(じょせい)はきれいでたまりませんね That woman is extremely beautiful.
- 旅行(りょこう)に行(い)きたくてたまらないよ I'm dying to go on a trip.
- 孫(まご)と遊(あそ)びたくてたまらない I'm dying to play with my grandchild.

Conclusion

We have had the chance to review and study many usages of the ***-te*** form, one of the most useful constructions you can master. The table on the right gives a summary of all the main uses of the ***-te*** form, and where you can find them in the two volumes of this book.

Grammatical summary of the *-te* form		
Form	**Meaning**	**Example**
～ている	gerund (Lesson 24)	話している To be talking
～てください	please (Lesson 24)	話してください Please talk
～てもいい	permission (Lesson 32)	話してもいい You can talk
～てはいけない	prohibition (Lesson 32)	話してはいけない You must not talk
～てほしい	wish, order (Lesson 24)	話してほしい I want you to talk
～てあげる	to do a favor (Lessons 28, 49)	話してあげる I talk to you (doing you a favor)
～てもらう	receive something (Lessons 28, 49)	話してもらう (I'll have) you talk to me
～てくれる	receive something (from someone close) (Lessons 28, 49)	話してくれる You talk to me (doing me a favor)
(Connector)	(sentence connector)	話してだまる I talk and become silent
～てある	(finished action)	話してある It has been told
～ていく	to go to	話していく I'm going to talk (to him)
～てくる	to go and come back	話してくる I'll (go) talk (and return)
～てから	after doing...	話してから After talking...
～てみる	to try	話してみる I'll try to talk (to him)
～ておく	to do something beforehand, to decide on doing something	話しておく I'll tell it (for later)
～てしまう	to finish doing| to regret doing	話してしまう I talked (and I regret doing it)
～てたまらない	to be dying to	話したくてたまらない I'm dying to talk

漫画例 Manga Examples

In this lesson we have studied some of the many expressions available to you once you master the *-te* form. Here we have selected some manga panels that give examples of the *-te* form in use.

Manga Example 1: "Please" in the negative

One of most useful expressions we can construct with the ***-te*** form is the request "please," as we saw in Lesson 24: all you need to do is add ください (sometimes written in kanji: 下さい) to the ***-te*** form of a verb.

Let's look at the verb in this manga panel, 見る ***miru*** "to look." First, let's make its ***-te*** form (it belongs to Group 1, so we will get 見て) and add ください to obtain the sentence 見てください "look, please." In this lesson, we have learned a new feature: the negative of the ***-te*** form. To obtain this negative form, start with the simple negative of the verb (Lesson 20) and then add で. Thus 見る ⇒ 見ない (simple negative) ⇒ 見ないで. Adding ください we will obtain a "negative please": 見ないでください "don't look please." If we don't use ください, as in this manga example, the sentence will have exactly the same meaning, but it will be a lot more colloquial (just like in English, since "come here, please" is not the same as just "come here").

Studio Kōsen

Girl: だけど甘(あま)く見(み)ないでね
but sweet look EP
But don't underestimate me, OK?

Note: In this sentence we also have the ***-i*** adjective 甘い ***amai*** "sweet," transformed into an adverb (Lesson 22). Besides "sweet," 甘い can also mean "indulgent/optimistic." Therefore, the sentence would literally mean "don't look at me indulgently," although here we have chosen a more natural version: "don't underestimate me"

Manga Example 2: You don't have to

In Lesson 32 we saw the permission form 〜てもいい. From there we can move on to the creation of sentences such as "you don't have to," which are usually constructed with the ***-te*** form of the negative of the verb (which functions as an ***-i*** adjective) plus 〜てもいい. For example: 思い出す ***omoidasu*** "to remember" ⇒ 思い出さない "to not remember" ⇒ 思い出さなくて (***-te*** form of the negative) ⇒ 思い出さなくてもいい "you don't need to remember."

Xian Nu Studio

Note: In casual speech, we tend to do without も in 〜てもいい sentences, as in this example. The word 何も means "nothing."

Fritz: 何も思い出さなくていい！
nothing remember (don't have to)!
You don't need to remember anything!

Manga Example 3: Connecting sentences

Earlier in this lesson we saw sentences could be linked using the ***-te*** form. In this example we have two linkages, the first one with an ***-i*** adjective, and the second one with a verb. The ***-te*** form of the ***-i*** adjective うるさい "noisy" is うるさくて, and the ***-te*** form of the verb 落ち着く ***ochitsuku*** "to be calm/settle down" is 落ち着いて. Therefore, the sentence, formed by three elements would be うるさくて落ち着いて食う ***urusakute ochitsuite kuu*** "to eat calmly with noise." **Note:** 食えん ***kuen*** is the contracted form of 食えない ***kuenai***, the negative potential (Lesson 32) of the verb 食う ***kuu*** "to eat," the vulgar version of 食べる ***taberu***. The word だろう is the simple ***-ō*** form (Lesson 34) of the verb です (the formal would be でしょう). In this case it functions as a tag with a nuance of insistence or reassertion of what has been said.

J.M. Ken Niimura

Kuraki: ああ、うるさくて落ち着いて食えんだろう
aah, noisy calmly eat can I?
Argh, you are so noisy there's no way I can eat in peace, is there?

Manga Example 4: To try

Another of the many usages of the versatile ***-te*** form is 〜てみる, which gives a sentence the meaning of "try to do something," or "do something just to try." This form is widely used, specially in spoken Japanese. In the manga example we see it combined with the verb やる (a colloquial verb meaning "to do"), which belongs to Group 2 and so its ***-te*** form is やって. Therefore, やってみる would literally mean "to try to do/to try" as we propose here.

In the example sentence the verb is in the ***-ō*** form (with the connotation of invitation, see Lesson 34). Since the tag 〜てみる functions like any other verb, it can be conjugated in the same way. Note also how Helen uses the potential form (Lesson 32) of the verb 使う ***tsukau*** "to use," which becomes 使える "can use."

Helen: まだ使(つか)えるの？
still use (can) Q?
Is it still working?

Joey: さあ...やってみよう
(doubtful)... do (try)
I don't know... Let's try it.

Manga Example 5: Something irreparable

We saw earlier how the expression 〜てしまう has the connotation of "finish doing something completely" and "do something with consequences." This last connotation can be used with actions performed by oneself as well as with voluntary or involuntary actions performed by other people. Here, Yuki remarks the noodles will overcook and she uses 〜てしまう to give the sentence the connotation of "and it would be a shame."

In the colloquial register, 〜てしまう is usually contracted into 〜ちゃう or 〜じゃう (〜ちゃった and 〜じゃった in the past), as in this case. のびる "to overcook" ⇒ のびて (***-te*** form) ⇒ のびてしまう (〜てしまう form) ⇒ のびちゃう (spoken contraction).

Yuki: 食(た)べましょう、のびちゃうわ
eat (invitation), overcook EP
Let's eat, or they'll overcook.

Manga Example 6: To go (and come back)

Xian Nu Studio

In Lesson 27 we already saw the fixed expression 行ってきます ***itte kimasu***, which you say when you are leaving the house. The expression 〜てくる has several meanings, but they all somehow imply the idea of *coming back* or *coming*. In the case of 行ってくる, the sentence expresses the connotation that is very common in Japanese of "*I'm going (but I'll come back).*" The same connotations are found in sentences such as 東京へ行ってきます "*I'm going to Tokyo [and I'll come back later].*"

Sachiko: 行(い)ってきます！
go (and come back)
See you later!

Manga Example 7: It's a good thing...

To conclude, let's look at a new use of the ***-te*** form: the expression 〜てよかった, which implies the idea of "thank goodness" or "just as well." In other words, it's a way to express relief. よかった is the past form of いい (*well, good*), so the literal translation of these expressions would be *It has been good that . . .*

Xian Nu Studio

In this example we have two ***-te*** forms. The first one is the continuous form of the verb: 恋をしている ***koi o shite iru*** (literally "to be doing love" that is, "to be in love"). The resultant verb 恋をしている is also given in the ***-te*** form and then you add 〜よかった to express the idea of "thank goodness": 恋をしていてよかった (literally, "lucky I have been doing love" or, as we have translated here, "thank goodness I'm in love").

Chiaki: 恋(こい)をしていて ...... よかった。
love DOP do GER... good
Thank goodness I'm in love.

Exercises 練習

1 Give the *-te* forms (normal and negative) of the verbs うばう ***ubau***,"to steal"; おどる ***odoru***, "to dance" (Group 2); 泳ぐ ***oyogu***, "to swim"; 考える ***kangaeru***, "to think" (Group 1).

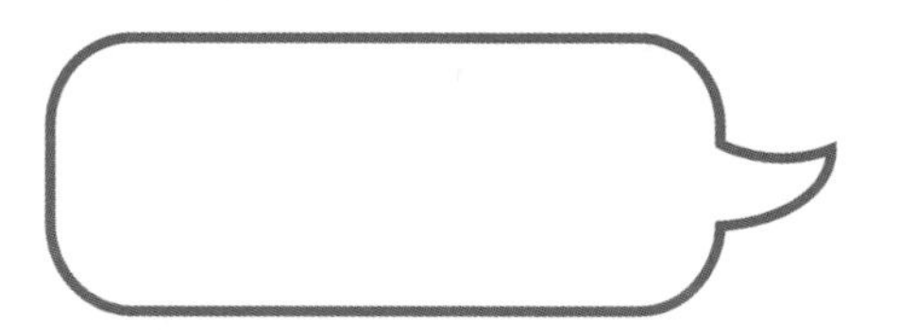

2 Translate into formal Japanese: "This food is delicious and nutritious." ("food": 料理 ***ryōri***, "delicious": おいしい , "nutritious": 栄養がある ***eiyō ga aru***)

3 Translate into English: 台所(だいどころ)の窓(まど)は開(あ)いてあるよ。(台所 : "kitchen", 窓 : "window", 開く : "to open")

4 Translate into Japanese: "After eating, let's go for a walk." ("to eat": 食べる ***taberu***, "to go for a walk": 散歩する ***sanpo suru***)

5 Translate into English: モンゴルに行(い)ってみたくてたまらないよ。(モンゴル : "Mongolia")

6 Translate into English: この本(ほん)を全部(ぜんぶ)読(よ)んでおいてしまおう。(全部 : "all," "the whole")

7 Translate into formal (and then colloquial) Japanese: "Don't turn the TV off." ("to turn off": 消す , "television": テレビ)

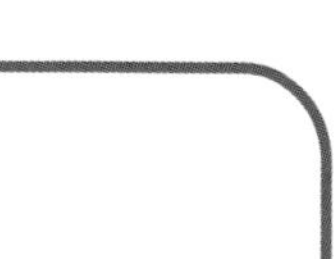

8 東京(とうきょう)へ行ってきた ; 東京へ行っておいた and 東京へ行ってしまった . What is the difference between these three sentences?

9 Translate into Japanese: "We don't have to write a thesis." ("to write": 書く ***kaku***, "thesis": 論文 ***ronbun***)

10 Translate into Japanese: "Just as well I've come to Sapporo." ("to come": 来る ***kuru***, "Sapporo": 札幌)

— Answers to all the exercises can be found online by following the link on page 9. —

影 The Kage Story

To finish Volume 1 of this two-volume series, we have the first episode of an exciting new manga story, which will continue in Volume 2. Titled ***Kage***, with art by J. M. Ken Niimura and words by J. M. Ken Niimura and Marc Bernabé, the story takes place in present-day Japan. Nuria, the main character, is a Spanish journalist and photographer, who has been sent to Tokyo by the newspaper where she works to write a feature on contemporary Japan. Once there, she meets Mina Tanimura, who works for a local newspaper, and who helps Nuria make the most of her stay in Japan, and carry out her work in the best possible conditions.

Characters

Nuria: Young Spanish photographer and journalist. She works for a newspaper in Madrid, and her boss sends her to Japan to write a feature story about the country.
Mina Tanimura: Young Japanese girl who works for a newspaper in Tokyo. She has been given the task of helping Nuria so that she can write her feature.
The Beggar: Mysterious Japanese vagrant who will be a key character in the story.
The Shadow: Nuria sees this shadow now and then during her stay in Japan. What could this shadow be, and why does it appear when it is least expected?

Nuria

Mina

The Beggar

The Shadow

Remember! The next episode of ***Kage*** continues in Volume 2 of *Learn Japanese with Manga*. If you want to enjoy the story, keep on studying!

KAGE
影
一日目
来日
ツーーン

平成17年10月5日
午後3時30分
ロシア
ドイツ
フランス
イタリ
スペイン
マドリッド

飲み物を持ってきましょうか？

はい、ちょっとね。
一時間後に到着しますよ。疲れていますか？

すみません、東京に何時に到着しますか？
韓国
日本
東京

いいですよ。ちょっと待ってくださいね。
お願いします。コーヒーを飲んでもいいですか？

ハァ
ハァ
すみません!!
通してください!!
タッタッタッ
あ、はい。ごめんなさい
ここで写真をとってはいけませんよ。カメラをしまっておいてください。
入国審査

パスポートを見せてください。

どうぞ。
国籍はスペインですね… 滞在の目的は何ですか？

ビジネスです。
私は新聞記者です。

荷物受け取り場所
ひいいいいっ、間に合わない！

すみませんが、私の荷物が見つかりません。
そうですか？搭乗券を見てもいいですか？
はい、これですね。
はい、どうも。

チェックインはマドリッドでしましたか？
はい、そうです。

ちょっと待ってください。

むっ

荷物をサンパウロに送ってしまいました。申し訳ないです。
え？サンパウロに？どうしてですか？

間違いがあったからです。すみません。
荷物をホテルに送ることができますか？
はい、できます。ホテルの名前は何ですか？

東京ビッグホテルです。よろしくおねがいします。

出口

ヌリアさん

谷村美奈です。よろしくお願いします。日本語が上手に話せますね。びっくりしました。
こんにちは。ヌリアです、はじめまして。すみません、遅くなりました。
いいえ、まだ勉強しています。もっと上手に話したいです。これからもっと勉強するつもりです。

どうして遅かったですか？何か問題がありましたか？

はい、荷物が届いてないよ。

本当ですか？困りましたね。コーヒーをゆっくり飲みたいですか？
はい、飲みたいよ。とても疲れた。少し休まなきゃ。

これはヌリアさんの携帯電話です。自由に使ってください。
サッ
この携帯ではスペインへかけられませんよ。急いでいますか？
ありがとう。家族に電話したい。大丈夫？

大変ですね。たくさん日本の写真をとらなければなりませんか？
そうだよ。6日間で仕事を終えて、スペインへ帰らなきゃならない。

あ、疲れた…
いいえ、ホテルに着いてから電話しよう。
りん
りん

Review for Lessons 31–35

Answers to all the review exercises can be found online by following the link on page 9.

KAGE – New vocabulary 新しい単語

しまる	to put away (Group 2)	問題（もんだい）	problem
とる	to take photos (Group 2)	届（とど）く	to arrive (packet)
記者（きしゃ）	journalist	困（こま）る	to be in trouble (Gp.1)
サンパウロ	São Paulo	携帯（けいたい）（電話（でんわ））	mobile phone
間違（まちが）い	mistake	自由（じゆう）な	free
送（おく）る	to send (Group 2)	着（つ）く	to arrive
かける	to telephone (Group 1)		

1. In this first episode of *Kage*, which city does Nuria depart from, and which city does she go to? Which country is the plane flying over in the first scene?

2. At what time will the plane reach its destination? (Specify am or pm.)

3. Why is Nuria visiting Japan? What sort of work does she do?

4. Where is Nuria's luggage when she reaches her destination? Why?

5. What does Nuria want to do with the mobile phone from Mina? Can she do it? Why?

6. After Nuria and Mina's first introductions, Nuria changes her speech to colloquial Japanese, while Mina keeps talking formally. How can we tell formal from colloquial Japanese? What does the formality of each character's language say about her personality?

7. Change the following sentences from formal to informal Japanese.

a) 飲み物（もの）を持ってきましょうか？ ____________________

b) ここで写真（しゃしん）をとってはいけません ____________________

c) 荷物（にもつ）をサンパウロに送（おく）ってしまいました ____________________

d) この携帯(けいたい)ではスペインへかけられません ________________

8. Change the following sentences from informal to formal Japanese.

a) 荷物(にもつ)が届(とど)いてないよ ________________

b) 少し休まなきゃ ________________

c) ホテルに着(つ)いてから電話(でんわ)しよう ________________

9. What connotation does ～てしまいました add to the sentence 荷物(にもつ)をサンパウロに送(おく)ってしまいました？

10. Make the potential form of these verbs: 疲(つか)れる , 待つ , 送(おく)る , 使(つか)う , とる , 着(つ)く .

11. Change the verbs in the previous question into the ～たい form.

12. Link the name of each country with its best matching word.

イタリア	ティー・タイム	スペイン	コアラ
中国	ピザ	フランス	テキーラ
アメリカ	ハリウッド	インド	ソーセージ
ブラジル	カンフー	オーストラリア	フラメンコ
ロシア	コサック	メキシコ	タージ・マハル
イギリス	サンバ	ドイツ	ワイン

13. Fill in the blanks of the following sentences with the correct question word.

a) A: 青木(あおき)先生は_______にいますか？ | B: 先生はそのレストランにいますよ。

b) A: この本は_______ですか？ | B: この本は 1500 円です。

c) A: 彼女(かのじょ)は_______車を持っているの？ | B: 赤くて小さい車だよ。

d) A: アキラさんは_______帰ったの？ | B: 3 時間前に帰った。

e) A: _______彼女(かのじょ)は来ませんでしたか？ | B: 仕事(しごと)をしなければならないからです。

f) A: あの人は＿＿＿＿ですか？ | B: あの人は青木(あおき)先生ですよ。

g) A: ＿＿＿＿のりんごを買おうか？ | B: ４つ。

14. Fill in the blanks with the appropriate word from the box below.

a) 私はコーヒーに 牛乳(ぎゅうにゅう) と＿＿＿＿＿＿＿を入れます。

b) A: あなたの＿＿＿＿＿＿＿は何(なん)ですか？ | B: 韓国(かんこく)です。

c) ＿＿＿＿＿＿＿、医者(いしゃ)になりたいよ！

d) A: ＿＿＿＿＿＿＿で払(はら)いますか？ | B: いいえ、カードでお願(ねが)いします。

e) ＿＿＿＿＿＿＿でアルゼンチンへ行こうよ！

f) 明日そちらへ行けないが、＿＿＿＿＿＿＿行ってもいいですか？

g) この漢字(かんじ)は＿＿＿＿＿＿＿書(か)いてはだめよ！

h) ワインに＿＿＿＿＿を入れるつもりか、お前？しないでよ、そんなこと ...

i) A: 食事(しょくじ)は＿＿＿＿＿＿にするつもりですか？ | B: 魚(さかな)が食べたいですね ...

j) 私は＿＿＿＿＿＿＿コーヒーはきらいだ！

将来(しょうらい)	こう	飛行機(ひこうき)	何(なん)	砂糖(さとう)
現金(げんきん)	こんな	氷(こおり)	国籍(こくせき)	あさって

15. Fill in the blanks with the most suitable word.

a) 飛行機(ひこうき)が＿＿＿＿＿＿＿します。シートベルトをしめてください。

1. 空港(くうこう) 2. 離陸(りりく) 3. 搭乗(とうじょう) 4. 通路(つうろ)

b) ＿＿＿＿＿＿＿でりんごを買うことができますよ。

1. あんな 2. こう 3. その 4. あそこ

c) ＿＿＿＿＿側(がわ)の座席(ざせき)に座(すわ)れた。しかし、くもっていて、何(なに)も見えなかった。

1. 通路(つうろ) 2. 窓(まど) 3. 到着(とうちゃく) 4. 予約(よやく)

d) A この雑誌(ざっし)は＿＿＿＿＿＿＿ですか？ | B: これは 20 ＿＿＿＿です。

1. いくら 2. いくつ 3. どれくらい 4. いつ

1. 肉(にく) 2. トイレ 3. ユーロ 4. 時差(じさ)

e) すみません、______________の月曜(よう)日、時間がありますか？

1. 来年　2. 来日(らいにち)　3. 来週(らいしゅう)　4. 来月

16. Choose the phrase that has the same meaning as the underlined part of the sentence.

a) ジョンさんはチェックインしたいです。

1. 荷物(にもつ)を買いたいです。　2. 荷物(にもつ)を食べたいです。
3. 荷物(にもつ)を見たいです。　4. 荷物(にもつ)をあずけたいです。

b) あさって、日本語を勉強(べんきょう)するつもりです。

1. 一日後　2. 二日後
3. 一日前　4. 二日前

c) 彼(かれ)は2000円をドルにかえました。

1. 為替(かわせ)した　2. 買った
3. 両替(りょうがえ)した　4. 留学(りゅうがく)した

d) 彼女(かのじょ)は英語(えいご)だけできます。

1. 国籍(こくせき)はスペインです　2. 国籍(こくせき)はイギリスです
3. 国籍(こくせき)はフランスです　4. 国籍(こくせき)は中国です

e) 僕(ぼく)の滞在(たいざい)の目的(もくてき)は留学(りゅうがく)です。

1. 勉強(べんきょう)したい　2. 食事(しょくじ)したい
3. 仕事(しごと)したい　4. ビジネスしたい

17. In each case, complete with a suitable question or answer, forming full sentences. For indirect questions, use the underlined part as the object of the question.

a) Q: メキシコ人はスペイン語ができますか？
A: はい、メキシコ人はスペイン語ができます。

b) Q: ______________________________?
A: 空港(くうこう)で飛行機(ひこうき)に乗(の)ります。

c) Q: ファーストクラスの航空券(こうくうけん)は安いですか？
A: ______________________________。

d) Q: ____?

A: 二年前に日本に来た。

18. This dialogue is out of order. Rewrite it in the correct order, below.

1) わかりました。いくら両替(りょうがえ)したいですか？
2) いいえ、日本円をユーロに替(か)えたいです。
3) 5万円です。
4) はい、お願(ねが)いします。
5) 今の為替(かわせ)レートで365ユーロになります。いいですか。
6) いらっしゃいませ。
7) はい。日本円をアメリカドルに替(か)えたいですか？
8) おはようございます。すみません、両替(りょうがえ)をしたいですが…

両替所(りょうがえじょ)の人: ____

私: ____

両替所(りょうがえじょ)の人: ____

私: ____

両替所(りょうがえじょ)の人: ____

私: ____

両替所(りょうがえじょ)の人: ____

私: ____

19. Complete this dialogue held at the airport with the most suitable words.

Clerk: Good morning. Can I help you?

Client: ごめんなさい、(1) ______________ が分かりません。(2) ______________ で話(はな)してください。

Clerk: 分かりました。日本語で話(はな)します。

Client: 荷物(にもつ)を持ってきました。(3) ______________ をしたいんですが…

Clerk: はい。あなたの (4) ______________ は何(なん)ですか？

Client: 山田(やまだ)年男(としお)です。

Clerk: パスポートと (5) ______________ 券(けん)をお願(ねが)いします。

Client: はい、どうぞ。

Clerk: どうも。(6) ______________ はいくつですか？

Client: 一つだけです。

Clerk: 荷物(にもつ)をここに置(お)いてください。座席(ざせき)は (7) ____________ 側(がわ)にしますか？

Client: いいえ、窓側(まどがわ)にしたいです。

Clerk: 分かりました。

Client: すみませんが、搭乗(とうじょう)時間は (8) ______________ ですか？

Clerk: ５時２５分です。

Client: (9) ______________ ゲートは何番(なんばん)ですか？

Clerk: ２４番(ばん)ゲートです。

Client: どうもありがとうございます。

Clerk: どういたしまして。どうぞ、これは搭乗(とうじょう)券です。

Client: この券(けん)を使(つか)って (10) ______________ に入れますか？

Clerk: はい、そうです。お気をつけて行ってらっしゃいませ。

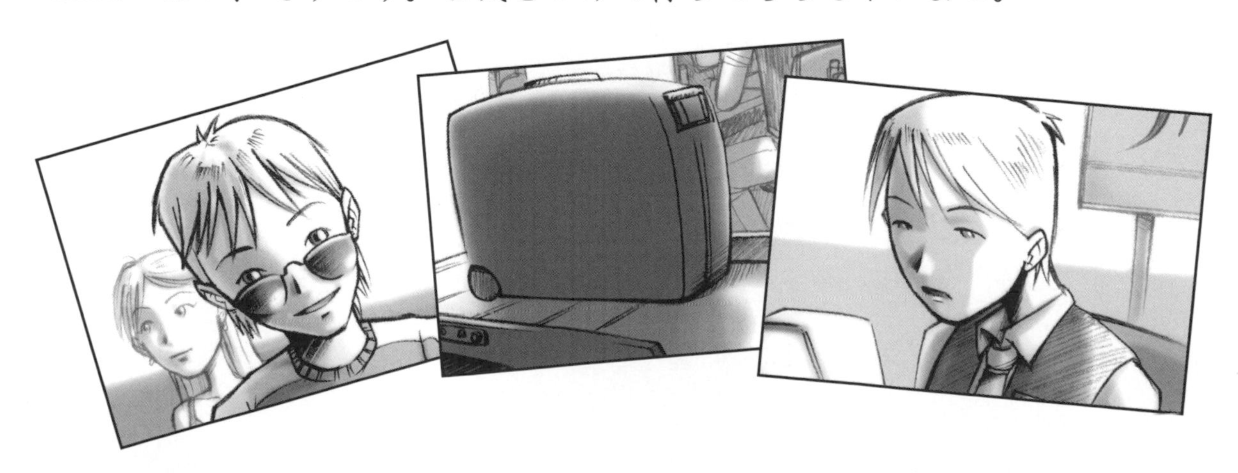

20. Following the example, convert the following sentences into a different version of the potential form.

a) 私は車を買うことができる。

私は車を買える____。

b) 彼はとてもおいしいラーメンを作ることができます。

____。

c) 本田さんは英語を教えることができませんでした。

____。

d) 春子ちゃんは速く走ることができない。

____。

e) あなたの息子さんは私の息子に勝つことができましたか？

____。

f) あの鳥はとても速く飛ぶことができなかった。

____。

21. Choose the sentence with the closest meaning to the original one.

a) このケーキを食べてはいけないよ。

1. このケーキを食べなければならないよ。
2. このケーキを食べてはだめだよ。
3. このケーキを食べることにしようよ。
4. このケーキを食べてもかまわないよ。

b) 来週、夏目先生の本を読まなくてはなりません。

1. 来週、夏目先生の本を読まなければなりません。
2. 来週、夏目先生の本を読んではなりません。
3. 来週、夏目先生の本を読んでもかまいません。
4. 来週、夏目先生の本を読まないでください。

c) あの学生はレストランに入りたがっている。

1. あの学生はレストランに入らなければならない。
2. あの学生はレストランに入ってほしい。
3. あの学生はレストランに入りたいと思っている。
4. あの学生はレストランに入ってはいけない。

22. Change the verb in each sentence into the form indicated (Af: affirmative, N: Negative, P: Past, F: Formal, C: Colloquial, Q: Question). Then, translate the resulting sentence into English.

a) 将来(しょうらい)、中国語を＿＿話(はな)したいです＿＿。(話(はな)す, ***-tai***, Af/F)

In the future, I want to speak Chinese.＿＿。

b) 明日、彼(かれ)の家へ＿＿＿＿＿＿＿＿！(行く ***-ō***, Af/C)

＿＿＿＿＿＿＿＿＿＿＿＿＿＿＿＿＿＿。

c) このカメラは高いですね。私は＿＿＿＿＿＿＿＿。(買う, potential, N/F)

＿＿＿＿＿＿＿＿＿＿＿＿＿＿＿＿＿＿。

d) 先生は新しい本を＿＿＿＿＿＿＿＿。(書(か)く, ***-garu***, AfP/C)

＿＿＿＿＿＿＿＿＿＿＿＿＿＿＿＿＿＿。

e) 明日、朝の５時に＿＿＿＿＿＿＿＿。(起(お)きる, obligation, Af/F)

＿＿＿＿＿＿＿＿＿＿＿＿＿＿＿＿＿＿。

f) 私は日本語を＿＿＿＿＿＿＿＿。(勉強(べんきょう)する, ***-tai***, N/F)

＿＿＿＿＿＿＿＿＿＿＿＿＿＿＿＿＿＿。

g) 彼女(かのじょ)はトマトと魚(さかな)が＿＿＿＿＿＿＿＿。(食べる, potential, NP/F)

＿＿＿＿＿＿＿＿＿＿＿＿＿＿＿＿＿＿。

h) オレはこのマンガを＿＿＿＿＿＿＿＿。(読(よ)む, ***tsumori***, Af/C)

＿＿＿＿＿＿＿＿＿＿＿＿＿＿＿＿＿＿。

i) このマンガを＿＿＿＿＿＿＿＿よ！(読(よ)む, prohibition, F)

＿＿＿＿＿＿＿＿＿＿＿＿＿＿＿＿＿＿。

j) 僕はこのプレゼントは ________________ ぞ！ (***hoshii***, NP/C)

____。

k) 今日はビールをたくさん ________________ ！(飲む, ***-ō***, Af/F)

____。

l) 田中先生はフラメンコを ________________。(おどる, potential, N/C)

____。

m) マリコちゃん、ここで ________________。(待つ, ***-te hoshii***, Af/F)

____。

n) すみませんが、ここに ________________。(座る, permission, Q/F)

____。

23. Fill in the gaps with a ***-te*** form verb from the box that follows.

a) A: お母さん。まだ寝ないの？

B: うるさいね！お母さんは本を 読んで (読む) いる。あんた、寝なさい。

b) 寒いか？じゃ、(私は) 君にセーターを ______(貸す)______。

c) 仕事を ______(する)______、遊びに行く。

d) 銀行に ______(行く)______。ちょっと待ってください。

e) A: どうして勉強しなかったか？

B: 昨日、夜までゲームを ______(する)______ からです。(past)

f) 中国語を勉強している。「こんにちは」と ______(言う)______ ね。ニーハオ！

g) おいしいチョコレートを買ったよ！ ______(食べる)______ わ！

h) A: すみません、一万円を ______(貸す)______ ！

B: だめだ、貸さない！

i) スパゲッティはたくさん ______(作る)______。食べてもいいよ。

j) A: すみません。トイレへ ______(行く)______ の？

B: いいよ。トイレはあちらです。

〜てから	〜てみる	〜てたまらない	〜てある	〜てもいい
〜てあげる	〜てしまう	〜てくる	〜ている	〜てください

24. Correct the mistakes in the following sentences, as in the example.

a) この牛乳(ぎゅうにゅう)を飲まない~~て~~でください。

b) 私の彼女(かのじょ)は美(うつく)しいで、静(しず)かなで、やさしいです。

c) マリオさんは学校(がっこう)へ行きたいです。

d) 私は10時まで家へ帰られませんでした。

e) この変態(へんたい)マンガをよんでもだめだよ！

f) あのレストランへ行かないでもいいです。

25. Choose the most suitable answer for each sentence.

a) 彼女(かのじょ)に手紙(てがみ)を ______。

1. 書(か)かよう　2. 書(か)こう　3. 書(か)きこう　4. 書(か)きよう

b) 私は先生に「バカだ、お前！」と ______。

1. 言ってあげた　2. 言ってから　3. 言ってしまった　4. 言いたがっている

c) あなたの家には犬(いぬ)が ______ いますか？

1. 何匹(なんびき)　2. いくつ　3. いくら　4. 何(なに)

d) 学生は学校(がっこう)へ勉強(べんきょう)をしに ______。

1. 行かなきゃならない　　2. 行かなくてもいい

3. 行ってもいい　　4. 行ってはならない

e) 西山(にしやま)さんはお酒(さけ)を ______ か？

1. 飲みれます　2. 飲められます　3. 飲まられます　4. 飲めます

f) 私は日本へ飛行機(ひこうき)で ______ です。

1. 行く　2. 行こうつもり　3. 行きたい　4. 行ってくる

g) あの山は ＿＿＿ 美しいね。

1. 高くて　2. 高い　3. 高て　4. 高くない

h) 青いセーターと赤いセーターがあるよ。どれに ＿＿＿ の？

1. してくる　2. しないで　3. する　4. できる

i) 明日、日本語の試験(しけん)があります。たくさん勉強(べんきょう) ＿＿＿。

1. してつもりです　2. ことができません

3. しておきたいです　4. すればなりません

j) 明日は朝の５時に出発(しゅっぱつ)するつもりか？おい、オレはそんな朝早(はや)く ＿＿＿ よ！

1. 起(お)けない　2. 起(お)きられない　3. 起(お)かない　4. 起(お)きれらない

k) すみません、君(きみ)のケーキを ＿＿＿。ごめんなさい！

1. 食べちゃった　2. 食べないで　3. 食べてしまた　4. 食べてある

l) ここから川が ＿＿＿。きれいだね！

1. 見える　2. 見えられる　3. 見る　4. 見れる

Kanji

話 (127)	聞 (128)	書 (129)	読 (130)	始 (121)	終 (122)	使 (136)	着 (148)	送 (254)	通 (255)	空 (154)
仕 (140)	事 (141)	物 (149)	者 (142)	暑 (98)	寒 (99)	何 (161)	天 (162)	写 (219)	真 (220)	勉 (232)

26. Practice writing the kanji below. Find the stroke order in the online Kanji Compilation section via the link on page 9.

書										
使										
終										
寒										
物										

27. Link each kanji with its most common reading (usually, the ***kun'yomi***).

空	なに	暑い	さむい
何	かく	送る	うつる
聞く	きく	写る	とおる
物	もの	寒い	あつい
書く	そら	通る	きる
事	こと	着る	おくる

28. Choose the correct kanji or kanji combination for each reading.

a) よむ

1. 話む 2. 書む 3. 読む 4. 売む

b). つかう

1. 問う 2. 使う 3. 便う 4. 聞う

c) しんぶん

1. 新聞 2. 親聞 3. 新問 4. 親問

d). はなす

1. 読す 2. 言す 3. 語す 4. 話す

e) かいわ

1. 会話 2. 令話 3. 今話 4. 合話

f). あつい

1. 暑い 2. 者い 3.箸い 4. 著い

29. Choose the correct reading for each kanji or kanji combination.

a) あの学者は書道を勉強している。

学者：1. かくしゃ　2. がくしゃ　3. かくじゃ　4. かぐしゃ

書道：1. しょどう　2. しょうどう　3. しゅどう　4. しゅうどう

勉強：1. ぺんきょ　2. べんきょ　3. ぺんきょう　4. べんきょう

b) 空手の先生にプレゼントを送りたいです。

空手：1. くうしゅ　2. そらて　3. あきて　4. からて

送りたい：1. とりたい　2. おくりたい　3. とおりたい　4. あまりたい

c) あなた、大事な 話があります。別(わか)れたいです。

大事な：1. だいじな　2. おおごとな　3. たいごとな　4. おおじな

話：1. はなす　2. わ　3. はなし　4. しゃべり

30. Give the ***furigana*** reading of the underlined kanji.

a) 新聞で着物を着た女の写真をみた。

b) 天の川と天文学の本を書店で読んだ。

c) その物語の終わりにヒーローが「寒いけど、天気がいいね」と言う。

d) 真夏に、私はいつも水着で仕事へ通います。

e) 何人の読者がその道の真ん中を通っていた？

31. Write the following words in kanji, and give their meanings. (**Note:** The words marked with an asterisk appear in kanji tables studied in previous lessons.)

そら ______ __________　　はじめる ______ __________

べんきょう ______ __________　　しゃしん ______ __________

てんし ______ __________　　*しょくじ ______ __________

“Books to Span the East and West”

Tuttle Publishing was founded in 1832 in the small New England town of Rutland, Vermont [USA]. Our core values remain as strong today as they were then—to publish best-in-class books which bring people together one page at a time. In 1948, we established a publishing outpost in Japan—and Tuttle is now a leader in publishing English-language books about the arts, languages and cultures of Asia. The world has become a much smaller place today and Asia's economic and cultural influence has grown. Yet the need for meaningful dialogue and information about this diverse region has never been greater. Over the past seven decades, Tuttle has published thousands of books on subjects ranging from martial arts and paper crafts to language learning and literature—and our talented authors, illustrators, designers and photographers have won many prestigious awards. We welcome you to explore the wealth of information available on Asia at **www.tuttlepublishing.com**.

Published by Tuttle Publishing, an imprint of Periplus Editions (HK) Ltd.

www.tuttlepublishing.com

Originally published as : JAPONÉS EN VIÑETAS: VOLUME 1

Library of Congress Control Number: 2022940733

ISBN 978-4-8053-1689-4

First edition, 2022

26 25 24 23 6 5 4 3

Printed in Singapore 2306TP

Distributed by

North America, Latin America & Europe
Tuttle Publishing
364 Innovation Drive
North Clarendon,
VT 05759-9436 U.S.A.
Tel: 1 (802) 773-8930
Fax: 1 (802) 773-6993
info@tuttlepublishing.com
www.tuttlepublishing.com

Japan
Tuttle Publishing
Yaekari Building, 3rd Floor,
5-4-12 Osaki, Shinagawa-ku,
Tokyo 141 0032
Tel: (81) 3 5437-017
Fax: (81) 3 5437-0755
sales@tuttle.co.jp
www.tuttle.co.jp

Asia Pacific
Berkeley Books Pte. Ltd.
3 Kallang Sector #04-01
Singapore 349278
Tel: (65) 6741-2178
Fax: (65) 6741-2179
inquiries@periplus.com.sg
www.tuttlepublishing.com